mikhail bakhtin

problems of

dostoevsky's
poetics

translated by
r. w. rotsel

ardis

ISBN 0-88233-040-3 cloth
ISBN 0-88233-041-1 paper

This book was set in IBM Univers
by William Kalvin.

Manufactured in the United States of America

TRANSLATOR'S NOTE

This is a translation. Its language is at times quite odd, a trait which it shares, however, with the original. Bakhtin tends to invent rather unusual expressions for his ideas and to use them without giving much explanation. I hope one need not spend as much time with the book as I have in order to appreciate it.

For some, the translation will presumably be much too literal. But I have sought only to render Bakhtin in English, not to render him more transparent or less redundant. The temptation to "improve" the text was great, but I trust that the readership of this book will have the courage to persevere and will ultimately be grateful for the unadulterated Bakhtin.

I am grateful to Professor Friedrich Scholz, Director of the Slavisch-Baltisches Seminar at the Westfälische Wilhelms-Universität in Münster, where I am an Assistent, for arranging my work load and schedule so as to make this translation possible.

Westfälische Wilhelms-Universität   R. Wm. R.
Münster, West Germany

TABLE OF CONTENTS

FOREWORD

The present work is devoted to the problems of Dostoevsky's *poetics* * and examines his creative work *only* from that point of view. We consider Dostoevsky one of the most brilliant innovators in the realm of literary form. He created, we believe, a wholly new type of artistic thought, which we have conditionally called *polyphonic.* This type of artistic thought found expression in Dostoevsky's novels, but its importance extends beyond the bounds of the novelistic genre, affecting certain basic principles of general European esthetics as well. One might even say that Dostoevsky created, as it were, a new artistic model of the world, in which many of the fundamental aspects of the old esthetic forms are radically transformed. The present work seeks, by means of a theoretical literary analysis, to expose Dostoevsky's *fundamental* innovations.

The basic features of Dostoevsky's poetics could not, of course, remain unmentioned in the voluminous critical literature (the first chapter of this book gives a survey of the most pertinent contributions in that area). But their fundamental novelty and organic unity in the whole of Dostoevsky's artistic world have been by no means sufficiently elucidated. The literature on Dostoevsky has been devoted chiefly to the ideological problems of his work, and the transcient currency of those problems has overshadowed the deeper, more timeless structural aspects of his artistic vision. It was often almost completely forgotten that Dostoevsky was first of all an *artist* (of a special sort, it is true), and not a philosopher or publicist. So the specific study of Dostoevsky's poetics remains an urgent task of literary scholarship.

For this second edition our book, originally published in 1929 under the title *Problemy tvorchestva Dostoevskogo (Problems of Dostoevsky's Art),* has been revised and considerably expanded. But of course even in the new edition the book does not pretend to be an exhaustive study of the problems raised, especially of such complex problems as that of the *entirety* of the polyphonic novel.

---

* Bakhtin's emphasis will throughout be indicated by italics, while the emphasis of quoted authors will be in bold type.

PROBLEMS OF DOSTOEVSKY'S POETICS

CHAPTER ONE

DOSTOEVSKY'S POLYPHONIC NOVEL

AND ITS ILLUMINATION IN THE CRITICAL LITERATURE

An acquaintance with the voluminous literature on Dostoevsky creates the impression that the subject under discussion is not a *single* author-artist who wrote novels and novellas *(povesti)*, but a whole series of philosophical statements made by *several* author-thinkers—Raskolnikov, Myshkin, Stavrogin, Ivan Karamazov, the Grand Inquisitor, and others. In literary criticism Dostoevsky's work has been broken down into a series of independent and self-contradictory philosophical positions, each defended by one or another of his heroes. The philosophical views of the author himself figure among them as well, though they are by no means accorded primary importance. For some scholars Dostoevsky's voice merges with the voices of certain of his heroes, for others it is a unique synthesis of all of the heroes' ideological voices, and for still others it is simply drowned out by the heroes' voices. The critics indulge in polemics with the heroes; they become their pupils, and they seek to develop their views into a completed system. The hero is ideologically authoritative and independent; he is perceived as the author of his own valid ideological conception, and not as the object of Dostoevsky's finalizing artistic vision. In the consciousness of the critics, the direct validity and significance of the heroes' words destroy the monological surface of the novel and encourage a direct answer, as if the hero were not the object of the author's word, but rather a full-valued, full-fledged carrier of his own private word.

B. M. Engelgardt quite accurately noted this characteristic of the literature on Dostoevsky.

When examining the Russian critical literature on Dostoevsky's works one readily notes that, with few exceptions, it never rises above the spiritual level of Dostoevsky's favorite characters. It does not rule the material at hand, the material masters it completely. It is still taking lessons from Ivan Karamazov and Raskolnikov, Stavrogin and the Grand Inquisitor, and becoming entangled in the same contradictions which entangled them as they came to a bewildered standstill in the face of

[3]

the problems which they had to solve, bowing respectfully before their complex and agonizing experiences.[1]

J. Meier-Gräfe has made a similar observation: "Who would ever think of taking part in one of the numerous conversations in *L'education sentimentale?* But we dispute with Raskolnikov, and not only with him, but with every bit-player as well."[2]

This peculiarity of the critical literature on Dostoevsky cannot, of course, be explained solely by the methodological helplessness of critical thought, nor should it be considered the complete destruction of the author's will. Such an approach on the part of the critical literature, as well as the unbiased perception of those readers who are constantly debating with Dostoevsky's *heroes,* does in fact correspond to a basic structural characteristic of that author's works. Dostoevsky, like Goethe's Prometheus, creates not voiceless slaves (as does Zeus), but rather *free* people who are capable of standing *beside* their creator, of disagreeing with him, and even of rebelling against him.

The plurality of independent and unmerged voices and consciousnesses and the genuine polyphony of full-valued voices are in fact characteristics of Dostoevsky's novels. It is not a multitude of characters and fates within a unified objective world, illuminated by the author's unified consciousness that unfolds in his works, but precisely the *plurality of equal consciousnesses and their worlds,* which are combined here into the unity of a given event, while at the same time retaining their unmergedness. In the author's creative plan, Dostoevsky's principle heroes are indeed *not only objects of the author's word, but subjects of their own directly significant word* (neposredstvenno znachashchee slovo) *as well.* Therefore the hero's word is here by no means limited to its usual functions of characterization and plot development,[3] but neither does it serve as the expression of the author's own ideological position (as in Byron, for example). The hero's consciousness is given as a separate, a *foreign* consciousness, but at the same time it is not objectified, it does not become closed off, it is not made the simple object of the author's consciousness. In this sense the image of Dostoevsky's hero is not the same as the usual objectivized image of the hero in the traditional novel.

Dostoevsky is the creator of the *polyphonic novel.* He originated an essentially new novelistic genre. Therefore his work cannot be confined within any boundaries and does not submit itself to any of the historical-literary schemata which we are accustomed to apply to manifestations of the European novel. In his works there appears a hero whose voice is constructed in the same way that the voice of the author himself is constructed in the usual novel. The hero's word about himself and about the world is every bit as valid as the usual authorial word; it is not subordinated to the objectivized image of the hero as one of his characteristics, nor does it serve as mouthpiece for the author's voice. It possesses an exceptional independence in the structure of the work, standing as if *alongside* the author's word and in a peculiar way combining

[4]

with it and with the full-valued voices of the other heroes.

It follows therefrom that the usual material or psychological bonds necessary for the pragmatic development of the plot are insufficient for Dostoevsky's world: they presuppose the heroes' objectivization and materialization as integral to the author's plan and they connect and combine completed images of people in the unity of a monologically perceived and understood world. Dosotevsky's plan presupposes the plurality of consciousnesses of equal value, together with their worlds. In Dostoevsky's novels the usual plot pragmatics play a secondary role and fulfill special functions, different from their usual ones. The final bonds which create the unity of his novelistic world are of another sort; the basic event disclosed by his novel is not amenable to the usual plot-pragmatic *(siuzhetno-pragmaticheskoe)* interpretation.

Further, the very orientation of the narration—whether it is carried out by the author, a narrator, or one of the heroes—must be completely different than in novels of the monological type. The position from which the story is told, the image is constructed, or the information is given must be oriented in a new way to this new world, the world of full-fledged subjects, not objects. The narrational, representational, and informational word must work out some sort of new relationship to its object.

Thus, all of the elements of Dostoevsky's novelistic structure are profoundly original; they are all determined by that new artistic task which only he succeeded in setting and fulfilling in all its breadth and depth: the task of constructing a polyphonic world and destroying the established forms of the basically *monological* (homophonic) European novel.[4]

From the point of view of a consistent monological vision and comprehension of the represented world and of the monological canon of novelistic construction, Dostoevsky's world may appear to be chaotic, and the construction of his novels a conglomerate of alien materials and incompatible principles of design. The profound organicism, consistency and unity of Dostoevsky's poetics can become clear only in light of his basic artistic task as we have formulated it.

This is our thesis. Before developing it on the basis of the material of Dostoevsky's works, we shall retrace the way in which the basic characteristic of his work, as put forward by us, has been interpreted in the critical literature. We have no intention here of giving an even remotely complete outline of the literature on Dostoevsky. We shall examine only a few works from the twentieth century, namely those which, firstly, touch upon questions of Dostoevsky's *poetics,* and, secondly, come closest to the basic characteristics of his poetics as we understand them. Thus the selection will be made from the point of view of our thesis, and, consequently, will be subjective. But a subjective selection is in this case unavoidable and justified: what we are giving here is not an historical outline and not even a survey. We wish only to orient our thesis and our point of view among the other points of view toward Dostoevsky's poetics which already exist in the literature. In the process of this orientation we shall clarify the various aspects of our thesis.

■

Until very recently the critical literature on Dostoevsky has been a to-direct ideological response to the voices of his heroes for it to be able to objectively perceive the distinguishing artistic characteristics of his new novelistic structure. Moreover, in attempting to gain a theoretical understanding of this new multi-voiced world, it has found no other course than to monologize this world according to the usual type, i.e., to perceive a work of an essentially new artistic will from an old and accustomed point of view. Some critics, enslaved by the content of the various heroes' ideological views, strove to reduce those views to a systematic monological whole, ignoring the essential plurality of unmerged consciousnesses, a deliberate part of the author's artistic intention. Other critics, while resisting the charm of unadulterated ideology, turned the full-valued consciousnesses of the heroes into materialized psyches perceived in an objectified way, and perceived Dostoevsky's world as the ordinary world of the European social-psychological novel. In the first instance the result was a philosophical monolog in place of the event of the interaction of full-valued consciousnesses; in the second it was a monologically understood objectified world, correlative to a single and unified authorial consciousness.

Impassioned co-philosophizing with the heroes and the dispassionate psychological or psychopathological analysis of the heroes as objects are equally incapable of penetrating the artistic archetechtonics of Dostoevsky's works. The passion of the co-philosophizers is incapable of an objective, genuinely realistic vision of the world of others' consciousnesses, and the realism of the analyzers is "in over its head." It is quite clear that in both cases the artistic problems proper are either avoided altogether or treated merely accidentally and superficially.

The chief method in the critical literature on Dostoevsky is philosophical monologization. Rozanov, Volynsky, Merezhkovsky, Shestov and others have travelled this path. In trying to force the plurality of consciousnesses depicted by the author into the systematic monological limits of a unified *Weltanschauung,* these scholars were compelled to resort either to antinomy or to dialectics. Out of the concrete and unified consciousnesses of the characters (and of the author himself) they mined ideological theses, which they either arranged in dynamic dialectical series or juxtaposed one to another as irreducable absolute antinomies. The interaction of several unmerged consciousnesses was replaced by the interaction of ideas, thoughts and positions adequate for a single consciousness.

Both dialectics and antinomy are in fact present in Dostoevsky's world. The thinking of his heroes is in fact sometimes dialectic or antinomic. But all of the *logical* bonds remain within the bounds of the individual consciousnesses and do not govern the interrelationships of events which relate the

[6]

consciousnesses to each other. Dostoevsky's world is profoundly personalized. He perceives and represents every thought as the position of a personality. Therefore, even within the bounds of each individual consciousness, a dialectical or antinomical series is merely an abstract aspect which is inseparably intertwined with the other aspects of the integral, concrete consciousness. Through this concrete consciousness, embodied in the *living voice of an integral person,* the logical series becomes part of the unity of the event depicted. A thought, drawn into an event, itself becomes part of the event and takes on the peculiar character of an "idea-feeling" or "idea-force" which creates the inimitable uniqueness of the "idea" in Dostoevsky's creative world. An idea, removed from the interrelationship of events of consciousnesses and forced into a systematic monological context, even of the most dialectical sort, inevitably loses its uniqueness and becomes an inferior philosophical assertion. For this reason all the large monographs based on the philosophical monologization of Dostoevsky's works contribute little toward an understanding of the distinguishing artistic characteristic of his world as we have formulated it. That characteristic did, it is true, give rise to all of these scholarly works, but it is in them least of all recognized.

Its recognition begins at the point where a more objective approach not to Dostoevsky's work is attempted, an approach not only to the ideas as such, but to the works as artistic entities as well.

The basic structural peculiarity of Dostoevsky's artistic world was first gropingly—but only gropingly—discovered by Vyacheslav Ivanov.[5] He defined Dostoevsky's realism as being based not on (objectified) cognition, but on "penetration." The principle of Dostoevsky's *Weltanschauung* is to affirm the next man's "I" *(chuzhoe "ia")* not as an object, but as another subject. The affirmation of another man's "I"—"Thou art"—is, according to Ivanov, the task which Dostoevsky's heroes must fulfill in order to overcome their ethical solipsism, their reclusive "idealistic" consciousness, and to transform the other person from a shadow into true reality. The solipsistic reclusiveness of the hero s consciousness and his seclusion in his own world always lie at the root of the tragical catastrophe in Dostoevsky's works.[6]

Thus the affirmation of the other's consciousness as a full-fledged subject, and not as an object, becomes the ethico-religious postulate which defines the *content* of the novel (the catastrophe of the reclusive consciousness). This is the principle of the author's *Weltanschauung,* from which point of view he comprehends his heroes' world. Consequently Ivanov shows only the purely thematic aspect of this principle in the content of the novel, and in a predominantly negative way, at that: the heroes are devastated because they cannot completely affirm the other—"Thou art." Affirmation—and non-affirmation—of the other's "I" by the hero is the theme of Dostoevsky's works.

But this theme is altogether possible in a novel of a purely monological type as well, and is in fact more than once treated in such novels. As the author's ethico-religious postulate and as the theme of the work's content, the

[7]

affirmation of another's consciousness does not constitute a new form or a new type of novelistic construction.

Vyacheslav Ivanov did not demonstrate how this principle of Dostoevsky's *Weltanschauung* becomes the principle of his *artistic* vision of the world and of the artistic construction of a *linguistic* unit—the novel. This principle is relevant for the literary scholar only as the principle of a concrete literary construction, and not as the ethico-religious principle of an abstract *Weltanschauung*. And only in such a form can it be objectively dissected on the basis of the empirical material of concrete literary works.

But Vyacheslav Ivanov did not do this. In the chapter devoted to the "principle of form," despite a series of valuable observations, he persists in perceiving Dostoevsky's novel within the bounds of the monological type. The radical artistic upheaval which Dostoevsky accomplished remained in its essence uncomprehended. Ivanov's basic definition of Dostoevsky's novel as a "novel-tragedy" seems to us incorrect.[7] It is characteristic as an attempt to reduce a new artistic form to an already-familiar artistic will. As a result, Dostoevsky's novel appears to be a sort of artistic hybrid.

Thus, while arriving at a profound and correct definition for Dostoevsky's basic principle—to affirm the other's "I" not as object, but as another subject— Vyacheslav Ivanov monologized this principle, i.e., he made it part of the author's monologically formulated *Weltanschauung* and perceived it merely as the contentual theme of a world depicted from the point of view of the author's monological consciousness.[8] In addition, he connected his idea with a series of direct metaphysical and ethical assertions which are not subject to any kind of verification based on the material of Dostoevsky's works themselves.[9] The artistic task of constructing a polyphonic novel, first fulfilled by Dostoevsky, remained undiscovered.

■

S. Askoldov gives a definition of Dostoevsky's basic distinguishing characteristics similar to that of Ivanov.[10] But he, too, remains within the bounds of Dostoevsky's monologized religious-ethical *Weltanschauung* and the monologically perceived content of his works.

"Dostoevsky's first ethical thesis," says Askoldov, "is at first glance something extremely formal, but at the same time is, in a certain sense, something of utmost importance. By all of his judgements and sympathies he says to us:'Be a personality!' "*("Bud' lichnost'iu!").*[11] Personality, according to Askoldov, differs from character, type, and temperament—which usually serve as the object of representation in literature—by virtue of its exceptional inner freedom and absolute independence from the external environment.

This is, then, the ethical principle of the author's *Weltanschauung*. Askoldov makes a direct transition from this *Weltanschauung* to the content of Dostoevsky's novels and shows by what means Dostoevsky's heroes become personalities in life and how they manifest themselves as such. Thus the personality inevitably comes into conflict with the external environment, above all a conflict with conventions of every sort. Hence the "scandal"—that first and most external manifestation of the pathos of the personality—plays an enormous role in Dostoevsky's works.[12] Crime, according to Askoldov, is a deeper manifestation of the pathos of the personality in life. He says: "Crime in Dostoevsky's novels is the statement in life of the religious-ethical problem. Punishment is the form of its solution. Therefore the two together constitute the basic theme of Dostoevsky's work..."[13]

Thus the methods of revealing the personality in life itself are constantly under discussion here, rather than the methods of visualizing and representing it artistically under the conditions of a specific artistic construction—the novel. Besides, the very interrelationship between the author's *Weltanschauung* and the world of his heroes is incorrectly represented. The direct transition from the pathos of the personality in the author's *Weltanschauung* to the real-life pathos *(zhiznennychi pafos)* of his heroes, and from there again to the author's monological deduction is the typical path of the monological novel of the romantic type. But this is not Dostoevsky's path. Askoldov says:

Dostoevsky, in all of his artistic sympathies and judgements, proclaims one very important proposition: the villain, the saint, and the ordinary sinner, if they have developed their personal quintessence to its utmost, all possess a certain equal worth, precisely in the quality of their personalities, which resist the murky currents of the all-equalizing "environment."[14]

Proclamations of this sort are characteristic of the romantic novel, which saw consciousness and ideology merely as the author's pathos and the author's deduction *(vyvod)*, and saw the hero merely as the executor of the author's pathos or the object of the author's deduction. It is precisely the romantics who give direct expression to their artistic sympathies and judgements in the very reality which they are representing, and who objectivize and materialize everything to which they cannot give the accent of their own voice.

Dostoevsky's originality lies not in the fact that he monologically proclaimed the worth of the personality—others had done so before him,—but in the fact that he was able to see and to show it with artistic objectivity as another, a foreign, personality, without lyricizing it or merging it with his own voice, while at the same time not reducing it to materialized psychic reality. The high appraisal of the personality's worth did not appear for the first time in Dostoevsky's *Weltanschauung,* but the artistic image of a foreign personality (if we accept Askoldov's term) and of multiple unmerged personalities joined in the unity of a given spiritual event, was realized for the first time in his novels.

The astonishing inner independence of Dostoevsky's heroes, correctly mentioned by Askoldov, is achieved by specific artistic means. It is achieved above all through the heroes' freedom and independence vis-a-vis the author in

[9]

the very structure of the novel, or, more precisely, through their freedom and independence in relation to the usual externalizing and finalizing authorial definitions. This does not, of course, mean that the hero disappears from the author's plan. No, his independence and freedom are precisely a part of the author's plan which, as it were, predestines him to be free (relatively speaking, of course) and introduces him as a free man into the strict and calculated plan of the whole. The hero's relative freedom no more destroys the strict specificity of the novel's construction than the presence of irrational or transfinite quantities destroys the strict specificity of a mathematical formula. This new position is not achieved by the abstract choice of theme (thought the theme, of course, has its significance, too), but by the totality of the special artistic devices of novelistic construction first introduced by Dostoevsky.

Thus Askoldov, too, monologized Dostoevsky's world, transforming the dominant of that world into a monological sermon, thereby reducing the heroes to the state of simple illustrations of that sermon. Askoldov correctly understood that the basic feature in Dostoevsky is a totally new vision and representation of the inner man and, consequently, of the event which binds inner men together. But he carried his explanation over into the plane of the author's *Weltanschauung* and into the plane of the characters' psychology.

One of Askoldov's later articles—"Psikhologiia kharakterov u Dostoevskogo" ("The Psychology of Dostoevsky's Characters")[15]—is also limited to an analysis of the purely characterological features of his heroes and does not reveal the principles of their artistic visualization and representation. The distinction between personality on the one hand and character, type, and temperament on the other is, as before, handled in the psychological plane. However, in this article Askoldov comes much closer to the concrete material of the novels, and therefore it contains numerous valuable observations on Dostoevsky's various artistic characteristics. But Askoldov's conception does not go beyond isolated observations.

It must be said that Vyacheslav Ivanov's formula—to affirm the other's "I" not as object, but as another subject, "Thou art,"—despite its philosophical abstractness, is much more adequate than Askoldov's formula "Be a personality." Ivanov's formula shifts the dominant to the other's personality, and in addition it better corresponds to Dostoevsky's *inwardly dialogical* approach to the represented consciousness of the hero, while Askoldov's formula is more monological and shifts the center of gravity to the realization of the individual personality, which, in the realm of artistic creation—if it had, in fact, been Dostoevsky's postulate—would have led to a subjective romantic type of novelistic construction.

■

Leonid Grossman approaches this same basic characteristic of Dostoevsky from another viewpoint—from the viewpoint of the novels' artistic construction itself. For Grossman Dostoevsky is first and foremost the creator of a new

[10]

and extremely original breed of novel.

Upon surveying his voluminous creative activity and all of the varied aspirations of his spirit, one must, I should think, agree that Dostoevsky's
chief significance lies not so much in philosophy, psychology, or mysti-
cism as in the creation of a new, truly brilliant page in the history of the
European novel.[16]

L. P. Grossman must be recognized as the founder of the objective and consistent study of Dostoevsky's *poetics* in our literary scholarship.

Grossman finds the basic distinguishing characteristic of Dostoevsky's
poetics in the destruction of the organic unity of material required by the conventional canon, in the joining of the most varied and incompatible elements in the
unity of a novelistic construction, and in the destruction of the unified and
integral narrative fabric. He says:

This is the basic principle of his novelistic composition: to subordinate
polarly incompatible narrative elements to the unity of the philosophical
plan and to the whirlwind movement of events. To combine philosophical
confessions with criminal adventures in a single artistic creation, to include
a religious drama in the plot of a vulgar story, to traverse all the peripeteia
of an adventure narrative and arrive at the revelation of a new mystery—
these were the kinds of artistic tasks which lay before Dostoevsky and which
challenged him to complex creative work. Dostoevsky merges opposites
in spite of the age-old traditions of an esthetic which required a correspondence between the material and its treatment, which took for granted unity
and, certainly, homogeneity and kindredness of the structural elements of a
given work of art. He issues a decisive challenge to the basic canon of the
theory of art. His task is to overcome the greatest difficulty facing the artist:
to create a unified and integral work of art from heterogeneous, profoundly
foreign materials of unequal value. This is why the Book of Job, the Revelation of St. John, the New Testament texts, St. Simeon the New Theo-
logian, and everything that feeds the pages of Dostoevsky's novels and lends
the tone to one or another of their chapters is combined here in a unique
way with the newspaper page, the anecdote, the parody, the street scene, the
grotesque, and even the pamphlet. He boldly casts into his crucibles ever
more elements, knowing and believing that in the heat of his creative work
the raw chunks of everyday reality, the sensations of cheap boulevard
stories and the divinely inspired pages of holy writ will melt and fuse in a
new substance and take on the profound stamp of his personal style and
tone.[17]

This is a brilliant descriptive characterization of the generic and compositional
features of Dostoevsky's novels. Almost nothing can be added to it. But the

explanations which Grossman gives seem to us insufficient.

In fact, the whirlwind movement of events, however mighty it may be, and the unity of the philosophical plan, however profound it may be, are hardly sufficient to fulfill that complex and contradictory compositional task which Grossman has so concisely and graphically formulated. The most banal contemporary film can outdo Dostoevsky in whirlwind movement of events. And unity of the philosophical plan in and of itself cannot serve as the final basis of artistic unity.

Grossman's assertion that Dostoevsky's entire heterogeneous material takes on "the profound stamp of his personal style and tone" is also, in our opinion, false. If that were the case, then how would Dostoevsky's novel differ from the ordinary novel, from the "epopee of the Flaubertian manner, hewn as if from a single piece, polished and monolithic"? A novel such as *Bouvard et Pécouchet,* for example, unites material of the most heterogenous content, but this heterogeneity does not appear in the structure of the novel, and it cannot appear very clearly because it is subordinated to the pervasive unity of a personal style and tone, to the unity of a single world and a single consciousness. The unity of Dostoevsky's novel is *above* personal tone and *above* personal style as they were known in the pre-Dostoevskian novel.

Given a monological understanding of the unity of style (and that is as yet the only such understanding), Dostoevsky's novel is *multi-styled* or styleless; given a monological understanding of tone, Dostoevsky's novel is *multi-accented* and embraces contradictory values. Contradictory accents intertwine in every word of his works. If Dostoevsky's utterly heterogenous material were developed in a unified world corresponding to a unified monological authorial consciousness, then the task of joining the incompatible would not have been solved and Dostoevsky would be an inferior, styleless artist. Such a monological world

...fatally breaks down into its component, dissimilar, mutually alien parts, it expands motionlessly, ridiculously and helplessly before us, a page from the Bible side by side with a note from someone's diary or a lackey's chastushka side by side with a Schillerian dithyramb of joy.[18]

In fact, the utterly incompatible elements of Dostoevsky's material are distributed among several worlds and several full-fledged consciousnesses; they are presented not within one field of vision, but within several complete fields of vision of equal value, and not the material directly, but rather these worlds and these consciousnesses with their fields of vision, are joined in a higher unity of a second order, the unity of the polyphonic novel. The world of the chastushka is joined with the world of the Schillerian dithyramb, Smerdyakov's field of vision is joined with that of Dmitry and Ivan. Thanks to these *varied worlds* the material is able to fully develop its uniqueness and specificity without interrupting or mechanizing the unity of the whole. It is as if varying systems of calculation were joined here in the complex unity of an Einsteinian universe. (The juxtaposition of Dostoevsky's world with that of Einstein is, of course, only an artistic comparison, not a scientific analogy.)

In another of his works L. Grossman comes closer to the multivoicedness of Dostoevsky's novel. In the book *Put' Dostoevskogo* (Dostoevsky's Path) he underscores the exceptional significance of the dialog in Dostoevsky's works. He says:

> The form of the conversation or the argument, in which diverse points of view can predominate one after another and can reflect the varying nuances of contradictory beliefs, is particularly appropriate for the embodiment of Dostoevsky's philosophy, which is constantly in the process of being formed, and never grows stiff and cold. This form of philosophical thought, in which every opinion becomes like a living being and is expounded by an impassioned human voice, must have appeared to such an artist and contemplator of images as Dostoevsky in a moment of profound meditation on the meaning of existence and the secret of the universe.[19]

Grossman tends to explain the dialogism of Dostoevsky's works by saying that his *Weltanschauung* contains a contradiction which he never completely overcame. Two mighty powers—faith and humanistic skepticism—collided early on in his consciousness and carry on a constant struggle for predominance in his *Weltanschauung*.[20]

One can disagree with this explanation, since it in essence exceeds the bounds of the objectively available material, but the presence of the plurality (in this case, the duality) of unmerged consciousnesses is correctly noted. Grossman also correctly points out that Dostoevsky perceives ideas in a very personalized way. Every opinion does indeed become a living being and is inseparable from a personified human voice. If introduced into an abstract systematic monological context, the opinion ceases to be what it was.

If Grossman had made the connection between Dostoevsky's compositional principle—the unification of utterly heterogenous and incompatible materials—and the plurality of consciousness-centers which are not reduced to a common denominator, he would have arrived at the artistic key to Dostoevsky's novels—polyphony.

It is symptomatic that Grossman conceives of dialog in Dostoevsky's works as a dramatic form, and every dialogization as necessarily a dramatization. Recent literature knows only the dramatic dialog and, to some extent, the philosophical dialog, but weakened to such a degree that it becomes a mere expository form, a pedagogical device. The dramatic dialog in the drama and the dramatized dialog in the narrative genres are always enclosed in a solid and unshakable monological framework. This monological framework does not, of course, have a direct verbal expression in the drama, but it is precisely in the drama that it is especially monolithic. The speeches in a dramatic dialog do not disrupt the world that is being depicted, nor do they make it multileveled; on the contrary, they require the monolithic unity of that world in order to be truly dramatic. The world of the drama must be made of a single piece. Any weakening of the monolith leads to a weakening of the dramatic effect. The characters meet in the unified field of vision of the author, the director and the audience, against the clear-cut backdrop of a unistructural *(odnosostavnyi)* world.[21] The concept of dramatic action as the resolver of all dialogical conflicts is a purely monological one. True multileveledness would destroy the drama, because dramatic action rests upon the unity of the world and is incapable of tying together and resolving multiple levels. In the drama the combination of integral fields of vision in a unity which stands above those fields of vision is impossible because the dramatic construction offers no support for such unity. Therefore the true dramatic dialog can play only a quite secondary role in Dostoevsky's polyphonic novel.[22]

More relevant is Grossman's assertion that Dostoevsky's later novels are in fact mystery plays.[23] The mystery play is truly multileveled and, to a degree, polyphonic. But the multileveledness and polyphony of the mystery play are strictly formal, and its very construction prohibits the development of a plurality of consciousness and their worlds. From the very beginning everything is pre-ordained, closed and finalized, although, it is true, not finalized in a single plane.[24]

In Dostoevsky's polyphonic novel the important thing is not the ordinary dialogical form of unfolding the material within the limits of its monological conception against the firm background of a unified material world. No, the important thing is the final dialogicality, i.e. the dialogical nature of the total work. As we have said, the dramatic work is, in this sense, monological, and Dostoevsky's novel is dialogical. It is not constructed as the entirety of a single consciousness which absorbs other consciousnesses as objects, but rather as the entirety of the interaction of several consciousnesses, of which no one fully becomes the object of any other one. This interaction does not assist the viewer to objectify the entire event in accordance with the ordinary monological pattern (thematically, lyrically, or cognitively), and as a consequence makes him a participant. The novel not only gives no solid support outside the dialogical conflict for a third, monologically engulfing consciousness—on the contrary, everything in it is so constructed as to make the dialogical opposition perpetual.[25] Not a single element of the work is constructed from the viewpoint of a non-participating "third party," and in the novel itself this "third party" is in no way represented. There is no place for him either in the composition or in the sense and meaning of the novel. This is not the author's weakness, but his greatest strength; it makes possible a new authorial position, higher than the monological one.

■

Otto Kaus, in his book *Dostoewski und sein Schicksal,* also points out the plurality of equally authoritative ideological positions and the extreme heterogeneity of material as the basic characteristic of Dostoevsky's novels. According to Kaus, no other author concentrated in himself so many contradictory and mutually exclusive concepts, judgements and evaluations as did Dostoevsky. But the most astounding fact is that Dostoevsky's works seem to vindicate all of these contradictory points of view: each of them finds support for itself in his novels.

Kaus characterizes Dostoevsky's many-sidedness and multileveledness thus:

Dostoevsky is the kind of host who gets on splendidly with the motleyest of guests; he can command the attention of the most mixed company and can hold them all in equal suspense. An old-fashioned realist can rightfully be enchanted with his description of forced labor, the streets and squares of Petersburg, and the arbitrary rule of the autocracy, but a mystic can with equal justification be intrigued by spiritual contact with Alyosha, with Prince Myshkin, and with Ivan Karamazov, who is visited by the devil. Utopians of every stripe can find joy in the dreams of the "ridiculous man," of Versilov or of Stavrogin, and religious people can strengthen their spirit through the struggle for God carried on in these novels by both the saints and the sinners. Health and strength, extreme pessimism and burning faith in salvation, the thirst for life and the thirst for death—all of these things fight a never-ending battle here. Violence and lovingkindness, arrogance and sacrificial meekness—the boundless fulness of life is embodied in vivid form in every particle of his work. Even the strictest critical conscientiousness cannot hinder each reader in interpreting the author's final word in his own way. Dostoevsky is many-sided and unpredictable in every motion of his artistic thought; his works are saturated with powers and intentions which, it would seem, are divided by insurmountable chasms.[26]

How does Kaus explain this characteristic of Dostoevsky?

Kaus maintains that Dostoevsky's world is a pure and genuine expression of the spirit of capitalism. Those worlds and those planes—social, cultural and ideological—which collide in Dostoevsky's work were in the past self-sufficient, organically self-enclosed, consolidated, and had inner significance as separate units. There was no real, material plane in which their essential contact and mutual penetration could take place. Capitalism destroyed the isolation of those worlds and broke down the seclusion and inner ideological self-sufficiency of those social spheres. With its tendency to make everything level, leaving no other divisions but the division into proletarians and capitalists, capitalism caused those worlds to collide and welded them together in its own contradictory, evolving unity. Those worlds had not yet lost their individual mien which had been acquired over the centuries, but they were no longer self-sufficient. Their blind co-existence and their blissful and self-assured state of mutual ideological ignorance came to an end; their mutual contradictoriness and, at the same time, their mutual connectedness were exposed with utmost clarity. Every atom of life trembles with the contradictory unity of the capitalist world and the capitalist consciousness, allowing nothing to rest easily in its isolation, but at the same time not resolving anything. The spirit of this world-being-formed found its fullest expression in the works of Dostoevsky.

Dostoevsky's powerful influence in our time, and everything unclear and undefined in that influence, finds its explanation and its only justification in the basic characteristic of his nature: Dostoevsky is the most decisive, consistent and implacable singer of capitalist man. His art is not the funeral dirge, but the cradlesong of our contemporary world, a world born of capitalism's fiery breath.[27]

Kaus's explanations are in many respects correct. The polyphonic novel could, indeed, have come into being only in the capitalist epoch. The most favorable soil for its development was, moreover, precisely in Russia, where capitalism's near-catastrophic arrival found an untouched variety of social worlds and groupings which had not, as was the case in the West, had their individual self-enclosedness weakened in the process of the gradual advent of capitalism. In Russia the contradictory nature of the evolving social life, which no longer fit into limits of a self-assured and calmly reflective monological consciousness, was bound to be particularly rash, and at the same time the individuality of the worlds that were thrown off their ideological balance and were colliding with one another was bound to be particularly complete and striking. In this manner the objective preconditions for the essential multileveledness and multivoicedness of the polyphonic novel were met.

But Kaus's explanations fail to elucidate the very fact which he is trying to explain. The "spirit of capitalism" is, after all, reflected in artistic language, specifically in the language of a particular variety of the novelistic genre. It is first of all necessary to discover the structural characteristics of this multileveled novel which is devoid of familiar monological unity. Kaus does not carry out this task. Having accurately pointed out the fact of the novel's multileveledness and the multivoicedness of its meaning, he transfers his explanations directly from the plane of the novel itself to the plane of reality. Kaus's merit lies in the fact that he refrains from monologizing this world and from any attempt to unite and reconcile the contradictions contained in it; he accepts its multileveledness and contradictoriness as an essential element of its very construction and its creative plan.

∎

V. Komarovich treats another aspect of the same basic characteristic of Dostoevsky's works in his article "Roman Dostoevskogo *Podrostok,* kak xudozhestvennoe edinstvo" ("Dostoevsky's Novel *A Raw Youth* as an Artistic Unit"). In analyzing this novel he uncovers five distinct themes which are only very superficially connected by a plot-determined bond *(fabuliar naja svjaz').*This forces him to assume some other sort of bond beyond the realm of plot pragmatics.

Dostoevsky snatches out shreds of reality and extends their 'empiricism' to the extreme, not allowing us to forget ourselves even for a minute in joyous recognition of that reality (as in Flaubert or Tolstoy); instead he frightens us, precisely because he snatches and tears all of these things out of the natural chain of reality. In transferring these shreds to his **own** purview,

[16]

Dostoevsky does not carry over the natural connections of our experience: it is not by means of the plot that the Dostoevskian novel is forged into an organic unity.[28]

The monological unity of the world is indeed violated in the Dostoevskian novel, but the torn-out chunks of reality are by no means directly combined in the unity of the novel: these chunks are germane to the integral field of vision of one or another character and have significance within the plane of one or another consciousness. If these chunks of reality, devoid of pragmatic connections, were directly combined in the unity of a single monological field of vision because of their emotional-lyrical or symbolical harmony, then we would have before us the world of a romanticist, of Hoffmann, for example, but not the world of Dostoevsky.

Komarovich gives a monological (extremely monological, even) interpretation of the ultimate plot-external unity *(vnesjuzhetnoe edinstvo)* of Dostoevsky's novel, despite the fact that he introduces an analogy with polyphony and with the contrapuntal combination of voices in the fugue. Under the influence of Broder Christiansen's monological esthetics he comprehends the plot-external, non-pragmatic unity of the novel as the dynamic unity of a volitional act:

Thus the teleological coordination of pragmatically disconnected elements (themes) is the genesis of the Dostoevskian novel's artistic unity. And in this sense it can be compared to the artistic whole of polyphonic music: the five voices of the fugue, entering into and developing in contrapuntal accord, are reminiscent of the 'voice coordination' *('golosovedenie')* of the Dostoevskian novel. Such a comparison—if it is a proper one—leads to a more generalized definition of the very genesis of unity. The law of unity embodied in music and in Dostoevsky's novel is the same law that is embodied in us, in the human "I"—the law of purposeful activity. In *A Raw Youth* this principle of unity corresponds exactly with the material which is symbolically represented in the novel: Versilov's 'love-hate' for Akhmatova is symbolic of the individual will's tragic outbursts into the supra-personal; consequently the entire novel is constructed on the model of the individual volitional act.[29]

Komarovich's basic error, it seems to us, lies in the fact that he looks for *direct* connections between separate elements of reality or between separate plot lines, while the important thing is the combination of full-valued consciousnesses with their worlds. Therefore, in place of unity of events, in which there are several full-fledged participants, he arrives at the empty unity of the individual volitional act. In this sense he interprets polyphony completely falsely. The essence of polyphony is precisely in the fact that the voices remain independent and, as such, are combined in a unity of a higher order than in homophony. If we are going to talk about the individual will, then it is precisely in polyphony that the combination of several individual wills occurs and that the bounds of an individual will are fundamentally exceeded. One could say that the polyphonic artistic will is the will to combine many wills, the will to the event *(volja k sobytiju)*.

It is just as inadmissable to equate the unity of Dostoevsky's world to an individual emotional-volitional accentual will as it is to do so with musical polyphony. As a result of such an equation, *A Raw Youth* appears in Komarovich's criticism as a sort of lyrical unity of a simplified monological type, since the thematic unities are combined according to their emotional-volitional accents, i.e. according to the lyrical principle.

It must be noted that our comparison of the Dostoevskian novel to polyphony is intended as a graphic analogy, nothing more. The image of polyphony and counterpoint simply indicates the new problems which arise when the structure of the novel goes beyond the bounds of ordinary monological unity, just as new problems arose in music when the bounds of the single voice were exceeded. But music and the novel are too unlike for there to be more than a figurative analogy, a simple metaphor, between them. But for lack of a more appropriate designation we shall turn this metaphor into the term "polyphonic novel." The metaphorical origin of the term should, in any case, not be forgotten.

■

The basic distinguishing characteristic of Dostoevsky's art was, it seems to us, profoundly understood by B. M. Engelgardt in his article "Ideologicheskij roman Dostoevskogo" ("Dostoevsky's Ideological Novel").

B. M. Engelgardt proceeds from the sociological and cultural-historical definition of Dostoevsky's hero. Dostoevsky's hero is the intellectual—*raznochinec*, cut off from the cultural tradition, the soil and the land—the representative of an "accidental tribe" *(sluchajnoe plemja)*. Such a man enters into a special relationship with the idea: he is defenseless before it and its power, for he is not firmly rooted in life and has been robbed of his cultural tradition. He becomes the "man of an idea," a man possessed by an idea. The idea becomes in him an "idea-force" which omnipotently defines and distorts his consciousness and his life. The idea leads an independent life in the hero's consciousness: it is in fact not he who lives, but the idea, and the novelist describes not the hero's life, but the life of the idea in him; the historian of the "accidental tribe" becomes the "historiographer of an idea." Therefore, in place of the biographical dominant of the usual type (as in Tolstoy or Turgenev, for example), the dominant of the hero's representation is the idea which possesses him. Hence originates the definition of Dostoevsky's novel as an "ideological novel." It is, however, not an ordinary ideological novel, a "novel with an idea."

Dostoevsky, says Engelgardt,

depicted the life of the idea in the individual and social consciousness, because he considered it to be the determining factor of cultured society. But this must not be understood to mean that he wrote ideological novels or stories with a bias and was a tendentious artist, more a philosopher than a poet. He wrote

[18]

not 'novels with an idea,' not philosophical novels in the style of the 18th century, but rather **novels about an idea.** Just as the central object for other novelists may have been the adventure, the anecdote, a psychological type, a picture from everyday life or from history, for him the central object was the 'idea.' He cultivated and raised to extraordinary heights a completely unique type of novel which, in contrast to the adventure novel, the sentimental, psychological, or historical novel, can be called **ideological.** In this sense, his work, despite its inherent polemical nature, was not surpassed in objectivity by the work of the other great artists of the word: he was himself such an artist, and in his novels he posed and resolved first and foremost purely artistic problems. It was his material that was extremely unusual: his heroine was the idea.[30]

The idea as the object of representation and as the dominant in the construction of the heroes' images leads to the dissolution of the world of the novel into the worlds of the heroes, organized and formed by the ideas which possess them. Engelgardt clearly reveals the multileveledness of Dostoevsky's novel:

The principle of the hero's purely artistic **orientation in his milieu** is the respective form of his **ideological attitude to the world.** Just as the complex of idea-forces which have dominion over the hero serves as the dominant of his artistic representation, so in like manner the point of view from which the hero sees the world is the dominant in the representation of surrounding reality. The world is presented to each hero in a particular aspect, according to which its image is then constructed. One cannot find in Dostoevsky a so-called objective description of the external world; strictly speaking, there are in his novels neither manners and customs *(byt)*, nor city or country life, nor nature, but there is the milieu, the soil, or the earth, depending on the plane on which the characters observe all of these things. Thus develops that multileveledness of reality in a work of art which in the work of Dostoevsky's successors leads in part to a characteristic disintegration of life, so that the action of the novel unfolds simultaneously or consecutively in completely different ontological spheres.[31]

Engelgardt differentiates three planes in which the novel's action can unfold, depending on the nature of the idea governing the consciousness and life of the hero. The first plane is "the milieu." Mechanical necessity prevails here; here there is no freedom, for every act of the will is a natural product of external conditions. The second plane is "the soil." This is the organic system of the developing spirit of the people. And, finally, the third plane is "the earth." Engelgardt says:

The third concept—"the earth"—is one of the most profound which we find in Dostoevsky. It is that earth which differs not from the children, that earth which Alyosha Karamazov kissed, weeping and sobbing and watering it with his tears, and ecstatically promised to love; it is everything—all of nature, and man, and the animals, and the birds—that wonderful garden which the Lord grew, taking the seeds from other worlds and sowing them on this earth.

It is the highest reality, and at the same time the world in which the earthly life of the spirit unfolds, having achieved the state of true freedom... It is the third kingdom, the kingdom of love, and therefore of complete freedom as well, the kingdom of eternal joy and merriment.[32]

Such is the plan of the novel, according to Engelgardt. Every element of reality (of the external world), every experience and every action necessarily fits into one of these three planes. Engelgardt also distributes the basic themes of Dostoevsky's novels among these three planes.[33]

How are these planes connected in the unity of the novel? What are the principles of their combination one with another?

These three planes and their corresponding themes, examined in their relationship one to another, represent, according to Engelgardt, the various *stages of the dialectical development of the spirit.* He says:

In this sense they form the **only path** by which, amid great suffering and danger, the seeker may pass in his search for the unconditional affirmation of existence. And it is not difficult to show the subjective significance of this path for Dostoevsky himself.[34]

This is Engelgardt's conception. It quite lucidly illuminates the most essential structural characteristics of Dostoevsky's works, and it consistently strives to overcome ideological one-sidedness and abstractness in the perception and evaluation of those characteristics. However, not everything in his conception seems correct to us. And the conclusions concerning Dostoevsky's work as a whole, which he reaches at the end of his article, seem to us totally incorrect.

Engelgardt was the first to correctly define the way in which the idea is stated in the Dostoevskian novel. The idea here is indeed not the *principle of the representation* (as in any novel), not the leitmotiv of the representation and not a conclusion drawn from it (as in the ideological, philosophical novel), but the *subject of the representation.* The idea is the principle of seeing and understanding the world and its formulation from the viewpoint of a given idea only for the characters,[35] not for the author himself, not for Dostoevsky. The heroes' worlds are built according to the ordinary ideological-monological principle; they are constructed as if by the heroes themselves. "The earth" is also only one of the worlds which form the unity of the novel, only one of its planes. Even if "the earth" receives a particular, hierarchically greater emphasis than "the soil" or "the milieu," it is nonetheless only the ideological aspect of such characters as Sonya Marmeladov, the Elder Zosima, and Alyosha.

The heroes' ideas which make up the basis of this plane of the novel are just as much the subject of the representation, are just as much "idea-heroines," as are the ideas of Raskolnikov, Ivan Karamazov and others. They by no means become the principles of the representation and of the construction of the entire novel as a whole, i.e. the principles of the author himself as an artist. If that were the case, the result would be an ordinary philosophical-ideological novel. The hierarchical accent given these ideas does not turn Dostoevsky's novel into an ordinary monological novel, which is ultimately always uni-accentual. From the point of view of the novel's artistic construction, these ideas are merely equal-valued participants in the action, along with the ideas of Raskolnikov, Ivan Karamazov and others. Moreoever, precisely such characters as Raskolnikov and Ivan Karamazov seem to set the tone for the construction of the novel as a whole; that is why the hagiographic tones in the speeches of the lame woman *(Khromonozhka),* in the stories and speeches of the pilgrim Makar Dolgoruky, and, finally, in the "Life of Zosima" stand out so sharply. If the author's world coincided with the plane "earth," then his novels would be constructed in the corresponding hagiographic style.

Thus not a single one of the characters' ideas—neither of the "positive," nor of the "negative" heroes— becomes the author's principle of representation or determines the form of the world of the novel in its entirety. Which raises the question: how are the heroes' worlds and their respective basic ideas united in the author's world, i.e. in the world of the novel? Engelgardt answers this question incorrectly, or, more precisely, he avoids it, in essence giving an answer to an altogether different question.

In reality, the interrelationships of the worlds or planes of the novel—"the milieu," "the soil," and "the earth," in Engelgardt's terms—are not presented as links in a unified dialectical series or as stages in the development of a unified spirit at all. For if the ideas in each individual novel—the planes in the novel are determined by the ideas basic to them—were in fact arranged as the links in a unified dialectical series, then each novel would be a complete philosophical whole, constructed according to the dialectical method. Then we would have, at best, a philosophical novel, a "novel with an idea" (even if a dialectical one), and at worst, philosophy in the form of a novel. The final link in the dialectical series would inevitably be the author's synthesis, which would cancel out the preceeding links as being abstract and fully superceeded.

In actuality, such is not the case: the dialectical development of a unified spirit is not present in any of Dostoevsky's novels, and development and growth are completely absent, in the same degree that they are absent from the tragedy (in this sense the analogy between Dostoevsky's novels and the tragedy is correct).[36] Each novel contains the opposition (an opposition which is not dialectically cancelled out) of many consciousnesses, which do not merge in the unity of a developing spirit, just as the souls and spirits do not merge in Dante's formally polyphonic world. As in Dante's world, they could, without losing their individuality and by combining instead of merging, form at best a static figure, a frozen event, as it were, similar to Dante's image of the cross (the souls of the crusaders),

[21]

the eagle (the souls of the emperors), or the mystical rose (the souls of the blessed). Neither does the author's spirit develop or evolve within the bounds of the novel itself, but, as in Dante's world, is either a spectator or becomes one of the participants. Within the bounds of the novel the heroes' worlds are interrelated by events, but, as we have already stated, their interrelationships cannot be reduced to thesis, antithesis and synthesis.

But neither can Dostoevsky's oeuvre as a whole be thought of as the dialectical development of a spirit. For his creative path is the artistic evolution of his novel, connected, it is true, with an ideological evolution, but not revealed in it. A dialectical development of the spirit, passing through the stages of "the milieu," "the soil," and "the earth," can be speculated upon only from beyond the limits of Dostoevsky's artistic work. His novels, as artistic units, do not depict or express the dialectical development of the spirit.

In the final analysis, B. M. Engelgardt monologizes Dostoevsky's world just as his predecessors had done, reducing it to a dialectically developing philosophical monolog. A unified, dialectically evolving spirit, understood in Hegelian terms, can give rise to nothing but the philosophical monolog. The plurality of unmerged consciousnesses can blossom least of all on the soil of monistic idealism. In this sense the unifed evolving spirit, even as an image, is organically foreign to Dostoevsky. Dostoevsky's world is profoundly *pluralistic.* If one were to look for an image toward which this whole world gravitates, an image in the spirit of Dostoevsky's own *Weltanschauung,* such an image would be the church, the communion of unmerged spirits, the meeting place of the sinner and the righteous man, or, perhaps, Dante's world, where multileveledness is carried over into eternity, where there are the penitent and the unrepentant, the saved and the damned. This is an image in Dostoevsky's own style, or, rather, in the style of his ideology, while the image of the unified spirit is profoundly foreign to him.

But the image of the church, too, remains only an image, explaining nothing of the structure of the novel itself. The artistic problem which the novel solves is essentially independent from that secondary ideological aspect which, perhaps, sometimes accompanied it in Dostoevsky's consciousness. The concrete artistic connections between the planes of the novel and their combinations in the unity of the work must be explained and demonstrated on the basis of the material of the novel itself, and both the "Hegelian spirit" and the "church" distract equally from this task.

If we raise the question of the extra-artistic causes and factors which made possible the construction of the polyphonic novel, then here, too, the least appropriate course of action would be to turn to subjective facts, profound though they may be. If multileveledness and contradictoriness were given to or preceived by Dostoevsky merely as a fact of his personal life, as multileveledness or contradictoriness of the spirit—his own and of others—then Dostoevsky would have been a romantic and would have created a monological novel about the contradictory development of the human spirit, truly in tune with the Hegelian conception. But in fact Dostoevsky found and perceived multileveledness and contradictoriness not in the spirit, but in the objective social world. In that social world the various planes were not stages, but *opposing camps,* and the contradictory relationships between them were not the rising or descending path of an individual, but rather the *state of society.* The multileveledness and contradictoriness of social reality were presented as an objective fact of the age.

The age itself made the polyphonic novel possible. Dostoevsky was *subjectively* involved in the contradictory multileveledness of his time; he changed camps, he switched from one to another, and in this respect the planes which existed in the objective social life were for him stages on his life's path and in his spiritual evolution. This was a profound personal experience, but Dostoevsky did not give it direct monological expression in his art. It only helped him to more profoundly comprehend the coexistent, extensively manifest contradictions between people, but not between ideas in a single consciousness. Thus the objective contradictions of the age determined Dostoevsky's art not in that he was able to overcome them within the history of his own spirit, but in that he came to objectively view them as simultaneously coexisting forces. (His vision was, of course, made more profound by personal experience.)

We now approach a very important characteristic of Dostoevsky's artistic vision, a characteristic which has been either totally uncomprehended or underestimated in the critical literature. Underestimation of this characteristic was what led to Engelgardt's false conclusions. The principle category of Dostoevsky's artistic vision is not evolution, but *coexistence* and *interaction.* He saw and conceived his world chiefly in space, not in time. Hence his strong inclination to the dramatic form.[37] He strives to extensively reveal all the sense-and reality-material available to him, organizing it in a single point in time in the form of dramatic juxtaposition. An artist like Goethe, for example, is organically inclined to the developing series. He strives to perceive all of the coexisting contradictions as various stages of some unified development and to see in every manifestation of the present traces of the past, the epitome of contemporaneity, or a tendency of the future; consequently, nothing for him is situated in a single extensive plane. Such, in any case, was the basic tendency of his vision and understanding of the world.[38]

In contrast to Goethe, Dostoevsky strove to perceive these very stages in their *simultaneity,* to *juxtapose* and *counterpose* them, and not to stretch them out into a developing series. To orient oneself in the world meant for him to think of all its contents as being simultaneous and to *guess at their interrelationships in a single point in time.*

This persistent urge to see all things as being coexistent and to perceive and depict all things side by side and simultaneously, as if in space rather than time, leads him to dramatize in space even the inner contradictions and stages of development of a single person, causing the characters to converse with their doubles, with the devil, with their alter egos, with caricatures of themselves (Ivan and the devil, Ivan and Smerdyakov, Raskolnikov and Svidrigailov, etc.). This characteristic explains the frequent appearance of paired heroes in Dostoevsky's works. It can be said that Dostoevsky strives to make two persons out of every contradiction

[23]

within a single person, in order to dramatize the contradiction and reveal it extensively. This characteristic is outwardly expressed in Dostoevsky's predilection for mass scenes and in his urge to concentrate as many characters and themes as possible in a single time and place, often at the expense of verisimilitude; i.e. to concentrate in a single split second the greatest possible qualitative diversity. Hence also Dostoevsky's tendency to observe the dramatic unity of time in his novels. And hence the catastrophic swiftness of action, the "whirlwind motion," the dynamics of Dostoevsky. Dynamics and speed here (as, by the way, everywhere) signify not the triumph of time, but the triumph over time, for speed is the only means of overcoming time in time. The ability to exist simultaneously and the ability to stand side by side or face to face opposite one another is for Dostoevsky the criterion for differentiating the essential from the non-essential. Only those things which can conceivably be presented simultaneously, which can conceivably be interconnected in a single point in time, are of the essence and enter into Dostoevsky's world; such things are also capable of being carried over into eternity, for in eternity, according to Dostoevsky, all is simultaneous, everything coexists. That which has significance only as "formerly" or as "later," that which satisfies only its own moment, which is justified only as past or future, or as present in relation to past and future, is for him non-essential and does not enter into his world. For the same reason his characters recall nothing, they have no biography, in the sense of something in the past or of something fully experienced and endured. They remember from their past only those things which have not ceased to be current for them and which continue to be experienced in the present: an unexpiated sin or crime, an unforgiven insult. Dostoevsky introduces only this sort of biographical fact into his novels, because it is compatible with his principle of simultaneity.[39] Therefore there is no causality in the Dostoevskian novel, no origination, no explanations based on the past, on the influence of the environment or of upbringing, etc. The hero's every act is in the present, and in this sense is unpredetermined; it is conceived of and depicted by the author as being free.

The characteristic of Dostoevsky under discussion is not, of course, a characteristic of his *Weltanschauung* in the usual sense of the word; it is a characteristic of his artistic perception of the world: he knew how to see and represent the world only in the category of coexistence. But, of course, this characteristic was necessarily reflected in his abstract *Weltanschauung* as well. And in it we note analgous phenomena: in Dostoevsky's thinking there are not genetic or causal categories. He constantly, and with a sort of organic hostility, polemicized against the theory of environmental causality *(teorija sredy),* in whatever forms it appeared (for example, in lawyers' appeals to the environment in justifying their clients). He almost never appeals to history as such, and he treats every social and political question within the realm of contemporaneity, and this not only because his status as a journalist required currency in his interpretations; on the contrary, we believe that the basic characteristics of Dostoevsky's artistic vision themselves explain his predilection for journalism, his love for the newspaper page, and his profound and subtle understanding of the newspaper page as a living reflection of contemporary social contradictions in the cross-section of a single day, where the most diverse and contradictory material is extensively revealed side by side and face to face.[40] And finally, in the realm of abstract *Weltanschauung,* this characteristic was manifested in Dostoevsky's tendency toward eschatalogy, both political and religious, and in his tendency to bring the "ends" together, feeling them out already in the present, making conjectures as to the future on the basis of its presence in the struggle of coexisting forces.

Dostoevsky's extraordinary artistic capacity for seeing all things in terms of their coexistence and interaction is his greatest strength, and at the same time his greatest weakness. It made him deaf and blind to a great many essential things; many aspects of reality could not gain access to his artistic field of vision. But on the other hand this capacity sharpened to the utmost his perception in the cross-section of a given moment and allowed him to see many and varied things where everyone else saw one and the same thing. Where others saw a single thought, he was able to feel out and find two thoughts, a divarication; where others saw a single quality he revealed in that quality the presence of another, contradictory one. All that was simple became in his world complex and multistructural *(mnogosostavnoe).* In every voice he could hear two contending voices, in every expression a split and a willingness to immediately turn into another, contradictory expression. In every gesture he perceived confidence and lack of confidence simultaneously; he perceived the profound ambiguity *(dvusmyslennost' i mnogosmyslennost')* of every phenomenon. But all of these contradictions and divarications did not become dialectical, they were not developed temporally, in an evolutionary series, but rather were manifested as standing side by side or opposed face to face in a single plane, either consonant but not merging, or irreconcilably contradictory; either the eternal harmony of unmerged voices, or a ceaseless, hopeless argument. Dostoevsky's vision was locked up in that instant in which this diversity manifests itself, and it remained locked up there, organizing and formulating this diversity within the cross-section of a given moment.

Dostoevsky's special gift for immediately and simultaneously hearing and understanding all of these diverse voices, a gift equalled only by Dante's, made it possible for him to create the polyphonic novel. The objective complexity, contradictoriness and multivoicedness of the epoch in which Dostoevsky lived, the situation of the non-noble intellectual *(raznochinec)* and social outcast, the profound biographical and inner involvement in the objective multileveledness of life, and, finally, the gift for seeing the world in interaction and coexistence—all these things prepared the soil out of which grew Dostoevsky's polyphonic novel.

The characteristics of Dostoevsky's vision which we have discussed, his special artistic conception of space and time, also found (as we shall show in greater detail below, in chapter four) support in the literary tradition with which Dostoevsky was organically connected.

Thus, Dostoevsky's world consists of the artistically organized coexistence and interaction of spiritual diversity, and not of stages of an evolving unified spirit. Therefore, despite their unique hierarchical values, the worlds of the heroes, the planes of the novel, lie side by side on the plane of coexistence (as in Dante's world) and interaction (which was absent from Dante's formal polyphony), and not one behind another as stages of evolution. This does not, of course, mean that logical vicious circles *(durnaja logicheskaja bezysxodnost')*, incompleted thoughts and *subjective* contradictoriness prevail in Dostoevsky's world. No, Dostoevsky's world is in its own way just as finished and rounded off as Dante's. But it is futile to seek in it a *systematic monological philosophical* finalizedness, even of a dialectical nature, not because the author failed to achieve it, but because it was not a part of his intention.

What caused Engelgardt to seek in Dostoevsky's works "individual links in a complex philosophical construction expressing the history of the gradual evolution of the human spirit,"[41] i.e. what caused him to take the well-worn path of philosophical monologization of Dostoevsky's works?

It seems to us that Engelgardt's basic error came at the very beginning with his definition of Dostoevsky's "ideological novel." The idea as the object of representation occupies an immense place in Dostoevsky's work, but it is nonetheless not the heroine of his novels. His hero was man, and, in the final analysis, he depicted not the idea in man, but, to use his own words, "the man in man." The idea was for him either the touchstone for testing the man in man, the form of his revelation, or—and this is the most important—the "medium," the milieu, in which the human consciousness is revealed in its most profound essence. Engelgardt underestimates Dostoevsky's deep personalism. Dostoevsky does not know, does not see, and does not represent the "idea for its own sake" in the Platonic sense or the "ideal existence" in the phenomenologists' sense. For Dostoevsky there are no ideas, thoughts, or situations which belong to no one, which exist "for their own sakes." He presents "truth for its own sake" in the spirit of Christian ideology, i.e. as a person who enters into interrelationships with other persons.

Therefore Dostoevsky depicted not the life of ideas in an isolated consciousness and not the interrelationships of ideas, but rather the interaction of consciousnesses in the sphere of ideas (but not only of ideas). And since in Dostoevsky's world the consciousness is not presented in the process of its evolution and growth, i.e. not historically, but *side by side* with other consciousnesses, it cannot concentrate on itself and its own idea and its idea's immanent logical development; instead, the consciousness is drawn into interaction with other consciousnesses. In Dostoevsky's works the consciousness is never self-sufficient; it always finds itself in an intense relationship with another consciousness. The hero's every experience and his every thought is internally dialogical, polemically colored and filled with opposing forces or, on the other hand, open to inspiration from outside itself, but in any case does not simply concentrate on its own object; it is accompanied by a constant sideward glance at the other person. One might say that Dostoevsky presents, in artistic form, the sociology of the consciousness, albeit only within the plane of coexistence. But regardless, Dostoevsky the artist achieves an *objective* vision of the life of the consciousness and the forms of its living coexistence, and therefore he presents the material that is valuable for the sociologist as well.

[26]

From the very beginning every thought of Dostoevsky's heroes (the "underground man," Raskolnikov, Ivan, etc.) feels itself to be a *speech* in an uncompleted dialog. Such a thought does not pursue a rounded-off and finalized monological whole. It lives a tense life on the border of another idea and another consciousness. It has its own special character as an event and is inseparable from man.

The term "ideological novel" seems, therefore, inadequate and distractive from Dostoevsky's real artistic task.

Thus Engelgardt, too, failed to fully recognize Dostoevsky's artistic will; while noting a number of its essential aspects, in general he interprets it as a philosophical-monological will, thereby transforming the polyphony of coexisting consciousnesses into the homophonic evolution of a single consciousness.

■

The problem of polyphony was very concisely and amply stated by A. V. Lunacharsky in his article "O 'mnogogolosnosti' Dostoevskogo" ("On Dostoevsky's 'Multivoicedness' ").[42]

In general, Lunacharsky shares our thesis concerning Dostoevsky's polyphonic novel. He says:

I agree that M. M. Bakhtin has succeeded in establishing with greater clarity than anyone before him the enormous significance of multivoicedness in the Dostoevskian novel and the role of multivoicedness as its most essential characteristic feature; in addition, he has correctly defined the extraordinary (and, in the works of the overwhelming majority of other writers, unthinkable) autonomy and full-valuedness *(polnocennost')* of every 'voice' that so startlingly developed in Dostoevsky's works.[43]

Lunacharsky further correctly emphasizes that

all of the 'voices' which play a truly significant role in the novel are 'convictions' or 'points of view toward the world.'

Dostoevsky's novels are brilliantly staged dialogs.

Under these conditions the profound independence of the individual 'voices' becomes, so to speak, especially piquant. One must assume that Dostoevsky sought to put forward various vital problems for discussion by these peculiar 'voices' which tremble with passion and blaze with the fire of fanaticism. He himself is, as it were, present at these convulsive disputes only as a spectator who watches curiously to see what turn the matter will take and how it will all end. And this is the case, to a significant degree.[44]

Lunacharsky further poses the question of Dostoevsky's forerunners in the realm of polyphony. He considers Shakespeare and Balzac to be such.

This is what he says of polyphony in Shakespeare:

Being an untendentious writer (as he was for a long time considered, at least), Shakespeare is polyphonic in the extreme. One could cite a long list of the opinions of his best critics, imitators and followers, who admire precisely his ability to create an incredible variety of personages who are all independent of him, all the while maintaining an incredible inner logic in all of the assertions and actions of every character in this endless circle dance...

One cannot say of Shakespeare that his plays sought to prove a certain thesis, nor that the 'voices' introduced into the great polyphony of the Shakespearian dramatic world sacrificed their autonomy for the sake of the dramatic intention or the structure as such.[45]

According to Lunacharsky, the social conditions of Shakespeare's age are analogous to those of Dostoevsky's age.

What sorts of social facts were reflected in Shakespeare's polyphony? Well, in the final analysis, of course, the same ones, in their main features, as in Dostoevsky. That colorful Renaissance, subdivided into myriad glittering splinters, which gave birth to Shakespeare and to the other dramatists of his time, was, of course, also the result of the stormy incursion of capitalism into comparatively quiet medieval England. And here, too, in precisely the same way, began a gigantic breakdown, gigantic changes and unexpected collisions of social structures and systems of consciousness which had never before come into contact with one another.[46]

Lunacharsky is, in our opinion, in so far correct that certain elements, certain rudiments, certain germs of polyphony can be discovered in Shakespeare's dramas. Shakespeare, together with Rabelais, Cervantes, Grimmelshausen and others, belongs to that line of development in European literature in which the germs of polyphony ripened and of which Dostoevsky became the culminator. But in our opinion it is simply impossible to speak of a completely formed and deliberate polyphony in Shakespeare's plays for the following reasons.

First of all, the drama is by nature alien to genuine polyphony; the drama can be multileveled, but cannot contain *multiple worlds;* it allows for only one, not several, systems of measurement.

Secondly, if one can speak at all of a plurality of full-valued voices in Shakespeare, it is only in relation to his work as a whole, and not in relation to the individual plays. In each play there is essentially only a single full-valued hero's voice, while polyphony requires a plurality of full-valued voices within the bounds of a single work; only then do the principles of polyphony apply to the construction of the whole.

Thirdly, the voices in Shakespeare's works are not points of view vis-à-vis the world in the same degree as they are in Dostoevsky's; Shakespeare's heroes are not ideologists in the full sense of the word.

One can speak of elements of polyphony in Balzac's work as well, but only of elements. Balzac occupies a place in the same line of development of the European novel as Dostoevsky, and is one of his direct forebears. The features common to the work of Balzac and Dostoevsky have often been noted (especially amply and well by L. Grossman), and there is no need to return to them. But Balzac did not overcome the objectivization of his characters and the monological finalization of his world.

It is our conviction that Dostoevsky alone can be considered the creator of the polyphonic novel.

Lunacharsky devotes most of his attention to an explanation of the social and historical causes of Dostoevsky's multivoicedness.

Like Kaus, Lunacharsky exposes the extraordinarily acute contradictoriness of Dostoevsky's age, of the age of young Russian capitalism, and, further, exposes the contradictoriness and *duality* of Dostoevsky's own social personality and his oscillations between revolutionary materialistic socialism and a conservative (reactionary) religious *Weltanschauung,* oscillations which never brought him to a final decision. We shall quote the conclusion of Lunacharsky's historical-genetic analysis.

It was only the inner dichotomy of Dostoevsky's consciousness, together with the dichotomy in the young Russian capitalist society, that caused him to turn again and again to the process of socialist principles and socialist reality, but in so doing the author created the least favorable conditions for those processes, so far as materialistic socialism was concerned.[47]

A little further on he says:

But that **unheard-of freedom of the 'voices'** which so amazes the reader in Dostoevsky's polyphony is precisely a result of the fact that, in essence, Dostoevsky's power over the spirits which he has called into life is limited...

If Dostoevsky is his own master as a writer, is he his own master as a person?

No, Dostoevsky is not his own master as a person, and the disintegration of his personality, its dichotomy—the fact that he would like to believe in something which instills no true faith in him, and would like to refute something which constantly instills doubt in him—this is what subjectively qualifies him to be the agonizing and necessary reflector of the confusion of his age.[48]

Lunacharsky's genetic analysis of Dostoevsky's polyphony is, without doubt, profound and, in so far as it remains within the limits of a historical-genetic analysis, raises no serious doubts. But doubts begin to form at the point where he draws from his analysis direct conclusions about the artistic worth and historical progressiveness (in artistic terms) of Dostoevsky's new type of polyphonic novel. The exceptionally harsh contradicitons of early Russian capitalism and Dostoevsky's duality as a social personality—his personal inability to make a particular ideological decision—

when taken by themselves are negative and historically transcient phenomena, but they provided the optimal conditions for the creation of the polyphonic novel and of "that unheard-of freedom of the voices...in Dostoevsky's polyphony," which was without doubt a step forward in the development of the Russian and European novel. Both Dostoevsky's epoch, with its concrete contradictions, and his biological and social person, with its epilepsy and its ideological duality, have long since faded into the past, but the new structural principle of polyphony, *discovered* under those conditions, retains and will continue to retain its artistic significance under the totally different conditions of subsequent epochs. Great discoveries of the human genius are possible only under the specific conditions of specific epochs, but they never perish and lose their value along with the epoch which gave them birth.

Lunacharsky draws no clearly false conclusions about the extinction of the polyphonic novel from his genetic analysis, but the final words of his article could give rise to such an interpretation. Here are those words: "Dostoevsky has not yet died here nor in the West, because capitalism is not yet dead, not to mention the vestiges of capitalism...Thus it is important to examine all the problems of that tragic 'Dostoevskyism' *(dostoevshchina)*."[49]

This formulation seems to us unacceptable. Dostoevsky's discovery of the polyphonic novel will outlive capitalism.

"Dostoevskyism," against which Lunacharsky, following Gorky's example, rightfully issues a call to battle, must, of course, under no circumstances be equated with polyphony. "Dostoevskyism" is a reactionary, *purely monological* extract from Dostoevsky's polyphony. It is always confined within the bounds of a single consciousness, it digs its way in and creates a cult of the duality of an *isolated* personality. The important thing in Dostoevsky's polyphony is what takes place *between various personalities,* i.e. their interaction and interdependence. One should not learn from Raskolnikov or Sonya, not from Ivan Karamazov and not from Zosima, isolating their voices from the polyphonic whole of the novels (and thereby distorting them),—one should learn from Dostoevsky himself, as the creator of the polyphonic novel.

In his historical-genetic analysis Lunacharsky reveals only the contradictions of Dostoevsky's epoch and his personal duality. But a protracted preparation of the general esthetic and literary tradition was required before those content-related factors could be transformed into a new form of artistic vision, before they could give birth to the new structure of the polyphonic novel. New forms of artistic vision take shape slowly, over centuries; a single epoch only creates the optimal conditions for the final maturation and realization of a new form. To reveal the process of the artistic genesis of the polyphonic novel is the task of historical poetics. Poetry cannot, of course, be divorced from social and historical analyses, but neither can it be revealed in them.

■

In the following two decades, i.e. in the 1930s and 1940s, problems of Dostoevsky's poetics took a back seat to other important tasks in the study of his art. Textological work continued, valuable publications of the manuscripts and notebooks of Dostoevsky's various novels took place, work on the four-volume collection of his letters continued, and the history of the writing of the individual novels was studied.[50] But specific theoretical works on Dostoevsky's poetics, which would have been interesting from the point of view of our thesis (the polyphonic novel), did not appear in that period.

In this respect, certain observations made by V. Kirpotin in his short work *F. M. Dostoevskii* deserve attention.

In contrast to very many scholars, who see one single soul—the soul of the author himself—in all of Dostoevsky's works, Kirpotin emphasizes Dostoevsky's special ability to *see* the souls of *others*.

> Dostoevsky had the ability to *see directly into the psyches of others*. He looked into their souls as if he were equipped with a magnifying glass which allowed him to discern the subtlest nuances and to observe the most inconspicuous changes and transitions in man's inner life. By seemingly passing over the external barriers, Dostoevsky directly observes the psychological processes which take place in man, and he commits them to paper...
>
> There was nothing a priori in Dostoevsky's gift of seeing the psyches, the 'souls' of others. This gift took on extraordinary proportions, but it was based on introspection, on observation of other people, and on the diligent study of man in Russian and world literature, i.e. it was based on internal and external experience, and had therefore *objective significance.*[51]

In refuting the false conceptions concerning the subjectivism and individualism of Dostoevsky's psychology, Kirpotin emphasizes his *realistic* and *social* character.

> In contrast to the degenerate decadent psychology of Proust or Joyce, which signaled the decline and fall of bourgeois literature, *Dostoevsky's psychology* in his positive works is not *subjective,* but *realistic.* His psychology is his special artistic method of penetrating into the objective essence of the *contradictory human collective* and into the very heart of the *social relationships* which trouble him, and his method for reproducing those things in the art of the word...Dostoevsky thought in psychological images, but he thought *socially.*[52]

Kirpotin's correct understanding of Dostoevsky's psychology as the objective realistic vision of the collective of others' psyches leads him consequently to a correct understanding of Dostoevsky's *polyphony* as well, although he himself does not use that term.

> The history of each individual soul is given by Dostoevsky not in

isolation, but together with the description of many other individuals' psychological experiences. Regardless of whether the story is being told in the first person, in the form of a confession, or by a narrator-author, we see that the writer proceeds from the assumption of the *equality* of **simultaneously existing,** experiencing people. His world is the world of a multitude of objectively existing and interacting psychologies, and this fact excludes decadent bourgeois subjectivism and solipsism from his interpretation of psychological processes.[53]

These are the conclusions of Kirpotin, who, following his own path, arrived at a position similar to ours.

■

In the last decade the literature on Dostoevsky has been enriched by a series of valuable synthesizing studies (books and articles) embracing all aspects of his work (V. Ermilov, V. Kirpotin, G. Fridlender, A. Belkin, F. Evnin, Ia. Bilinkis, and others). But prevalent in all of these studies are historical-literary and historical-sociological analyses of Dostoevsky's work and of the social reality reflected in it. Problems of a strictly poetic nature are treated as a rule merely in passing (although valuable, if somewhat random, observations are made in some of these studies on various aspects of Dostoevsky's artistic form).

From the point of view of our thesis, Viktor Shklovsky's book *Za i protiv. Zametki o Dostoevskom (Pro and Contra. Remarks on Dostoevsky)* is of particular interest.[54]

Shklovsky proceeds from the position, first established by L. Grossman, that it is precisely the *conflict,* the struggle of ideological voices, that lies at the core of the artistic *form* of Dostoevsky's works, at the core of his *style.* But Shklovsky is interested not so much in Dostoevsky's polyphonic form as in the historical (epochal) and biographical sources of the ideological conflict which gave birth to that form. In his polemical remarks "Contra" he defines the nature of his book thus:

> The peculiarity of my book is not in the fact that I emphasize those stylistic characteristics which I consider self-evident—they were emphasized by Dostoevsky himself in *Brothers Karamazov* when he titled one of the books of the novel "Pro and contra." I have tried to explain something else in my book: what caused that conflict which resulted in Dostoevsky's literary form, and, at the same time, what constitutes the universality of Dostoevsky's novels, i.e. who is interested in that conflict today.[55]

Shklovsky brings massive and diverse historical, literary-historical, and biographical material to bear, and in his characteristic lively and witty form he reveals the conflict of the historical forces, the social, political and ideological voices of the epoch, a conflict which runs through all of the stages of Dostoevsky's life and creative work, penetrating all the events of his life and organizing both the form and the content of all of his works. That conflict nonetheless remained unresolved for Dostoevsky's epoch and for him personally. "Dostoevsky died without having resolved anything, avoiding solutions and remaining unreconciled."[56]

One can agree with all of this (although it is, of course, also possible to question certain of Shklovsky's propositions). But we must emphasize that, if Dostoevsky died "without having resolved" any of the ideological questions posed by his epoch, he did not die without having created a new form of artistic vision— the polyphonic novel, which will retain its artistic significance even after the epoch with all of its contradictions has faded into the past.

Shklovsky's book contains valuable observations on questions of Dostoevsky's poetics as well. From the point of view of our thesis, two of his observations are interesting.

The first of them concerns characteristics of Dostoevsky's creative process and the rough drafts of his works.

> Fyodor Mikhailovich was fond of sketching out plans of things; he was even fonder of developing, mulling over and complicating his plans, and he did not like to *finish* his manuscripts...
>
> Not, of course, because he was in too great a 'hurry'—Dostoevsky worked with numerous drafts, 'being inspired **several times** by it (by a scene— V. Sh.)' (1858, Letter to M. Dostoevsky). But Dostoevsky's plans are by their very nature incomplete, and this in effect negates them.
>
> I assume that he had too little time not because he signed too many contracts or because he procrastinated the completion of his works. *As long as a work remained multileveled and multivoiced, as long as the people in it were still arguing, despair over the absence of a conclusion was postponed.* The conclusion of a novel signified for Dostoevsky the collapse of a new Tower of Babylon.[57]

This observation is quite correct. In Dostoevsky's rough drafts the polyphonic nature of his works and the fundamentally unfinalized nature of his dialogs are visible in raw and naked form. Dostoevsky's creative process, as revealed in his rough drafts, differs sharply from the creative process of other writers (of L. Tolstoy, for example). Dostoevsky does not work at making objectivized images of people, he seeks no objectified speeches for *characters* (characteristic and typical ones), he seeks no expressive, graphic, finalizing authorial words. Above all he seeks—*for his hero*—words which are maximally pregnant with meaning and seemingly independent of the author, words which express not the hero's character (or his typicality) and not his position in given real-life situations, but rather his final ideological position in the world, his point of view vis-à-vis the world. *For the author as author* he seeks words and plot situations which provoke, tease, and elicit response. Herein lies the profound originality of Dostoevsky's creative process.[58]

The study of his manuscripts from this angle is an interesting and important task.

In the passage which we have quoted, Shklovsky touches on the complex problem of the fundamental unfinalizability of the polyphonic novel. In Dostoevsky's novels we do in fact observe a unique conflict between the internal unfinalized nature of the heroes and the dialog on the one hand, and the *external* (in most cases compositional and thematic) *completeness* of every individual novel. We cannot delve deeply into this difficult problem here. We shall say only that almost all of Dostoevsky's novels have a *conventionally (uslovno) literary, conventionally monological* ending (especially characteristic in this respect is the ending of *Crime and Punishment).* In essence only *The Brothers Karamazov* has a completely polyphonic conclusion, and precisely for that reason it remains, from the ordinary, i.e. monological, point of view, uncompleted.

No less interesting is Shklovsky's second observation. It concerns the dialogical nature of all the elements of Dostoevsky's novelistic structure.

It is not only Dostoevsky's heroes who disagree; individual elements of the plot development seem to stand in mutual contradiction: facts are unriddled in different ways and the psychology of the heroes is self-contradictory; the form is the result of the essence *(sushchnost').*[59]

The essential dialogicality of Dostoevsky's works is indeed not limited to the outward, compositionally expressed dialogs carried on by his heroes. *The polyphonic novel as a whole is thoroughly dialogical.* Dialogical relationships obtain between all the elements of its structure, i.e. the elements are contrapuntally counterposed. For dialogical relationships constitute a much more far-reaching phenomenon than merely the relationships between speeches in a literary composition; they are an almost universal phenomenon which permeates all of human speech and all relationships and manifestations of human life and, in general, everything that has meaning and significance.

Dostoevsky could perceive dialogical relationships everywhere, in all the manifestations of conscious and intelligent human life; for him dialog begins at the same point where consciousness begins. Only purely mechanistic relationships are not dialogical, and he categorically denied their significance for an understanding and interpretation of life and of man's acts (viz. his struggle against mechanistic materialism, against the fashionable psycho-physiological theories, against Claude Bernard, against the theory of environmental causality, etc.). Therefore all of the relationships of the internal and external parts and elements of his novel have a dialogical character, and the whole of the novel is constructed as a *"great dialog" (bol'shoi dialog).* The "great dialog" is illuminated and intensified by the dialogs of the heroes which take place within it, within the composition of the novel, and ultimately the dialog goes to the very core, into every word of the novel, making it double-voiced, into every gesture, every mimical movement of the hero's face, making the novel irregular and erratic; here we have already the "microdialog" which determines the characteristics of Dostoevsky's verbal style.

[34]

■

The last critical work which we will consider in our survey is the collection of essays published in 1959 by the Institute for World Literature of the Academy of Sciences of the USSR under the title *Tvorchestvo F. M. Dostoevskogo (F. M. Dostoevsky's Work)*.

Almost all of the works of the Soviet literary scholars included in this volume contain a number of valuable individual observations and broader theoretical generalizations on the question of Dostoevsky's poetics,[60] but for us, from the point of view of our thesis, of greatest interest is L. P. Grossman's copious work "Dostoevskii-xudozhnik" ("Dostoevsky the Artist"), and within that work the chapter entitled "The Laws of Composition." In this new work Grossman expands, deepens and enriches with new observations those conceptions which he had developed already in the 30s, and which we have analyzed above.

According to Grossman, the basis of the composition of all of Dostoevsky's novels is "the principle of two or several converging stories" which in contrasting ways augment each other and are connected in accordance with the musical principle of polyphony.

Following the lead of Vogüe and Vyacheslav Ivanov, whom he sympathetically quotes, Grossman emphasizes the musical character of Dostoevsky's composition.

We shall quote Grossman's most interesting observations and conclusions.

Dostoevsky himself drew attention to this direction (musical direction—M. B.) in his composition, and once drew an analogy between his structural system and the musical theory of 'modulations' or counterpositions. He was, at the time, writing a novella with three chapters, each with a different content, but internally unified. The first chapter was a polemical and philosophical monolog, the second a dramatic episode which prepared the way for the tragic denouement in the third. Is it possible to publish these chapters separately, asks the author. They are internally related, they have unlike, but inseparable, motifs which allow an organic change of tonalities, but not their mechanistic severance. This is a possible interpretation of Dostoevsky's brief but meaningful remarks made in a letter to his brother on the subject of the forthcoming publication of *Notes from the Underground* in the journal *Vremia (Time)*: 'The novella is divided into three chapters...The first chapter is perhaps one-and-one-half printed sheets in length...Should we really print it separately? People will laugh at it, the more so since without the other two (main) chapters it loses all of its juice. You know what a modulation is in music. It is exactly the same thing here. The first chapter is obviously idle chatter; but suddenly this idle chatter is resolved by an unexpected catastrophe in the last two chapters.' (*Letters*, 1, p. 365.)

Here Dostoevsky with great subtlety transfers the law of musical transition from one tonality to another into the realm of literary composition.

The novella is built on the principles of artistic counterpoint. The psychological torment of the fallen girl in the second chapter corresponds to the insult suffered by her tormentor in the first, but at the same time, because of her meekness, it contradicts his feelings of wounded and embittered pride. This is point versus point (punctum contra punctum). *These are different voices singing in different ways on the same theme.* This is 'multivoicedness,' which reveals the variety of life and the complexity of human experience. One of Dostoevsky's favorite composers, M. I. Glinka, said in his 'Notes:' *'Everything in life is counterpoint, i.e. antithesis.* [61]

Grossman's observations on the musical nature of Dostoevsky's composition are very correct and subtle. If we transpose Glinka's statement that "everything in life is counterpoint" from the language of musical theory into the language of poetics, we can say that for Dostoevsky *everything in life is dialog, i.e. dialogical antithesis.* And in essence, from the point of view of philosophical esthetics, contrapuntal relationships in music constitute only the musical variety of broadly understood *dialogical relationships.*

Grossman thus concludes the observations quoted above:

> This was the realization of the law, discovered by the novelist, which provides that 'some other story,' tragic and terrible, always forces its way into the word-for-word description of real life. In accordance with his poetics, these two stories can be thematically augmented by others, which often makes for the well-known multileveledness of Dostoevsky's novels. But the principle of the two-sided elucidation of the main theme remains predominant. With this two-sidedness is connected the much-studied phenomenon of the double in Dostoevsky which, in its conception, fulfills not only an important ideological and psychological function, but an important compositional one as well.[62]

These are Grossman's valuable observations. They are especially interesting for us because Grossman, in contrast to other scholars, approaches Dostoevsky's polyphony from the standpoint of composition. He is interested not so much in the *ideological* multivoicedness of Dostoevsky's novels as in the strictly compositional application of counterpoint as the bond between the various stories included in the novel, the various plots, the various planes.

■

Such is the interpretation of Dostoevsky's polyphonic novel in that part of the critical literature which at all concerned itself with problems of his poetics. The majority of critical and historical-literary studies of his works even now continue to ignore the uniqueness of his artistic form and instead seeks his originality in the content—in the theme, ideas, and individual images taken from the novels and

[36]

evaluated only from the point of view of their life-related content. But in the process, the content itself inevitably becomes less rich: the most essential of its elements is lost, namely those *new* things which Dostoevsky saw. Without understanding a new form of vision, it is impossible to correctly understand those things which have been seen and discovered by means of that new form. Artistic form, correctly understood, does not formulate content which has already been prepared and discovered, but rather allows it to be found and seen for the first time.

That which in the Russian and European novel prior to Dostoevsky constituted the ultimate whole—the unified monological world of the author's consciousness—becomes in Dostoevsky's novel a part, an element of the whole; that which was all of reality becomes here one ot the aspects of reality; that which bound the whole together—the pragmatic progression of the plot and the personal style and tone—becomes here a subordinate element. There arise new principles for the artistic combination of elements and the construction of the whole, there arises—to speak metaphorically—novelistic counterpoint.

The consciousness of critics and scholars is today still enslaved by the ideology of Dostoevsky's heroes. The author's artistic will does not receive clear theoretical recognition. It seems that everyone who enters the labyrinth of the polyphonic novel loses his way and cannot hear the whole for all the individual voices. Often even the vague outline of the whole goes unnoticed; the artistic principles of the combination of voices are simply not captured by the ear. Everyone interprets Dostoevsky's final word in his own way, but they all interpret it as a *single* word, a *single* voice, a *single* accent, and therein lies their basic mistake. The unity of the polyphonic novel which stands above the word, above the voice, above the accent remains undiscovered.

CHAPTER TWO

THE HERO AND THE AUTHOR'S POSITION

IN RELATION TO THE HERO IN DOSTOEVSKY'S WORK

We have advanced a thesis and given a rather monological (in light of our theory) revue of the most pertinent attempts to define the basic features of Dostoevsky's art. In the process of this critical analysis we have made our point of view clear. Now we must move on to a more detailed and conclusive development of that point of view, based on the material of Dostoevsky's works.

We will concentrate consecutively on the three aspects of our thesis: on the relative freedom and independence of the hero and his voice in the framework of the polyphonically conceived novel; on the special means of stating ideas in the polyphonic novel; and finally on the new principles of connection *(sviaz')* which bind together the whole of the novel. The present chapter is devoted to the hero.

The hero interests Dostoevsky not as a manifestation of reality possessing specific, fixed social-typical and individual-characterological traits, not as a specific figure constructed of unambiguous and objective features, an aggregate answer to the question "Who is he?" No, the hero interests Dostoevsky as a *particular point of view* in relation to the world and in relation to the hero himself, as the semantic and judgement-passing position of a man in relation to himself and to surrounding reality. For Dostoevsky the important thing is not how the hero appears to the world, but, most importantly, how the world appears to the hero and how the hero appears to himself.

This is an important and fundamental characteristic of the hero's perception. The hero as point of view, as position vis-à-vis the world and vis-à-vis himself, requires unique methods of development and literary characterization. That which must be developed and characterized is not the hero's specific milieu nor a fixed image of him, but rather the *sum total of his consciousness and self-consciousness*, in the last analysis *the hero's final word about himself and about his world*.

Therefore the elements from which the image of the hero is constructed are not the facts of reality—the reality of the hero himself and of his environment,— but rather the *significance* of those facts for the *hero himself,* for his self-consciousness. All of the hero's fixed, objective qualities, his social position, his sociological and characterological typicality, his habitus, his spiritual mien and even his physical appearance, i.e. everything usually employed by the author in creating a concrete and substantive image of the hero—"Who is he?"—in Dostoevsky becomes the object of the hero's own reflection, the subject of his own self-consciousness. Thus the *function* of the hero's self-consciousness becomes the subject of the author's vision and representation. While self-consciousness is usually only an element of the hero's reality, merely one aspect of his integrated image, here all of reality becomes an element of the hero's self-consciousness. The author does not retain for himself, that is exclusively for his own field of vision, a single essential definition, a single characteristic, a single trait of the hero. He introduces all of these into the hero's field of vision, casting them all into the crucible of the hero's self-consciousness. This pure self-consciousness in its totality remains within the author's purview as the matter of his vision and representation.

Already in the earliest, the "Gogolian" period of his literary career, Dostoevsky depicts not the "poor government clerk," but the *self-consciousness* of the poor clerk (Devushkin, Golyadkin, even Prokharchin). That which in Gogol's field of vision was given as the aggregate of objective traits forming the hero's fixed social-characterological image is introduced by Dostoevsky into the field of vision of the hero himself and becomes the object of his agonizing self-awareness. Dostoevsky even forces his "poor government clerks," whose external appearance was depicted by Gogol, to contemplate themselves in the mirror.[63] As a result of this method all the concrete features of the hero, while retaining their content, are transferred from one descriptive plane to another and take on an entirely new artistic significance: they can no longer finalize and enclose the hero, giving the artist's answer to the question "Who is he?" We see not who he is, but *how* he perceives himself; our artistic vision focuses not on the reality of the hero, but on the pure function of his perception of that reality. Thus the Gogolian hero becomes Dostoevsky's hero.[64]

The following somewhat simplified formula could be given for the way in which the young Dostoevsky revolutionized Gogol's world: he transferred the author and the narrator with the totality of their points of view and the descriptions, characterizations and definitions of the hero given by them, to the purview of the hero himself, thereby turning the finalized integrated reality of the hero into the material of the hero's own self-consciousness. It is not without purpose that Dostoevsky causes Makar Devushkin to read Gogol's "Overcoat" and to perceive it as a story about himself, a slander against him. Thus Dostoevsky literally introduces the author into the hero's field of vision.

Dostoevsky caused, as it were, a small-scale Copernican upheaval by making what had been the author's firm and finalizing definition of the hero an aspect of the hero's self-definition. Gogol's world, the world of "The Overcoat," "The Nose," "Nevsky Prospect" and "Notes of a Madman," remains in content unchanged in Dostoevsky's first works—in *Poor Folk* and *The Double.* But the distribution of Gogol's material among the structural elements of the work is in Dostoevsky completely different. The functions that were performed by the author are now performed by the hero as he elucidates himself from all possible points of view; the author no longer elucidates the reality of the hero, but rather his self-consciousness as reality of a second order. The dominant of the entire literary vision and structure was shifted, the world took on a new visage, despite

[39]

the fact that Dostoevsky introduced almost no essentially new, non-Gogolian material.[65]

Not only the reality of the hero himself, but also the external world and way of life surrounding the hero are drawn into the process of self-awareness and are transferred from the author's field of vision to that of the hero. They no longer reside in the same plane as the hero, beside him and external to him in the unified world of the author. Therefore they cannot be the causal, genetic factors defining the hero and cannot fulfill an explanatory function in the work. Only another consciousness can stand as equal in the same plane with the all-encompassing consciousness of the hero; only another point of view can stand equal to his point of view. *Only the objective world—the world of other equal consciousnesses—can be counterposed by the author to the all-engulfing consciousness of the hero.*

One must not think of self-consciousness in the social-characterological plane or see it simply as a new trait of the hero, or see Devushkin or Golyadkin, for example, as Gogolian heroes with self-consciousness added. Belinsky perceived Devushkin in just that way. He was impressed by the passage with the mirror and the popped button, but he did not catch its structural literary significance. Self-consciousness for him merely enriches and humanizes the portrait of the "poor clerk," taking its place beside the other characteristics in the concrete image of the hero, constructed within the author's ordinary field of vision. Perhaps this hindered Belinsky in correctly assessing "The Double" as well.

Self-awareness, as the *artistic dominant* of the hero's construction, cannot lie in the same plane as the other features of his image; self-awareness draws the other features into itself, taking them as its material and depriving them of any power to define and finalize the hero. Self-awareness can be the dominant in the portrayal of any individual. But not all individuals provide equally favorable material for such a portrayal. In this respect Gogol's clerk offered excessively narrow possibilities. Dostoevsky sought a predominantly perceiving hero, a hero whose entire life was concentrated in the pure function of perceiving himself and the world. Thus the "dreamer" and the "underground man" appear in his works. "Dreaminess" and membership in the "underground" are both social-characterological traits, but they fit into Dostoevsky's artistic dominant. The consciousness of an unfulfilled dreamer (who is also incapable of fulfillment) or of an underground man is such favorable soil for Dostoevsky's artistic purposes that it allows the author to unite the artistic dominant of the portrayal with the social-characterological dominant of the person portrayed.

"Oh, if only it were out of pure laziness that I don't do anything. Lord, how I would respect myself then. I would respect myself precisely because then I would at least be capable of being lazy; then I would have at least one definite trait which I myself could be sure of. Question: 'Who is he?' Answer: 'A lazy lout.' How awfully pleasant it would be to hear that about myself. That would mean that I'm definitely defined, that would

[40]

mean that there is something to say about me. 'A lazy lout!'—that's already
a calling and a purpose. That's a career!" (IV, 147)

The "underground man" does not merely dissolve in himself all possible
concrete traits of his image by making them the subject of his own reflection—
he has no such traits at all, he has no fixed definition, there is nothing to say about
him; he figures not as a person taken from life, but rather as the subject of consciousness and dream. And for the author he is not a carrier of qualities and characteristics which are neutral in relation to his self-consciousness and capable of
finalizing him; no, the vision of the author is directed precisely at his self-consciousness and at the inescapable unfinalizability and vicious circle *(durnaia beskonechnost')* of that self-consciousness. Thus the social-characterological definition of the "underground man" and the artistic dominant of his image merge into
one.

Only in the classicists, only in Racine, can one find such a deep and total
concurrence between the form of the hero and the form of the man, between the
dominant of the hero's image and the dominant of his character. The comparison
of Dostoevsky with Racine sounds paradoxical because the material upon which,
in each respective case, the completeness of artistic compatibility is built is too
diverse. Racine's hero is all objective existence, stable and firm, like a sculpture.
Dostoevsky's hero is all self-consciousness. Racine's hero is infinite function.
Racine's hero is equal to himself. But artistically the Dostoevskian hero is as precise as Racine's. Self-consciousness as the artistic dominant of the hero's image
is enough in itself to break down the monological unity of the artistic world, given
the condition that the hero as self-consciousness is in fact "depicted," and not
"expressed," i.e. that the hero does not merge with the author, does not become
his mouthpiece. Consequently, monological unity is broken when the accents of
the hero's self-consciousness are in fact objectivized and when in the work itself
a distance between the hero and the author is maintained. If the umbilical cord
binding the hero to his creator is not cut, then we have before us not a work of
art, but a personal document.

In this sense Dostoevsky's works are profoundly objective. Having become
the dominant, the hero's self-awareness breaks down the monological unity of
the work, without destroying, of course, the artistic unity of a new, non-mono-
logical type. The hero becomes relatively free and independent because everything
in the author's design which defined and, so to speak, predestined the hero, everything which qualified him once and for all as a completed image of reality,—now
all of that functions no longer as a finalizing form, but as material of his self-consciousness.

In a monological design the hero is closed and the limits of his meaning are
sharply outlined: he acts, experiences, thinks and perceives within the boundaries
of what he is, i.e. within the boundaries of his image defined as reality; he cannot
stop being himself, i.e. he cannot exceed the boundaries of his character, his typicality and his temperament without in the process violating the author's monological

[41]

design. Such an image is constructed in the world of the author, which is objective in relation to the hero's consciousness; the construction of the author's world, with its perspectives and finalizing definitions, requires a firm external position, a firm authorial field of vision. The hero's self-consciousness is presented against the fixed background of the external world and is contained within the fixed framework of the author's consciousness, which defines and portrays the hero and remains inaccessible to him from within.

Dostoevsky renounces all of these monological premises. Everything that the monological author retained for himself and used to create the ultimate unity of the novel and of the world portrayed in it Dostoevsky presents to his hero, turning it all into an aspect of the hero's self-consciousness.

There is literally nothing we can say about the hero of *Notes From the Underground* that he does not already know himself: his typicalness for his time and social position, the sober psychological, or even psychopathological, definition of his inner constitution, the characterological category of his consciousness, his comicality and tragicalness, all the possible moral definitions of his personality, etc. In Dostoevsky's design he knows all of these things perfectly well himself, and he persistently and agonizingly absorbs all of these definitions from within. The external perspective is, as it were, made impotent in advance and deprived of the final word.

Since in this work the dominant of the portrayal coincides perfectly with the dominant of that which is portrayed, the author's formal task finds clear expression in the content. The "underground man" thinks most about what others think or might think about him and strives to keep one step ahead of every other consciousness, everyone else's thoughts about him, every other point of view toward him. At all essential points in his confession he strives to anticipate possible definitions and assessments of him by others, to guess the sense and tone of those assessments, and to carefully formulate the potential words of others, interrupting his own speech with the imagined remarks of others.

" 'Isn't that shameful! Isn't that degrading!' perhaps you would say to me, scornfully shaking your heads. 'You thirst for life, but you solve the problems of life with jumbled logic...Yes, there is some truth in you, but no modesty; out of the pettiest pride you make a show of your truth, you expose it to disgrace, to the market place...You do indeed have something to say, but out of fear you hide your final word because you haven't the courage to pronounce it; you possess only cowardly insolence. You boast of your consciousness, but you vacillate because, although your mind functions, your heart is clouded over with depravity, and without a pure heart a real consciousness is impossible. And how importunate you are, how you force yourself on people, how you put on airs! Nothing but mendacity and more mendacity!

Of course I've made up all of your words myself. That's also from the underground. *For forty years straight I've listened through a crack in the*

[42]

underground to these words of yours. I thought them up myself, but they were the only ones that came to me. It's no wonder that I've learned them by heart and given them literary form..." (IV, 164-165).

The hero from the underground listens in on every word said about him by others, he looks in all the mirrors of others' consciousnesses and knows all the possible refractions of his own image in those mirrors. He is aware of his objective definition, neutral both to foreign consciousnesses and to his own self-consciousness, and he takes into account the viewpoint of a "third party." But he also knows that all of these definitions, both biased and objective, rest in his hands and cannot finalize him, precisely because he himself perceives them; he can go beyond their limits and make them invalid. He knows that he has the *final word,* and he seeks, come what may, to retain for himself this final word about himself, the word of his self-consciousness, in order through it to become what he is not. His self-consciousness lives on its unfinalizedness, its open-endedness and indeterminacy.

And this is not merely a characterological trait of the "underground man's" self-consciousness; it is the dominant of his construction by the author. The author indeed leaves the final word to his hero. And precisely it, or, more exactly, the tendency toward it, is necessary to the author's design. The author constructs his hero not out of words that are foreign to him [i.e. to the hero], and not out of neutral definitions, he constructs not a character, a type, a temperament, not an objectified image of the hero, but precisely the hero's *word* about himself and about his world.

Dostoevsky's hero is not an objectified image, but rather an autonomous word, a *pure voice;* we do not see him, we hear him. Everything that we see and know independently of his word is non-essential and is swallowed up as material by the word, or remains outside it as a stimulative and provocative factor. We will further see that the entire artistic construction of the Dostoevskian novel is directed toward the exposition and elucidation of the hero's word, and fulfills a provocative and directive function in relation to that word. The epithet "a cruel talent" applied to Dostoevsky by N. K. Mikhailovsky has a basis, though not so simple a one as Mikhailovsky imagined. The sort of moral torture to which Dostoevsky subjects his heroes in order to force from them the word of ultimate self-consciousness allows him to expose in the portrayal of a character all that is material and objectivized, all that is firm and immutable, all that is external and neutral, within the sphere of the character's self-consciousness and his self-utterances.

A comparison with recent enthusiastic imitators of "the cruel talent"— the German expressionists Kornfeld, Werfel, etc.—provides sufficient evidence of the artistic depth and subtlety of Dostoevsky's provocative artistic devices. In most cases the imitators cannot progress beyond the depiction of hysterical frenzies, because they are incapable of creating around the hero that particularly complex and subtle social atmosphere which causes him to reveal and explain himself dialogically, to perceive aspects of himself in the consciousness of others, and to create loop-holes for himself, prolonging his final word and laying it bare in highly tense interaction with other consciousnesses. The artistically most restrained imitators, such as Werfel, create a symbolic situation for the hero's self-revelation. Such, for example, is the trial scene in Werfel's *Spiegelmensch,* in which the hero tries himself while the judge takes the transcript and calls the witnesses.

The expressionists accurately comprehend the dominant of self-consciousness in the construction of the hero, but they are incapable of making the self-consciousness reveal itself spontaneously and in an artistically convincing way. The result is either an obvious, crude experiment with the hero, or a symbolical drama.

In Dostoevsky the hero's self-elucidation, his self-revelation and his own words about himself are not pre-determined by a neutral image of the hero conceived by the author as the final goal of his characterization. It is for this reason that even some of Dostoevsky's situations are occasionally a bit fantastical. Verisimilitude of character is for Dostoevsky verisimilitude of the hero's own inner word about himself in all its purity. But in order to sense and express that inner word and in order to introduce it into the field of vision of another individual, the laws of that individual's field of vision must be violated, because the normal field of vision can encompass the objectified image of another individual, but not another field of vision in its entirety. The author must find some fantastical viewpoint outside the normal field of vision.

Dostoevsky says the following in his foreword to "A Gentle Creature":

And now about the story itself. I titled it fantastic' although I myself consider it utterly realistic. But there is in fact something of the fantastic in the very form of the story, which I find necessary to explain in advance.

The point is that this is not a story and not a sketch. Imagine a husband whose wife, a suicide who several hours earlier has thrown herself out a window, is laid out on a table before him. He is distraught and has not yet had time to gather his thoughts. He paces to and fro from one room to another trying to comprehend what has taken place, to 'get his thoughts together.' In addition, he is a confirmed hypochondriac, one of those who talk to themselves. So he talks to himself, relating what has happened, **explaining** it to himself. Despite the apparent continuity of what he says, he contradicts himself several times, both in his logic and in his emotions. He justifies himself and blames his wife; he enters into extraneous explanations, now displaying crudity of thought and of heart, now deep emotion. Gradually he does in fact **explain** matters to himself and does 'get his thoughts together.' The series of recollections which he has evoked leads him irresistably to the **truth;** the truth irresistably edifies his mind and his heart. Toward the end even the tone of the story is modified, in relation to its disorderly beginning. The truth reveals itself rather clearly and definitively to the bereaved, or at least it seems so to him.

Such is the theme. Of course the action of the story takes place over

[44]

several hours, with fits and starts and in a confused and erratic form: first he speaks to himself, then he addresses an invisible listener, as if addressing a judge. And so it is in reality. If a stenographer could have overheard him and taken down all that he said, the result would have been a little rougher and less polished than I represent it, but the psychological sequence would, it seems to me, remain the same. This assumption of a stenographer taking notes (which I would then put into polished form) is what I call the fantastic in this story. But such a procedure has in part already been permitted in works of art: Victor Hugo, for example, employed an almost identical device in his masterpiece *Le dernier jour d'un condamné*. And although he did not introduce a stenographer, he allowed an even greater implausibility by assuming that a condemned man would be able (and have time) to keep his diary not only on his final day, but even in his final hour and literally in his final minute. But if Hugo had not allowed this fantasy, then the work itself—the most real and true of all that he wrote—would not exist. (X, 378-379).

We have included this foreword in its entirety because of the extreme importance of the propositions expressed in it for an understanding of Dostoevsky's art. That "truth" at which, having explained events to himself, the hero must— and finally does—arrive can be for Dostoevsky essentially only the truth of the *hero's own consciousness.* It cannot be neutral to his self-consciousness. In the mouth of another individual the contentually identical word, the identical definition, would take on another meaning and another tone, and would no longer be the truth. According to Dostoevsky the final word about an individual, truly adequate to him, can be given only in the form of a confessional self-utterance.

But how can this word be introduced into the story without destroying the identity of the word, and at the same time not destroying the fabric of the story and not reducing the story to a simple motivation for the introduction of the confession? The fantastical form of "A Gentle Creature" is only one possible solution to this problem, a solution limited by the scope of the novella. But what artistic efforts were required of Dostoevsky to synthesize the function of a fantastic stenographer in an entire multivoiced novel!

The problem here, of course, is not one of pragmatic difficulties or of external compositional devices. In Tolstoy, for example, the last thoughts of a dying hero, his final burst of consciousness and his final words, are simply introduced directly from the author into the fabric of the story. (Such was the case already in "Sevastopol Stories," but the later works—"Death of Ivan Ilych" and "Master and Man"—are particularly exemplary of this.) No problem arises for Tolstoy. For him it is not necessary to apologize for the fantasticality of his device. Tolstoy's world is monolithically monological; the hero's word is contained in the firm framework of the author's words about him. The hero's final word is given as an external (authorial) word: the hero's self-consciousness is merely an aspect of his firm image and is in essence predetermined by that image even when thematically the consciousness undergoes crisis and radical inner upheaval ("Master and Man").

[45]

Self-awareness and spiritual rebirth remain in Tolstoy purely in the realm of content, assuming no form-determining significance; the ethical unfinalizedness of a character up until his death does not become structural unfinalizability of the hero. The artistic structure of Brekhunov's or Ivan Ilych's image differs in no way from that of old prince Bolkonsky's or Natasha Rostov's image. The hero's self-consciousness and his word do not become the dominant of his construction, despite their thematic importance in Tolstoy's works. A second full-fledged voice (next to the author's voice) does not appear in his world, and therefore neither the problem of combination of voices, nor that of the particular formulation of the author's point of view arises. Tolstoy's monologically naive point of view and his word penetrate everywhere, to every corner of the world and of the spirit, subordinating everything to their unity.

In Dostoevsky the authorial word stands opposite the full-valued, unsullied word of the hero. Consequently the problem of the formulation of the author's word arises, i.e. the problem of its formal artistic position in relation to the hero's word. This problem lies deeper than the question of the superficial compositional authorial word and of its elimination by means of the *Icherzählung* (first-person narration), by introducing a narrator, by constructing the novel in scenes, and by reducing the authorial word to the status of a stage direction. All of these compositional devices of eliminating or weakening the compositional authorial word do not of themselves touch the heart of the problem; their real artistic meaning can vary radically, depending on the varying artistic tasks they are designed to carry out. The *Icherzählung* of *The Captain's Daughter* is infinitely far removed from the *Icherzählung* in *Notes from the Underground,* even if we abstractly think away the content of these forms. Pushkin constructs Grinev's story within a fixed monological field of vision, although that field of vision itself is not outwardly expressed, since there is no direct authorial word. But precisely this field of vision determines the entire construction. As a result, *Grinev's firm image* is an image, and not a word; Grinev's word is an element of his image, i.e. it functions only in his characterization and in the pragmatic development of the plot. Grinev's position in relation to the world and to events is only a component of his image: he is presented as *characteristic reality,* and not at all as a directly significant, valid *semantic position.* Direct and immediate significance belongs exclusively to the author's point of view, which is the basis of the structure; all else is merely its object. The introduction of a narrator does not necessarily at all weaken the author's monological way of seeing and thinking, nor at all increase the weight or independence of the hero's word. Such is, for example, Pushkin's narrator Belkin.

Thus all of these compositional devices are in themselves incapable of altering the monological character of the artistic world. But in Dostoevsky they do in fact fulfill this function, becoming the instrument for the realization of his polyphonic artistic intention. We will further see how and by what means they perform this function, but for the moment we are interested only in the artistic intention itself, not in the means of its concrete realization.

[46]

■

Self-consciousness, as artistic dominant in the construction of the hero's image, demands a radically new *authorial position* in relation to the character depicted. We repeat, the point is not to discover new characteristics or new human types of some sort or other which could be perceived and depicted within the bounds of the ordinary monological artistic approach to man, i.e. without a radical alteration of the author's position. No, the point is precisely to discover a *new integral view of man*—"the personality" (Askoldov) or "man in man" (Dostoevsky)— which is possible only through an approach to man from a correspondingly new and *integral* authorial position.

We shall attempt to elucidate in somewhat greater detail this integral position, this fundamentally new *form* of the artistic view of man.

Already in his first work Dostoevsky shows how the hero himself revolts against literature in which the "little man" is externalized and finalized without himself being consulted *(zaochno)*. As we have already noted, Makar Devushkin read Gogol's "Overcoat" and was *personally* deeply insulted by it. He recognized himself in Akaky Akakievich and was outraged by the fact that his poverty had been *spied upon,* that his entire life had been found out and described, that he had been defined totally once and for all, and that he was left no prospect for the future.

> You hide sometimes, you sneak away, you hide in your own inade-
> quacies, you're afraid to show your face anywhere at all sometimes, because
> you're afraid of gossip, because they'll turn everything on earth into slander
> against you, and here your whole public and private life is paraded through
> fiction, it's all printed and read and laughed at and ridiculed!" (I, 146).

Devushkin is especially outraged because Akaky Akakievich died the way he was, an unchanged man.

In the image of "The Overcoat's" hero Devushkin saw himself totally quantified and measured and defined to the last detail: you're all here, there is nothing more in you, there is nothing more to be said about you. He felt himself hopelessly pre-determined and completed, almost as if he were dead and buried. At the same time he felt the falsity of the author's approach to Akaky Akakievich. The hero's characteristic "revolt" against his literary finalization is represented by Dostoevsky in the sustained primitive forms of Devushkin's consciousness and speech.

The serious, deeper sense of this revolt can be expressed thus: one dare not turn a living person into the voiceless object of a secondhand *(zaochnoe)* finalizing perception. *In every person there is something which only he himself can reveal in a voluntary act of self-consciousness and expression, something which is not amenable to an externalizing, secondhand definition.* In *Poor Folk* Dostoevsky made the first attempt, in a still imperfect and unclear form, to show *something innerly unfinalizable in man,* something which Gogol and other authors cᶠ "stories about poor clerks" could not capture from their monological authorial positions. Thus already in his first work Dostoevsky begins to grope at his future radically new position in relation to the hero.

In Dostoevsky's subsequent works the heroes no longer carry on a *literary* polemic with finalizing secondhand definitions of one individual by another (although the author sometimes does this for them in an extremely subtle ironical-parodical form), though they all struggle furiously against such secondhand definitions of their personalities. They all acutely feel their own inner unfinalizedness and their capacity to outgrow and make *untrue* any definition that externalizes and finalizes them. So long as a man is alive he lives on the fact that he is not yet finalized and has not yet pronounced his last word. We have already noted how agonizingly the "underground man" listens in on all actual and potential words others say about him, and how he strives to guess and anticipate all possible definitions of his personality on the part of others. The hero of *Notes from the Underground* is the first hero-ideologist in Dostoevsky's work. One of his basic ideas, which he sets forth in his polemic with the socialists, is precisely the idea that man is not a final and determinate quantity upon which stable calculations can be made; man is free and therefore can overturn any rules which are forced upon him.

Dostoevsky's hero always seeks to shatter the finalizing, deadening framework of *others'* words about him. Occasionally this struggle becomes an important tragic motif in the hero's life (Nastasya Filippovna, for example).

In the case of the leading characters (the protagonists of the great dialog, such as Raskolnikov, Sonya, Myshkin, Stavrogin, Ivan and Dmitry Karamazov), the profound sense of personal unfinalizedness and indeterminacy is realized through the very complex means of ideological thought, crime, or heroic feat.[66]

Man is never coincident with himself. The equation of identity A=A is inapplicable to him. In Dostoevsky's artistic thought, the genuine life of the personality is played out in the point of non-intersection of man with himself, at the point of his departure beyond the limits of all that he is in terms of material being which can be spied out, defined and predetermined without his will, "at second hand" *(zaochno)*. The genuine life of the personality can be penetrated only *dialogically,* and then only when it mutually and voluntarily opens *itself.*

The truth about an individual in the mouths of others, nondialogical, *secondhand* truth, becomes a degrading and deadening lie when it concerns his "holy of holies," i.e. the "man in man."

We shall cite several statements of Dostoevsky's heroes in regard to *secondhand analyses* of the human soul.

In *The Idiot* Myshkin and Aglaya are discussing Ippolit's attempted suicide. Myshkin delivers an analysis of the deepseated motivations of Ippolit's act. Aglaya says to him:

> I find all of this very mean on your part; it is so *rude to examine and judge a person's soul* as you are judging Ippolit. You lack tenderness: the *truth by itself, after all, is unjust.* (VI, 484)

The truth is unjust when it concerns the depths of *another person's personality.*

The same motif, in a somewhat more complex form, rings even more clearly in *Brothers Karamazov* in Alyosha's conversation with Liza about Captain Snegirev, who had trampled underfoot the money offered him. Having told of this action, Alyosha analyzes Snegirev's emotional state and, as it were, *predetermines* his future actions by *foretelling* that the next time he will *undoubtedly* take the money. To this Liza replies:

> Listen, Aleksei Fyodorovich, isn't there in this whole discussion of ours, that is, of yours...no, better, of ours...isn't there an element of *contempt* for him, for that unfortunate, in the fact that we are *picking his soul apart* like this *from on high?* In the fact that we have so *positively* decided that he will take the money? (IX, 271-272).

An analogous motif of the inadmissability of penetration by an *outsider* into the depths of another's personality is heard in Stavrogin's angry words, spoken in Tikhon's cell, whence he has come with his "confession":

> Listen, I can't stand spies and psychologists, at least ones who go boring into my soul.[67]

It should be mentioned that in this case Stavrogin is completely mistaken in regard to Tikhon. Tikhon approaches him in a deeply *dialogical* way and understands the *unfinalizedness* of his inner personality.

■

At the very end of his creative career Dostoevsky, writing in his notebook, defines the nature of his realism thus: "To find with absolute realism the *man in man...* I am called a *psychologist*—it is *not true.* I am merely a realist in a higher sense, i.e. I depict all the *depths of the human soul.[68]*

We shall return more than once to this remarkable formula, but for now we are interested in emphasizing three of its aspects.

Firstly, Dostoevsky considers himself a realist, not a subjective romanticist, trapped in the world of his own consciousness. He carries out his new task— "to depict all the depths of the human soul"—with absolute realism, i.e. he perceives these depths *outside* himself, in the souls of *others.*

Secondly, Dostoevsky believes that his new task cannot be fulfilled through realism in the usual sense, or, to use our terminology, through *monological* realism. A unique approach to the "man in man," a "higher form of realism" must be found.

Thirdly, *Dostoevsky categorically denies that he is a psychologist.*

This third aspect must be treated in a bit more detail.

[49]

Dostoevsky had a negative attitude toward contemporary psychology, both in scientific literature and in fiction, as well as toward the way it was practiced in the law courts. In psychology he saw a degrading *materialization* of the human soul, a sacrifice of the soul's freedom, its unfinalizability, and that unique *indeterminacy* and *indefiniteness* which constitute the chief object of representation in Dostoevsky: he always depicts man *on the brink* of a final decision, in a moment of crisis, at an *un-predeterminable* turning point in the life of his soul.

Dostoevsky constantly and harshly criticized mechanistic psychology, both its pragmatic line, based on concepts of *common-sense* and *utility,* and particularly its physiological line, which equated psychology with physiology. He ridiculed it in his novels as well. We need only recall the "lumps on the brain" in Lebezyatnikov's explanations of Katerina Ivanovna's spiritual crisis *(Crime and Punishment),* or the use of Claude Bernard's name as a pejorative symbol of man's liberation from responsibility—the "Bernards" of Mitenka Karamazov.

But particularly revealing for an understanding of Dostoevsky's artistic position is his criticism of legal investigative psychology, which is at best a "double-edged weapon," i.e. it allows with equal probability the acceptance of mutually exclusive alternatives, and at worst is a degrading lie.

The remarkable detective Porfiry Petrovich in *Crime and Punishment* (it was he who called psychology a "double-edged weapon") is guided not by legal investigative psychology, but rather by a special *dialogical intuition* which permits him to penetrate Raskolnikov's unfinalized, undecided soul. Porfiry's three meetings with Raskolnikov do not at all resemble the usual investigative interrogations, not because they do not "follow the form" (as Porfiry constantly emphasizes), but because they violate the very bases of the traditional psychological relationship between investigator and criminal (a fact which Dostoevsky emphasizes). All three of Porfiry's meetings with Raskolnikov are genuine and remarkable polyphonic dialogs.

The most profound picture of false psychology in practice is given in the scenes of the preliminary investigation and the trial of Dmitry in *The Brothers Karamazov.* The investigator, the judges, the prosecutor, the defense attorney, and the expert witnesses are all incapable of even approaching the unfinalized, undetermined nucleus of Dmitry's personality, Dmitry being throughout his whole life essentially on the brink of monumental inner decisions and crises. For this live and burgeoning nucleus they substitute a sort of *ready-made definitiveness,* "naturally" and "normally" *predetermined* in its every word and act by the "laws of psychology." All of Dmitry's judges are devoid of a genuine dialogical approach to him and of a dialogical penetration into the unfinalized nucleus of his personality. They seek and see in him only the factual, *material definiteness* of experiences and actions, which they subordinate to already defined concepts and schemes. The true Dmitry remains outside their power to judge—he will pass judgement on himself.

For these reasons Dostoevsky refused to consider himself a psychologist in any sense. We are not, of course, interested in the philosophical-theoretical side of his criticism as such—it is unsatisfactory and suffers from a basic lack of under-standing of the dialectic of freedom and necessity in man's actions and conscious-ness.[69] Important for us here is the direction of his *artistic* interest and the new *form* of his artistic vision of the inner man.

It is pertinent here to note that the major inspiration of all of Dostoevsky's work, from the standpoint of form and of *content,* is the struggle against the *materialization* of man, of human relations, and of all human values under the conditions of capitalism. Dostoevsky did not, it is true, clearly comprehend the deep economic roots of materialization and he did not, so far as is known, ever use the term "materialization" *(oveshchestvlenie)* itself, but precisely this term best expresses the profound meaning of his struggle for man. Dostoevsky per-ceived with great insight the penetration of this *materializing denigration* of man into every pore of contemporary life and into the very foundations of human thinking. In his critique of this materializing mode of thinking he sometimes "addresses himself to the wrong party," to use V. Ermilov's phrase;[70] for example, he accuses the revolutionary-democratic movement and the Western socialists, whom he considered an outgrowth of the capitalist spirit, of materialization. But as has been said, important for us here is not the abstract theoretical or publi-cistic aspect of his critique, but rather the liberating and de-materializing signi-ficance of his *artistic form.*

The new artistic position of the author vis-à-vis the hero in Dostoevsky's polyphonic novel is a *consequent* and *fully realized dialogical position* which confirms the hero's independence, inner freedom, unfinalizedness and indeter-minacy. For the author the hero is not "he" and not "I", but a full-valued "thou," that is, another full-fledged "I" ("Thou art"). The hero is the subject of a pro-foundly serious *actual* dialogical mode of address, as opposed to a rhetorically *acted-out* or *conventional* literary one. And this dialog—the "great dialog" of the novel as a whole—takes place not in the past, but now, in the *present* of the creative process.[71] It is, however, not a stenographic report of a *completed* dia-log which the author, no longer a participant, views from the commanding height of his authorial position: such an approach would immediately turn a genuine and unfinalized dialog into the objectivized and finalized *image of a dialog,* com-mon to every monological novel. The great dialog in Dostoevsky's work is artis-tically organized as the *unclosed entirety* of life itself, of life *on the brink.*

The dialogical relationship to the hero is realized by Dostoevsky in the course of the creative process and in the moment of its culmination. It is part of the author's design and consequently it remains in the completed novel as an indis-pensable form-determining aspect.

The authorial word about the hero is conceived in Dostoevsky's novels as a word *about someone who is present,* someone who can hear the author and can *answer him.* This conception of the authorial word in Dostoevsky's works is not a conventional device; it is rather the author's unconditional *final* position. In the fifth chapter of this book we shall attempt to show that Dostoevsky's dis-tinctive verbal style is also determined by the overriding significance of precisely

[51]

such a dialogically oriented word, and by the insignificance of the role played by the monologically inhibited word, which waits for no answers from its object.

In Dostoevsky's plan the hero is the carrier of a full-valued word, not the dumb, voiceless object of the author's word. The author's intention in regard to the hero is in fact an intention in regard to his *word.* Therefore the author's word about the hero is a word about a word. It is oriented to the hero as if to a word, and therefore is *dialogically addressed* to him. By the very construction of the novel the author speaks not *about* the hero, but *with* him. And it cannot be otherwise: only a dialogical, participatory orientation takes the word of another person seriously and approaches it as a semantic position, as another point of view. My word can maintain a close bond with the word of another, and at the same time not become one with it, not engulf it nor dissolve its significance (i.e. maintain completely its independence as a word) only within the framework of an interior dialogical orientation. To maintain distance within this intense semantic bond is by no means a simple matter. But distance is an integral aspect of the author's intention, for only this distance assures genuine objectivity in the representation of the hero.

Self-consciousness as dominant in the construction of the hero's image requires the creation of an artistic atmosphere in which his word can unfold and elucidate itself. Not a single element of this atmosphere can be neutral: it must all touch his sore spot, provoke and question him, even polemize and taunt him. All must be turned and directed toward the hero, all must be perceived as a *word about someone present,* as the word of a "second," not a "third" party. The semantic point of view of a "third party," around which the stable image of the hero is built, would destroy this atmosphere, and therefore it does not enter into Dostoevsky's creative world. The "third party" point of view is absent not because it is beyond Dostoevsky's reach, due, for example, to the heroes' autobiographical character or to the author's extraordinarily polemical nature, but simply because it does not fit into Dostoevsky's plan. The plan requires total dialogization of all structural elements. Hence the apparent nervousness and the extreme unevenness and agitation of Dostoevsky's novels, which conceal from the superficial reader the most subtle artistic calculation, balance and necessity of every tone, every accent, every unexpected turn of events, every scandalous scene, every eccentricity. Only in light of the artistic task which Dostoevsky set for himself can one comprehend the true function of such compositional elements as the narrator and his tone, dialog conceived as compositional component, or the nature of direct narration from the author's perspective (in those instances where it is present), etc.

Such is the hero's relative independence within the bounds of Dostoevsky's creative plan. At this point we must move to forestall a possible misunderstanding. It may seem that the hero's independence contradicts the fact that he exists merely as an aspect of a work of art and is consequently created from beginning to end by the author. In fact this contradiction does not exist. We recognize the heroes' freedom within the bounds of the artistic plan, and in that sense their freedom is indeed just as created as the un-freedom of the objectivized hero. But to create does not mean to invent. Every act of creation is bound by the laws of the material on which it operates as well as by its own laws. Every creative act is determined by its object and by the object's structure, and therefore permits of no arbitrariness and, in essence, invents nothing new, but simply reveals what is present in the object itself. One can arrive at a correct conclusion, but that conclusion has its own logic, and therefore it cannot be invented, i.e. fabricated from beginning to end. In like manner, no artistic image, regardless of what sort, can be invented, because each possesses its own artistic logic and inherent order (zakonomernost'). Having set a specific task for himself, the creator must subordinate himself to its inherent order.

Dostoevsky's hero is not an invented hero, just as the hero of the common realistic novel, the romantic hero, and the classical hero are not invented. But each has his own inherent order and logic which belong to the realm of the author's artistic will, and yet are not subject to his whim. Having chosen a hero and the dominant of his representation, the author has already bound himself to their inner logic, which he must then reveal in his depiction. The logic of the self-consciousness permits only certain artistic means of revelation and representation. The self-consciousness must be interrogated and provoked to self-expression, but must not be given a pre-determining or finalized image. Such an objectified image would fail to depict precisely that which the author has chosen as his subject.

Thus the hero's freedom is an aspect of the author's intention. The hero's word is created by the author, but created in such a way that it can freely develop its own inner logic and independence *as the word of another person, as the word of the hero himself.* As a result it is removed not from the author's intention entirely, but simply from his monological field of vision, the elimination of which is part and parcel of Dostoevsky's plan.

■

In his book *O iazyke xudozhestvennoi literatury (On Literary Language)* V. V. Vinogradov refers to the extremely interesting, almost *polyphonic* plan of an unfinished novel by N. G. Chernyshevsky. Vinogradov uses it as an example of the search for the maximally objective construction of the *author's image.* Chernyshevsky's manuscript bore several titles, one of which was *Perl sozdaniia (The Pearl of Creation).* In his foreword to the novel Chernyshevsky describes the essence of his intention thus:

> It is a very difficult matter to write a novel without romantic interest, without a single female character. But I felt the need to try my hand at a still more difficult task: *to write a purely objective novel devoid not only of every trace of my own personal attitudes, but devoid of every trace of my personal sympathies as well. There is no such novel in all of Russian literature. Onegin* and *A Hero of Our Time* are clearly subjective. *Dead Souls* contains no personal portraits of the author or his friends, but the author's

personal sympathies are present—they are responsible for the strength of the impression which the novel makes. I think that for me, a man of strong and fixed beliefs, there would be nothing more difficult than to write as Shakespeare wrote: *he depicts life and people without betraying his own views on the problems which his characters confront, each in his own way.* Othello says 'Yes,' Iago says 'No,' Shakespeare says nothing; he has no desire to state his preference for 'yes' or 'no.' (I refer, of course, to the manner, not to the magnitude of the talent under discussion.) *Try to discover with whom I sympathize and with whom I don't—you'll not find out.* In *The Pearl of Creation* every poetic situation is examined from all four sides— try to discover which views are sympathetic to me and which are not. *Try to discover how one view is transmuted into another totally incompatible one.* Here is the true sense of the title 'The Pearl of Creation'—here, as in mother-of-pearl, we have the intermingling of all the colors of the rainbow. But, as in mother-of-pearl, all the shades slip past one another, playing on a background of snowy whiteness. Therefore the verse of the epigraph is appropriate to my novel:

> Wie Schnee, so weiss,
> Und kalt, wie Eis,—

The second line applies to me.

'White as snow' is the novel, and 'cold as ice' is the author. For me, a man who loves passionately that which he loves, it was not easy to be cold as ice. But I managed. Which proves that I possess the creative power required of a novelist...*My characters have very diverse faces...Think of each one what you will. Each says of himself: "I am totally in the right"—you be the judge of these conflicting claims. I do not judge.* These characters praise one another and they condemn one another—all of that is none of my business.[72]

Such is Chernyshevsky's intention (in so far as we can judge from his foreword). We see that Chernyshevsky here touched on an essentially new structural form for the "objective novel," as he calls it. He himself emphasizes the absolute novelty of this form ("There is no such novel in all of Russian literature") and contrasts it with the ordinary "subjective"novel (which we would call "monological").

What, according to Chernyshevsky, is the essence of this new novelistic structure? The author's subjective viewpoint must not be represented in it: neither his sympathies and antipathies, nor his agreement or disagreement with the various characters, nor his personal ideological position ("his own views on the problems which his characters confront").

This does not mean, of course, that Chernyshevsky planned a novel without an authorial position. Such a novel cannot be written. Vinogradov is quite correct when he says: "The tendency to 'objectivity' of reproduction and the various devices of 'objective' construction are all merely special, but correlative, principles of the construction of the *author's image."73* We are dealing here not with the absence, but with the *radical alteration of the author's position,* and Chernyshevsky himself emphasizes that this new position is much more difficult than the usual one and requires enormous "creative power."

This new "objective" authorial position (realized, in Chernyshevsky's view, only by Shakespeare) allows the complete and independent unfolding of the heroes' points of view. Each character *freely* (without the author's interference) develops and substantiates the validity of his own position: "each says *of himself:* 'I am totally in the right'— you be the judge of these conflicting claims. I do not judge."

Chernyshevsky sees the chief advantage of the new "objective" novelistic form precisely in the *free self-elucidation of the characters' points of view* and in the absence of finalizing authorial judgements. We would emphasize that Chernyshevsky saw here no unfaithfulness to his "strong and fixed beliefs." Thus we can say that Chernyshevsky came very close to the concept of polyphony.

In addition, Chernyshevsky approaches the concept of counterpoint and of the "idea-image" *[obraz idei]*. He says,

> *Try to discover how one view is transmuted into another totally incompatible one.* Here is the true sense of the title 'The Pearl of Creation'—here, *as in mother-of-pearl, we have the intermingling of all the colors of the rainbow.*

This is, in essence, a marvelous graphic definition of counterpoint in literature.

This interesting conception of a new structure for the novel belongs to a contemporary of Dostoevsky who sensed the extraordinary multi-voicedness of his epoch just as keenly as did Dostoevsky. Actually his conception cannot be termed polyphonic in the full sense of the word. In it the new authorial position is characterized essentially negatively, as the absence of the author's usual subjectivity. There is no mention of the author's dialogical activity, without which the new authorial position cannot be realized. In any case, Chernyshevsky distinctly felt the need to go beyond the limits of the novel's prevailing monological form.

It is appropriate here to again underscore the *positive activeness* of the new authorial position in the polyphonic novel. It would be absurd to contend that the author's consciousness is nowhere expressed in Dostoevsky's novels. The consciousness of the polyphonic novel's creator is omnipresent and active in the extreme in the novel. But the function of his consciousness and the forms of its activity are different than in the monological novel: the author's consciousness does not turn others' consciousnesses (i.e. the consciousnesses of the heroes) into its objects and does not attach secondhand finalizing definitions to them. It senses the proximity of other consciousnesses of equal value which are as limitless and unfinalizable as it is. It reflects and re-creates other consciousnesses and their worlds and re-creates them in their genuine *unfinalizability* (which is after all their very essence), rather than creating a world of objects.

The consciousnesses of others cannot be contemplated and analyzed and defined like objects or things—one must *relate dialogically* to them. To think about them means *to converse with them; otherwise they immediately turn their objectivized side to us:* they fall silent and grow cold and retreat into their finalized objectivized images. An enormous and intense dialogical activity is required of the polyphonic novel's author; the minute this activity weakens, the characters begin to grow cold and become materialized, and monologically formulated chunks of life appear in the novel. Such non-polyphonic chunks can be found in all of Dostoevsky's novels, but they, of course, do not determine the nature of the whole.

The author of the polyphonic novel need not renounce himself and his consciousness, but he must in an unusual degree broaden and deepen and reorganize his consciousness (in a specific way) so that it can encompass the full-fledged consciousnesses of others.This was a very difficult matter and, as Chernyshevsky realized in his plan for an "objective novel," had not yet been attempted. But it was necessary for the artistic re-creation of the polyphonic nature of life itself.

Every *true* reader of Dostoevsky, everyone who can escape the monological mode and is capable of rising to Dostoevsky's new authorial position, feels a peculiar *active broadening* of his consciousness, not only in the sense of acquiring new objects (human types, characters, natural and social phenomena), but primarily in the sense of a special, completely new dialogical contact with the full-fledged consciousnesses of others and the active dialogical penetration into the unfinalizable depths of man.

The finalizing activity of the monological author is particularly evident in the fact that he casts his objectifying shadow on every viewpoint which he does not share, thus materializing it to a certain degree. In contrast to this, Dostoevsky's authorial activity is evident in his developing each of the contending viewpoints to its maximum strength and depth, to the maximum of plausibility. He strives with exceptional power to reveal and develop every possible meaning contained in a given point of view. (As we have seen, Chernyshevsky strove for the same thing in *The Pearl of Creation.*) This authorial activity, which intensifies the thoughts of others, is possible only on the basis of a dialogical relationship with the other's consciousness and point of view.

It is hardly necessary to mention that the polyphonic approach has nothing in common with relativism (nor with dogmatism). It should be noted that both relativism and dogmatism equally exclude all argumentation and all genuine dialog, either by making them unnecessary (relativism) or impossible (dogmatism). Polyphony as an *artistic* method lies in a completely different plane.

■

The author's new position in the polyphonic novel can be made plain by juxtaposing it with a clearly expressed monological authorial position in any given work.

Therefore we shall briefly analyze L. Tolstoy's story "Three Deaths" from our particular point of view. This rather short, but nonetheless tri-leveled story is quite typical of Tolstoy's monological manner.

Three deaths are depicted in the story—the deaths of a grand lady, a coachman, and a tree. Tolstoy presents each death as the summation and illumination of a life, as the optimum vantage point for understanding and assessing that life in its entirety. Therefore it can be said that the story essentially depicts three lives, totally finalized in their meaning and value. These three lives and their three planes in Tolstoy's story are *self-enclosed and do not "know" one another.* They are related only by the purely external pragmatic bond necessary for the unity of the structure and plot: the coachman Seryoga, who is transporting the sick lady, takes the boots of an old coachman who is dying in a hut by the post station (the boots are of no more use to the dying man) and then, after the old man's death, he cuts down a tree in the forest to make a cross for his grave. Thus the three lives and the three deaths appear to be externally connected.

But no inner bond, *no bond connecting the consciousness* is present. The dying lady knows nothing of the life and death of the coachman and of the tree; they do not enter into her field of vision and her consciousness. And neither the lady nor the tree enters the consciousness of the dying coachman. The lives and deaths of all three characters and their worlds reside side by side in a unified, objectified world and even come into *external* contact with one another, but they know nothing about each other and are not reflected in one another. They are self-enclosed and deaf, they neither hear nor answer one another. There is and can be no dialogical relationship among them. They neither argue nor agree.

But all three characters and their self-enclosed worlds are united, juxtaposed and interpreted in the *author's* unified, all-embracing field of vision and consciousness. He, the author, knows everything about them, he juxtaposes and counterposes and assesses all three lives and deaths. The three lives and deaths illuminate each other, but only for the author, who is *external* to them and takes advantage of his *external location* to definitively interpret and finalize them. His all-embracing field of vision enjoys an overwhelming superiority of information over the characters' field of vision. The rich lady sees and comprehends only her own little world, her own life and death, without even suspecting that the old coachman and the tree might similarly live and die. Therefore she cannot by herself understand and evaluate the *lie* of her life and death—she lacks the necessary dialogical background. In like manner the old coachman cannot understand and appreciate the wisdom and truth of his life and death. All these things are revealed only in the author's better-informed field of vision. The tree is, of course, by nature incapable of comprehending the wisdom and beauty of its death—that the author does for it.

Thus the finalizing total meaning of each character's life and death is revealed only in the author's field of vision and only because of the superior knowledge of that field of vision, that is, because the characters can neither see nor understand. Such is the finalizing monological function of the omniscient authorial field of vision.

As we have seen, there is no dialogical relationship between the characters and their worlds. But the author does not relate dialogically to him, either. A dialogical relationship to his heroes is foreign to Tolstoy. He does not (and fundamentally cannot) extend his point of view vis-à-vis the hero to the hero's own consciousness, and the hero cannot respond to the author's point of view. In a monological work the ultimate finalizing authorial evaluation of the hero is by nature a *secondhand evaluation* which neither supposes nor considers the hero's own potential *response* to such an evaluation. The hero is not given the final word. He cannot break out of the fixed, finalizing framework of the author's secondhand evaluation. The author's approach meets no inner dialogical resistance from the hero.

Tolstoy's authorial consciousness and word are nowhere directed toward the hero, they do not question him and they expect no answer from him. The author neither argues with his hero nor agrees with him. He speaks about him, not with him. The final word belongs to the author and can never meet in one dialogical plane with the hero's word because it is based on material which the hero cannot see or understand, material which remains external to the hero's consciousness.

The external world in which the story's characters live and die is the *world of the author,* an objective world in relation to the characters' consciousnesses. Everything in it is perceived and depicted within the author's all-embracing and omniscient field of vision. The rich woman's world—her apartment, its furnishings, her acquaintances and their experiences, the doctors, etc.—is described from the author's point of view and not the way she herself sees it (although when reading the story we are fully aware of her *subjective attitude* toward her world). The coachman's world (the hut, the stove, the cook) and the world of the tree (nature, the forest)—all of these things are, like the rich lady's world, components of one and the same objective world and are perceived and depicted from *one and the same authorial position.* There is no point at which the author's field of vision intersects or collides dialogically with the heroes' fields of vision and attitudes. The author's word nowhere experiences resistance from the hero's potential word, which would interpret the same phenomena differently, in its own way, i.e. from the point of view of *its own truth.* The author's point of view cannot meet in one plane, on one level with that of the hero. The hero's point of view, in so far as it is revealed by the author, remains the object of the author's point of view.

Thus, despite the multiple planes in Tolstoy's story, it is neither polyphonic nor contrapuntal (in our sense). It contains but one *cognitive subject,* all else being merely the *object* of its cognition. Under these conditions a dialogical relationship between the author and his heroes is impossible. Therefore the "great dialog," in which the heroes and the author participate on equal footing, is absent. Instead

[58]

we have the characters' objectivized dialogs, compositionally expressed within the author's field of vision.

We chose to discuss "Three Deaths" because in it Tolstoy's monological position is quite clear and *obvious*. In Tolstoy's novels and larger novellas the case is, of course, by no means so clear-cut.

The novels' major characters and their worlds are not self-enclosed and deaf to one another; they intersect and intertwine in various ways. The characters know each other, they exchange their individual "truths," they argue and agree, and they carry on dialogs with one another, submitting their *Weltanschauungen*, as well as more minor matters, for discussion. Such characters as Andrei Bolkonsky, Pierre Bezukhov, Levin and Nekhlyudov have their own highly developed fields of vision which sometimes *almost* coincide with the author's (i.e. the author sometimes sees the world as if through their eyes); their voices sometimes *almost* merge with the author's voice. But none of them resides in the same plane with the author's word and the author's truth, and the author does not enter into a dialogical relationship with any of them. All of them, together with their fields of vision, their truths, their quests and their controversies, are immutably inscribed into the finalizing *monolithic monological whole* of the novel, which in Tolstoy's work, unlike Dostoevsky's, never consists of the "great dialog." All the bonds and finalizing factors of the monological whole lie in the area of the author's superiority of information, an area which is fundamentally inaccessible to the heroes' consciousnesses.

Let us return to Dostoevsky. How would "Three Deaths" look if we make for a moment the strange assumption that Dostoevsky had written it? That is, what would a polyphonic "Three Deaths" be like?

Dostoevsky would first of all cause the three planes to be reflected in one another and would tie them together by means of dialogical relationships. He would introduce the life and death of the coachman and of the tree into the field of vision and consciousness of the grand lady, and would introduce the lady's life into the coachman's consciousness. He would cause all of his characters to perceive and understand all those essentials which he—the author—perceives and understands. He would leave for himself no *essential* superiority of information (as far as the sought-after truth is concerned). He would arrange a face-to-face confrontation of the respective truths of the lady and the coachman, he would cause them to come into dialogical contact (although not necessarily in direct dialogs within the composition of the work) and would himself assume a position of dialogical equality in relation to them. He would construct the whole work in the form of a large dialog, which the author organizes and in which he participates, without retaining the final word for himself. He would reflect in his work the dialogical nature of human thought and human life itself. And not only the pure *intonations of the author* would be heard in the words of the story; the intonations of the lady and of the coachman would be heard as well, i.e. the words would become double-voiced. A conflict of opinion (a microdialog) could be heard in every word, every word would be an echo of the great dialog.

[59]

...vsky would never depict three *deaths.* In his world, where
... the dominant in the representation of a human being, and
...edged consciousnesses is the major occurrence, death is
...nd illuminating life. Death as Tolstoy conceives of it is
...oevsky's world.[74] Instead of the deaths of his heroes,
...be the crises and turning points in their lives, i.e. he
... depict life *on the brink.* His heroes would remain inwardly *unfinalized,*
because the self-consciousness cannot, after all, be finalized *from without.* Such
would be the polyphonic manner of the story.

Nothing which is in the least essential is ever left outside the realm of the
consciousness of Dostoevsky's leading characters (i.e. of those characters who
participate as equals in the great dialogs of his novels); they are confronted dialogically with every essential element that enters into the world of his novels.
The individual "truth" of every major character in a given novel is without fail
introduced into the *dialogical field of vision* of all the other major characters.
Ivan Karamazov, for example, knows and understands Zosima's truth and that
of Dmitry and Alyosha as well as the "truth" of the voluptuary—his father
Fyodor Pavlovich. Dmitry understands all of these truths, too, and Alyosha understands them very well. In *The Devils* there is not a single idea which does
not find a dialogical response in Stavrogin's consciousness.

Dostoevsky never retains for himself an essential *superiority of information,* but only that indispensable minimum of pragmatic, purely informative
omniscience which is necessary for the development of the plot. An essential
superiority of information on the part of the author would turn the great dialog of the novel into a merely rhetorical dialog or into a finalized and objectivized one.

We shall cite some excerpts from Raskolnikov's first long interior monolog at the beginning of *Crime and Punishment.* The subject under discussion is
Dunechka's decision to marry Luzhin:

"It is clear that none other than Rodion Romanovich Raskolnikov is involved here and is in the foreground. Yes, well, and we can arrange his happiness, pay his way at the university, make him a partner at the office, assure
his whole future; perhaps in time he'll be a rich man, honored, respected,
perhaps he'll even end his days a famous man! But what of mother? Well,
after all, this is her Rodya, her precious Rodya, her firstborn! Well, for
such a firstborn son, how could she hesitate to sacrifice even such a daughter?
Oh, kind and unjust hearts! But what of it—we won't refuse Sonya's fate,
will we? Sonechka, Sonechka Marmeladova, eternal Sonechka, so long as
the world stands. Have either of you measured the sacrifice fully? Is it right?
Can you manage it? Is it of any use? Does it make sense? Do you know,
Dunechka, that Sonya's fate is no more wretched than your fate with Mr.
Luzhin? 'There is no question of love here,' writes mama. And what if,
besides love, there can be no respect, either, what if, on the contrary,

there already exists revulsion, contempt and loathing? What then? Then it turns out again, no doubt, one will have to **"keep oneself clean."** Isn't that the way it is? Do you understand what this cleanliness means? Do you understand that Luzhin's cleanliness is the same as Sonya's, and maybe even worse, more disgusting, more base, because you, Dunechka, at least you can count on some surplus of comfort, while with her it is a matter of naked death, pure and simple! 'It costs a lot, Dunechka, it costs a lot, this cleanliness!' Well, and if you can no longer bear it later on, will you be sorry? How much grief and sorrow, how many curses there'll be, and tears hidden from everyone, because you are no Marfa Petrovna [Svidrigailova] ! And what will happen to mother then? She's already upset and tormented; what will it be like when she sees it all clearly? And what about me? What did you think about me, anyway? I don't want your sacrifice, Dunechka, I don't want it, mama! It won't happen as long as I'm alive, it won't happen, it won't! I don't accept it!"

" 'Or else renounce life completely,' he shouted suddenly in a fit of rage, 'obediently accept fate as it comes, once and for all, stifle everything within yourself, renouncing any right to act, to live and to love!' "

'Do you understand, do you understand, my dear sir, what it means when there's nowhere left for you to go?' he suddenly remembered Marmeladov's voice from yesterday, 'because every man has to have at least somewhere to go...' " (V, 49, 50, 51)

This interior monolog, as we said, took place at the very beginning, on the second day of the novel's action, before the final decision to kill the old woman had been made. Raskolnikov had just received his mother's letter in which she writes in detail of Dunya and Svidrigailov and in which she informs him of Luzhin's courtship of Dunya. On the previous evening Raskolnikov had met with Marmeladov and had learned Sonya's entire history from him. Thus all of these future major characters in the novel were already reflected in Raskolnikov's consciousness; they entered into his fully dialogized interior monolog together with their "truths" and existential positions, and he engaged them in an intense and fundamental interior dialog, a dialog of ultimate questions and ultimate vital decisions. From the very beginning he knows everything, anticipates everything and takes everything into consideration. He has already entered into dialogical contact with his entire milieu.

The dialogized interior monolog which we have cited is a brilliant model of the *microdialog:* every word in it is double-voiced, every word contains a conflict of voices. In fact, at the beginning of the passage Raskolnikov re-creates Dunya's words and the intonations through which she passes judgement or seeks to convince, and to them adds his own ironic, indignant, or precautionary intonations. In his words two voices resound simultaneously—that of Raskolnikov and that of Dunya. In the words which follow ("Well, after all, this is her Rodya, isn't it, her precious Rodya, her firstborn!" etc.) his mother's voice with her intonations

[61]

of love and tenderness is heard, and at the same time we hear Raskolnikov's voice with the intonations of bitter irony, indignation (at the thought of Dunya's self-sacrifice) and melancholy reciprocal love. Subsequently we hear in Raskolnikov's words Sonya's voice and that of her father. Dialog penetrates every word, giving rise to conflicts and interruptions of one voice by another. This is a microdialog.

Thus at the very beginning of the novel all the leading voices of the great dialog have already been heard. These voices are not self-enclosed and are not deaf to one another. They constantly hear each other, call out to one another, and are mutually reflected in one another (especially in the microdialogs). Not a single essential action takes place, nor is a single essential thought expressed outside this dialog of "conflicting truths."

Throughout the novel nothing that plays a part in it—people, ideas, objects—remains external to Raskolnikov's consciousness; everything is contrasted to him and dialogically reflected in him. All possible evaluations and attitudes toward his personality, his character, his idea and his actions are extended into his consciousness and are addressed to him in dialogs with Porfiry, Sonya, Svidrigailov, Dunya and others. Everyone else's views of the world intersect with his view. Everything that he sees and observes—the slums of Petersburg and the monumental Petersburg, all of his chance meetings and various insignificant events— is drawn into a dialog, it answers his questions and puts new ones to him, it provokes him and disputes with him or confirms him in his own thoughts. The author retains for himself no essential superiority of information and enters as Raskolnikov's equal into the great dialog that is the novel.

This is the new authorial position in relation to the hero in Dostoevsky's polyphonic novel.

CHAPTER THREE

THE IDEA IN DOSTOEVSKY'S WORKS

Let us move on to the next element of our thesis—the statement of the idea in Dostoevsky's artistic world. The concept of polyphony is incompatible with the representation of a single idea *(odnoideinost')* executed in the ordinary way. Dostoevsky's originality must be manifested with particular sharpness and clarity in the statement of the idea. In our analysis we shall avoid discussing the content of the ideas which Dostoevsky introduces—we are interested in their artistic function within the work.

The hero in Dostoevsky is not only a word about himself and about his immediate environment, but also a word about the world: he has not only a consciousness, but an ideology, too.

Already the "underground man" is an ideologist, although the ideological creativity of the heroes attains its full significance in the novels, where the idea does in fact almost become the heroine of the work. Nonetheless, the dominant of the hero's representation remains unchanged—it is the self-consciousness.

Therefore the hero's word about the world merges with his confessional word about himself. The truth about the world, according to Dostoevsky, is inseparable from the truth of the personality. The categories of self-consciousness which determined life already in the case of Devushkin, and especially in the case of Golyadkin,—acceptance or non-acceptance, revolt or meekness—in the novels become the basic categories of thought about the world. Therefore the loftier principles of *Weltanschauung* are the same as the principles of the most concrete personal experience. Thus is achieved the artistic merging of personal life with *Weltanschauung*, of intimate experience with the idea, which is so characteristic of Dostoevsky. Personal life becomes uniquely unselfish and principled, and lofty ideological thinking becomes intimately personal and passionate.

The merging of the hero's word about himself with his ideological word about the world greatly elevates the direct significance of his self-utterance and strengthens his resistance to every external finalization. The idea aids the self-consciousness in asserting its sovereignty within Dostoevsky's artistic world and helps it triumph over every firm and stable image.

But on the other hand the idea is able to retain its significance, its full meaning, only when the self-consciousness is the dominant of the hero's artistic representation. In a monological artistic world an idea, placed in the mouth of a hero who is depicted as a firm and finalized image of reality, inevitably loses

[63]

its direct significance and becomes an aspect, a predetermined feature of reality no different from any other of the hero's traits. Such an idea is a social-typical or an individual-characteristic one, or a mere intellectual gesture on the part of the hero, the intellectual expression on his spiritual face. The idea ceases to be an idea and becomes a simple artistic characteristic. As such, it becomes a part of the hero's image.

If an idea in a monological world retains its significance as an idea, it is inevitably separated from the firm image of the hero and ceases to be artistically combined with him: it is merely placed in his mouth, but could with equal success be placed in the mouth of any other hero. The author merely wants to be sure that a particular correct idea is expressed in the context of a given work; who expresses it and when is determined by the compositional considerations of convenience and appropriateness, or on the basis of purely negative criteria: in such a way that it does not destroy the speaker's verisimilitude. Such an idea *belongs to no one.* The hero is a mere carrier of the independent idea; as a true, significant idea, it gravitates toward a certain apersonal systematic-monological context, or in other words, toward the author's own systematic-monological *Weltanschauung.*

The monological artistic world does not recognize the thoughts and ideas of others as an object of representation. In such a world everything ideological is divided into two categories. Certain thoughts—the true, significant ones—correspond to the author's consciousness and strive to take form in the purely semantic unity of the *Weltanschauung;* such thoughts are not represented, they are asserted; their assertion is objectively expressed in their special accent, their special position in the work as a whole, in the very verbal-stylistic form of their expression and by a whole series of other methods of advancing a confirmed, significant thought. We always detect such a thought in the context of the work: a confirmed thought has a different sound than an unconfirmed thought. The other ideas and thoughts—from the author's points of view incorrect or indifferent ones, ones which do not fit into his *Weltanschauung*—are not asserted, but rather are either polemically negated or lose their direct significance and become mere elements of characterization, the hero's intellectual gestures or his more permanent intellectual qualities.

In the monological world *tertium non datur:* a thought is either confirmed or negated; otherwise it simply ceases to be a thought of full significance. In order to become a part of the artistic structure, an unconfirmed thought must be deprived of its significance and become a psychic fact. Thoughts which are polemically negated are also not represented, because negation, in whatever form it may take, excludes the possibility of the genuine representation of an idea. A negated foreign thought *(otricaemaia chuzhaia mysl')* does not break out of the monological context, but on the contrary, becomes the more harshly and implacably shut up within its own borders. A negated foreign thought is not capable of creating a full-fledged foreign consciousness side by side with another consciousness, so long as this negation remains the purely theoretical negation of a thought as such.

The artistic representation of an idea is possible only when it is stated in terms beyond confirmation and negation, but at the same time is not reduced to a mere psychological experience, devoid of direct significance. In a monological world such a statement of an idea is impossible: it contradicts the most basic principles of that world. Those basic principles go far beyond the bounds of art alone; they are the principles of the entire ideological culture of modern times. But what are those principles?

The principles of ideological monologism found their most striking and theoretically distinct expression in idealistic philosophy. In idealism the monistic principle, i.e. the assertion of the unity of *existence,* is transformed into the principle of the unity of the *consciousness.*

For us, of course, the important thing is not the philosophical side of the question, but rather a certain characteristic of ideology in general, a characteristic manifested in the idealistic transformation of the monism of existence into the monologism of consciousness. And this characteristic is, in turn, important for us only from the viewpoint of its further artistic application.

The unity of consciousness, which replaces the unity of existence, is inevitably transformed into the unity of a *single* consciousness; it makes no difference what metaphysical form it takes: "consciousness in general" ("*Bewusstsein uberhaupt*"), "the absolute I,", "the absolute spirit," "the normative consciousness," etc. Alongside this unified and inevitably *single* consciousness is to be found a multitude of empirical human consciousnesses. From the point of view of "consciousness in general" this plurality of consciousnesses is accidental and, so to speak, superfluous. Everything that is essential and true in those consciousnesses becomes part of the unified context of "consciousness in general" and is deprived of its individuality. That which is individual, that which distinguishes one consciousness from another one and from other ones, is unessential for cognition and falls within the sphere of the individual human being's psychic organization and limitation. From the point of view of truth, there are no individual consciousnesses. The only principle of the individualization of cognition recognized by idealism is *error.* Every correct judgement corresponds to a particular unified systematic-monological context, rather than being attached to a personality. Only error individualizes. Everything that is true finds a place for itself within the bounds of a single consciousness, and if it does not in fact find a place, it is for reasons incidental and extraneous to truth itself. Ideally a single consciousness and a single mouth are completely sufficient for total fulness of cognition; there is no need and no basis for a multitude of consciousnesses.

It should be pointed out that the inevitability of a single and unified consciousness by no means necessarily follows from the concept of the one and only truth *(edinaia istina)* itself. It is completely possible to imagine and to assume that this one and only truth requires a plurality of consciousnesses, and that it has, so to speak, the nature of an *event* and is born in the point of contact of various consciousnesses. Everything depends on one's conception of the truth and its

[65]

relationship to the consciousness. The monological conception of cognition and truth is only one of the possible conceptions. It arises only where the consciousness is placed below existence and where the unity of existence is transformed into the unity of consciousness.

On the basis of philosophical monologism genuine interaction of consciousnesses is impossible, and therefore genuine dialog is also impossible. In essence, idealism knows only a single form of cognitive interaction between consciousnesses: he who knows and possesses the truth instructs him who errs and is ignorant of it, i.e. the interaction of teacher and pupil. Consequently only a pedagogical dialog is possible.[75]

The monological conception of the consciousness prevails in other spheres of ideological creative work as well. All that is significant and valuable is everywhere concentrated around a single center—the carrier. All idealistic creative work is thought of and perceived as a possible expression of a single consciousness, a single spirit. Even where the matter under discussion is a collective of a variety of creative forces, unity is still illustrated by the image of a single consciousness: the spirit of a nation, the spirit of a people, the spirit of history, etc. All that has significance can be collected in a single consciousness and subordinated to a unified accent; everything which is not amenable to such a reduction is accidental and unessential. In modern times European rationalism with its cult of unified and exclusive *(edinyi i edinstvennyi)* reason, and particularly the Enlightenment, during which the basic genres of European prose were formed, abetted the consolidation of the monological principle and its penetration into all spheres of ideological life. European utopism is also based on this monological principle. Utopian socialism with its faith in the omnipotence of convictions belongs here, too. Unity of meaning is everywhere represented by a single consciousness and a single point of view.

Faith in the self-sufficiency of a single consciousness in all spheres of ideological life is not a theory created by some thinker or other; no, it is a profound structural characteristic of the ideological creativity of modern times, the determinate of its inner and outer form. We can be interested here only in the literary manifestations of this characteristic.

The statement of an idea in literature is, as we have already seen, usually totally monologistical. An idea is either confirmed or negated. All confirmed ideas merge in the unified vision and representation of the author's consciousness; the unconfirmed ideas are distributed among the heroes and are no longer significant ideas, but social-typical or individually characteristic manifestations of thought. The primary knower, understander and seer is the author alone. Only he is an ideologist. The author's ideas are marked by the stamp of his own individuality. Thus *individuality and direct and valid ideological significance are combined* in the author *without detracting from each other.* But only in the author. In the heroes, individuality kills the significance of their ideas, or, if the significance of those ideas is retained, they are separated from the hero's individuality and combine with that of the author. Hence the work's *single ideological accent;* the

[66]

appearance of a second accent is inevitably perceived as an inadmissable contradiction within the author's *Weltanschauung.*

A confirmed and full-valued authorial idea can perform a triple function in a monological work: firstly, it is the *principle of the vision and representation of the world,* the principle of the *choice* and unification of material, the principle of the *ideological singletonedness* of all elements of the work. Secondly, the idea can be given as a more or less distinct or conscious *conclusion* drawn from that which is being represented. Thirdly, the author's idea can be given direct expression in the *ideological position of the central hero.*

The idea as a principle of representation becomes one with the form. It determines all the formal accents and all the ideological assessments which constitute the formal unity of artistic style and the unified tone of the work.

The deeper strata of this form-determining ideology, the factors which determine the basic characteristics of a work's genre, are of a traditional nature, they take shape and develop over the course of centuries. Artistic monologism belongs to this realm of the deeper strata of form.

Within a monological framework, ideology seen as a conclusion, as a summation of the meaning of that which is represented, inevitably transforms the represented world into the *voiceless object of that conclusion.* The forms of the ideological conclusion themselves can be most varied. The statement of the represented material depends upon those forms: the material can be the simple illustration of an idea, a mere example; it can be the basis for an ideological generalization (the experimental novel); or, finally, it can have a more complex relationship to the final sum. If the representation is oriented entirely toward an ideological conclusion, the result is an ideological, philosophical novel (Voltaire's *Candide,* for example), or—at worst—simply a crudely tendentious novel. And even if this direct orientation is absent, an element of ideological conclusion is nonetheless present in every representation, however modest or concealed the formal functions of that conclusion may be. The accents of the ideological conclusion must not contradict the form-determining accents of the representation itself. If such a contradiction exists, it is perceived as a shortcoming, for within a monological world contradictory accents collide in a single voice. Unity of viewpoint must weld together the most formal elements of style as well as the most abstract philosophical conclusions.

The hero's philosophical position can lie in the same plane as the form-determining ideology and the final ideological conclusion. The hero's point of view can be transferred from the objective sphere to the sphere of principle. In that case the ideological principles which lie at the basis of the structure no longer depict only the hero and determine the author's point of view toward him; those principles are now also expressed by the hero himself and determine his own point of view toward the world. Such a hero is formally very different from the ordinary type of hero. It is not necessary to go beyond the bounds of a given work to find other documentation of the concurrence of the author's ideology with that of the hero. Moreover, such a concurrence of content, having no basis in the work, is in itself possessed of no power to convince. The unity of the author's ideo-logical principles of representation and the hero's ideological position must be revealed in the work itself, as the *single-accentedness of the representation and the speeches and experiences of the hero,* rather than as the concurrence of the hero's thoughts with the ideological views of the author, as stated in some other place. The very words and experiences of such a hero are presented differently: they are not materialized, they characterize not only the speaker himself, but the object at which they are directed as well. Such a hero's word lies in the same plane as the author's word.

The absence of distance between the position of the author and that of the hero is manifested in a whole series of other formal characteristics as well. The hero, for example, is, like the author himself, not closed and inwardly fi-nalized, and therefore does not fit wholly into the Procrustian bed of the plot, which is thought of as only one of many possible plots, and is consequently for the given hero an accidental one. This open-ended hero is typical of the Roman-ticists, of Byron and Chateaubriand; Lermontov's Pechorin is in some ways such a hero.

And finally, the author's ideas can be sporadically scattered throughout the entire work. They can appear in the author's speeches as isolated apothegms, maxims, or entire discourses, or they can be put into the mouth of one or ano-ther hero, sometimes in large quantities, without, however, merging with his in-dividuality (Turgenev's Potugin, for example).

This whole mass of organized and unorganized ideology, from the princi-ples which determine the form, to the chance and easily ignored maxims of the author, must be subordinated to a single accent and must express a single and unified point of view. Everything that remains is the object of this point of view, i.e. is subordinated to the accent. Only ideas which fall into the groove of the author's point of view can retain their significance without destroying the single-accented unity of the work. *None* of these authorial ideas, regardless of their function, are *represented:* they either represent and internally direct the repre-sentation, or they shed light on that which is represented, or, finally, they ac-company the representation as separable semantic ornaments *(otdelimyi smys-lovoi ornament). They are expressed directly, without distance.* And within the bounds of the monological world which they represent, a foreign idea cannot be represented. It is either assimilated or polemically refuted, or ceases to be an idea altogether.

■

Dostoevsky was capable of *representing a foreign (chuzhaia) idea,* while still maintaining its full meaning as an idea, and at the same time maintaining distance as well, not confirming the idea and not merging it with his own ex-pressed ideology.

In his work the idea becomes an *object of artistic representation,* and

[68]

Dostoevsky himself became a great *artist of the idea.*

It is characteristic that the image of an artist of the idea occurred to Dostoevsky already in 1846-47, i.e. at the very beginning of his creative path. We have in mind the image of Ordynov, the hero of "The Landlady." He is a lonesome young scholar. He has his own creative system, his own unusual approach to the scientific idea:

> He was creating a system for himself; it grew within him over a period of years, and in his soul a still vague and obscure, but somehow wonderfully joyful *image of an idea* was gradually taking shape, an idea embodied in a *new, blissful form,* and that form struggled to burst out of his soul, tearing at it and tormenting it; he still timidly *sensed* its originality, its *truth* and its uniqueness: creativity was already revealing itself to his powers; it was taking form and gaining strength. (I, 425).

And at the end of the story:

> Perhaps a complete, original, unique idea would have been born in him. Perhaps he was destined to become an *artist in science. (I, 498)*

Dostoevsky was also destined to become an artist of the idea, not in science, but in literature.

What are the conditions which make the artistic representation of an idea possible for Dostoevsky?

First of all we must be reminded that the image of the idea is inseparable from the image of the person, the carrier of that idea. It is not the idea in and of itself which is the "heroine of Dostoevsky's works," as B. M. Engelgardt asserts, but rather the *man of an idea (chelovek idei).* We must again emphasize that Dostoevsky's hero is the man of an idea; this is not a character or temperament, not a social or psychological type: the image of a *full-valued* idea has, of course, nothing to do with such externalized and finalized images of people. It would, for example, be foolish to even attempt to combine Raskolnikov's idea, which we understand and *feel* (according to Dostoevsky an idea can and must be not only understood, but "felt" as well), with his finalized character or his social typicality as a *raznochinec* of the '60's: his idea would immediately lose its direct significance as a full-valued idea and would be removed from the conflict in which it *lives* in ceaseless dialogical interaction with other full-valued ideas— those of Sonya, Porfiry, Svidrigailov, etc. The carrier of a full-valued idea can be none other than the "man in man," with his free unfinalizedness and indeterminacy, about whom we spoke in the previous chapter. It is precisely to this unfinalized inner nucleus of Raskolnikov's personality that Sonya, Porfiry and others dialogically address themselves. It is also to this unfinalized nucleus of Raskolnikov's personality that the author, by virture of the whole structure of his novel, addresses himself.

[69]

Consequently only the unfinalizable and inexhaustible "man in man" can become the man of an idea, whose image is combined with the image of a full-valued idea. This is the first condition of the representation of the idea in Dostoevsky.

But this condition contains, as it were, its inverse as well. We can say that in Dostoevsky's works man overcomes his "thingness" *(veshchnost')* and becomes "man in man" only by entering the pure and unfinalized sphere of the idea, i.e. only by becoming the selfless man of an idea. Such are all of Dostoevsky's leading characters, i.e. all of the participants in the great dialog.

In this respect Zosima's definition of Ivan Karamazov's personality is applicable to all of these characters. Zosima of course couched his definition in his theological language, i.e. it stemmed from that sphere of the Christian idea in which he lived. We shall quote the appropriate passage from that—for Dostoevsky—very characteristic *penetrant (proniknovennyi)* dialog between the Elder Zosima and Ivan Karamazov.

"Is that really your conviction regarding the consequences of the whithering of people's faith in the immortality of their souls?" the Elder Zosima asked Ivan suddenly.

"Yes, I have asserted that. If there is no immortality, there is no virtue."

"You are blissfully happy if you really believe that. Or terribly unhappy."

"Why unhappy?" smiled Ivan.

"Because in all probability you do not yourself believe either in the immortality of your soul, nor in the things that you have written about the church and the religious question."

"Perhaps you are right!...But nonetheless it was not all merely a jest...," suddenly admitted Ivan strangely, blushing quickly, by the way.

"Verily, it was not all merely a jest. *This idea is not yet resolved in your heart, and it torments you.* But he who is tormented is also fond at times of amusing himself with his despair, as if also out of despair. For the time being you, too, are amusing yourself with your despair—and with newspaper articles and worldly arguments, without yourself believing in your dialectic, under your breath laughing at it with pain in your heart... *This question is unresolved in you, and that is your great misfortune, for it persistently demands a resolution...*"

"But perhaps it is already resolved? Resolved in a positive direction?" Ivan continued to ask strangely, gazing steadily at the elder with some sort of inexplicable smile.

"If it cannot be resolved in a positive direction, it will never be resolved in a negative one, either; you yourself know this characteristic of your heart. Therein lies all its torment. But thank the Creator for giving you an *extraordinary heart, a heart capable of suffering such sufferings,* of *'setting its mind on things above, not on things on the earth, seeking those things which are above,* for our home is in the kingdom of heaven.' May God grant that the resolution of your heart come while you are still on earth, and may God bless your path!" (IX, 91-92)

In his discussion with Rakitin Alyosha defines Ivan similarly, only in more worldly language.

"Ach, Misha, his soul [Ivan's—M.B.] is a stormy one. His mind is held captive. He is filled with a great and unresolved idea. *He is one of those who don't need millions, they just need to get an idea straight."* (IX, 105)

All of Dostoevsky's leading characters have the capacity to "set their minds on things above" and to "seek those things which are above;" each of them is filled with a "great and unresolved idea," all of them must above all "get an idea straight." And in this resolution of an idea lies their entire real life and their personal unfinalizedness. If one were to think away the idea in which they live, their image would be totally destroyed. In other words, the image of the hero is inseparably linked with the image of the idea. We *see* the hero in and through the idea, and we *see* the idea in and through the hero.

All of Dostoevsky's leading characters, as people of an idea, are absolutely unselfish, in so far as the idea has in fact taken command of the deepest core of their personality. This unselfishness is not a trait of their objective character and not an external description of their actions; unselfishness expresses their real life in the sphere of the idea (they "don't need millions, they just need to get an idea straight"). Living an idea *(ideinost')* is somehow synonymous with unselfishness. In this sense even Raskolnikov is absolutely unselfish when he kills and robs the old woman usurer, as is the prostitute Sonya and the accomplice in the murder of Ivan Karamazov's father; the "raw youth's" *idea* to become a Rothschild is also absolutely unselfish. We repeat again: the important thing is not the ordinary classification of a person's character and actions, but rather the indicator of the dedication of his whole personality to the idea.

The second condition for the creation of the image of the idea in Dostoevsky is his profound understanding of the dialogical nature of human thought, the dialogical nature of the idea. Dostoevsky was able to see, reveal and depict the true sphere of the life of an idea. An idea does not *live* in one person's *isolated* individual consciousness—if it remains there it degenerates and dies. An idea begins to live, i.e. to take shape, to develop, to find and renew its verbal expression, and to give birth to new ideas only when it enters into genuine dialogical relationships with other, *foreign,* ideas. Human thought becomes genuine thought, i.e. an idea, only under the conditions of a living contact with another foreign thought, embodied in the voice of another person, that is, in the consciousness of another person as expressed in his word. It is in the point of contact of these voice-consciousnesses that the idea is born and has its life.

The idea, as *seen* by Dostoevsky the artist, is not a subjective individual-psychological formulation with a "permanent residence" in a person's head; no, the idea is interindividual and intersubjective. The sphere of its existence is not the individual consciousness, but the dialogical intercourse *between* consciousnesses. The idea is a *living event* which is played out in the point where two or more consciousnesses meet dialogically. In this respect the idea resembles the *word,* with which it forms a dialogical unity. Like the word, the idea wants to be heard, understood and "answered" by other voices from other positions. Like the word, the idea is by nature dialogical, the monolog being merely the conventional form of its expression which arose from the soil of the ideological monologism of modern times, as characterized above.

Dostoevsky saw and artistically represented the *idea* as precisely such a living event, played out between consciousness-voices. The artistic revelation of the dialogical nature of the idea, the consciousness, and of every human life that is illuminated by a consciousness (and therefore is at least marginally acquainted with ideas) made Dostoevsky a great artist of the idea.

Dostoevsky never sets forth completed ideas in monological form, but neither does he depict their *psychological* evolution within a *single* individual consciousness. In both cases the ideas would cease to be living images.

We recall, for example, Raskolnikov's first interior monolog, which we quoted in the preceding chapter. Here we find no psychological evolution of the idea within a *single* self-enclosed consciousness. On the contrary, the consciousness of the solitary Raskolnikov becomes the field of battle for the voices of others; the events of recent days (his mother's letter, the meeting with Marmeladov), reflected in his consciousness, take on the form of an intense dialog with absentee interlocutors (with his sister, his mother, Sonya, and others), and in this dialog he, too, seeks to "get his ideas straight."

Already before the action of the novel begins, Raskolnikov has published a newspaper article containing an exposition of the theoretical bases of his idea. Dostoevsky nowhere gives us this article in monological form. We first become acquainted with its content, and consequently with Raskolnikov's main idea, in Raskolnikov's tense and, for him, terrible, dialog with Porfiry (Razumikhin and Zametov also participate in the dialog). Porfiry is the first to give an account of the article, and he does so in a deliberately exaggerated and provocative form. This internally dialogized account is constantly interrupted by questions put to Raskolnikov, and by the replies of the latter. Then Raskolnikov himself describes his article, but he is constantly interrupted by Porfiry's provocative questions and remarks. And, from the point of view of Porfiry and his like, Raskolnikov's account is saturated with inner polemics. Razumikhin also gives his comments. As a result, Raskolnikov's idea appears before us in the interindividual zone of intense struggle between several individual consciousnesses, while the idea's theoretical side is indissolubly combined in the ultimate life-principles of the dialog's participants.

This same idea of Raskolnikov appears again in his no less tense dialogs with Sonya; here it takes on a different tonality, entering into dialogical contact with another very strong and integral life-principle, that of Sonya, thus revealing new facets and potentialities. Next we hear this idea in Svidrigailov's dialogized presentation in his conversation with Dunya. But in the voice of Svidrigailov, who is one of Raskolnikov's parodical doubles, the idea has a completely different sound, and it turns another of its sides toward us. And lastly, Raskolnikov's idea comes into contact throughout the entire novel with various manifestations of life, it is tried and tested, and it is confirmed or refuted by them. This aspect was discussed in the preceeding chapter.

Let us also recall Ivan Karamazov's idea that "everything is permissible" ("vse pozvoleno") as long as the soul is not immortal. What an intense dialogical life this idea lives throughout the entire novel *The Brothers Karamazov!* What a variety of voices expresses it and what unexpected dialogical contacts it makes!

Both of these ideas (Raskolnikov's and Ivan Karamazov's) reflect other ideas, just as in painting a certain color, because of the reflections of the surrounding colors, loses its abstract purity, but in return begins to live a truly colorful life. If one were to withdraw these ideas from the dialogical sphere of their lives and give them a monologically completed theoretical form, what cachetic and easily-refuted ideological constructions would result!

■

As an artist Dostoevsky did not create his ideas in the same way that philosophers and scholars create theirs—he created living images of the ideas which he found, detected, or sometimes divined in *reality itself,* i.e. images of already-living ideas, ideas already existing as idea-forces. Dostoevsky possessed a brilliant gift for hearing the dialog of his age, or, more precisely, for perceiving his age as a great dialog, and for capturing in it not only individual voices, but above all the *dialogical relationships* between voices, their dialogical *interaction.* He heard both the dominant, recognized, loud voices of the age, that is to say, the dominant, leading ideas (both official and unofficial), and the still-weak voices, the ideas which had not yet reached full development, the latent ideas which no one else had yet discerned, and the ideas which were only beginning to mature, the embryos of future *Weltanschauungen.* Dostoevsky himself wrote: "Reality is not limited to the familiar, the commonplace, for it consists in huge part of a *latent, as yet unspoken future Word.*"[76]

In the dialog of his times Dostoevsky heard the resonances of the voice-ideas of the past, too—both of the recent past (the 1830s and 40s), and of the more remote. He also strove, as we have just said, to discern the voice-ideas of the future, seeking to divine them, so to speak, in the place prepared for them in the dialog of the present, in the same way that it is possible to foresee a reply which has not yet been uttered in a dialog which is already in progress. Thus,

[73]

the past, the present, and the future came together and confronted one another in the plane of contemporaneity.

We repeat: Dostoevsky never created his idea-images out of nothing, he never "invented" them, any more than a painter invents the people he paints; he was able to hear and divine them in existing reality. Therefore it is possible to find and point out the specific *prototypes* of the ideas in Dostoevsky's novels, as well as those of his heroes. The prototypes of Raskolnikov's ideas, for example, were the ideas of Max Sterner as expressed in his tract "Der Einzige und sein Eigentum," and the ideas of Napoleon III, developed in his book *Histoire de Jules César* (1865);[77] one of the prototypes for Petr Verkhovensky's ideas was *Catechism of a Revolutionary;*[78] the prototypes of Versilov's ideas (in *A Raw Youth*) were the ideas of Chaadaev and Herzen.[79] Not all of the prototypes for Dostoevsky's idea-images have as yet been discovered. We must emphasize that we are not referring here to Dostoevsky's "sources"—that term would be inappropriate—but precisely to the *prototypes* of his images of ideas.

Dostoevsky in no way copied or expounded on these prototypes; he freely and creatively re-worked them into living artistic images of ideas, in the very same way that an artist works with his human prototypes. Above all, he destroyed the self-enclosed monological form of his idea-prototypes and made them part of the great dialog of his novels, where they begin to live a new, eventful artistic life.

As an artist, Dostoevsky revealed in the image of a given idea not only the actual and historical traits which were present in the prototype (in Napoleon's *Histoire de Jules César,* for example), but its *potentialities* as well, and it is just these potentialities that are of prime importance for an artistic image. Dostoevsky often made artistic conjectures as to how a given idea would develop and behave under certain altered conditions, or as to the unexpected directions its further development and transformation would take. For this purpose Dostoevsky placed the idea at the vertex of dialogically intersecting consciousnesses. He brought together ideas and *Weltanschauungen* which were in real life completely divergent and deaf to one another, and caused them to dispute. He as it were extended these ideas by means of a dotted line to their point of intersection. Thus he anticipated the future convergence of ideas which were as yet divergent. He foresaw new combinations of ideas, the emergence of new idea-voices, and changes in the arrangement of all the idea-voices in the universal dialog. This is why the Russian—and universal—dialog of Dostoevsky's works, a dialog of already-living idea-voices with idea-voices that are still being born, that are still unfinalized and fraught with new possiblities, continues to involve the minds and voices of Dostoevsky's readers in its tragic and exalted game.

Thus the idea-prototypes used in Dostoevsky's novels alter the form of their existence, without losing the significance of their meaning: they become completely dialogized, not monologically finalized, images of ideas, i.e. they enter a new sphere of *artistic* existence.

Dostoevsky was not only an artist who wrote novels and stories, but also a publicist-thinker who published articles in *Vremia, Epoxa, Grazhdanin* and *Dnevnik pisatelia (Time, The Epoch, The Citizen* and *Diary of a Writer)*. In those articles he expressed specific philosophical, religious-philosophical, social-political, and other ideas; in the articles he expressed *his own confirmed* ideas in *systematic-monological* or rhetorical-monological (i.e. *publicistic*) form. He sometimes expressed the same ideas in letters to various people. Here, in the articles and letters, he give, of course, not images of ideas, but direct, monologically confirmed ideas.

But we meet these "Dostoevskian ideas" in his novels as well. How should we regard them there, i.e. in the artistic context of his creative work?

In exactly the same way as we regard Napoleon III's ideas in *Crime and Punishment* (ideas with which Dostoevsky the thinker was totally at variance), or the ideas of Chaadaev and Herzen in *A Raw Youth* (ideas with which Dostoevsky the thinker was in partial agreement); i.e. we should regard the ideas of Dostoevsky the thinker as *idea-prototypes* for certain idea-images in his novels (the images of the ideas of Sonya, Myshkin, Alyosha Karamazov, Zosima).

Actually, the ideas of Dostoevsky the thinker change the very form of their existence when they become part of his polyphonic novel; they are turned into artistic images of ideas: they become indissoluably combined with the images of people (Sonya, Myshkin, Zosima), they are freed from their monological isolation and finalization, becoming completely dialogized and entering into the great dialog of the novel *on completely equal terms* with other idea-images (the ideas of Raskolnikov, Ivan Karamazov and others). It is totally inadmissable to ascribe to them the finalizing function of the author's ideas in a monological novel. As equal participants in the great dialog, they simply do not have such a function. If a certain partiality of Dostoevsky the publicist for various ideas or images is sometimes felt in the novels, it is manifested only in superficial ways (as in the conventional-monological epilogue to *Crime and Punishment,* for example) and cannot destroy the powerful artistic logic of the polyphonic novel. Dostoevsky the artist always wins out over Dostoevsky the publicist.

Thus Dostoevsky's private ideas, expressed in monological form outside the artistic context for his work (in articles, letters and conversations), are only the prototypes of certain images of ideas in his novels. For this reason it is totally inadmissable to substitute a criticism of these monological idea-prototypes for a genuine analysis of Dostoevsky's polyphonic artistic thought. It is important that the *function* of ideas in Dostoevsky's polyphonic world be revealed, and not only their *monological substance*.

■

For a correct understanding of the representation of the idea in Dostoevsky's works it is imperative to consider one more characteristic of the ideology which determined their form. We have in mind above all that ideology which was the principle of Dostoevsky's vision and representation of the world, the ideology which indeed determined the form of his works, because it is what, in the final analysis, determines the function of abstract ideas and thoughts in those works.

The two basic elements on which any ideology is founded were absent from Dostoevsky's form-determining ideology: the *individual thought* and a unified *system* of thoughts in relation to the subject matter. An ordinary ideology contains separate thoughts, assertions and propositions which of themselves can be either correct or incorrect, depending on their relationship to the subject matter, and regardless of who is their carrier, regardless of whom they belong to. These "no-man's" thoughts, correct in relation to the subject matter *("nich'i" predmetno-vernye mysli),* are unified in the subject matter's systematic oneness. In the unity of the system, thought brushes against thought and one thought is bound to another on the basis of the subject matter. For the thought, the system is the ultimate whole, and the elements which form the system are the individual thoughts.

In this sense Dostoevsky's ideology contains neither the separate thought, nor a systematic unity. For him the basic, indivisible unit was not the individual thought, proposition or assertion, based on and limited to the subject matter *(predmetno-ogranichenaia),* but rather the integrated point of view, the integrated position of a personality. For him subject-oriented meaning is inseparably combined with the position of the personality. The personality presents itself full-blown in every thought. Therefore the combining of thoughts is the combining of integrated positions, the combining of personalities.

To speak paradoxically, Dostoevsky thought not in thoughts, but in points of view, in consciousnesses, in voices. He strove to perceive and formulate every thought in such a way that the whole man could express himself and resonate within it, thus expressing in compressed form his entire *Weltanschauung,* from alpha to omega. Only thoughts which squeezed an entire spiritual orientation into themselves were taken by Dostoevsky as elements of his artistic *Weltanschauung;* such thoughts were for him indivisible units, and such units combined to form a concrete event of organized human orientations and voices, not merely a unified system based on the subject matter. In Dostoevsky's works two thoughts are already two people, for there are no no-man's thoughts—every thought represents a whole person.

Dostoevsky's effort to perceive every thought as an integrated personal position and to think in voices can be clearly seen even in the composition of his publicistic articles. His manner of developing a thought is everywhere the same: he develops its dialogically, not in a dry logical dialog, but by juxtaposing deeply individualized integral voices. Even in his polemical articles he essentially does not try to persuade; rather he organizes voices and couples philosophical orientations, in most cases in the form of an imagined dialog.

Here is the typical structure of one of his articles.

In the article "Sreda" ("The Environment") Dostoevsky begins by stating a series of propositions in the form of questions and assumptions about the psychological state and orientation of jury members, interrupting and illustrating his thoughts, as usual, with the voices and semi-voices of individuals; for example:

> It would seem that one of the feelings (among others, of course)
> common to all jury members in the world, but to ours in particular, is
> the feeling of power, or, to put it better, the feeling of absolute might.
> This is sometimes an obscene feeling, i.e. when it dominates all others...
> In my daydreams I have imagined court sessions in which almost all of the
> jurors are, for example, peasants, who were only yesterday serfs. The pro-
> secutor and the attorneys for the defense appeal to them and curry their
> favor and glance at them, but our old peasants sit there and say to them-
> selves: "Well, now then, if I want to, I'll let 'em go, and if I don't—off to
> Siberia with 'em..."
> Others will decide, as we have sometimes heard, "It's a pity to ruin
> somebody's life; they're people, too, after all. The Russian folk is merciful..."

Further on Dostoevsky orchestrates his theme with the aid of an imaginary dialog.

> I hear a voice saying, "Even if we assume that those weighty prin-
> ciples of yours (i.e. Christian ones) are still the same and that it is true that
> one must be a citizen first of all, and hold up the flag, as you said, and so
> on; even if we assume so for now without an argument, just think, where
> are our citizens supposed to come from? Just imagine what things were
> like only yesterday! All these civil rights (and what generous ones, at that!)
> have suddenly come crashing down on the peasant like an avalanche. They've
> crushed him, they're as yet nothing but a burden for him, a burden!"
> "Of course there is justice in what you say," I answer the voice,
> hanging my head a bit, "but still, the Russian folk..."
> "The Russian folk? If you please," I hear another voice speaking,
> "someone says that gifts came crashing down on the peasant like an ava-
> lanche and crushed him. But maybe he feels not only that he received so
> much power as a gift, but beyond that maybe he feels that he got it for
> nothing, that is, that he is not yet worthy of these gifts..." (This point of
> view is then developed further.)
> "This is in part a slavophile voice," I think to myself. This thought
> is indeed comforting, and the conjecture about the peasant's meekness
> before the power which he has received as a gift, and of which he is not
> yet 'worthy' is certainly more charitable than the conjecture about his
> desire to make fun of the public prosecutor..." (Development of the an-
> swer.).
> "Well, see here," says a caustic voice, "you seem to be forcing some
> new-fangled philosophy of environment on the peasantry, but where does
> that come from? Sometimes all twelve of these jurors are peasants, and
> every last one of them thinks it's a mortal sin to eat the forbidden foods

during Lent. And you want to go accusing them of social tendencies."

"Of course, of course, how should they have any idea about the 'environment,' that is, the whole lot of them," I think to myself, "but still, there are ideas in the air, and ideas have something penetrating about them..."

"Well I never," laughs the caustic voice.

"And what if our peasantry is particularly inclined to the doctrine of the environment, by nature, perhaps, or because of its Slavic tendencies? What if the Russian folk is the most favorable material in all of Europe for the propagandists?"

The caustic voice laughs louder yet, but it is somehow not convincing.[80]

This theme is further developed by means of semi-voices and with concrete, everyday scenes and situations, each having as its final goal the characterization of some human orientation or another: that of the criminal, the lawyer, the juror, etc.

Many of Dostoevsky's publicistic articles are constructed in this way. His thought always finds its way through the labyrinth of voices and semi-voices and the words and gestures of other people. He never proves his propositions on the material of other abstract propositions, nor does he combine thoughts according to subject matter, but instead juxtaposes orientations and among them builds his own orientation.

Of course in such articles the form-determining characteristic of Dostoevsky's ideology is not able to manifest itself with sufficient depth. In the articles it is simply the form of the exposition, and the monological mode of thinking is not overcome. Publicistics offers the least favorable conditions for overcoming mono-logism. Nonetheless, Dostoevsky here, too, is not able, and does not want, to separate the thought from the man and his living lips in order to bind it to another thought in a purely objective *(predmetnyi)*, impersonal plane. While the usual ideological orientation sees the objective sense, the objective "treetops" in an idea, Dostoevsky sees above all its "roots" in man; for him an idea has two sides, and these two sides, according to Dostoevsky, cannot be even abstractly sepa-rated. His entire material unfolds before him as a series of human orientations. His path leads not from idea to idea, but from orientation to orientation. For him, to think means to question and to listen, to try out orientations, incorpor-ating some and unmasking others. It should be emphasized that in Dostoevsky's world even *agreement (soglasie)* retains its *dialogical* character, i.e. it never leads to a *merging* of voices and truths in a single *impersonal* truth, as is the case in the monological world.

It is characteristic that Dostoevsky's works are completely devoid of *separate* ideas, propositions and formulations, such as maxims, apothegms and aphorisms, which, when removed from their context and separated from their voice, retain their significance in an impersonal form. But how many such separate, true thoughts can be (and usually are) culled from the novels of L.

[78]

Tolstoy, Turgenev, Balzac, etc., where they are sprinkled throughout the speeches of the characters and in the author's speech; separated from their voice, they retain their entire impersonal aphoristic significance.

In the literature of classicism and of the Enlightenment there developed a special aphoristic way of thinking, i.e. thinking in separate well-rounded and self-sufficient thoughts which were purposely independent of their context. The Romanticists developed another type of aphoristic thinking.

Such forms of thinking were particularly foreign and antagonistic to Dostoevsky. His form-determining *Weltanschauung* recognizes no *impersonal truth,* and in his works there are no detached, impersonal verities. There are only integral, indivisible idea-voices or viewpoint-voices, but they, too, cannot be detached from the dialogical fabric of the work without distorting their nature.

True, there are among Dostoevsky's characters representatives of the worldly, epigonic style of aphoristic thinking, or, rather, aphoristic babbling, who, like old prince Sokolsky (in *A Raw Youth)* spout banal witticisms and aphorisms. To their number belongs Versilov, but only partly, only because of a periferal side of his personality. These worldy aphorisms are, of course, objectivized. But there is a special type of hero in Dostoevsky's works—Stepan Trofimovich Verkhovensky. He is an epigone of a higher style of aphoristic thinking—the enlightened and romantic. He spouts his "verities" because he lacks a "dominant idea" which would determine the core of his personality; he possesses separate impersonal verities which because of their impersonality, cease to be completely true, but he lacks a truth of his *own.* In the hours before his death he defines his own relationship to the truth:

> "My friend, I've been a liar all my life. Even when I spoke the truth. I never spoke for truth's sake, only for my own; I used to know it, but only now do I see..." (VI, 678)

Out of context none of Stepan Trofimovich's aphorisms retains its full meaning, they are to a certain degree objectivized, and they are stamped with the author's irony (i.e. they are double-voiced).

There are also no separate thoughts or propositions in the dialogs of Dostoevsky's characters which take place within the composition of his works. They always argue on the basis of *integrated points of view,* rather than over *separate points;* they put themselves and their whole idea body and soul into even the shortest speech. They almost never take apart and analyze their integrated ideological positions.

Also in the great dialog of the novel the separate voices and their worlds are counterposed as inseparable wholes, rather than being broken down into separate points and propositions.

Dostoevsky very aptly characterizes his method of integral dialogical contrapositions in a letter to Pobedonostsev on the subject of *The Brothers Karamazov:*

[79]

"For I intend this sixth book, 'A Russian Monk,' which will appear on August 31, to be the answer to this **negative** *side.* And I tremble for it for this reason: will it be an adequate answer? All the more so because the *answer is not a direct one aimed at propositions which have already been stated point-by-point* (in the Grand Inquisitor or earlier), but merely an oblique one. It will be something directly [and inversely] opposite to the *Weltanschauung* which has been stated already, but again, it is presented *not point-by-point,* but, so to speak, in an *artistic picture." (Letters,* vol. IV, p. 109)

■

The characteristics of Dostoevsky's form-determining ideology hold true for all sides of his polyphonic creative work.

As a result of this ideological approach it is not a world of objects, illuminated and ordered by his monological thinking, that unrolls before Dostoevsky, but a world of mutually illuminating consciousnesses, a world of coupled human philosophical orientations. He searches among them for the highest, most authoritative orientation, and he thinks of it not as his own true thought, but as another true person and his word. The image of the ideal man or the image of Christ represents for him the solution of ideological quests. This image or this highest of voices must crown the world of voices, organize it and subdue it. Precisely the image of a man and his voice (a voice not the author's own) was the ultimate ideological criterion for Dostoevsky: not faithfullness to his own convictions, and not the merit of the convictions themselves, taken abstractly, but precisely faithfulness to the authoritative image of the man.[81]

In answer to Kavelin, Dostoevsky jotted in his notebook:

"It is not enough to define morality as faithfulness to one's convictions. One must constantly ask oneself: are my convictions just? There is only one test for them—Christ. This is no longer philosophy, but faith, and faith is a red light...

I cannot call a burner of heretics a moral man, because I do not recognize your thesis that morality is agreement with inner convictions. That is only **honesty** (Russian is a rich language), not morality. I have a moral model and ideal—Christ. I ask—would he have burned heretics?—no. That means that the burning of heretics is an immoral act...

Christ was mistaken—it's been proved! A burning feeling tells me: better to remain with a mistake, with Christ, than with you...

Living life has flown away from you, and only formulas and categories are left, but that seems to make you happy. That way one has more peace and quiet, you say (laziness)...

You say that only acting according to convictions is moral. But where did they come from? I simply do not believe you, and I say, on the contrary, it is immoral to act according to convictions. And of course you cannot prove me wrong."[82]

The important thing in these thoughts is not Dostoevsky's Christian confession of faith in and of itself, but the living *forms* of his artistic and ideological thinking which are here recognized and clearly expressed. Formulas and categories are foreign to his thinking. He prefers to err, but remain with Christ, i.e. to be without truth in the theoretical sense, without truth-as-formula or truth-as-proposition. His *putting a question* (What would Christ do?) to his ideal image is extremely characteristic; it illustrates his inner dialogical orientation to the image: he does not merge with it, but follows in its path.

Characteristic of Dostoevsky's form-determining ideology are the following: distrust of convictions and their usual monological function; the quest for truth not as a conclusion of one's consciousness, but rather in the ideal, authoritative image of another person; an orientation toward the voice and word of another person. The author's idea or thought must not have the function of totally illuminating the world represented in the work; it must take its place in the work as the image of a person, an orientation among other orientations, a word among other words. This ideal orientation (the true word) must be kept in view, but it must not taint the work with the author's personal ideological tone.

In the plan for *The Life of a Great Sinner* we find the following very revealing section:

1. THE OPENING PAGES. 1) **Tone**, 2) squeeze in the thoughts artistically and concisely. The first notabene is the *Tone* (the story is a Life, i.e. although told by the author, but concisely, not skimping on explanations, but presenting it in scenes. Harmony is needed here). *The dryness of the story should sometimes approach that of* **Gil Blas. As if** there were nothing special in the spectacular and dramatic sections.

But the *dominant idea* of the Life must be visible, i.e. the *whole dominant idea will not be explained in words* and will always remain a puzzle, but the reader should always be aware that this is a pious idea, and that the Life is such an important thing that I was justified to begin with the childhood years.—Also, *through the choice* of the **story's** *subject matter* and all of the facts in it, the *man of the future* will be constantly exposed to view and put on a pedestal.[83]

The "dominant idea" was indicated already in the plan of every one of Dostoevsky's novels. In his letters he often emphasized the extraordinary importance of the basic idea for him. In a letter to Strakhov he says of *The Idiot:* "Much in the novel was written hurriedly, much is too drawn out and did not turn out well, but some of it did turn out well. I do not stand behind the novel, but I do stand behind my idea."[84]

[81]

Of *The Devils* he writes to Maikov: "The *idea* has seduced me and I've fallen terribly in love with it, but if I state it, won't I emaciate the whole novel?—this is my problem!"[85] But the function of the dominant idea is a special one even in the plans of the novels. It does not extend beyond the bounds of the great dialog, and does not finalize it. It determines only the choice and distribution of the material ("through the choice of the story's subject matter"), and that material is the voices and viewpoints of other people, among which "the man of the future will be constantly put on a pedestal."[86]

We have already said that the idea functions as the ordinary monological principle of seeing and understanding the world only for the characters. Everything that could serve as direct expression or support for the idea is distributed among them. The author stands before the hero, before his unadulterated voice. In Dostoevsky there is no objective representation of milieu, of manners and customs, of nature, of things, i.e. of all that which could be a support or prop for the author. The diverse world of things and the relationships of things which is a part of Dostoevsky's novel is presented from the heroes' viewpoint, in their spirit and tone. The author, as carrier of his own idea, does not come into direct contact with a single thing, only with people. It is clear that both the ideological leitmotif and the ideological conclusion, which turns its material into an object, are impossible in this world of subjects.

In 1878 Dostoevsky wrote to one of his correspondents:

"Add to this [he had been speaking of man's non-submission to a universal law of nature—M.B.] my 'I', which perceived everything. If it perceived all of this, i.e. the whole earth and its axiom [the law of self-preservation—M. B.], then my 'I' is higher than all of this, or at least is not limited to this, but stands, as it were, off to the side, above all of this, judging and perceiving it...In that case this 'I' not only is not subject to the earthly axiom and earthly law, it goes beyond them and has a higher law."[87]

This chiefly idealistic assessment of the consciousness was not monologically applied in Dostoevsky's artistic works. He presents the perceiving and discriminating "I" and the world as its object not in the singular, but in the plural. Dostoevsky overcame solipsism. He reserved the idealistic consciousness not for himself, but for his heroes, and not for one of them, but for all of them. In place of the relationship of the perceiving and discriminating "I" to the world, the problem of the interrelationships of these perceiving and discriminating "I's" stood at the center of his creative work.

CHAPTER FOUR

CHARACTERISTICS OF GENRE

AND PLOT COMPOSITION IN DOSTOEVSKY'S WORKS

Those features of Dostoevsky's poetics which we have sought to reveal in the preceeding chapters take for granted, of course, a totally new treatment of the aspects of genre and plot composition by Dostoevsky as well. Neither the hero, the idea, nor the polyphonic principle of the construction of the whole fit into the genre and compositional forms of the biographical, social-psychological, or family novel, or the novel of everyday life *(bytovoi roman)*, i.e. into the dominant literary forms of Dostoevsky's times, forms developed by such of his contemporaries as Turgenev, Goncharov and L. Tolstoy. In relation to them, Dostoevsky's works obviously belong to a completely different genre, foreign to that of his contemporaries.

The plot *(siuzhet)* of the biographical novel is inadequate to Dostoevsky's hero, for it rests wholly on social and characterological definitiveness and on the hero's complete embodiment in life. There must be a deep organic unity between the hero's character and the theme of his life. The biographical novel revolves around that unity. The hero and the objective world that surrounds him must be made of a single piece. In this sense Dostoevsky's hero is not, and cannot be, concretely embodied and dream of joining in a normal-life plot *(normal'nyi zhiznennyi siuzhet)*. The longing for embodiment of the "dreamer," a man born of the idea of "the underground man," or the "hero from an accidental family" *("geroi sluchainogo semeistva")* is one of Dostoevsky's major themes.

Dostoevsky's polyphonic novel is built on a different plot-compositional base and is connected with other traditions of genre in the development of European prose.

In the literature on Dostoevsky the characteristics of his work are often connected with the traditions of the European adventure novel. And there is a measure of truth in this.

A formal similarity, very important for the structure of the novel, exists between the adventure hero and the Dostoevskian hero. As with Dostoevsky's hero, one cannot say who the adventure hero is. He has no firm social-typical and individual-characterological qualities from which a stable image of his character, type or temperament could be formed. Such a definitive image would weigh down the adventure plot and limit the possibilities for adventure. Anything can happen to the adventure hero, and he can become anything. He, too, is not substance, but pure function of risk and adventure. The adventure hero is as unfinalized and unpredetermined by his image as the Dostoevskian hero.

True, this is an external and very crude similarity. But it is sufficient to make Dostoevsky's heroes potential carriers of adventure plots. The possible connections which the heroes can make and the possible events in which they can participate are determined and limited neither by their character, nor by the social world in which they would otherwise be concretely embodied. Therefore Dostoevsky was unhindered in using the most extreme and consistent devices not only of the respectable adventure novel, but of the boulevard novel as well. Only one thing is excluded from the life of Dostoevsky's hero—the social seemliness of the completely embodied hero of family and biographical novels.

For this reason Dostoevsky was unable to in any way follow or approach the style of Turgenev, Tolstoy, or the Western European representatives of the biographical novel. On the other hand, all the variations of the adventure novel left their mark on his work. Grossman says:

In the first place, he reproduced—and this is the only such incidence in the entire history of the classic Russian novel—the typical story lines of adventure literature. The traditional patterns of the European novel of adventure more than once served Dostoevsky as models for the construction of his intrigues.

He even employed the cliches of that literary genre. In the heat of meeting deadlines he was seduced by the current types in the adventure story, made use of by boulevard novelists and newspaper satirists...

No, it would seem that Dostoevsky did not leave a single attribute of the old adventure novel unused. Besides secret crimes and mass catastrophes, titled characters and unexpected situations, we find here the most typical feature of the melodrama—aristocrats who go slumming and then fraternize with the dregs of society. This is not a trait of Stavrogin alone among Dostoevsky's heroes. It is just as characteristic of Prince Valkovsky, Prince Sokolsky, and even to some extent of Prince Myshkin.[88]

But why did Dostoevsky need the world of the adventure? What function does it fulfill in his work as a whole?

In answering this question, Leonid Grossman indicates three major functions for the adventure theme. First of all, the introduction of the adventure world brought with it exciting narrative interest, which made the difficult trip through the labyrinth of philosophical theories, images and human relations, all contained within a single novel, easier for the reader. Secondly, Dostoevsky found in the novel-feuilleton "that spark of sympathy for the insulted and injured which makes itself felt behind all the adventures of redeemed outcasts and beggars-made-happy." Finally, it expresses one of the "primordial traits" of Dostoevsky's art:

the urge to introduce the extraordinary into the very thick of the commonplace; to merge, according to the romantic principle, the sublime with the grotesque; and, by means of an almost imperceptible transformation, to push the images and manifestations of everyday reality to the limits of the fantastic.[89]

We cannot help agreeing that all of the functions which Grossman has indicated are indeed performed by the adventure material in the Dostoevskian novel. Nonetheless, it seems to us that the matter by no means ends here. To be entertaining was, for Dostoevsky, never a goal in itself, nor was the romantic intertwining of the sublime with the grotesque or the extraordinary with the commonplace. Even if, by introducing slums, forced labor and hospitals, the authors of the adventure novel did indeed pave the way for the social novel, Dostoevsky had at his disposal models of the genuine social novel—the social-psychological, biographical novel and the novel of everyday life,—to which, however, he paid little attention. Grigorovich and others who began writing at the same time as Dostoevsky followed completely different models in their approach to the same world of the insulted and injured.

The functions indicated by Grossman are secondary ones. They do not contain the basic, most important point.

The plot *(siuzhetnost')* of the social-psychological, family, and biographical novels and the novel of everyday life bind hero to hero not as person to person, but as father to son, husband to wife, rival to rival, lover to loved one, or as landlord to peasant, proprietor to proletarian, the well-to-do bourgeois with the déclassé vagrant, etc. Family and biographical relationships of social standing and class form the firm, all-determining bases for all contacts among characters in the plot; chance is excluded here. The hero is assigned to the plot as a person concretely embodied and strictly localized in life, in the concrete and impermeable accouterments of his class or station, his domestic situation, his age, and his goals in life. His *humanity* is so concretized and specified by his position in life that it is deprived of any determining influence on the thematic relationships within the plot. It can be revealed only within the strict limits of those relationships.

The heroes' positions are determined by the plot, and they can meaningfully come together only on specific, concrete grounds. Their interrelationships are created by the plot, and finalized by the plot as well. Their consciousnesses and self-consciousnesses as persons cannot encompass any in any way meaningful bonds outside the plot itself. The plot can never become the simple material for the intercourse of consciousnesses outside the plot, because the hero and the plot are made of a single piece. The heroes as heroes are born of the plot itself. The plot is not only their clothing, it is their body and soul. And conversely: their body and soul can be revealed and finalized only within the plot.

The adventure plot, on the contrary, is precisely the hero's clothing, clothing which he can change as often as he pleases. The adventure plot rests not on what the hero is and on his position in life, but sooner on what he is not and what, from the point of view of any already-existing reality, is unexpected and not predetermined. The adventure plot does not rest on existing and stable situations—domestic, social, biographical; it develops in spite of them. The adventure situation is a situation in which any person may appear as a person. Moreover, the adventure plot makes use of every stable social localization not as a finalizing life-form *(zhiznenaia forma),* but as a "situation." Thus the aristocrat in a boulevard novel has nothing in common with the aristocrat in a social-domestic novel. The aristocrat in the boulevard novel is a situation in which a person has found himself. The person behaves as a person in aristocrat's clothing: he shoots, he commits crimes, flees his enemies, overcomes obstacles, etc. All social and cultural institutions, establishments, estates, classes and domestic relationships are only situations in which the eternal man can be himself. The problems dictated by his eternal human nature—by the instinct for self-preservation, the thirst for victory and triumph, the thirst for dominion, and erotic love—are what determines the adventure plot.

It is true that the eternal man of the adventure plot is, so to speak, a corporeal and corporeal-spiritual man. Therefore, outside the plot itself he is empty, and consequently he establishes no bonds with other characters outside the plot. The adventure plot cannot, therefore, be the ultimate bond in Dostoevsky's novelistic world, but as plot it offers favorable material for the realization of his artistic design.

The adventure plot in Dostoevsky is combined with the statement of profound and acute problems; above and beyond that it is placed wholly at the service of the idea: it puts persons into extraordinary situations which reveal and provoke them, it brings them together and collides them with other persons under unusual and unexpected conditions, precisely for the purpose of *testing* an idea and the man of an idea, i.e. the "man in man." And this allows the author to combine with the adventure story such other seemingly foreign genres as the confession, the lives of saints, etc.

Such a combination of the adventure story, often of the boulevard sort at that, with the idea, the problematic dialog, the confession, the Life and the sermon seemed, from the point of view of the conceptions of genre dominant in the 19th century, unusual, and was regarded as a crude and completely unjustified violation of the "esthetic of genre." And indeed, in the 19th century these genres and elements of genre were strictly delimited and seemed alien to one another. We should recall L.P. Grossman's excellent characterization of the alien quality of Dostoevsky's material (see Chapter 1, pp. 10-11). We have tried to show that the alien quality of genre and style is given meaning and is overcome by Dostoevsky through the consistent polyphonism of his work. But now the time has come to elucidate this question from the point of view of the *history* of genre, i.e., to transfer our attention to the plane of *historical poetics.*

The point is that the combination of the adventure story with the statement of acute problems, with the dialogical approach, with the confession, the Life and the sermon, is by no means something absolutely new and unheard of.

[86]

Only Dostoevsky's polyphonic application and perception of this combination
of genres was new. Its roots reach back to the most remote antiquity. The 19th
century adventure novel is only one of the branches—and an impoverished and
deformed one, at that—of a mighty and widespread tradition of genre which
reaches, as we said, into the depths of the past, to the very sources of European
literature. We believe that it is very important to trace this tradition back to its
sources; we dare not limit ourselves to an analysis of the genres closest to Dostoevsky. We even intend to concentrate our chief attentions precisely on the
sources. Therefore we must leave Dostoevsky for a time in order to leaf through
some of the ancient pages of the history of genre, which have been almost
totally neglected in our criticism. This historical digression will help us to more
profoundly and correctly understand the genre and plot-compositional characteristics of Dostoevsky's works, characteristics which until now have remained
essentially unrevealed in the literature on him. In addition, it seems to us that
this question has a wider significance for the theory and history of literary genres.

  A literary genre,by its very nature reflects the most stable, "eternal" tendencies in the development of literature. The undying elements of the *archaic*
are always preserved in the genre. True, these archaic elements are preserved in
the genre only thanks to their constant *renewal* and, so to speak, contempori-
zation. Genre is always the same and not the same, always old and new simultaneously. A genre is reborn and renewed at every stage in the development of
literature and in every individual work of the given genre. This gives the genre
life. Therefore the archaic elements preserved in the genre are not dead, but
eternally living, i.e. capable of renewal. A genre lives in the present, but is
always *remembers* its past, its beginnings. Genre is the representative of the creative memory in the process of literary development. Precisely for this reason it
is genre which is capable of providing *unity* and *continuity* in this development.

  This is why it is necessary to return to the sources for a correct understanding of genre.

                                    ■

  At the close of classical antiquity, and then in the epoch of Hellenism,
there arose and developed numerous genres which were externally fairly diverse,
but bound by an inner kinship, and which therefore formed a special realm in
literature which the ancients themselves very expressively called "σπουδογέλοιον"
i.e. the realm of the serio-comical. Into this category the ancients put the mimes
of Sophron, the "Socratic dialog" (as a special genre), the voluminous literature
of the Symposiasts (also as a special genre), the early literature of the memoir (Ion
of Chios, Critias), pamphlets, all of bucolic poetry, the "Menippian satire" (as
a special genre), and several other genres. It is hardly possible to establish distinct and stable boundaries within the realm of the serio-comical. But the ancients
themselves distinctly felt its fundamental peculiarity, and they counterposed it to
the more serious genres: the epopee, the tragedy, history, classical rhetoric, etc.

And in fact the distinction of this realm from the rest of the literature of classical antiquity is very substantial.

What are the distinctive characteristics of the serio-comic genres?

Despite their great external diversity, they are united by a profound bond to *carnivalistic folklore.* They are all—to a greater or lesser degree—imbued with a specific *carnival attitude to the world,* some of them being direct literary variants of oral carnival folk genres. The carnival attitude to the world, which permeates these genres through and through, determines their basic characteristics and establishes the particular relationship of the image and the word in them to reality. True, in all the serio-comical genres there is a strong rhetorical element, but that element is radically altered in the atmosphere of *jolly relativity (veselaia otnositel'nost')* of the carnival attitude: its one-sided rhetorical seriousness, rationality, singleness of meaning, and dogmatism are made weaker.

The carnival attitude possesses an indestructable vivacity and the mighty, life-giving power to transform. That is why even in our time those genres which have even the most remote connection with the traditions of the serio-comical preserve within themselves the carnivalistic yeast (leaven) which sharply differentiates them from other genres. These genres always carry a special stamp by which we can recognize them. A critical ear always perceives even the most distant echoes of the carnival attitude to the world.

We shall give the name *carnivalized literature* to those genres which have come under the influence—either directly or indirectly, through a series of intermediary links—of one or another variant of carnivalistic folklore [ancient or medieval). The whole realm of the serio-comical is the first example of such literature. It is our opinion that the problem of the carnivalization of literature is one of the most important problems of historical poetics, and of the poetics of genre in particular.

However, we shall address the problem of carnivalization itself somewhat later (after analyzing the carnival [i.e. *carneval,* the phenomenon of pre-Lenten, Shrovetide, or Mardis-Gras merrymaking—trans.] and the carnival attitude). Here we shall pause to discuss several external characteristics of genre of the serio-comical which are in fact the result of the carnival attitude's power to transform.

The prime characteristic of all the serio-comic genres is their new relationship to reality: their object or—what is more important—their starting point for understanding, evaluating and formulating reality is the *present,* often the topicality of the immediate present. For the first time in ancient literature the object of a *serious* (though at the same time comical) representation is presented without epical or tragical distance, presented not in the absolute past of myth and legend, but on the contemporary level, in direct and even crudely familiar contact with living contemporaries. In these genres mythical heroes and historical figures out of the past are deliberately and emphatically contemporized, and they act and speak in familiar contact with the unfinalized present. Consequently, in the realm of the serio-comic a radical change takes place in the structuring of time and values in the artistic image. This is the prime characteristic of the serio-comical.

The second characteristic is inseparably bound up with the first: the serio-comical genres are not based on *legend* and do not elucidate themselves by means of the legend—they are *consciously* based on *experience* (although insufficiently mature experience) and on *free imagination;* their relationship to legend is in most cases deeply critical, and at times bears the cynical nature of the exposé. Thus for the first time there appears an image that is almost completely liberated from legend and is based on experience and free imagination. This is indeed an upheaval in the history of the literary image.

The third characteristic is the deliberate multifariousness and discordance of all of these genres. They reject the stylistic unity (or, strictly speaking, the limitation to a single style) of the epopee, the tragedy, lofty rhetoric and the lyric. For them multiplicity of tone in a story and a mixture of the high and low, the serious and the comic, are typical; they make wide use of introductory genres—letters, manuscripts which have been found, parodically reconstructed quotations, and the like. In some of these genres the mixture of prose and poetic speech is observed, living dialects and slang are introduced (in Roman times—bilingualism), and various authorial masks appear. The *represented* word *(izobrazhennoe slovo)* appears alongside the representational word *(izobrazhaiushchee slovo),* and in certain genres double-voiced words play a leading role. Thus there appears here a radically new attitude to the word as the material of literature.

These are the three basic characteristics common to all of the serio-comical genres. From them it is plain to see what enormous significance this realm of ancient literature had for the development of the future European novel and for the other prose genres which gravitated toward the novelistic form and developed under its influence.

Speaking in a rather simplified and schematic fashion, one could say that the genre of the novel has three basic roots: the *epic,* the *rhetorical* and the *carnivalistic* (with many transitional forms in between, of course). The starting points for the development of the various varieties of the third, i.e. the carnivalistic line of the novel, including the variety which leads to Dostoevsky, must be sought in the realm of the serio-comical.

Two genres from the realm of the serio-comical have definitive significance for the formation of that variety in the development of the novel and of artistic prose which we shall conditionally call "dialogical," and which, as we have said, leads to Dostoevsky; the *"Socratic dialog"* and the *"Menippean satire."* We must treat them in rather greater detail.

The "Socratic dialog" was a special and, in its time, widespread genre. "Socratic dialogs" were written by Plato, Xenophon, Antisthenes, Aeschines, Phaedo, Euclid, Alexamenos, Glaucon, Simias, Criton, and others. Only the dialogs of Plato and Xenophon have survived; of the others we have only reports and a few fragments. But on this basis we can form a conception of the character of this genre.

The "Socratic dialog" is not a rhetorical genre. It grows out of a carnivalistic folk foundation and is deeply imbued with the carnivalistic attitude to the world, particularly, of course, in the *oral* Socratic stage of its development. We shall return later to the carnivalistic foundation of this genre.

Originally the "Socratic dialog"—at the literary stage of its development—was very close to the genre of the memoir: it consisted of reminiscences of actual discussions in which Socrates had taken part, records of recollected discussions, placed in the framework of a brief story. But very soon the free creative attitude to the material liberates the genre from the limitations of history and the memoir form, retaining only the Socratic method of dialogically arriving at the truth, and the external form of a dialog written down within the framework of a story. Plato's "Socratic dialogs" have this free, creative character, as do, to a lesser extent, the dialogs of Xenophon and the fragmentary dialogs of Antisthenes.

We shall concentrate on those aspect of the "Socratic dialog" which have particular significance for our conception.

1. The Socratic concept of the dialogical nature of truth and of human thought about it lies at the foundation of the genre. The dialogical means of seeking the truth is counterposed to the *official* monologism which claims *to possess the ready-made truth;* and it is counterposed to the naive self-confidence of people who think that they know something, i.e. who think that they possess certain truths. The truth is not born and does not reside in the head of an individual person; it is born of the dialogical intercourse *between people* in the collective search for the truth. Socrates called himself a "pander": he brought people together and caused them to collide in a dispute, as a result of which the truth was born; in relation to this newborn truth Socrates called himself a "midwife," because he assisted with the birth. For this reason he called his method an "obstetric" one. But Socrates never called himself the exclusive possessor of ready-made truth. We would emphasize that the Socratic concepts of the dialogical nature of truth lay at the carnivalistic folk foundations of the "Socratic dialog" genre and determined its *form,* but are by no means always represented in the content of the individual dialogs. The content often took on a monological character which contradicted the genre's form-determining idea. In Plato's dialogs of his first and second periods the recognition of the dialogical nature of truth is retained also in his philosophical *Weltanschauung,* albeit in a weakened form. The dialog in those periods has not yet been turned into a simple means of elucidating ready-made ideas (for pedagogical ends), so that Socrates has not yet been turned into a "teacher." That takes place in Plato's final period: the monologism of the content begins to destroy the form of the "Socratic dialog." Consequently, when the "Socratic dialog" entered the service of the already-formed, dogmatic *Weltanschauungen* of various philosophical schools and religious doctrines, it lost all contact with the carnivalistic attitude to the world and became a simple form for expressing already-discovered, ready-made, indisputable truth, and finally degenerated into the question-and-answer form of training neophytes (i.e. the catechism).

2. The two basic devices of the "Socratic dialog" were the syncrisis (συ 'γχρισις)

and the anacrisis ($\overset{\prime}{\alpha}\nu'\alpha\chi\rho\iota\sigma\iota\varsigma$). Syncrisis was understood as the juxtaposition of various points of view toward a given object. This technique of juxtaposing various word-opinions was, because of the very nature of the "Socratic dialog," accorded very great importance. Anacrisis consisted of the means of eliciting and provoking the words of one's interlocutor, forcing him to express his opinion, and express it fully. Socrates was a great master of the anacrisis: he was able to force people to *speak*, i.e. to put into words their hazy, but stubborn, pre-formed opinions, elucidating them by means of the word, and thereby exposing their falseness or incompleteness; he had the ability to drag the accepted truths out into the light of day. Anacrisis is the provocation of the word by the word (and not by means of the plot situation, as in the "Menippean satire," of which we shall speak in due course). Syncrisis and anacrisis dialogize thought, they bring it outside, turn it into a *speech* in a dialog, and turn it over to the dialogical intercourse between people. Both of these devices originate from the concept of the dialogical nature of truth which lies at the foundation of the "Socratic dialog." Within this carnivalized genre syncrisis and anacrisis lose their narrow, abstract-rhetorical character.

3. *Ideologies* are the heroes of the "Socratic dialog." The ideologist is first of all Socrates himself, but all of his interlocutors are also ideologists— his pupils, the Sophists, or simple people, whom he involves in the dialog and makes into unwilling ideologists. The very event which takes place (or, more accurately, is reproduced) in the "Socratic dialog" is a purely ideological event of searching for and *testing* the truth. This event sometimes unfolds with genuine (but its own peculiar) dramatic effect (the peripetations of the idea of the immortality of the soul in Plato's *Phaedo*, for example). Thus the hero-ideologist is first introduced into European literature by the "Socratic dialog."

4. In addition to anacrisis, i.e. the provocation of the word by the word, the plot situation of the "Socratic dialog" is sometimes used for the same purpose. In Plato's *Apology* the situation of the trial and the expected death sentence determines the special character of Socrates' speech as the summing-up and confession of a man *on the threshold*. In *Phaedo* the discussion of the immortality of the soul, with all its internal and external peripetations, is directly defined by the situation of impending death. In both cases there is present a tendency to create *extraordinary* situations, which cleanse the word of all automatism and objectivization and force the person involved to reveal the deepest layers of his personality and thought. Of course the freedom to create extraordinary situations which provoke the profound word is in the "Socratic dialog" (at its literary stage) severely limited by the genre's historical nature and its relation to the literature of the memoir. Nonetheless, we can already speak of the origin of a special type of dialog, the "dialog on the threshold" *(Schwellendialog),* which subsequently had wide currency in Hellenistic and Roman literature, then in the Middle Ages, and finally in the literature of the Renaissance and the Reformation.

5. The idea in the "Socratic dialog" is organically combined with the image

[91]

of a person, its carrier (Socrates and the other essential participants in the dialog). The dialogical testing of the idea is simultaneously a testing of the person who represents it. Thus we can speak here of a rudimental *image of an idea.* We also observe here the free creative attitude to that image. The ideas of Socrates, the leading Sophists, and other historical personages are not quoted and are not paraphrased, but are presented in free creative development against the dialogizing background of other ideas. To the degree that the genre's historical basis and its relation to the memoir are weakened, foreign ideas become more and more plastic, and people and ideas which in reality never came into actual contact (but could have done so) begin to meet in the dialogs. This is only one step away from the "dialog of the dead," in which people and ideas divided by centuries confront one another on a dialogical plane. But the "Socratic dialog" does not yet take that step. In the *Apology* Socrates does, however, seem to foretell that dialogical genre when, in his pre-vision of the death sentence, he speaks of the dialogs that he will carry on in the nether world with the shadows of the past, just as he had done here on earth. It must be emphasized that the *image of the idea* in the "Socratic dialog," as opposed to the image of the idea in Dostoevsky, has a *syncretic* character: at the time of the creation of the "Socratic dialog" the differentiation of the abstract-scientific and philosophical *concept* from the artistic *image* had not yet taken place. The "Socratic dialog" is still a syncretic philosophical-artistic genre.

These are the basic characteristics of the "Socratic dialog." They provide us with justification for considering this genre one of the origins of that line of development of European prose, and of the novel in particular, which leads to the works of Dostoevsky.

The "Socratic dialog" existed for only a short time as a specific genre, but in the process of its decay other dialogical genres were formed, among them the "Menippean satire." Of course the "Menippean satire" cannot be considered purely the product of the "Socratic dialog's" disintegration (as is sometimes done), because its roots reach *directly* back into carnivalistic folklore, whose definitive influence is even more significant here than in the "Socratic dialog."

Before analyzing its particulars, we shall give some general information about the "Menippean satire."

The genre takes its name from the philosopher Menippos of Gadara (3rd century B.C.), who gave it its classical form,[90] although the term itself was first used to denote a specific genre by the Roman scholar Varro (1st century B.C.), who called his satires "saturae menippeae." But the genre itself arose much earlier; its first representative was, perhaps, Antisthenes, a pupil of Socrates and an author of "Socratic dialogs." "Menippean satires" were also written by Aristotle's contemporary Heracleides Ponticus, who, according to Cicero, was also the founder of a related genre, the logistoricus (a combination of the "Socratic dialog" with fantastic stories). An undoubted representative of the "Menippean satire" was Bion Borysthenes, i.e. from the banks of the Dnepr (3rd century B.C.). Then come Menippos, who gave the genre greater clarity, and Varro, of whose satires numerous fragments have survived. Seneca's *Apokolokyntosis,* i.e. *The Pumpkinization,* is a classical "Menippean satire." Petronius' *Satyricon* is a "Menippean satire" extended almost to the status of a novel. The well-preserved "Menippean satires" of Lucian give us the most complete notion of what the genre was (although not all of its varieties are represented). Apuleius' *Metamorphoses (The Golden Ass),* which, like its Greek source, is known to us through Lucian's summary, is an extensive "Menippean satire." Another interesting example of the "Menippean satire" is the so-called "Hippocratian novel" (the first epistolary European novel). The ancient stage of the "Menippean satire's" development is culminated by Boethius' *De Consolatione Philosophiae.* We find elements of the "Menippean satire" in certain varieties of the "Greek novel," in the ancient utopian novel, and in the Roman satire (Lucilius and Horace). Within the "Menippean satire's" orbit there developed certain related genres, genetically connected with the "Socratic dialog": the diatribe, the already-mentioned logistoricus, the soliloquium, the aretalogical genres, etc.

The "Menippean satire" exercised a very strong influence on ancient Christian literature (of the antique period) and on Byzantine literature (and through it, on Old Russian writing as well). It continued its development, in various forms and under various names, in post-antique times also: in the Middle Ages, during the Renaissance and the Reformation, and in modern times; it continues, actually, to develop even now (both with a clear-cut recognition of its genre and without it). This carnivalized genre, extraordinarily flexible and as versatile as Proteus, and capable of penetrating other genres, has had enormous, but as yet underestimated significance for the development of European literatures. The "Menippean satire" became one of the chief carriers and implementors of the carnival attitude toward the world and has remained so up until the very present. We shall return later to this aspect of its significance.

Now, after our short (and, of course, far from complete) review of antique "Menippean satires," we must reveal the basic characteristics of this genre, as they came to be defined in antiquity. Henceforth we shall call the "Menippean satire" simply the *menippea.*

1. In comparison to the "Socratic dialog," the specific weight of the comic element is greater in the menippea, althought it vascillates significantly in the various varieties of this flexible genre: the comical element is very great in Varro, for example, but it disappears, or, rather, is reduced in Boethius.[91] We shall in due course consider in greater detail the specific *carneval* character (in the broad sense of the word) of the comical element.

2. The menippea is fully liberated from the limitations of the historical and memoir forms which were characteristic of the "Socratic dialog" (although externally the memoir form is sometimes preserved); it is free of legend and is not bound by any requirements of external verisimilitude. The menippea is characterized by *extraordinary freedom of philosophical invention and of invention within the plot.* The fact that the leading heroes of the menippea are historical and legendary figures (Diogenes, Menippos and others) does not at all restrict this

[93]

freedom. Indeed, in all of world literature we would not be able to find a genre with greater freedom of invention or fantasy than the menippea.

3. The most important characteristic of the menippea lies in the fact that the most daring and unfettered fantasies *(fantastika)* and adventures are internally motivated, justified and illuminated here by a purely ideological and philosophical end—to create *extraordinary situations* in which to provoke and test a philosophical idea—the word or the *truth,* embodied in the image of the wise man, the seeker after this truth. We emphasize that the fantastic serves here not in the positive *embodiment* of the truth, but in the search after the truth, its provocation and, most importantly, its *testing.* To this end the heroes of the "Menippean satire" ascend into heaven, descend into the nether world, wander through unknown fantasy lands, and are placed into other extraordinary situations (Diogenes, for example, sells himself into slavery on the market place, Perigrinus triumphantly immolates himself at the Olympic Games, and Lucian the Ass constantly appears in extraordinary situations, etc.). The fantastic very often takes on the character of an adventure story, and sometimes a symbolical or even mystical-religious character (in Apuleius). But in every case it is subordinated to the purely ideological function of provoking and testing the truth. The wildest fantastical adventures are brought into organic and indissoluble artistic unity with the philosophical idea. It must be further emphasized that we have in mind the testing of an *idea,* of the *truth,* not the testing of a specific individual or social-typical human character. The testing of the wise man is the testing of his philosophical position in the world, not of one or another trait of his character, independent of that position. In this sense it can be said that the content of the menippea consists of the adventures of an *idea* or the *truth* in the world: either on earth, in the nether regions, or on Olympus.

4. A very important characteristic of the menippea is the organic combination within it of free fantasy, symbolism, and—on occasion—the mystical-religious element, with extreme and (from our point of view) crude *underworld naturalism (trushchebyi naturalizm).* Truth's earthly adventures take place on highroads, in brothels, dens of thieves, taverns, market places, prisons, and at secret cults' erotic orgies, etc. The idea here has no fear of the underworld or of the filth of life. The man of an idea—the wise man—is confronted with the extreme expression of worldly evil, depravity, baseness and vulgarity. This underworld naturalism is present, apparently, already in the early menippea. The ancients said of Bion Borysthenes that he was the first to "deck out philosophy in the many-colored dress of a hetaera." There is a great deal of underworld naturalism in Varro and Lucian. But underworld naturalism could develop to its broadest and fullest only in the menippea of Petronius and Apuleius, who gave the genre novelistic scope. The organic combination of philosophical dialog, lofty symbolism, fantastic adventure and underworld naturalism is a remarkable characteristic of the menippea which was preserved at all subsequent stages in the development of the dialogical line of novelistic prose right up until Dostoevsky.

5. Boldness of invention and fantasy combines in the menippea with

extraordinary philosophical universalism and extreme ideologism *(mirosozercatel' nost')*. The menippea is a genre of "ultimate questions." In it ultimate philosophical positions are put to the test. The menippea seeks to present a person's ultimate, decisive words and actions, each of which contains the whole person and his whole life in its entirety. This feature of the genre was, apparently, particularly clear-cut in the early menippea (of Heracleides Ponticus, Bion, Teles, and Menippos), but was preserved, although sometimes in a weakened form, as the typical characteristic in all of the genre's varieties. In the menippea the nature of the philosophical problems dealt with was necessarily much different than in the "Socratic dialog": all problems which were in the least "academic" (gnoseological and esthetic) fell by the wayside, as did complex and extensive argumentation, leaving, essentially, only bare "ultimate questions" with an ethico-practical inclination. In the menippea syncrisis (i.e. juxtaposition) of precisely such stripped-bare "ultimate positions in the world" is typical. Take, for example, the carnivalistic-satirical representation of the "Vitarum auctio," i.e. of the ultimate positions of life, in Lucian, the fantastic voyages over ideological seas in Varro (Sesculixes), travels through all of the philosophical schools (already apparent in Bion), and the like. In all of them the *pro et contra* of the ultimate questions of life are laid bare.

6. In connection with the philosophical universalism of the menippea, there appears in it a tri-levelled construction: action and dialogical syncrisis are transferred from earth to Olympus and to the nether world. This tri-levelled construction is given with great external obviousness in, for example, Seneca's *Pumpkinization,* where "threshold dialogs" are also given with great external clarity: at the gates of Olympus (where Claudius was refused admittance) and on the threshold of the nether world. The menippea's tri-levelled construction exercised a definitive influence on the corresponding construction of the medieval mystery play and the mystery-scene. The "threshold dialog" genre was also extremely widespread in the Middle Ages, both in serious and in comical genres (the famous fabliau of the peasant arguing at the gate of heaven, for example), and is particularly widely represented in the literature of the Reformation—the "literature of the heavenly gates" *("Himmelspforten-Literatur"),* as it was called. The representation of the *nether world* took on great importance in the menippea: the special genre of the "dialog of the dead," so widespread in European literature of the Renaissance in the 17th and 18th centuries, came into existence.

7. A special type of *experimental fantasticality,* totally alien to the antique epos and tragedy, appears in the menippea: observation from an unusual point of view, from a high altitude, for example, coupled with radical changes in the scale of the observed phenomena (Lucian's *Ikaromenippos,* for example, or Varro's *Endymiones*—observation of the life of the city from a high altitude). This line of experimental fantasticality continues, under the definitive influence of the menippea, in the following epochs as well—in Rabelais, Swift, Voltaire *(Micromégas)* and others.

8. What might be called moral-psychological experimentation appears for

the first time in the menippea: the representation of man's unusual, abnormal moral and psychic states—insanity of all sorts ("maniac themes"), split personalities, unrestrained daydreaming, unusual dreams, passions bordering on insanity,[92]suicide,etc. In the menippea these phenomena are not narrowly thematic, but rather have a formal, genre-connected character. Dreams, daydreams and insanity destroy the epic, tragic integrity of a man and his fate: in him the possibilities of another man and another life are revealed, he loses his finalizedness and singleness of meaning, he ceases to coincide with himself. Dreams are common also in the epos, but there they are meant to prophesy, motivate or warn—they do not take the dreamer beyond the bounds of his fate and his character, they do not destroy his integrity. Of course man's unfinalizability and his non-coincidence with himself are still rather elementary and rudimentary in the menippea, but they are already apparent and they afford a new vision of man. The dialogical attitude of man to himself (containing the seeds of the split personality) which appears in the menippea also contributes to the destruction of his integrity and finalizedness. In this respect Varro's menippea *Bimarcus,* i.e. *The Double Marcus,* is very interesting. As in all of Varro's menippea, the comic element here is very strong. Marcus had promised to write a work on tropes and figures, but does not keep his promise. Marcus Number Two, i.e. his conscience, his double,constantly reminds him of his promise, giving him no peace. Marcus Number One tries to fulfill his promise, but he cannot concentrate: he is distracted by reading Homer, he begins to write verse himself, etc. In Varro the dialog between the two Marcuses, i.e. between a man and his conscience, has a comical character, but nonetheless, as an artistic discovery it exercised an essential influence on the *Soliloquia* of Augustine. We should mention in passing that in the representation of the double, Dostoevsky, too, always retains an element of the *comic* alongside the tragic (in *The Double,* as well as in Ivan Karamazov's conversation with the devil).

9. Characteristic of the menippea are scandalous scenes and scenes of eccentric behavior, incongruous speeches and performances, i.e. all violations of the generally accepted, ordinary course of events and of the established norms of behavior and etiquette, including the verbal. The artistic structure of these scandalous scenes sharply distinguishes them from epical events and tragical catastrophes. They also differ essentially from comical brawls and exposés. It can be said that in the menippea there appear new artistic categories of the scandalous and the eccentric which are completely alien to the classical epos and the dramatic genres. (We shall subsequently discuss the carnivalistic character of these categories.) Scandals and eccentricities destroy the epical and tragical integrity of the world, they form a breach in the stable, normal ("seemly") course of human affairs and events and free human behavior from predetermining norms and motivations. The consultations of the gods on Olympus are full of scandals and eccentric performances (in Lucian, Seneca, Julian the Apostate and others), as are scenes in the nether world and on earth (Petronius' scandals on the square, in the inn, in the bath, for example). The "incongruous word"—incongruous either because of its cynical frankness, because it profanely exposes something which is holy, or because it crudely violates

etiquette—is also quite characteristic of the menippea.

10. The menippea contains many sharp contrasts and oxymoronic combinations: the virtuous hetaera, the true freedom of the wise man contrasted with his status as a slave, the emperor who becomes a slave, moral downfall and purification, luxury and povery, the noble bandit, etc. The menippea is fond of playing with sharp transitions and changes, ups and downs, rises and falls, unexpected comings together of distant and divided things, mesalliances of all sorts.

11. The menippea often includes elements of *social utopia* which are introduced in the form of dreams or journeys to unknown lands; on occasion the menippea grows into a utopian novel (*Abaris* by Heracleides Ponticus). The utopian element combines organically with all the other elements of the genre.

12. The menippea characteristically makes wide use of other genres: novellas, letters, oratory, symposia, etc.; the mixture of prose and verse diction is also characteristic. The inserted genres are presented at various distances from the author's ultimate position, i.e. with various degrees of parody and objectivization. The verse parts are almost always to a certain degree parodical.

13. The presence of inserted genres intensifies the variety of styles and tones in the menippea; there is formed here a new attitude to the word as the material of literature, an attitude characteristic of the whole dialogical line in the development of literary prose.

14. Finally, the menippea's last characteristic—its topicality and publicistic quality. This is in its way the "journalistic" genre of antiquity, pointedly reacting to the ideological issues of the day. The satires of Lucian taken as a whole make up an entire encyclopedia of the contemporary life of his time: they are full of both open and hidden polemics with the various philosophical, religious, ideological and scientific schools, tendencies and currents of the time; full of the images of contemporary or recently deceased public figures, the "masters of thought" in all spheres of social and ideological life (under their own names or disguised); full of allusions to the great and small events of the epoch; they feel out new tendencies in the development of everyday life, and show newly arising types in all social strata, etc. It is a sort of "Diary of a Writer" which seeks to discover and evaluate the general spirit and tendency of evolving contemporary life. Taken in their entirety, the satires of Varro make up a similar "Diary of a Writer" (albeit with a sharp preponderence of the carnivalistic-comical element). We find the same characteristics in Petronius, Apuleius and others. A journalistic, publicistic, feuilletonistic, and pointedly topical quality is characteristic to a greater or lesser degree of all representatives of the menippea. This final characteristic is organically combined with all of the other traits of the genre.

These are the basic characteristics of the genre of the menippea. We must again emphasize the organic unity of all of these seemingly very heterogeneous traits and the profound internal integrity of this genre. It was formed in an epoch of the decay of the tradition of a nation and the destruction of those ethical norms which made up the antique ideal of "seemliness" ("beauty and nobility"), in an epoch of intense struggle among multitudinous heterogeneous religious and philosophical schools and tendencies, when disputes over "ultimate questions" of *Weltanschauung* became everyday mass phenomena in every stratum of the population and took place wherever people gathered—in market squares, on streets and highroads, in taverns and baths, on the decks of ships, etc.—in a time when the figure of the philosopher and wise man (the Cynic, the Stoic, the Epicurean) or of the prophet and miracle-worker became typical and was encountered more often than the figure of the monk in the Middle Ages during the epoch of the greatest flowering of the monastic orders. It was the epoch of the preparation and formation of a new world religion—Christianity.

Another side of this epoch is the depreciation of all external human positions in life and their transformation into *roles* played out according to the will of blind fate on the stage of the theater of the world (a profound philosophical recognition of this situation is found in Epictetus and Marcus Aurelius, and on the literary plane in Lucian and Apuleius). This led to the destruction of the epical and tragical integrity of man and his fate.

Therefore the genre of the menippea is perhaps the most adequate expression of the characteristics of the epoch. In it the content of life is poured into the stable form of the genre, which commands an *inner logic* determining the inseparable coupling of all its elements. For this reason the genre of the menippea was able to gain such an immense influence, as yet almost totally unrecognized by scholarship, in the history of the development of European novelistic prose.

While possessing inner integrity, the genre of the menippea at the same time possesses great external plasticity and the remarkable ability to absorb related smaller genres and to penetrate as a component part into other large genres.

Thus the menippea absorbs such related genres as the diatribe, the soliloquy and the symposium. The relatedness of these genres is determined by the external and *internal dialogical nature* of their approach to human life and human thought.

The diatribe is an internally dialogized rhetorical genre, usually constructed in the form of a discussion with an interlocutor who is not present, a fact which led to the dialogization of the process of speech and thought itself. The founder of the diatribe was considered by the ancients to be that same Bion Borysthenes who was also considered the founder of the menippea. It should be mentioned that it was precisely the diatribe, and not classical rhetoric, which exercised a definitive influence on the characteristics of the genre of the ancient Christian sermon.

The dialogical attitude to oneself defines the genre of the soliloquy. It is a discussion with oneself. Already Antisthe es (he was a pupil of Socrates and may himself have written menippea) considered the greatest achievement of his philosophy the "ability to relate dialogically to himself." Epictetus, Marcus Aurelius and Augustine were remarkable masters of this genre. At the basis of the genre lies the *inner man*—"oneself," which is accessible not to passive self-observation, but only to an active *dialogical approach to oneself,* an approach which destroys the naive integrity of one's conception of oneself that is the basis of the lyrical, epical and tragical image of man. The dialogical approach to oneself breaks down the outer shell of the self's image that exists for other people, determines the external assessment of a person (in the eyes of others), and clouds the clarity of the self-consciousness.

Both genres—the diatribe and the soliloquy—developed within the orbit of the menippea, intertwining with it and penetrating it (particularly at the Roman and early Christian stages).

The symposium—the banquet dialog—existed already in the epoch of the "Socratic dialog" (there are examples of it in Plato and Xenophon), but developed widely and with considerable variety only in the following epochs. The dialogical word spoken at the banquet had certain privileges (originally of a cultic character): the right of special freedom, ease and familiarity, of special openness, eccentricity and ambivalence, i.e. the combination of praise and abuse or of the serious and the comical within the word. The symposium is by nature a purely carnivalistic genre. The menippea was sometimes directly formulated as a symposium (apparently already by Menippos; three of Varro's satires are formulated as symposia, and there are elements of the symposium in Lucian and Petronius).

As we have said, the menippea had the capacity to insinuate itself into large genres, subjecting them to a certain transformation. Thus, elements of the menippea can be detected in the "Greek novels." For example, the scent of the menippea distinctly wafts from certain images and episodes of Xenophon of Ephesos' *Ephesian Tales.* The representation of the lower strata of society is given in the spirit of underworld naturalism:jails, slaves, thieves, fishermen, etc. Internal dialogism and elements of parody and reduced laughter are characteristic of other novels. Elements of the menippea also penetrate the utopian works of antiquity and the works of the aretalogical genre (Philostratus' *The Life of Apollonius of Tyana,* for example). The menippea's power to penetrate and transform has great significance for the narrative genres of ancient Christian literature as well.

Our description of the characteristics of the genre of the menippea and the connected, related genres is extremely close to the description which could be given of the characteristics of the genre of Dostoevsky's works (cf., for example, L. P.Grossman's description quoted on pp. 10-11). In essence all of the menippea's characteristics (with appropriate modifications and complications) are found in Dostoevsky as well. And, indeed, we have here the world of one and the same genre; in the menippea it is at the *beginning* of its development, and in Dostoevsky it is at its very *peak.* But we already know that the beginning, i.e. the archaic elements of the genre, are preserved in a renewed form in the highest stages of the genere's development. Moreover, the higher a genre develops and the more complex it becomes, the better and more fully it remembers its past.

Does this mean that Dostoevsky proceeded directly and consciously from the antique menippea? Of course not! He was by no means a *stylizer* of ancient genres. Dostoevsky made connection with the chain of the given genre tradition at the point where it was passing through his time, although the earlier links of the chain, including the antique one, were, to a greater or lesser degree, familiar and congenial to him (we shall return again to the question of Dostoevsky's genre sources). Speaking rather paradoxically, one might say that it was not Dostoevsky's subjective

nory, but the objective memory of the genre in which he was working, which
served the characteristics of the ancient menippea.

The genre characteristics of the menippea were not only reborn, they were
renewed in Dostoevsky's works. In his creative utilization of the possibilities of the
genre Dostoevsky departed widely from the authors of antique menippea. In the
philosophical and social problems with which they deal, as well as in their artistic
qualities, the antique menippea seem primitive and bland in comparison with
Dostoevsky. The most important distinction is that the antique menippea does not
yet know *polyphony.* The menippea, like the "Socratic dialog," was able only to
prepare certain conditions present in the genre which were conducive to the emergence of polyphony.

■

Now we must turn out attention to the problem, mentioned earlier, of the
carnival and the carnivalization of literature.

The problem of carnival (in the sense of the totality of all the various festivals, rituals and forms of a carnival type), its essence, its roots deep in the primordial order and the primordial thinking of man, its development under the
conditions of the class society, its extraordinary vitality and undying fascination
is one of the most complex and interesting problems of cultural history. We
cannot, of course, treat it exhaustively here. We are here essentially interested
only in the problem of carnivalization, i.e. of the definitive influence of carnival
on literature, or, precisely, on literary genre.

Carnival itself (we repeat: in the sense of the totality of all the various festivals of a carnival type) is, of course, not a literary phenomenon. It is a *syncretic
pageant* form of a ritual nature. It is a very complex and diverse form, having many
variations and nuances based on the general carnival principle and depending on
various epochs, peoples and individual festivals. Carnival developed an entire
language of symbolic, concretely sensuous (konkretno-chuvstvennye) form, ranging
from large, complicated mass performances to individual carnivalistic gestures. This
language differentially and, one might say, articulately (like any language) expressed the
unified (but complex) carnival attitude which penetrates all of its forms. This language
cannot be in any degree fully or adequately translated into a verbal language, much
less into a language of abstract concepts, but it is amenable to a certain transposition into the language of artistic images (i.e. the language of literature), which is
related to it by its concretely sensuous nature. We call the transposition of carnival into the language of literature the carnivalization of literature. We shall iso-
late and examine the individual aspects and characteristics of carnival from the
viewpoint of this transposition.

Carnival is a pageant without a stage and without a division into performers
and spectators. In the carnival everyone is an active participant, everyone com-
munes in the carnival act. Carnival is not contemplated, it is, strictly speaking, not
even played out; its participants *live* in it, they live according to its laws, as long

as those laws are in force, i.e. they live a *carnivalistic life.* The carnivalistic life is life drawn out of its *usual rut,* it is to a degree "life turned inside out," "life the wrong way 'round" *("monde à l'envers").*

The laws, prohibitions and restrictions which determine the system and order of normal, i.e. non-carnival, life are for the period of carnival suspended; above all, the hierarchical system and all the connected forms of fear, awe, piety, etiquette, etc. are suspended, i.e. everything that is determined by social-hierarchical inequality among people, or any other form of inequality, including age. All *distance* between people is suspended and a special carnival category goes into effect—the *free, familiar contact among people.* This is a very important aspect of the carnival attitude. People who are in life separated by impenetrable hierarchical barriers enter into free, familiar contact on the carnival square. The special character of the organization of mass performances, the free carnival gesticulation, and the frank carnivalistic word are also made possible by this category.

In carnival there develops, in a concretely sensuous, half-real, half-play-acted form, a *new modus of interrelationship of man with man* which is counterposed to the omnipotent hierchical social relationships of non-carnivalistic life. Man's behavior, gesture and word are liberated from the authority of all hierarchical positions (of estate, rank, age, property status) which define them totally in non-carnivalistic life, and therefore they become, from the point of view of normal, non-carnival life, eccentric and inappropriate. *Eccentricity* is a special category of the carnival attitude which is organically connected with the category of familiar contact; it permits the latent sides of human nature to be revealed and developed in a concretely sensuous form.

A third category of the carnival attitude is connected with familiarization— the category of *carnivalistic mésalliances.* The unfettered familiar attitude encompasses everything: all values, thoughts, phenomena and things. All the things that were closed off, isolated, and separated from one another by the non-carnivalistic hierarchical attitude enter into carnivalistic contacts and combinations. Carnival brings together, unites, weds and combines the sacred with the profane, the lofty with the lowly, the great with the insignificant, the wise with the stupid, etc.

With this is connected yet a fourth carnivalistic category—*profanation:* the carnivalistic blasphemies, a whole carnivalistic system of lowering of status and bringing down to earth, the carnivalistic obscenities connected with the reproductive power of the earth and the body, the carnivalistic parodies of sacred texts and apothegms, etc. These carnivalistic categories are *not abstract thoughts* on equality and freedom, on the interrelatedness of all things, or on the unity of opposites, etc. No, these are concretely sensuous ritual-pageant "thoughts," experienced and played out in life itself, which have taken shape and survived over a period of millenia in the broadest masses of the European peoples. They were therefore able to exercise such an immense *formal, genre-determining* influence on literature.

These carnivalistic categories, above all the category of the free familiari-

zation of man and the world, were transposed over a period of millenia into literature, particularly into the dialogical line in the development of novelistic prose.
Familiarization furthered the destruction of epical and tragical distance and the
transferal of the material that is being represented to the zone of familiar contact; it was decisively reflected in the organization of the plot and the situations
of the plot, it determined the special familiarity of the authorial position in relation to the heroes (impossible in the higher genres), it introduced the logic of
mésalliances and profanatory lowerings of status, and, finally, it exercised a powerful transforming influence on the verbal style of literature itself. All of these things
are clearly manifested in the menippea, too. We shall return to this again, but
first we must touch upon several aspects of carnival, starting with the *carnival
performances (karnaval'nye deistva)*.

The primary carnival performance is the *mock crowning* and subsequent
discrowning of the king of carnival. This ritual is found in one or another form
in all festivals of the carnival type: in the most highly developed forms—the saturnalia, the European carnival, and the festival of fools (in which, in place of a king,
mock priests, bishops, or popes were chosen, depending on the rank of the local
church), and in less-developed forms—all of the other festivals of this type, even
in the festive carouse, which included the selection of ephemeral kings and queens
of the fest.

The basis of the ritual performance of crowning and discrowning the king
is the very core of the carnivalistic attitude to the world—*the pathos of vicissi-
tudes and changes, of death and renewal.* Carnival is the festival of all-destroy-
ing and all-renewing time. The basic meaning of carnival can be expressed in this
way. But we would emphasize again: this is not an abstract meaning, but rather
a living attitude to the world, expressed in the experienced and play-acted concretely sensuous form of the ritual performance.

Crowning and discrowning is a two-in-one *(dvuedinyi)*, ambivalent ritual
expressing the inevitability, and simultaneously the creativity, of change and renewal, the *jolly relativity* of every system and order, every authority and every
(hierarchical) position. The idea of immanent discrowning is contained already
in the crowning: it is ambivalent from the very beginning. The antipode of a real
king—a slave or a jester—is crowned, and this seems to reveal and sanctify the inside-out world of the carnival. In the ritual of coronation all the elements of the
ceremony itself, the symbols of authority which are handed over to the crownee,
and the clothes in which he is dressed become ambivalent and acquire an air of
jolly relativity, almost taking on the nature of theatrical props (albeit ritualistic
ones); their symbolic significance becomes bilevelled (as actual symbols of authority, in the non-carnival world, they are single-levelled, absolute, weighty, and
monolithically serious). From the outset the discrowning shows through the coronation. All carnivalistic symbols are of this nature: they always include within
themselves the perspective of negation (death), or its opposite. Birth is fraught
with death, and death with new birth.

The ritual of discrowning as it were finalizes the coronation, and is insepa-

[102]

rable from it (I repeat: this is a two-in-one ritual). And a new coronation shows through it. Carnival celebrates change itself, the very process of replacability *(smeniaemost')*, rather than that which is replaced. Carnival is, so to speak, functional, not substantive. It absolutizes nothing; it proclaims the jolly relativity of everything. The ceremonial of the ritual of discrowning is counterposed to the ritual of coronation: the regal vestments are stripped from the discrownee, his crown is taken off, the remaining symbols of authority are removed, and he is ridiculed and beaten. All the symbolic elements of the ceremonial have a second, positive aspect—it is not naked, absolute negation and destruction (absolute negation, like absolute affirmation, is unknown to carnival). Moreover, it was precisely in the ritual of discrowning that the carnival pathos of change and renewal and the image of the creativity of death stood out especially clearly. Therefore it is the ritual of discrowning that was most often transposed into literature. But, we repeat, crowning and discrowning are inseparable, they are two-in-one, and they transmute into one another; if they are absolutely divided, their carnivalistic significance is completely lost.

The carnival performance of crowning-discrowning is, of course, permeated with the carnival categories (the logic of the carnivalistic world): free, familiar contact (this is very clearly manifest in the discrowning), the carnival mésalliances (slave-king), profanation (making light of the symbols of higher authority), etc.

We shall not dwell here on the details of the crowning-discrowning ritual (although they are of interest), nor on its different variations in various epochs and various celebrations of the carnival type. Neither shall we analyze the various secondary rituals of carnival, that of disguise, for example, i.e. the carnivalistic changing of clothing, positions, and destinies in life, or the carnivalistic mystifications, the bloodless carnival wars, the verbal agons and cursing matches, the exchanges of gifts (abundance as an aspect of carnivalistic utopia), etc. All of these rituals were also transposed into literature, imbuing the corresponding plots and plot situations with symbolic depth and ambivalence, or with jolly relativity and the levity and rapidity of change of carnival.

But, of course, the ritual of crowning and discrowning had an extraordinarily great influence on literary-artistic thinking. It determined the special *discrowning type (razvenchivaiushchyi tip)* of construction of artistic images and whole works, in which the discrowning was essentially ambivalent and bilevelled. If the carnivalistic ambivalence faded from the images of discrowning, then those images were turned into a purely negative *exposé* of a moral or social-political nature, they became single-levelled, lost their artistic character and were turned into naked journalism.

We must yet touch upon the ambivalent nature of carnival images. All of the images of carnival are two-in-one images, they unite within themselves both poles of change and crisis: birth and death (the image of pregnant death), benediction and damnation (the benedictory carnival curses, with simultaneous wishes of death and rebirth), praise and condemnation, youth and age, top and bottom, face and backside, stupidity and wisdom. Paired images, chosen for contrast (high

[103]

and low, fat and thin, etc.) and for similarity (doubles and twins) are characteristic of the carnival mode of thinking. The utilization of things in reverse is also
characteristic: putting on clothing inside out, trousers on the head, dishes in
place of headgear, the use of household utensils as weapons, etc. This is a special
manifestation of the carnival category of *eccentricity;* it is the violation of the
usual and the accepted, it is life drawn out of its usual rut.

The image of *fire* is profoundly ambivalent in carnival. Fire simultaneously
destroys and renews the world. In European carnivals there was almost always a
special edifice or structure (usually a vehicle festooned with all sorts of carnival
bric-a-brac) called "hades," and at the end of carnival this "hades" was ceremon-
iously set on fire (sometimes the carnival "hades" was ambivalently combined
with the horn of plenty). The ritual of "moccoli" of the Roman carnival is typical: every participant in the carnival carried a lighted candle ("a candle stub"), and
each tried to put out the candle of the other, crying "Sia ammazzato!" ("Death
to thee!"). In his famous description of the Roman carnival (in *Italienische Reise)*
Goethe, attempting to reveal the profound meaning behind the carnivalistic images,
relates a profoundly symbolic scene: during the "moccoli" a boy puts out his
father's candle with the merry carnival cry, "Sia ammazzato, il Signore Padre!"

The *laughter* of carnival is itself deeply ambivalent. It is genetically related
to the most ancient forms of ritual laughter. Ritual laughter was directed toward
a higher order: the sun (the chief god), the other gods, and the highest earthly
authority were disparaged and ridiculed, and thereby forced to *renew themselves.*
All forms of ritual laughter were connected with death and rebirth, with the act
of reproduction, and with the symbols of reproductive power. Ritual laughter
reacted to *crises* in the life of the sun (the solstices), in the life of the deity, in
the life of the world, and of man (funery laughter). In it mockery was fused with
rejoicing.

The directedness of ancient ritual laughter toward a higher order (deity and
authority) explains the privileges of laughter in antiquity and in the Middle Ages.
Much was permitted in the form of laughter that was impermissable in serious
form. In the Middle Ages "parodia sacra," i.e. parody of sacred texts and rituals,
was possible under the cover of the legitimized freedom of laughter.

Carnivalistic laughter is also directed toward a higher order—toward the
change of authorities and truths, toward the change of world orders. Laughter
encompasses both poles of change, and it relates to the very process of change,
to *crisis* itself. In the act of carnival laughter death and rebirth, negation (ridicule)
and affirmation (joyful laughter) are combined. This is profoundly ideological
and universal laughter. So much for the character of ambivalent carnival laughter.

In connection with laughter we shall touch on yet another question—the
carnivalistic nature of *parody.* Parody, as we have already mentioned, is an integral element in the "Menippean satire," and in all carnivalistic genres in general.
Parody is organically alien to pure genres (the epopee, the tragedy), but to the
carnivalized genres it is, on the contrary, organically compatible. In antiquity
parody was inseparably connected with the carnival attitude to the world. Parody

is the creation of a *double which discrowns its counterpart (razvenchivaiushchii dvoinik);* it is that same "inside-out world." Therefore the parody is ambivalent. Antiquity in essence parodied everything: the satyr drama, for example, was originally a parodical, comical aspect of the tragical trilogy which preceeded it. The parody here was not, of course, merely a negation of that which was parodied. Everything has its parody, i.e. its comical aspect, because everything is reborn and renewed through death. In Rome parody was an obligatory element of funery as well as of triumphant laughter (both were, of course, rituals of the carnival type). In carnival, parody was employed very widely, and had diverse forms and degrees: various images (carnival pairs of various sorts, for example) parodied one another in various ways and from various viewpoints, as in a system of trick mirrors which elongates and compresses and contorts in various directions and to various degrees.

Parodical doubles became a rather common phenomenon in carnivalized literature. This is particularly vividly expressed in Dostoevsky—almost all of the leading heroes in his novels have several doubles who parody them in different ways: Raskolnikov has Svidrigailov, Luzhin and Lebezyatnikov, Stavrogin has Petr Verkhovensky, Shatov and Kirilov, and Ivan Karamazov has Smerdyakov, the devil and Rakitin, In each of them (i.e. in each of the doubles) the hero dies (i e. is negated) in order to be born again (i.e. to be purified and to rise above himself).

In the narrowly formal literary parody of modern times the link with the carnivalistic attitude to the world is almost completely broken. But in the parodies of the Renaissance (in Erasmus, Rabelais and others) the carnival fire burned still: parody was ambivalent and was aware of its bond with death and renewal. Therefore the womb of parody could conceive one of the greatest, and at the same time most carnivalistic, novels of world literature—Cervantes' *Don Quixote.* Dostoevsky thus evaluated this novel:

> There is nothing in the world more profound or powerful than this work. This is the ultimate and greatest word that human thought has yet produced, it is the most bitter irony expressible by man, and if the world were to end and someone were to ask there, somewhere, "Well, did you understand your life on earth? What conclusions did you reach about it?" one could silently point to Don Quixote: "Here is my conclusion about life; can you judge me for it?"

It is characteristic that Dostoevsky constructs his evaluation of *Don Quixote* in the form of a typical "threshold dialog."

To conclude our analysis of carnival (from the viewpoint of the carnivalization of literature), a few words about the carnival square.

The main arena for the carnival performances was the square and the adjoining streets. True, carnival extended into homes as well, being limited, essentially, only in time, not in space; it knows neither platform nor stage. But the central area could only be the square, for by its very idea carnival *belongs to the whole people, it is universal, everyone* must take part in its familiar contact. The square was symbolic of the whole people. The carnival square—the square where the carnival performances took place—acquired an additional symbolic nuance which broadened and deepened its meaning. In carnivalized literature the square, as the setting of the plot's action, becomes bilevelled and ambivalent: it is as if, through the actual square, one could see the carnival square, the scene of free, familiar contact and of crownings and discrownings carried out by the whole people. Other places of action (ones which are, of course, motivated by the plot and by reality), if they can in any way be the scene of meetings and contacts of diverse people—streets, taverns, roads, baths, the decks of ships, etc.—take on the additional significance of the carnival square. (Given the naturalistic way in which these places are represented, the universal symbolism of carnival has no fear of naturalism.)

Celebrations of the carnival type occupied an enormous place in the life of the broadest masses of the people in antiquity, both in Greece, and especially in Rome, where the central (but not the only) celebration of the carnival type was the *saturnalia*. These celebrations had no smaller (and perhaps even a greater) significance in medieval Europe and during the Renaissance, being in part a direct, living continuation of the Roman saturnalia. In the realm of carnivalistic folk culture there was no break in tradition between antiquity and the Middle Ages. In all the epochs of their development, celebrations of the carnival type exercised an enormous, and as yet underrated and insufficiently studied influence on the entire culture, including literature, some of the genres and tendencies of which have undergone a particularly powerful *carnivalization.* In antiquity the ancient Attic comedy and the whole realm of the serio-comical was especially strongly carnivalized. In Rome all varieties of the satire and the epigram were even organizationally connected with the saturnalia, were written for saturnalia, or, at least, were created under the cover of the established carnivalistic liberties of that festival (the complete work of Martial, for example, was directly connected with the saturnalia).

In the Middle Ages the voluminous literature of comedy and parody in the vernacular languages and in Latin was in one way or another connected with celebrations of the carnival type—with carnival proper, with the "festival of fools," with the free "paschal laughter" (risus paschalis), etc. In the Middle Ages almost every religious holiday had its folkish, carnivalistic side (especially such holidays as Corpus Christi). Many national celebrations, such as the bullfight, for example, had a clearly expressed carnivalistic character. The carnival atmosphere held sway during fairs, on the festival of the gathering of grapes, on days when miracle and mystery plays and stories were staged, etc.; the entire medieval theatrical life was of a carnival nature. The large cities of the late Middle Ages (such as Rome, Naples, Venice, Paris, Lyon, Nurnberg, Cologne, etc.) lived a full carnival life in all about three months of the year (and sometimes more). It could be said (with certain reservations, of course) that the medieval man lived, as it were, *two lives:* one, the *official,* monolithically serious and gloomy life, subject to a strict hierarchical order, filled with fear, dogmatism, reverence and piety, and the other, the *life of the carnival square,* free, full of ambivalent laughter, blasphemy, the profanation of all that was holy, disparagement and obscenity, and familiar contact with everyone and everything. Both of these lives were legal and legitimate, but were divided by strict temporal limits.

If the alternation and mutual bestrangement *(ostranenie)* of these two systems of life and thought (the official and the carnivalistic) are not taken into consideration, it is impossible to correctly understand the peculiarity of medieval man's cultural consciousness, or to gain an understanding of many of the phenomena of medieval literature, of the "parodia sacra," for example.[93]

In this epoch the carnivalization of the *verbal life* of the European peoples took place: whole strata of language—the so-called *familiar speech of the street (famil'iarno-ploshchadnaia rech')*—were permeated with the carnival attitude to the world, and a huge fund of liberated carnivalistic gesticulation was created. The familiar speech of all the European peoples is filled to this day with relics of carnival, especially in its profanity and expressions of ridicule; contemporary gestures of invective and ridicule are also filled with the symbolism of carnival.

During the Renaissance the essence of carnival broke down many barriers and invaded many areas of the official life and *Weltanschauung.* And above all it took possession of almost all of the great literary genres, fundamentally transforming them. The whole of artistic literature was profoundly and almost totally carnivalized. The carnivalistic attitude toward the world, with all its categories, the laughter of carnival, the symbolism of the carnival rituals of crowning and discrowning, of changes and disguises, the ambivalence of carnival and all the nuances of the liberated carnival word—familiar, cynically frank, eccentric, lauditorily abusive, etc.—penetrated deeply into almost all literary genres. The complex forms of the Renaissance *Weltanschauung* are formed on the basis of the carnival attitude. Antiquity, as assimilated by the humanists of the time, was seen to a certain degree through the prism of the carnival attitude toward the world. The Renaissance is the zenith of carnivalistic life.[94] Thereafter began its decline.

Beginning with the 17th century the folk-carnival life begins to wane: it almost loses its quality of belonging to the whole people *(vsenarodnost'),* its specific weight in the life of the people is sharply reduced, its forms become impoverished, shallow, less complex. From the time of the Renaissance the culture of the *court masquerade* begins to develop, absorbing a whole series of carnival forms and symbols (predominantly of an external, decorative character). Subsequently there begins to develop a broader line of celebrations and entertainments (no longer limited to the court) which could be called the *masquerade line* of development; it preserved a few of the freedoms and a few faint reflections of the carnival attitude. Many of the carnival forms lost touch with their folk origins and retreated from the public square into the chamber masquerade, which still exists today. Many ancient forms of carnival have been preserved and continue to live and renew themselves in the *farcical* street comedy *(ploshchadnaia balagannaia komika)* and also in the *circus.* Certain elements of carnival are also preserved in the theatrical life of modern times. It is characteristic that even the theatrical subculture has retained something of the carnival liberties, the carnival attitude and the carnival charm; this was very well depicted by Goethe in *Wilhelm Meisters Lehrjahre,* or for our own time by Nemirovich-Danchenko in his memoirs. Under certain circumstances something of the carnival atmosphere was also preserved among the so-called bohemians, although in most cases they have degraded and banalized the carnival attitude (they have, for example, not a grain of the carnival spirit of belonging to the whole people).

Aside from the later emaciating offshoots from the carnival trunk, the street carnival in the true sense, as well as other celebrations of the carnival type, have continued to exist, but have lost their former significance and their former richness of forms and symbols.

As a result, carnival and the carnival attitude have deteriorated and dispersed, and have lost their nature of truly belonging to the whole people. Consequently the nature of the carnivalization of literature has also changed. Until the second half of the 17th century, people were *directly involved* in the carnival performances and the carnival attitude, they still *lived* in carnival, i.e. carnival was one of the forms of life itself. Therefore carnivalization had an immediate nature (certain genres were even directly used in carnival). *The source of carnivalization was carnival itself.* Moreover, carnivalization had a genre-determining significance, i.e. it provided not only the context, but the foundation of the work's genre as well. From the second half of the 17th century carnival almost completely ceases to be a direct source of carnivalization, relinquishing its place to already-carnivalized literature; thus carnivalization becomes a purely literary tradition. Already in Sorel and Scarron we observe, along with the direct influence of carnival, the strong influence of the carnivalized literature of the Renaissance (chiefly Rabelais and Cervantes), and the latter influence is predominant. Consequently carnivalization becomes part of the literary tradition of genre. The carnival elements in this literature, which is already cut off from carnival, its direct source, undergo certain changes of form and meaning.

Of course carnival in the true sense, and other celebrations of the carnival type (the bullfight, for example), the masquerade line of development, the farcical comedy, and other forms of carnivalistic folklore also continue to this day to exercise a certain direct influence on literature. But in most cases that influence is limited to the content of the work, not touching the foundation of its genre, i.e. it has been deprived of its genre-determining power.

■

Now we can return to the carnivalization of genres within the sphere of the serio-comical, which term is itself ambivalent in the manner of carnival.

Despite its very complicated literary form and its philosophical profundity, there can be no doubt as to the carnivalistic origins of the "Socratic dialog." The basis of the original nucleus of the genre was the carnivalistic-folkloristic

[108]

"debate" between life and death, darkness and light, summer and winter, etc.,
a debate permeated with the pathos of change and jolly relativity which did not
allow thought to stand still and grow cold in one-sided seriousness, useless exactness and singleness of meaning. This distinguishes the "Socratic dialog" both from
the purely rhetorical dialog and from the tragic dialog, but its carnivalistic origin
relates it in certain respects to the agons of ancient Attic comedy and to the
mimes of Sophron (there have even been attempts to reconstruct Sophron's mimes
on the basis of certain Platonic dialogs). The Socratic discovery of the dialogical
nature of thought and truth assumes the carnivalistic familiarization of the relationships among the participants in the dialog and the abolition of all distance
between them; it assumes, moreover, the familiarization of the attitude toward
the object of thought, lofty and important though it may be, and of the attitude
toward truth itself. Certain of Plato's dialogs are constructed on the model of
carnivalistic crowning and discrowning. Free mésalliances of thoughts and images
are typical of the "Socratic dialog." "Socratic irony" is reduced to carnival
laughter.

Socrates' image itself has an ambivalent character—it combines beauty and
ugliness (cf. his characterization by Alcibiades in Plato's *Feast);* his own self-characterization as a "pander" and "midwife" are also in the spirit of carnival debasement. And Socrates' personal life was surrounded with carnivalistic legends (his
relationship with his wife Xanthippe, for example). Carnivalistic legends are in
general profoundly different from heroic epic myths: they debase the hero and
bring him down to earth, they familiarize and humanize him and bring him up
close; the ambivalent laughter of carnival turns to ashes all that is stilted and stiff,
but in no way harms the genuinely heroic core of the image. It should be noted
that the images of novelistic heroes (Gargantua, Eulenspiegel, Don Quixote, Faust,
Simplizissimus, etc.) also took shape in the atmosphere of carnival legends.

The carnival nature of the menippea manifests itself even more clearly.
Both its external layers and its deepest core are permeated by carnivalization.
Certain menippea directly depict celebrations of the carnival type (Varro depicts
the Roman celebrations in two satires, for example; in one of Julian the Apostate's
menippea the celebration of saturnalia on Olympus is depicted). This is a purely
external (thematic, so to speak) connection, but it, too, is characteristic. More
to the point is the carnivalistic interpretation of the three planes of the menippea:
Olympus, the nether world, and Earth. The representation of Olympus has an
obviously carnivalistic character: free familiarization, scandals and eccentricities,
and crownings and discrownings are typical of the Olympus of the menippea.
Olympus is, as it were, turned into the carnival square (cf., for example, Lucian's
Iuppiter tragoedus). Sometimes scenes on Olympus are presented as carnivalistic
debasements or bringings-down-to-earth (also in Lucian). Still more interesting
is the consistent carnivalization of the nether world. The nether world equalizes
representatives of all earthly circumstances; there the emperor and the slave, the
rich man and the beggar meet on equal terms and enter into familiar contact;
death discrowns all those who wear crowns in life. In the representation of the

nether world the carnival logic of "the world upside down" was often applied: in the nether world the emperor becomes slave, and the slave—emperor, etc. The carnivalized nether world of the menippea determined the medieval tradition of a *happy hell* which culminated in the works of Rabelais. The deliberate interchanging of the nether world of antiquity and the Christian hell is characteristic of this medieval tradition. In the mystery plays hell and the devil (in the "diableries") are also consistently carnivalized.

The earthly plane, too, is carnivalized in the menippea: there is to be seen behind almost every scene and event of real-life, most of which are naturalistically depicted, a more or less obviously carnivalistic square with its specific carnival logic of familiar contacts, mésalliances, disguises and mystifications, contrasting paired images, scandals, crownings and discrownings, etc. Thus the carnival shows through all of the naturalistic underworld scenes of the *Satyricon* with greater or lesser clarity. And the very plot of the *Satyricon* is consistently carnivalized. We observe this also in Apuleius' *Metamorphoses (The Golden Ass)*. Sometimes carnivalization lies buried in deeper strata and allows us to speak only of *carnivalistic overtones* of individual images and events. But sometimes it comes to the surface, for example in the purely carnivalistic episode of the supposed murder *on the threshold*, in which Lucius stabs the wineskins filled with wine and mistakes the wine for blood, or in the following scene of carnival mystification depicting his trial. Carnivalistic overtones are heard even in a menippea of such a serious tone as Boethius' *De Consolatione Philosophiae*.

Carnivalization penetrates even to the deepest philosophico-dialogical core of the menippea. We have seen that extreme universality and the naked statement of the ultimate questions of life and death are characteristic of this genre (personal problems and involved philosophical argumentations are foreign to it). Carnivalistic thought lives also in the sphere of ultimate questions, but it plays them out in the concretely sensuous form of carnival performances and images, rather than providing them with an abstract philosophical or dogmatic religious solution. Therefore carnivalization made possible the transfer of ultimate questions from the abstract philosophical sphere, through the carnival attitude toward the world, to the concretely sensuous plane of images and events which are, in accord with the carnival spirit, dynamic, diverse and vivid. The carnival attitude made it possible to "clothe philosophy in the parti-colored garb of the hetaera." The carnival attitude is the drive shaft connecting the *idea with the artistic adventure image.* In modern European literature the philosophical novellas of Voltaire, with their ideological universalism and carnivalistic dynamism and diversity of color, serve as a vivid example of this *(Candide,* for example); these novellas reveal in quite obvious form the tradition of the menippea and of carnivalization.

Thus carnivalization penetrates to the very philosophical core of the menippea.

We can now draw such a conclusion. We have revealed in the menippea an astounding combination of what would seem to be absolutely diverse and incompatible elements: philosophical dialog, adventure and fantasy, underworld naturalism, utopia, etc. We can now state that the connecting principle which bound all of these diverse elements into the organic whole of the genre, a principle of extraordinary strength and tenacity, was carnival and the carnival attitude toward the world. And in the subsequent development of European literature carnivalization constantly assisted in the destruction of all barriers between genres, between self-enclosed systems of thought, between various styles, etc., it destroyed all manner of isolation and mutual neglect, it brought together things which were far apart, and it united things which were separated. This was the momentous function of carnivalization in the history of literature.

Now a few words about the menippea and carnivalization on Christian soil.

The menippea and the related genres which developed within its orbit exerted a definitive influence on the formation of ancient Christian literature—Greek, Roman and Byzantine.

The basic narrative genres of ancient Christian literature—the "gospels," the "acts of the apostles," the "apocalypse" and the "lives of the saints and martyrs"—are connected with ancient aretalogy which, in the first centuries after Christ, developed within the orbit of the menippea. Its influence increases sharply in the Christian genres, especially at the expense of the *dialogical element* of the menippea. In these genres, especially in the numerous "gospels" and "acts," classical Christian dialogical syncrises are developed: the syncrisis of the tempted (Christ or the righteous man) with the tempter, the believer with the non-believer, the righteous man with the sinner, the beggar with the rich man, the follower of Christ with the pharisee, the apostle (the Christian) with the heathen, etc. These syncrises are familiar to all through the canonical Gospels and Acts. Corresponding anacrises also develop (i.e. provocation by word or by plot situation).

In the Christian genres, as in the menippea, the *testing of an idea and its bearer*, testing by means of temptation and martyrdom (particularly, of course, in the hagiographic genre), is of enormous organizational significance. As in the menippea, rulers, rich men, thieves, beggars, hetaera, etc. meet on equal terms in a single, fundamentally dialogized plane. As in the menippea, dream visions, insanity and obsessions of all sorts have a certain significance here. Finally, Christian narrative literature absorbed other related genres: the symposium (the gospel meals) and the soliloquy.

Christian narrative also underwent direct carnivalization (independently of the influence of the carnivalized menippea). It is sufficient to recall the scene of the crowning and discrowning of the "King of the Jews" in the canonical Gospels. But carnivalization is much more strongly manifested in apocryphal Christian literature.

Thus ancient Christian narrative literature (including the canonical), too, was permeated by elements of the menippea and carnivalization.[95]

These are the sources, the "beginnings" (the "archaic elements"—*"arxaika"*) of the genre tradition of which Dostoevsky's work became one of the pinnacles.

These "beginnings" are preserved in a renewed form in his works.

But Dostoevsky is separated from these sources by two millenia, during which the tradition of genre continued to develop, became more complex, and changed in form and in meaning (preserving, however, its unity and continuity). Now a few words on the further development of the menippea.

We have seen that already in antiquity, including the ancient Christian period, the menippea displayed an extraordinary "protean" capacity for changing its external form (while preserving the inner essence of its genre), growing into an entire novel,combining with related genres, and taking root in other large genres (in the Greek and ancient Christian novel, for example). This capacity is manifested in the further development of the menippea in the Middle Ages as well as in modern times.

In the Middle Ages the characteristics of the menippea's genre continue to live and to renew themselves in certain genres of Latin ecclesiastical literature, which was a direct continuation of the ancient Christian literary tradition, especially in certain varieties of hagiographic literature. The menippea lives in a freer, more original form in such dialogized and carnivalized medieval genres as "arguments," "debates," ambivalent "panegyrics" (*desputaisons, dits, débats*), morality and miracle plays, and in the later Middle Ages in mystery plays and stories. Elements of the menippea can be detected in the parodies and semi-parodies of the Middle Ages: in parodied visions from beyond the grave, in parodied "gospel readings," etc. Finally, another very important aspect in the development of this tradition of genre was the novelistic literature of the Middle Ages and the early Renaissance, a literature thoroughly permeated with elements of the carnivalized menippea.[96]

The entire medieval development of the menippea is permeated with elements of *local* carnivalistic folklore and reflects the specific characteristics of the various periods of the Middle Ages.

During the Renaissance, an epoch of profound and almost complete carnivalization of all literature and philosophy, the menippea takes root in all of the large genres (in Rabelais, Cervantes, Grimmelshausen and others), while at the same time diverse Renaissance forms of the menippea develop, in most cases combining the antique and medieval traditions of the genre: Des Periers' *Cymbalum mundi,* Erasmus's *The Praise of Folly,* Cervantes' *Novelas ejemplares, Satyre Menippée de la vertue du Catholicon d'Espagne* (I594, one of the greatest political satires in world literature), the satires of Grimmelshausen, Quevedo, and others.

In addition to taking root in other carnivalized genres, the menippea continues in modern times to develop independently in various forms and under various names: "Lucian's dialog," "conversations in the kingdom of the dead" (variations in which antique traditions predominated), the "philosophical novella" (a variety of the menippea characteristic of the Renaissance), the "fantastical story" and the "philosophical fairy tale" (forms characteristic of Romanticism—of Hoffmann, for example), etc. It should be mentioned here that in modern times various literary schools and creative methods have made use of the genre characteristics of the menippea, renewing them in various ways, of course. Thus, for example, the rationalistic "philosophical novella" of Voltaire and the romantic "philosophical fairy tale" of Hoffmann share the traits of the menippea's genre and are equally heavily carnivalized, despite the profound differences in their artistic direction, ideological content, and, of course, their creative individuality (it suffices to compare, for example, *Micromégas* and *Klein Zaches*). It must be said that in modern literatures the menippea has been the predominant conduit for the most pronounced and vivid forms of carnivalization.

In conclusion it seems necessary to emphasize that the term "menippea," like the names of all the other antique genres—"epopee," "tragedy," "idyll," etc.— when applied to modern literature is intended as a designation of the *essence of a genre,* not of the specific canon of a genre (as in antiquity).[97]

With this we conclude our excursion into the area of the history of genre and return to Dostoevsky (although throughout our excursion he has not been lost from view for a single moment).

■

We have already mentioned in the course of our excursion that our characterization of the menippea and its related genres can be expanded almost *in toto* to include the genre characteristics of Dostoevsky's works. Now we must concretely illustrate this situation by means of an analysis of certain of his works which are of *key importance* so far as genre is concerned.

In two "fantastic tales" of the late Dostoevsky—"Bobok" (1873) and "The Dream of a Ridiculous Man" (1877)—the classical characteristics of the menippea are so clearly and fully manifested that the stories can be termed menippea almost in the strict antique sense of the word. Variants on the essence of the genre, freer and farther removed from its antique models, are presented in a number of other works (*Notes from the Underground,* "A Gentle Creature," etc.). Finally, the menippea takes root in all of Dostoevsky's larger works, especially in his five mature novels, and it takes root in the most essential and decisive aspects of these novels. Therefore we can flatly state that the menippea in essence sets the tone for Dostoevsky's entire work.

It would hardly be a mistake to say that "Bobok," with its depth and boldness, is one of the greatest menippea in all of world literature. But we shall not consider here the depth of its content—we are interested in the characteristics of the work's genre.

Above all, the image of the narrator and the tone of his story are characteristic. The narrator—"a certain person"[98] —is on the threshold of insanity (delirium tremens). But aside from that, he is a person unlike everyone else, i.e. one who deviates from the general norm, who has fallen out of the normal rut of life, who despises everyone and is despised by everyone—we have before us a new variant of the "underground man." His tone is unstable and equivocal, full of suppressed ambivalence, with elements of infernal buffoonery (after the manner of the devils in mystery plays). Despite the external form of short, "choppy," categorical sentences, he conceals his final word and tries to evade it. He himself quotes a characterization of his style that had been given by a friend:

Your style, you see, changes, it's choppy. You chop and chop, first an introductory clause, and then an introduction, then you'll stick something into parentheses, and then you'll start to chop again, and chop... (X, 343)

His speech is internally dialogized and shot through with polemics. The story begins with a polemic with a certain Semyon Ardalionovich, who accuses him of being a drunkard. He polemizes with the editors who refuse to print his works (he is an unrecognized author) and with the contemporary public, which is incapable of understanding humor; in essence, he polemizes with all of his contemporaries. And then, when the main action unfolds, he polemizes with "today's corpses." Such is the dialogized and equivocal verbal style and tone of the story, so typical of the menippea.

At the beginning of the story we have a discourse on a topic typical for the carnivalized menippea—the relativity and ambivalence of reason and insanity, of good sense and stupidity. And then follows the description of a cemetery and a funeral.

This whole description is permeated with a markedly *familiar and profanizing* attitude to the cemetery, the funeral, the clergy at the cemetery, the deceased, and to the "sacrament of death" itself. The whole description is built on oxymoronic combinations and carnivalistic mésalliances, it is filled with *debasements and bringings-down-to-earth,* and with carnivalistic symbolism, and at the same time with crude naturalism.

Here are several typical fragments:

"I came out to *enjoy myself,* and ran into a *funeral...* I haven't been in a graveyard for about 25 years, I bet. What a place!

First of all, the *scent (dux).* About fifteen corpses *arrived. Shrouds of various prices;* there were even two catafalques: for a general and for some rich lady or other. Many *mournful faces* and lots of feigned mourning, but also lots of *genuine jollity.* The clergy has nothing to complain about: *the money's coming in.* But the *scent, the scent (dux).* I wouldn't want to be the *spiritual (duxovnyi) leader* here." *(A profanatory pun typical of the genre.)*

I glanced cautiously into the faces of the other corpses, because I was afraid of my impressionability. There are some gentle expressions, and also some unpleasant ones. In general the *smiles* are disagreeable, and some of them are even awfully..."

I left during the *service* to wander about *beyond the gate.* And I found a little restaurant that wasn't bad: one could have a bite to eat and everything. Many of the *mourners* had also jammed in. I noticed much *jollity and genuine animation. I had something to eat and drink.* (X, 343-344)

We have set off the most striking nuances of familiarization and profanation, the oxymoronic combinations, the mésalliances, the bringings-down-to-earth, the naturalism and the symbolism. We can see that the text is heavily saturated with them. We have before us a fairly exaggerated example of the style of the carnivalized menippea. Let us recall the symbolic significance of the ambivalent combination: death-laughter (here jollity)-feast (here "had something to eat and drink").

Then follows a short, vacillating meditation by the narrator, who has sat down on a grave stone, on the subject of *wonder* and *respect,* which his contemporaries have renounced. This meditation is important for an understanding of the author's conception. And then the following simultaneously naturalistic and symbolical detail is given:

> "On the *stone* next to me lay a *half-eaten sandwich:* foolish and *out of place.* I threw it on the ground, because it is not *bread,* just a *sandwich.* Anyway, I don't think it's a sin to crumble bread on the *ground;* crumbling it on the *floor* is sinful. I'll look it up in Suvorov's calendar." (X, 345)

This especially naturalistic and profanatory detail—the half-eaten sandwich on the grave stone—gives us occasion to touch upon the subject of carnivalistic symbolism: to crumble bread on the ground is permissible—that is sowing of seed, fructification; to crumble it on the floor is forbidden—the floor is barren soil.

Further on begins the development of the fantastical plot, which creates an anacrisis of extraordinary power (Dostoevsky is a great master of the anacrisis). The narrator listens in on the conversation of the dead beneath the earth. It turns out that their lives continue for a time in the grave. The deceased philosopher *Platon* Nikolaevich (an allusion to the "Socratic dialog") explains this circumstance as follows:

> "He (Platon Nikolaevich—M.B.) explains this by the simplest fact, i.e. by the fact that *up there,* when we were still alive, we mistook the death up there for the real death. It's as if the body comes to life again here, the remnants of life become concentrated, but *only in the consciousness.* Life continues—I don't quite know how to express it—as if by inertia. In his opinion everything is concentrated somewhere in the consciousness, and it lasts for two or three months...sometimes even half a year...For example, there is one person here who is almost completely decomposed, but once in about six weeks he'll suddenly blurt out one word: of course it doesn't make sense, it's something about a bobok: 'Bobok, bobok,' but nonetheless there is still an invisible spark of life glowing in him..." (X, 354)

Thus an extraordinary situation is created: the *final life of the consciousness* (the two or three months before its complete loss), freed from all conditions, positions, obligations and laws of normal life, so to speak a *life outside of life.* And how will it be put to use by "today's corpses?" An anacrisis which provokes the corpses' consciousnesses to reveal themselves with *complete,* unlimited *freedom.* And reveal themselves they do.

A typical carnivalized menippean nether world unfolds: a rather motley crew of corpses which cannot immediately liberate themselves from their earthly hierarchical positions and relationships, together with the comical conflicts, scolding and scandals which consequently arise, and on the other hand, the carnivalistic liberties, the awareness of a complete absence of responsibility, frank graveyard eroticism, laughter in the graves ("*chuckling* pleasantly, the general's *cadaver* began to quiver"), etc. The marked carnival tone of this paradoxical "life outside of life" is set from the very beginning by the game of cards which is going on in the grave on which the narrator is sitting (of course it is a make-believe game, played "by rote"). All of these are typical traits of the genre.

The "king" of this carnival of corpses is a "ne'er-do-well of pseudo-high-society" (as he characterizes himself), a baron Klinevich. We shall quote him in order to illustrate the anacrisis and its use. Having disposed of the philosopher Platon Nikolaevich's moral interpretations (which are related by Lebedyatnikov), he declares:

"Enough! I am sure that all the rest ismonsense. The main thing is that we have two or three months of life, and then finally—bobok. I propose that we spend these two months as pleasantly as possible, and to that end that we establish new ground rules. Ladies and gentlemen! I *propose that we not be ashamed of anything!"*

Meeting with the corpses' unanimous approval, he develops his thought a bit further:

"I just *want everyone to tell the truth.* That is all that I ask, because that is the most important thing. *On earth it is impossible to live without lying, because life and lie are synonyms;* but here we will tell the truth *just for fun.* What the hell, the *grave* does mean something doesn't it! *We shall all tell our life's stories aloud, and we won't be ashamed of anything.* I'll tell you about myself first. I'm a carnivorous beast, you know. *Up there everything was tied together with rotten strings.* Away with all strings, let us live out these two months in *shameless truthfulness! Let's strip off our clothes and show ourselves naked!"*
"Let's strip, let's strip," they shouted at the top of their lungs.
(X, 355-356).

The corpses' dialog was, in true carnival manner, unexpectedly interrupted:

"And then I suddenly *sneezed*. It happened suddenly and unintentionally, but the effect was astounding: everything grew silent, *exactly like in a cemetery*, it disappeared like a dream. It became truly as quiet as a tomb."

I shall quote the narrator's concluding assessment, which is interesting for its tone:

"No, I can't accept it, I simply can't! Bobok doesn't bother me (it turned out to be a bobok, alright!).
Debauchery in such a place, debauchery of their last hopes, debauchery of flacid, rotting cadavers, and they didn't even spare their *final moments of consciousness!* They were given those moments as a gift, and... But the main thing, the main thing is—in such a place! No, I can't accept it..." (X, 357-358)

Here the almost unadulterated words and intonation of a completely different voice, the voice of the author, break into the narrator's speech, but then are immediately broken off with the word "and..."

The story's ending is in the manner of a feuilleton: "I'll take it to *Grazhdanin (The Citizen)*; a portrait of one of the editors was displayed there, too. Maybe they'll print it."

Such is Dostoevsky's almost classical menippea. The genre is sustained here with amazing integrity. One might even say that the menippea reveals its ultimate possibilities here, that it realizes its maximum. This is, of course, by no means a *stylization* of a dead genre. On the contrary, in this work of Dostoevsky the menippea *continues to live* a full life as a genre. For the life of a genre consists of its constantly being reborn and renewed in *original* works. Dostoevsky's "Bobok" is profoundly original. And he was not writing a parody on the genre, he used it in its straightforward sense. It should, however, be noted that the menippea, including its ancient, antique forms, always parodies itself to a degree. That is one of the identifying features of the menippea. The element of self-parody is one of the reasons for the unusual vitality of the genre.

Here we must touch on the question of Dostoevsky's possible genre sources. The essence of every genre is established and revealed in all its fullness only in the many diverse variants which arise during the entire historical development of the given genre. The greater the accessability of these variants to the artist, the richer and more flexible is his command of the given genre's language (for the language of a genre is concrete and historical).

Dostoevsky had a very good and subtle understanding of all of the possibilities of the menippea's genre. He commanded an extraordinarily profound and differentiated feeling for the genre. An investigation of all of Dostoevsky's possible contacts with the different variants of the menippea would be very important for a deeper understanding of the genre characteristics of his works, as well as for a more complete notion of the pre-Dostoevskian tradition of genre itself.

Dostoevsky was most directly and closely tied to the variants of the antique menippea through ancient Christian literature (i.e. through the "gospels," the "apocalypse," and the "lives," etc.). But he was also certainly acquainted with classical examples of the antique menippea. It is quite probable that he knew Lucian's menippea *Menippos, or a Journey to the Kingdom of the Dead* and his *Conversations with the Dead* (a group of dialogical satires). In these works are illustrated various types of behavior of the dead in the kingdom beyond the grave, i.e. in a carnivalized nether world. It should be noted that Lucian—the "Voltaire of antiquity"—was, beginning with the 18th century,[99] widely known in Russia and inspired numerous imitations, and that the genre situation of a "meeting in the world beyond the grave" became current in literature, down to the level of schoolroom exercises.

It is possible that Dostoevsky was also acquainted with Seneca's menippea "The Pumpkinization." We find in Dostoevsky three points which are in keeping with this satire: 1) the "open merriment" of the mourners at the cemetery in Dostoevsky is, perhaps, tinged with an episode from Seneca: Claudius, flying down from Olympus to the nether world through Earth, comes upon his own funeral on Earth and sees that all the mourners are very merry (except for the litigious ones); 2) the make-believe game of cards, played "by rote," is, perhaps, tinged with Claudius' game of dice in the nether world, also a make-believe game (the dice come tumbling out before they are thrown); 3) the naturalistic dis-crowning of death in Dostoevsky is reminiscent of the even cruder depiction of the death of Claudius, who dies (gives up the ghost) while defecating.[100]

There is no doubt about Dostoevsky's more or less close acquaintance with other antique works of the genre—with the *Satyricon, The Golden Ass,* etc.[101]

The European sources of genre which may have revealed to Dostoevsky the richness and variety of the menippea are very numerous and diverse. He probably knew Boileau's literary-polemical menippea *Dialogue des héros de romans,* and perhaps he knew Goethe's literary-polemical satire *Götter, Helden and Wieland,* too. He was probably acquainted with the "dialogs of the dead" of Fénelon and Fontenelle (Dostoevsky had an excellent knowledge of French literature). All of these satires are connected with the representation of the kingdom beyond the grave, and they all externally sustain the antique form of the genre (based predominantly on Lucian).

Diderot's menippea, which are free in their outer form, but typical in the essence of their genre, are of very substantial significance for an understanding of Dostoevsky's tradition of genre. Of course Diderot's tone and style (sometimes in the spirit of the erotic literature of the 18th century) differ from Dostoevsky's. In *Neveu de Rameau* (essentially a menippea, but without the fantastic element) the motif of extremely frank confessions without a single grain of remorse cor-responds to "Bobok." And the image of the nephew Rameau, a frankly "rapa-cious type" who, like Klinevich, considers social morality a batch of "rotten strings" and recognizes only "shameless truthfulness," corresponds to the image of Klinevich.

Dostoevsky was familiar with another variant of the free menippea via Voltaire's *Contes philosophiques*. This type of menippea was very close to some aspects of his own works (Dostoevsky even planned to write a *Russian Candide*).

We should recall the enormous significance for Dostoevsky of the *dialogical culture* of Voltaire and Diderot, which can be traced back to the "Socratic dialog," the antique menippea, and—in part—to the diatribe and the soliloquy.

Another type of free menippea, which included fantastic and fairytale elements, was represented in the work of Hoffmann, who exercised a significant influence already on the early Dostoevsky. The tales of Edgar Allen Poe, the essence of which was close to that of the menippea, also attracted Dostoevsky's attention. In his article *"Tri rasskaza Edgara Poe"* ("Three Tales of Edgar Poe") Dostoevsky quite correctly noted the kinship of that writer with himself:

> He almost always chooses the most extraordinary reality and *places his hero in the most extraordinary external and psychological situation,* and with what penetrating power, what amazing accuracy does he relate the state of that person's soul![102]

True, in this definition only one aspect of the menippea is singled out— the creation of an extraordinary plot situation, i.e. a provocative anacrisis, but it was precisely this aspect which Dostoevsky constantly singled out as the chief distinguishing characteristic of his own creative method.

Our survey (by no means a complete one) of Dostoevsky's genre sources shows that he knew, or could have known, diverse variants of the menippea, a genre of great plasticity, rich in possibilities and extraordinarily well suited to penetrate "the depths of the human soul" and to keenly and nakedly state the "ultimate questions."

On the basis of the story "Bobok" it can be shown to what degree the essence of the menippea genre was in accord with all of Dostoevsky's basic artistic aspirations. In so far as genre is concerned, this story is one of his key works.

We shall turn out attention first of all to the following. Little "Bobok," one of Dostoevsky's shortest stories, is nearly a microcosm of his entire work. Very many of the most important ideas, themes and images of his works—both preceeding and subsequent ones—appear here in a keen and naked form: the idea that "all is permitted" *("vse pozvoleno")* if there is no God and no immortality of the soul (one of the leading idea-images in his work); the related theme of confesssion without remorse and of "shameless truthfulness," which runs through all of Dostoevsky's works, beginning with *Notes from the Underground*; the theme of the final moments of consciousness (which is in other works related to the themes of capital punishment and suicide); the theme of a consciousness on the brink of insanity; the theme of sensuality which penetrates the loftiest spheres of consciousness and thought; the theme of the total "impropriety" and "unseemliness" of life cut off from its folk roots and faith, etc.—all of these themes and

[119]

ideas are contained in an intense and naked form within the seemingly narrow confines of this story.

The story's leading images (true, they are not many) are in keeping with the other images in Dostoevsky's works: Klinevich is a simplified, intensified repetition of Prince Valkovsky, Svidrigailov and Fyodor Karamazov; the narrator ("a certain person") is a variant of the "underground man;" we are also acquainted to a certain degree with General Pervoedov,[103] with the voluptuous elderly official who has squandered a huge sum of public funds intended for "widows and orphans," with the sycophant Lebezyatnikov, and with the engineer and believer in progress who wants to "organize life here on a rational basis."

"Simpleman" ("prostoliudin," a well-to-do shop-keeper) occupies a special place among the corpses; he alone has preserved his bond with the folk and its faith, and for that reason he conducts himself properly even in the grave, he accepts death as a sacrament, interprets the goings-on around him (among the licentious corpses) as the "visitation of trials and tribulations upon their souls," and impatiently awaits the "sorokoviny"[104] ("May our forty days pass quickly, then I shall hear their tearful voices weeping o'er me, my spouse's wail, my children's soft lament!..."). This simpleman's seemliness and his most reverential tone, which are counterposed to the impropriety and familiar cynicism of everyone else (both living and dead), anticipate in part the image of the pilgrim Makar Dolgoruky, although here, under the conditions of the menippea, the "seemly" simpleman is presented with a slight nuance of comicality and appears somewhat irrelevant.

Moreover, the carnivalized nether world of "Bobok" is *internally* quite in keeping with the scandalous scenes and catastrophes which have such an essential significance in almost all of Dostoevsky's works. Such scenes, which usually take place in drawing rooms, are, of course, much more complex and colorful, full of carnivalized contrasts, sharp mésalliances and eccentricities, and essential crownings and discrownings, but their inner essence is analagous: the "rotten strings" of the official and personal lie are snapped (or at the least weakened for a moment), and human souls, terrible ones, as in the nether world, or, on the contrary, bright and pure ones, are laid bare. People appear for a moment outside the normal situations of life, as on the carnival square or in the nether world, and a different—more genuine—sense of themselves and of their relationships one to another is revealed.

Such, for example, is the famous scene of Nastasya Filippovna's nameday party *(The Idiot)*. Here there are also external similarities with "Bobok": Ferdyshchenko (a petty mystery-play devil) proposes a *petit-joue*—everyone will tell the most wicked act of his whole life (compare this with Klinevich's proposal: "We shall all tell our life's stories aloud, and we'll not be ashamed of anything"). True, the stories which are told do not justify Ferdyshchenko's expectations, but this *petit-joue* helps to create the carnival-square atmosphere in which sharp carnivalistic changes in the people's fates and miens occur, cynical calculations are exposed, and Nastasya Filippovna's familiar, debasing speech takes on the sound of the public square. Here we shall not, of course, deal with the profound moral-psychological and social meaning of this scene—we are interested in the aspect of genre itself, in the *carnival overtones* which are felt in almost every image and every word (their realism and motivatedness notwithstanding), and in that second level of the carnival square (and of the carnivalized nether world) which, as it were, shows through the realistic fabric of this scene.

I shall mention also the sharply carnivalized scene of scandals and discrownings at Marmeladov's funeral feast (in *Crime and Punishment*). Or the even more complicated scene in Varvara Petrovna Stavrogina's grand drawing room in *The Devils*, in which the mad "lame girl" *("xromonozhka")* participates, her brother Lebyadkin takes part, the "devil" Petr Verkhovensky appears for the first time, Varvara Petrovna's perfervid eccentricity is seen, Stepan Trofimovich is exposed and banished, Liza becomes hysterical and falls unconscious, Shatov slaps Stavrogin in the face, etc. Everything here is unexpected, out of place, incompatible and inadmissable in the usual, "normal" course of life. It is completely impossible to imagine such a scene in, for example, a novel of L. Tolstoy or Turgenev. This is no grand drawing room, it is the public square. Finally, I would recall the extraordinarily vivid carnivalistic-menippeic color of the scandalous scene in the Elder Zosima's cell *(The Brothers Karamazov)*.

These scandalous scenes—and they occupy a very important place in Dostoevsky's works—almost always met with negative criticism from contemporaries,[105] and continue to do so today. They seemed and seem improbable in terms of real life and unjustified in artistic terms. They were often attributed to the author's predilection for purely external, false effects. In reality, these scenes are in both the spirit and the style of Dostoevsky's entire work. And they are deeply organic, there is nothing invented in them: as a whole, as well as in their *every detail,* they are determined by the consistent artistic logic of those carnival performances and categories which we have characterized above and which over the centuries were absorbed into the carnivalized line in the development of artistic prose. At their basis lies the profound carnival attitude to the world, which unites and makes sense of all that seems absurd and unexpected in these scenes and creates their artistic truth.

Because of its *fantastical* plot "Bobok" presents this carnival logic in a somewhat simplified (the genre required simplification), but sharp and naked form, and therefore can serve as a commentary on the more complicated but analagous phenomena in Dostoevsky's works.

In the story "Bobok" rays leading from Dostoevsky's preceeding works and to his succeeding ones come to a focus. "Bobok" was able to become this focal point precisely because it is a menippea. All aspects of Dostoevsky's creative work feel at home here. As we see, the narrow confines of this story proved to be very capacious.

We would recall that the menippea is the *universal* genre of *ultimate questions.* In it action takes place not only "here" and "now," but in the whole world and in all eternity: on earth, in the nether world, and in heaven. In

Dostoevsky the menippea converges with the mystery play. The mystery play is, after all, nothing more than a modified medieval dramatic variant of the menippea. In Dostoevsky the participants in the performance stand *on the threshold* (the threshold of life and death, truth and falsehood, sanity and insanity). And they are presented as *voices* which ring out "before heaven and earth." The central figurative idea here is also in the spirit of the mystery play (the Eleusinian mystery play): "today's corpses"—unfruitful seed, cast on the ground, but capable neither of dying (i.e. of cleansing itself of itself, of rising above itself), nor of being born anew (i.e. of bearing fruit).

■

The second key work, in so far as genre is concerned, is "The Dream of a Ridiculous Man" (1877).

This work is also traceable by the essence of its genre to the menippea, though to other of the menippea's variants: to the "dream satire" and to "fantastic journeys" with utopian elements. These two variants are often combined in the subsequent development of the menippea.

As we have said, it was via the "Menippean satire" (and in general via the realm of the serio-comical) that the element of dream was first given a special (non-epical) interpretation in European literature. In the epopee the dream did not destroy the unity of the represented world and did not create a second plane; not did it destroy the *simple* integrity of the hero's image. The dream is not counterposed to normal life as *another* possible life. Such a contraposition (from one or another viewpoint) appears for the first time in the menippea. In the menippea dream is introduced precisely as the *possibility* of a completely different life, organized according to different laws than normal life (sometimes as an "inside-out world"). Life seen in a dream makes normal life seem strange, forcing the dreamer to comprehend and evaluate it in a new way (in light of the other possibility seen in the dream). The person who dreams becomes a different person, he reveals in himself new possibilities (both worse ones and better ones), he tests and corrects himself by means of the dream. Sometimes the dream is constructed directly as a crowning and discrowning of the person and of life.

Thus there is created in the dream an *extraordinary situation* which is impossible in normal life and which serves the same basic goal of the menippea: to test the idea and the man of the idea.

The menippeic tradition of the artistic utilization of the dream continues to live in the subsequent development of European literature in diverse variants and with diverse nuances: in the "dream visions" of medieval literature, in the grotesque satires of the 16th and 17th centuries (especially vividly in Quevedo and Grimmelshausen), in its fairytale-symbolic application by the Romantics (including Heinrich Heine's distinctive dream lyrics), in the psychological and social-utopian application in realistic novels (George Sand, Chernyshevsky). It is especially imperative to take note of the important variation known as *crisis dreams* which lead the person to rebirth and renewal (the crisis variation of the dream was employed in dramaturgy as well: by Shakespeare, Calderon, and, in the 19th century, by Grillparzer).

Dostoevsky made wise use of the artistic possibilities of the dream in almost all of its variations and nuances. There is surely no other writer in all of European literature in whose works dreams play such a large and essential role. We recall the dreams of Raskolnikov, Svidrigailov, Myshkin, Ippolit, the raw youth, Versilov, Alyosha and Dmitry Karamazov, and the role which they play in the realization of the ideological plan of the respective novels. The crisis variation of the dream predominates in Dostoevsky. The dream of the "ridiculous man" belongs to this type.

As for the "fantastic journey" variety used in "The Dream of a Ridiculous Man," Dostoevsky may have been acquainted with Cyrano de Bergerac's work *Histoire comique des états et empires de la Lune* (1647-1650). This work describes an earthly paradise on the moon, from which the narrator has been banished for being disrespectful. He is accompanied on his journey about the moon by the "demon of Socrates," which allows the author to introduce a philosophical element (in the spirit of Gassendi's materialism). Judged by its external form, de Bergerac's work is a complete philosophico-fantastical novel.

Also interesting is Grimmelshausen's menippea *Der fliegende Wandersmann nach dem Monde* (c. 1659), which was taken from the same source as Cyrano de Bergerac's book. Here the utopian element occupies first place. The extraordinary purity and honesty of the moon's inhabitants is depicted; they know no vices, crimes or untruthfulness, it is always spring in their land, they live long lives, and they greet death with a merry feast within a circle of friends. Children born with evil tendencies are sent off to Earth so that they cannot corrupt lunar society. The exact date of the hero's arrival on the moon is given (just as Dostoevsky gives the date of the ridiculous man's dream).

Dostoevsky was also undoubtedly familiar with Voltaire's menippea *Micromégas,* which lies in the same fantastical line of the menippea's development (the bestrangement of earthly reality).

In "The Dream of a Ridiculous Man" we are first of all struck by the work's extreme universalism and at the same time by its extreme terseness and its amazing artistic and philosophical laconicism. There is no involved discursive argumentation in it whatever. Dostoevsky's extraordinary ability (discussed in the preceeding chapter) to artistically *see and feel an idea* is very clearly manifested here. We have before us a genuine *artist of the idea.*

"The Dream of a Ridiculous Man" gives a complete and profound synthesis of the universalism of the menippea, as a genre of ultimate philosophical questions, with the universalism of the medieval mystery play, which depicted the fate of the human race: paradise on earth, fall into sin, redemption. "The Dream of a Ridiculous Man" clearly reveals the inner kinship of these two genres, which are, of course, also bound by an historical-genetic kinship. But in so far as genre is concerned, the antique type of menippea predominates here. In general,

[123]

it is not the Christian, but the antique spirit which prevails in "The Dream of a Ridiculous Man."

From the point of view of style and composition "The Dream" differs rather signficantly from "Bobok": it contains essential elements of the diatribe, the confession and the sermon. Such a complex of genres is characteristic of Dostoevsky's work in general.

The central part of the work is the tale of a dream vision. We are given a marvelous characterization, as it were, of the compositional peculiarity of the dream:

> "...It all happened as it always does in a dream, when you *leap over space and time, over the laws of existence and reason, stopping* only on those *points which cause your heart to dream.*" (X, 429)

This is in essence a completely accurate characterization of the compositional method of the construction of the fantastic menippea. Moreover, this characterization can, with certain limitations and reservations, be applied to Dostoevsky's whole creative method. In his works Dostoevsky makes almost no use of relatively uninterrupted historical and biographical time, i.e. of strictly epical time; he "leaps" over it, concentrating action in *crisis points, turning points and catastrophes,* when the inner significance of the moment is equal to a "billion years," i.e. when the moment loses its temporal limitation. He also leaps over space, concentrating action in only two "points": *on the threshold* (in doorways, in entrances, on the stairs, in corridors, etc.), where crises and turning points occur, and on the *square,* or its substitute, the drawing room (reception room or dining room), where catastrophes and scandals occur. Precisely this is his artistic conception of time and space. He also often leaps over elementary empirical verisimilitude and superficial rational logic. That is why the menippea's genre is so congenial to him.

Also characteristic of Dostoevsky's creative method, as artist of the idea, are the "ridiculous man's" words:

> "...I have seen the truth—it is not as if I had invented it with my reason, I saw it, I saw it, and its **living image** has filled my soul for all time." (X, 440)

The themes of "The Dream" are almost an encyclopedia of all of Dostoevsky's leading themes, and at the same time all of these themes and the means of their artistic elaboration are quite characteristic of the carnivalized genre of the menippea. We shall pay special attention to several of them.

1. Clearly detectable in the central figure of the "ridiculous man" is the *ambivalent*—serio-comic—image of the "wise fool" and the "tragic clown" of carnivalized literature. But such ambivalence, although usually in a more subdued form, is characteristic of all of Dostoevsky's heroes. One might say that Dost-

oevsky's artistic sense could not imagine a human being of any significance without certain elements of eccentricity (in its diverse variants). This is most vividly seen in the image of Myshkin. But in all the rest of Dostoevsky's leading heroes—in Raskolnikov, Stavrogin, Versilov, Ivan Karamazov—there is always "something funny," although in a more or less reduced form.

We repeat, Dostoevsky, as an artist, could not imagine *singletoned (odnotonnaia)* human significance. In the preface to *The Brothers Karamazov* ("From the Author") he even asserts the *historical* importance of eccentricity:

"For the eccentric is not only 'not always' an exception and an isolated case, but on the contrary, it often happens that precisely he is the one who carries within himself the *marrow of the whole,* and the rest of the people of his time are all for some reason cut off from him for a time by some transitory wind..." (IX, 9)

In the image of the "ridiculous man" this ambivalence in keeping with the spirit of the menippea is revealed and emphasized.

The *fullness* of the "ridiculous man's" *consciousness* is also characteristic of Dostoevsky: he himself knows better than anyone that he is ridiculous ("...if there was a person on earth who knew better than anyone else that I was ridiculous, it was I myself..."). When he begins his preaching of *paradise* on earth, he knows very well that it is unattainable: "And what is more, so what, so what if it never comes true and there will never be a paradise (I understand that already!)—I'll go on preaching it anyway." (X, 441) This is an eccentric who keenly comprehends both himself and everything else; there is not a grain of naiveté in him; it is impossible to finalize him (for there is nothing which escapes his consciousness).

2. The story opens with the theme, typical for the menippea, of a person who *alone* knows the truth, and is therefore ridiculed by everyone else as a madman. Here is that brilliant opening:

"I am a ridiculous person. They call me a madman now. That would be a promotion in rank for me if I were no longer so ridiculous for them as I was before. But now I am not angry any more, now they are all dear to me, even when they laugh at me—then they are even somehow especially dear. I would laugh along with them—not at myself, but out of love for them—if it weren't so sad when I look at them. I am sad because they do not know the truth, and I know it. Oh, how difficult it is for one person alone to know the truth! But they will never understand that. No, they will never understand." (X, 420)

This is the typical position of the wise man in the menippea (Diogenes, Menippus, or Democritus in the "Novel of Hippocrates"), the carrier of truth, in relation to all others, for whom the truth is insanity or stupidity; but in "The

[125]

Dream" this position is deeper and more complex than in the antique menippea. But at the same time this position—in different variants and with deverse nuances— is characteristic of all of Dostoevsky's leading heroes, from Raskolnikov to Ivan Karamazov: being possessed by their "truth" determines their attitude to other people and creates the special sort of loneliness of these heroes.

3. The theme of absolute indifference to everything in the world, typical of the menippea of the Cynics and the Stoics, appears further on in the story:

> "...there grew in my soul a terrible melancholy because of a certain circumstance which was already infinitely greater than my whole self: it was, namely, the conviction which had taken hold of me that **nothing** anywhere in the world **matters.** I had had such a presentiment for a long time, but the complete conviction appeared somehow suddenly in the last year. I suddenly felt that it **would not matter** to me if the world existed or if there were nothing anywhere. I began to sense and to feel with my whole being that I **was all alone."** (X, 421)

This universal indifference and premonition of nonexistence leads the "ridiculous man" to the thought of suicide. We have before us one of Dostoevsky's many variations on the theme of Kirillov.

4. Then follows the theme of the last hours of life before suicide (one of Dostoevsky's leading themes). In keeping with the spirit of the menippea, this theme is here laid bare and intensified.

After the "ridiculous man" makes the final decision to kill himself, he meets in the street a little girl who begs him to help her. The "ridiculous man" rudely shoves her away, because he feels that he is already outside all the norms and obligations of human life (like the corpses in "Bobok"). Here are his reflections.

> "But if, for example, I'm going to kill myself in two hours, then what do I care about this little girl, and what does shame or anything else in the world have to do with me!...I began to stamp my feet and to scream like a wild man at the poor child because, I thought, 'not only do I feel no remorse, but even if I commit some inhumanly base act, I can do so now because in two hours all will be over with.' "

This moral speculation, typical of the menippea, is no less typical of Dostoevsky's works. The "ridiculous man's" reflections continue thus:

> "For example, a strange thought suddenly occurred to me: if I had lived sometime before on the moon or on Mars and had committed there the most shameful and dishonorable act imaginable, and had been debased and disgraced for it in such a way as could be imagined only in a dream or in a nightmare, and if I then turned up on earth, but continued to be aware of what I had done on the other planet, and if I knew that I would never for

any reason have to return there, would it, as I stood on the earth looking at the moon, **matter** to me or not? Would I be ashamed of that act or not?" (X, 425-426)

Stavrogin, in his discussion with Kirillov, asks himself a quite analagous speculative question about an act committed on the moon (VII, 250). This is all familiar to us as the problem of Ippolit *(The Idiot)*, of Kirillov *(The Devils)*, and of the shamelessness in the grave in "Bobok." Moreover, these are all simply various facets of one of the leading themes of all of Dostoevsky's works, the theme "all is permitted" (in a world where God and the immortality of the soul do not exist), and the related theme of ethical solipsism.

5. Further on the central (or genre-determining) *theme of the crisis dream* is developed; more precisely, it is the theme of a man's rebirth and renewal through a dream which permits him to *see* "with his own eyes" the possibility of a completely different human life on earth.

"Yes, that dream came to me then, my third-of-November dream! They make fun of me now by saying that it was just a dream. But isn't it all the same if it was a dream or not, as long as that dream revealed the truth to me? For if you've once found out the truth and seen it, then you know that it's the truth and that there is and can be no other, whether you're asleep or awake. Well, so it's a dream, so what, but this life which you so exalt I wanted to extinguish by suicide, and then my dream, my dream—oh, it revealed to me a new, a great, a renewed, a mighty life!" (X, 427)

6. In the "dream" itself the utopian theme of heaven on earth which the "ridiculous man" has seen with his own eyes and experienced on a distant, unknown star is developed in detail. The description of heaven on earth is carried through in the spirit of the antique Golden Age, and is therefore thoroughly permeated with the carnival attitude to the world. The depiction of heaven on earth is in many ways reminiscent of Versilov's dream in *A Raw Youth*. The "ridiculous man's" purely carnivalistic faith in the unity of mankind's aspirations and in the goodness of human nature is quite characteristic:

"And besides, everyone is on his way to the same goal, or at least everyone is striving for the same goal, *from the wise man down to the worst brigand;* it's just that they are on different paths. That is a venerable verity, but here is something new: I cannot much go astray. Because *I have seen the truth, I have seen* and I know that people can be beautiful and happy, and still be capable of living on earth. I cannot and do not want to believe that evil is the normal condition of man." (X, 440)

We emphasize again that truth, according to Dostoevsky, can only be the object of a living vision, not of an abstract comprehension.

[127]

7. At the end of the story the theme, very characteristic for Dostoevsky, of the *instantaneous* transformation of life into paradise is brought in (it is most profoundly to be seen in *The Brothers Karamazov*):

"And besides, it is so simple: in a single day, **in a single hour**—everything would immediately be worked out! The main thing is—love your neighbor as yourself, that's the main thing, and that's all there is to it, nothing else is necessary: you will see at once how it will all work out." (X, 441)

8. We shall also note the theme of the mistreated little girl which is found in a series of Dostoevsky's works: we meet it in *The Insulted and the Injured* (Nellie), in Svidrigailov's dream before his suicide, in "Stavrogin's Confession," in *The Eternal Husband* (Liza); the theme of the suffering child is one of the leading themes of *The Brothers Karamazov* (the images of suffering children in the chapter "Rebellion," the image of Ilyushechka, "the child is crying" in Dmitry's dream).

9. There are also elements of underworld naturalism here: the debauched captain who begs on the Nevsky (we are familiar with this image from *The Idiot* and *A Raw Youth*), drunkenness, a card game and a fight in the room next to the closet where the "ridiculous man" spent his sleepless nights in a Voltairean armchair, absorbed in solving ultimate questions, and where he has his dream of the fate of mankind.

We have, of course, not exhausted all the themes of "The Dream of a Ridiculous Man," but this suffices to demonstrate the enormous ideological capaciousness of this variety of the menippea and its adaptability to Dostoevsky's themes.

No actual dialogs take place in "The Dream of a Ridiculous Man" (except for the half-expressed dialog with the "unknown being"), but the narrator's entire speech is permeated by interior dialog: all of his words are directed to himself, to the universe, to his creator,[106] to all people. And here, as in the mystery play, the word rings out before heaven and earth, i.e. before the entire world.

These are the two key works of Dostoevsky which most clearly reveal the essence of his works' genre, which gravitates toward the menippea and the genres related to it.

We have analyzed "Bobok" and "The Dream of a Ridiculous Man" from the point of view of the historical poetics of genre. We were primarily interested in how the essence of the menippea's genre is manifested in these works. But at the same time we have tried to show how the traditional characteristics of the genre are organically combined with their unique and profound application in Dostoevsky.

■

We shall touch on several other of his works which are also, by their nature, close to the menippea, but are of a somewhat different type and lack the directly fantastic element.

Such a story is "A Gentle Creature" ("*Krotkaia*"). Here the cutting thematic anacrisis, sharp contrasts, mésalliances and moral experiments characteristic of the genre are formulated as a soliloquy. The story's hero says of himself: "I am a master at speaking without uttering a word, I have talked my whole life through without uttering a word and I have lived through entire tragedies by myself without uttering a word." The hero's image is revealed through his dialogical attitude toward himself. And he remains almost to the end by himself in utter loneliness and hopeless despair. He acknowledges no higher judgement above himself. He generalizes his loneliness and universalizes it as the ultimate loneliness of the whole human race:

> "Stagnation! Oh, nature! *Man is alone on earth—that is the misfortune!* Everything dead and dead men everywhere. Nothing there but people, and all around them—silence. This is the earth!"

Notes from the Underground (1864) is also in essence akin to this type of the menippea. It is constructed as a diatribe (a conversation with an interlocutor who is absent), it is saturated with both open and hidden polemics, and it contains the essential elements of the confession. In the second part a story with a cutting anacrisis is introduced. In *Notes from the Underground* we also find other familiar aspects of the menippea: cutting dialogical syncrises, familiarization and profanation, underworld naturalism, etc. This work too is characterized by extraordinary ideological capaciousness: almost all of the themes and ideas of Dostoevsky's subsequent works are outlined here in simplified and denuded form. We shall concentrate on the verbal style of this work in the following chapter.

We shall touch upon one more of Dostoevsky's works, one with a very characteristic title—"A Vile Tale" ("*Skvernyi anekdot,*"1861). This *thoroughly carnivalized* story is also akin to the menippea (of the Varronian type). An argument among three generals at a name-day party serves as the plot's ideological nodus. Afterward the story's hero (one of the three generals), as a test of his liberal-humanistic ideas, goes to the wedding celebration of one of his lowliest subordinates where, out of inexperience (he is not a drinking man), he becomes intoxicated. Everything is built on the extreme *inappropriateness and scandalousness* of all that occurs. Everything is full of sharp carnivalistic contrasts, mésalliances, ambivalence, debasement and discrowning. There is also the element of rather cruel moral experimentation. We shall not here touch upon the profound social-philosophical idea which is present in this work and which is not yet fully appreciated. The story has an intentionally uneven, ambiguous and mocking tone and is permeated by elements of hidden social-political and literary polemic.

There are elements of the menippea in all of Dostoevsky's early works (i.e. those written before his exile, largely under the influence of the genre tradition of Gogol and Hoffmann).

As we have said, the menippea takes root in Dostoevsky's novels as well. We shall cite only the most relevant instances (without particular argumentation).

In *Crime and Punishment* the famous scene of Raskolnikov's first visit to

Sonya (where the Gospels are read) is an almost perfect Christianized menippea: it has cutting dialogical syncrises (faith versus lack of faith, meekness versus pride), a cutting anacrisis, oxymoronic combinations (the thinker and the criminal, the prostitute and the righteous woman), the naked statement of ultimate questions, and the reading of the Gospels in an underworld setting. Raskolnikov's dream and the dream of Svidrigailov before his suicide are also menippea.

In *The Idiot* Ippolit's confession ("my necessary explanation") is a menippea framed by the carnivalized scene of the dialog on Prince Myshkin's terrace and ending with Ippolit's attempted suicide. In *The Devils* it is Stavrogin's confession together with the accompanying dialog between Stavrogin and Tikhon. In *A Raw Youth* it is Versilov's dream.

In *The Brothers Karamazov* the conversation between Ivan and Alyosha in the "Capital City" tavern on the market square of the remote provincial town is a wonderful menippea. The monk and the atheist solve ultimate universal questions to the sounds of the tavern organ, the clack of billiard balls and the uncorking of beer bottles. Into this "Menippean satire" a second satire is inserted—"The Legend of the Grand Inquisitor," which has its own independent meaning and is constructed on the New Testament syncrisis of Christ and the devil.107 Both of these interconnected "Menippean satires" belong to the most profound artistic-philosophical works of world literature. Finally, Ivan Karamazov's conversation with the devil (the chapter "The Devil. Ivan Fedorovich's Nightmare") is an equally profound menippea.

Of course all of these menippea are subordinated to the polyphonic plan of the whole of the novel which contains them, they are determined by it and are inseparable from it.

But aside from these relatively independent and relatively complete menippea, all of Dostoevsky's novels are permeated by elements of the menippea and of related genres—the "Socratic dialog," the diatribe, the soliloquy, the confession, etc. It goes without saying that all of these genres came down to Dostoevsky through two millenia of intensive development, but despite all of the changes which occurred, they retained their generic essence. Cutting dialogical syncrises, extraordinary and provocative plot situations, crises and turning points, moral experimentation, catastrophes and scandals, contrasting and oxymoronic combinations, etc., determine the entire compositional structure of the plots of Dostoevsky's novels.

Without a further, thoroughgoing study of the essence of the menippea and the other related genres, and also of the history of these genres and their manifold variations in modern literatures, a correct historico-genetic explanation of the genre characteristics of Dostoevsky's works (and not only of Dostoevsky's; the problem has a much broader significance) is impossible.

■

In analyzing the genre characteristics of the menippea in Dostoevsky's works we simultaneously revealed the elements of carnivalization in them. And that is quite understandable, since the menippea is a thoroughly carnivalized genre. But the phenomenon of carnivalization in Dostoevsky's works is, of course, not limited to the menippea; it has yet other genre sources, and therefore requires special attention.

It is difficult to say that carnival and its later derivatives (the masquerade line of development, or the farcical street comedy) exercised a fundamental, direct influence on Dostoevsky (although there were certainly experiences of a carnival type in his life).[108] Carnivalization influenced him, as it did the majority of other writers of the 18th and 19th centuries, primarily as a tradition of literary genre whose extra-literary source, i.e. carnival proper, he did not, perhaps, even clearly perceive.

But carnival, its forms and symbols, and above all the carnival attitude itself over many centuries seeped into numerous literary genres, merged with their characteristics, formed them, and became inseparable from them. Carnival, as it were, was reincarnated in literature, in a definite and vigorous line of its development. The carnival forms, transposed into the language of literature became *powerful means* of artistically comprehending life, they became a special language, the words and forms of which possess an extraordinary capacity for *symbolic* generalization, i.e. for *generalization in depth.* Many of the essential sides, or, more precisely, strata, of life, and profound ones at that, can be discovered, comprehended and expressed only with the help of this language.

In order to master this language, i.e. in order to assimilate the carnival tradition of literary genre, the writer need not know all the links and brances of that tradition. Genre possesses its own organic logic which can be to a certain extent understood and creatively mastered on the basis of a few models, or even fragments. *But the logic of genre is not an abstract logic.* Every new variety and every new work in a given genre always in some way enriches it and adds to the perfection of the genre's language. For this reason it is important to know the possible genre sources of a given author and the literary atmosphere in which his work was created. The fuller and more concrete our knowledge of an artist's *genre contacts,* the more profound will be our penetration into the characteristics of his form and the correcter our understanding of the interrelationships of tradition and innovation within that form.

The fact that we have touched upon questions of *historical* poetics obligates us to characterize at least those basic links of the carnival tradition of genre with which Dostoevsky was directly or obliquely connected and which determined the atmosphere of his works' genre, an atmosphere which is in many ways essentially different from that of Turgenev's, Goncharov's or L. Tolstoy's works.

The writers of the Renaissance—above all Boccaccio, Rabelais, Shakespeare, Cervantes and Grimmelshausen—became the chief sources of carnivalization for the literature of the 17th, 18th and 19th centuries.[109] The early picaresque novel (which was directly carnivalized) also became such a source. In addition, of course, the carnivalized literature of antiquity (including the "Menippean satire") and the

Middle Ages was also a source of carnivalization for those writers.

All of the basic sources of the carnivalization of European literature that we have named, with the possible exception of Grimmelshausen and the early picaresque novel, were very well known to Dostoevsky. But he was familiar with the characteristics of the picaresque novel through Lesage's *Gil Blas*, and it attracted his intense interest. It depicted life drawn out of its usual and, so to speak, legitimized rut, it debunked all of people's hierarchical positions, played with those positions, was filled with sudden changes, about-faces and mystifications, and perceived the entire world which it represented in the zone of familiar contact. As far as Renaissance literature is concerned, its direct influence on Dostoevsky was considerable (especially that of Shakespeare and Cervantes). We are speaking not of the influence of individual themes, ideas or images, but of the more profound influence of the *carnival attitude itself*, i.e. of the very *forms* of seeing the world and man and of the truly *divine freedom* of approach to them which is manifested not in individual thoughts, images and external structural devices, but in the creative work of these writers *as a whole.*

For Dostoevsky's mastery of the carnival tradition, the literature of the 18th century was of essential importance; primary were Voltaire and Diderot, for whom the combination of carnivalization with a high dialogical culture based on antiquity and on the dialogs of the Renaissance was characteristic. Here Dostoevsky found the organic combination of carnivalization with rationalistic philosophical ideas and, in part, with social themes.

Dostoevsky found the combination of carnivalization with the adventure plot and with burning current social themes in the social-adventure novels of the 19th century, mainly in Frédéric Soulié and Eugène Sue (and in part in Dumas fils and Paul de Kock). In these writers' works carnivalization has a more external character: it is manifested in the plot, in external carnivalistic antitheses and contrasts, in sudden turns of fate, mystifications, etc. The profound and free carnival attitude is almost totally absent here. The most important element in these novels was the application of carnivalization to the representation of contemporary reality and contemporary existence; *existence* was drawn into the carnivalized action of the plot, and the ordinary and constant were combined with the extraordinary and changeable.

Dostoevsky found a more profound assimilation of the carnival tradition in Balzac, George Sand and Victor Hugo. They display many fewer external manifestations of carnivalization, but have, on the other hand, a more profound carnival attitude toward the world and, most importantly, in their works carnivalization penetrates the very structure of great and mighty characters and the development of passions. The carnivalization of passion is manifested above all in its ambivalence: love combines with hatred, avarice with selflessness, love of power with self-depreciation, etc.

Dostoevsky found the combination of carnivalization and the sentimental perception of life in Sterne and Dickens.

Finally, Dostoevsky found the combination of carnivalization and the romantic idea (but not of the rationalistic type, as in Voltaire and Diderot) in Edgar Poe and especially in Hoffmann.

The Russian tradition occupies a particular place. Besides Gogol, it is imperative to point out the enormous influence exercised on Dostoevsky by the most carnivalized of Pushkin's works: *Boris Godunov,* the *Tales of Belkin,* "The Little Tragedies," and *The Queen of Spades.*

Our brief survey of the sources of carnivalization does not pretend to completeness. We sought only to trace the basic lines of the tradition. We emphasize again that we are not interested in the influence of individual authors, works, themes, ideas or images—we are interested rather in the influence of the *genre tradition itself,* which was transmitted through the given authors. The tradition is reborn and renewed in each of them in its own unique way. It is in this that the tradition lives. To use a simile, we are interested in the word of *language,* not in its *individual usage* in a particular *unique context,* although, of course, the one does not exist without the other. It is, naturally, possible to study the individual influences, i.e. the influence of one individual author upon another, the influence of Balzac on Dostoevsky, for example, but that is a special task which we have not set for ourselves here. We are interested only in the tradition itself.

In Dostoevsky's work the carnival tradition is, of course, also reborn in a new way: it takes on meaning in its own way, combines with other artistic elements, and serves its own particular artistic goals, those goals which we have sought to reveal in the preceeding chapters. Carnivalization is organically combined with all the other characteristics of the polyphonic novel.

Before moving on to an analysis of the elements of carnivalization in Dostoevsky (we shall concentrate on only a few works), we must first touch upon two questions.

For a correct understanding of the problems of carnivalization, a simplified conception of carnival in the spirit of the *masquerade* line of development of modern times must be avoided, and a trivially vulgar bohemian conception all the more so. Carnival is an eminent attitude toward the world which belonged to the *entire folk (velikoe vsenarodnoe mirooshchushchenie)* in bygone millenia. It is an attitude toward the world which liberates from fear, brings the world close to man and man close to his fellow man (all is drawn into the zone of liberated familiar contact), and, with its joy of change and its jolly relativity, counteracts the gloomy, one-sided official seriousness which is born of fear, is dogmatic and inimical to evolution and change, and seeks to absolutize the given conditions of existence and the social order. The carnival attitude liberated man from precisely this sort of seriousness. But there is not a grain of nihilism in carnival, nor, of course, a grain of shallow frivolity or trivially vulgar bohemian individualism.

The narrow theatrical-pageant conception of carnival, so characteristic of modern times, must also be avoided.

To correctly understand carnival one must take it at its *sources* and at its *heights,* i.e. in the form in which it found itself in antiquity, in the Middle Ages, and, finally, in the Renaissance.[110]

[133]

The second question concerns literary movements. Having once penetrated and, to a degree, defined the structure of a genre, carnivalization can be employed by various movements and creative methods. It is inadmissable to see in it only the specific characteristic of Romanticism. Every movement and creative method interprets and renews it in its own way. To convince oneself of this it is sufficient to compare carnivalization in Voltaire (realism of the Enlightenment), the early Tieck (Romanticism), Balzac (critical realism) and Ponson du Terrail (pure adventure). The degree of carnivalization in each of the authors named is almost the same, but in each case it is subordinated to special artistic tasks (connected with the given literary movement), and therefore it "sounds" differently (we are not speaking now of the individual characteristics of each of these authors). At the same time, the presence of carnivalization defines them as belonging to one and the same tradition of *genre* and creates, from the point of view of poetics, a very *fundamental commonality* among them (we repeat, despite all the differences in direction, individualism and artistic value among them).

■

In "Petersburg Dreams in Verse and Prose" (1861) Dostoevsky recalls the unique and vivid carnival feeling for life which he experienced at the very beginning of his artistic career. It was above all a special feeling for Petersburg, with all its sharp social contrasts, as a "fantastical magical vision," as a "dream," as something standing on the brink of reality and fantastical invention. An analagous, though less powerful and profound carnival feeling for a large city (Paris) can be found in Balzac, Sue, Soulié, and others, but the sources of this tradition reach back to the antique menippea (Varro, Lucian). Further on, on the basis of this feeling for the city and its throngs, Dostoevsky gives a sharply carnivalized picture of the coming into being of his first literary plans, including the plan of *Poor Folk*:

> And I began to look around, and suddenly I saw some strange faces. They were all strange, queer, totally prosaic figures, not a Don Carlos or a Posa among them, just titular counsellors, but at the same time they seemed somehow to be fantastical titular counsellors. Someone *grimaced* at me, hiding behind this whole *fantastical throng,* and *jerked at some strings and springs,* and these *dolls* moved, and he laughed, and *they all laughed!* And then another story came to me, in some dark corners some titular heart, honest and pure, moral and loyal to its superiors, and along with it some little girl, mistreated and melancholy, and their whole story rent my heart deeply. And if one could gather together that whole throng which I dreamed of then, it would make a marvelous *masquerade...* 111

Thus, according to these reminiscences of Dostoevsky, his art was born of a vivid carnivalistic vision of life ("I call the feeling I had on the Neva a vision," says Dostoevsky). Here we have the characteristic accessories of a carnival complex:

laughter and tragedy, a clown, a farcical street comedy *(balagan),* and a crowd of masqueraders. But the main thing here, of course, is the carnival attitude itself, which profoundly permeates "Petersburg Dreams." By the essence of its genre, this work is a variety of carnivalized menippea. The carnival *laughter* which accompanies the vision should be emphasized. We shall in due course see that in fact Dostoevsky's entire work is permeated by this laughter, though in a reduced form.

We shall not concentrate on the carnivalization in Dostoevsky's early works. We shall examine the elements of carnivalization only in several individual works published after his exile. We are setting ourselves a limited task here: to prove the presence of carnivalization and to reveal its basic functions in Dostoevsky. A deeper and more complete study of this problem, based on the material of his entire work, would go beyond the bounds of this book.

The first work of the second period—"Uncle's Dream"—is distinguished by vividly expressed, but somewhat simplified and *external* carnivalization. The center of the story is occupied by a scandal-catastrophe with a double discrowning—of Moskaleva and of the prince. And the very tone of the chronicler of Mordasov's story is ambivalent in the ironic glorification of Moskaleva, i.e. the carnivalistic mergence of praise and abuse.[112]

The scene of the scandal and discrowning of the prince—the carnival king, or, more precisely, the carnival bridegroom—is carried out as a *dismemberment,* as a typical carnivalistic "sacrificial" tearing to pieces:

> "If I'm a tub, you, sir, are a *no-legs...*"
> "What, I'm a no-legs?"
> "Well, yes, sir, a no-legs, and you're *toothless,* too, sir, that's what you are, sir."
> "And *one-eyed*, too!" shouted Marya Alexandrovna.
> "You have a corset in place of *ribs,* sir!" added Natalya Dmitrievna.
> "Your *face* is on springs!"
> "You don't have your own *hair!*"
> "And he has a pasted-on *moustache,* the fool!" screeched Marya Alexandrovna.
> "At least leave me with my real *nose,* Marya Stepanovna!—cried the prince, stunned by such sudden *frankness...*
> "Oh my Lord!" said the poor prince. "Take me away from here, old boy, before they tear me *limb from limb!...*" (II, 398-399)

We have here a typical "carnival anatomy"—the enumeration of the parts of a dismembered body. Such "enumerations" comprise a very widespread comic device in carnivalized literature of the Renaissance (it is found very often in Rabelais, and in a less developed form in Cervantes).

The heroine of the story, Marya Alexandrovna Moskaleva, also appeared in the role of the discrowned king of carnival::

The guests left with *shrieks* and *curses.* Marya Alexandrovna remained, finally, alone among the wreckage and ruin of her former glory! Alas! *Power, glory, importance—all had disappeared in this single evening!* (II, 399)

But after the scene of the *comical* discrowning of the *old* suitor follows a *paired* scene of the *tragic self-discrowning and death of the young suitor,* the schoolteacher Vasya. This *pairing* of scenes (and individual images) which mutually reflect one another or shine through one another, one being presented in the comical plane and the other in the tragical (as in this instance), one in a lofty and the other in a low plane,or where one affirms and the other denies, etc., is characteristic of Dostoevsky; taken together, these paired scenes create an ambivalent whole. In this is manifested the more profound influence of the carnival attitude. True, in "Uncle's Dream" this characteristic still has a rather external nature.

Carnivalization is much more profound and fundamental in the novella *The Village of Stepanchikovo and its Inhabitants,* although here too a good deal of it is external. It is around Foma Fomich Opiskin, the former *hanger-on and buffoon* who has become the *unlimited despot* on the estate of Colonel Rostanev, that life in Stepanchikovo is concentrated, i.e. it is concentrated around a *carnival king.* For this reason the entire life of the village of Stepanchikovo takes on a vividly expressed carnival character. This is life outside its normal rut, almost an "inside-out world."

And it cannot be otherwise, inasmuch as it is a carnival king—Foma Fomich— who sets the tone. And all of the other characters—the participants in this life—also have a carnival tint: the *mad rich woman* Tatyana Ivanovna, who suffers from an erotic mania (in a banal romantic style) and—existing simultaneously with her—the purest and kindest of souls, the *mad wife* of the general with her adoration of and devotion to Foma; the *fool (durachok)* Falalei with his *kamarinsky*[113] and his persistent dream about a white bull; the *mad footman* Vidoplyasov, who is constantly changing his surname to a more noble one—"Tantsev," "Esbuketov" (he is forced to do this because the house servants find an indecent rhyme for each new name); the *old man* Gavrila, who is forced in his old age to learn French; the malicious *jester* Ezhevikin; the *"progressive" fool* Obnoskin, who dreams of a wealthy bride; the *bankrupt hussar* Mizinchikov; the *eccentric* Bakhcheev, etc. All of these people, who have for one reason or another gotten out of the usual rut of life, are deprived of the situation in life which would normally correspond to them. The entire action of this novella is an uninterrupted series of scandals, eccentric escapades, mystifications, discrownings and crownings. The work is saturated with parodies and half-parodies, including a parody on Gogol's *Selected Passages from a Correspondence with Friends;* the parodies are organically combined with the carnival atmosphere of the entire novella.

Carnivalization allows Dostoevsky to see and depict aspects of the characters and behavior of people which in the normal course of life could not reveal themselves. The character of Foma Fomich is especially deeply carnivalized: he does not coincide with himself, he is not equal to himself, he cannot be given an unambiguous, finalizing definition, and in many ways he anticipates Dostoevsky's future heroes. He and Colonel Rostanev are, incidentally, presented as a carnivalistic contrasting pair.

■

We have concentrated on the carnivalization in two works of Dostoevsky's second period because it is of a somewhat external, and therefore very graphic character, obvious to everyone. In subsequent works carnivalization recedes into the deeper strata and its character changes. In particular, the *comic* aspect, here rather loud, there is muted and reduced almost to the extreme. We must concentrate on this point in somewhat more detail.

We have already mentioned the phenomenon, important in world literature, of reduced laughter. Laughter is a specific ethical attitude toward reality, but is untranslatable into logical language; it is a specific means of seeing and capturing reality, and consequently a specific means of constructing an artistic image, plot or genre. The ambivalent laughter of carnival possessed enormous creative, genre-forming power. This laughter could seize and capture a phenomenon in the process of change and transition and could fix both poles of evolution within a phenomenon in their continuous, creative, renewing changeability (*smeniaemost'*): death is foreseen in birth and birth in death, defeat in victory and victory in defeat, discrowning in coronation, etc. Carnival laughter does not allow any one of these elements of change to be absolutized or grow stiff and cold in one-sided seriousness.

When we say that birth is "foreseen" in death we inevitably "logicize" (*logiziruem*) and somewhat distort the ambivalence of carnival, for we thereby dichotomize death and birth and somewhat separate them one from another. In living carnival images death itself is pregnant and gives birth, and life-giving mother's loins become a grave. The creative, ambivalent laughter of carnival, in which derision and triumph, praise and abuse are inseparably fused, gives rise to precisely such images.

When the images and laughter of carnival are transposed into literature, they are to a greater or lesser degree transformed in accordance with specific literary-artistic tasks. But regardless of the degree or the fashion in which they are transformed, ambivalence and laughter remain in the carnivalized image. However, under certain circumstances and in certain genres laughter can be reduced. It continues to determine the structure of the image, but it itself is muted down to a minimum: it is as if we see laughter's footprints in the structure of represented reality, but we do not hear laughter itself. Thus in Plato's "Socratic dialogs" (of the first period) laughter is reduced (though not completely), but it remains in the structure of the image of the central hero (Socrates) and in the methods of developing the dialog, and—most importantly—in the genuine (not rhetorical) dialogicality itself, the dialogicality which engulfs thought in the jolly relativity of evolving existence and does not allow it to grow stiff and cold in dogmatic (monological) ossification. But here and there in the dialogs of the early period laughter goes beyond the structure

[137]

of the image and, so to speak, bursts out into a louder register. In the dialogs of the later period laughter is reduced to a minimum.

In Renaissance literature laughter is in general not reduced, but even there it has certain gradations of "volume." In Rabelais, for example, it rings out loudly as on the public square. In Cervantes it is no longer of public-square intensity, although in the first book of *Don Quixote* the laughter is still loud enough, while in the second it is significantly reduced (in comparison with the first). This reduction is also connected with certain changes in the structure of the main hero's image and in the plot.

In the carnivalized literature of the 18th and 19th centuries laughter is, as a rule, muted considerably—to the level of irony, humor, and other forms of reduced laughter.

Let us return to reduced laughter in Dostoevsky. As we have said, in the first two works of the second period laughter is still clearly heard, although elements of carnival ambivalence are, of course, retained in it.[114] But in Dostoevsky's subsequent large novels laughter is reduced almost to a minimum (especially in *Crime and Punishment*). But in all of his novels we find traces of the function of ambivalent laughter (which Dostoevsky absorbed together with the genre tradition of carnivalization) in artistically organizing and illuminating the world. We find such traces in the structure of images, in many plot situations, and in certain characteristics of verbal style. But reduced laughter is given its most important, one might say decisive, expression in the author's ultimate position, which excludes any possible one-sided, dogmatic seriousness and does not permit any one point of view or pole of life or thought to become absolutized. All one-sided seriousness (of life and of thought) and all one-sided pathos are turned over to the heroes, but the author, causing them to collide in the "great dialog" of the novel, leaves that dialog open, he places no finalizing period at its end.

It should be mentioned that the carnival attitude knows no final period, either; it is hostile to any *final ending*: for it every ending is merely a new beginning—carnival images are reborn again and again.

Certain scholars (Vyacheslav Ivanov, V. Komarovich) apply the antique (Aristotelean) term "catharsis" (purification) to Dostoevsky's works. If this term is understood in a very broad sense, then we can agree (without catharsis in the broad sense there can be no art). But tragical catharsis (in the Aristotelean sense) is inapplicable to Dostoevsky. The catharsis which completes Dostoevsky's novels could be—of course inadequately and somewhat rationalistically—expressed thus: *nothing definitive has yet taken place in the world, the final word of the world and about the world has not yet been said, the world is open and free, everything is still in the future and will always be in the future.*

But this is, after all, also the *purifying meaning* of ambivalent laughter.

It would, perhaps, not be superfluous to again emphasize that we are speaking here of Dostoevsky the artist. Dostoevsky the publicist was by no means a stranger to narrow-minded, one-sided seriousness, nor to dogmatism, nor even to eschatology. But the ideas of Dostoevsky the publicist, when introduced into a novel, become merely one of the personified voices in an unfinalized and open dialog.

In Dostoevsky's novels everything is directed toward the as yet unspoken and unpredetermined "new word," everything tensely awaits that word, and the *author* does not block its path with his own one-sided and clear-cut seriousness.

Reduced laughter in carnivalized literature by no means excludes the possibility of somber colors within a work. Therefore the somber colors of Dostoevsky's works should not confuse us: they are not the final word.

Occasionally reduced laughter comes to the surface in Dostoevsky's novels, especially when he introduces a narrator or chronicler, whose story is almost always constructed in parodical-ironical, ambivalent tones (the ambivalent glorification of Stepan Trofimovich in *The Devils*, for example, which is very close in tone to the glorification of Moskaleva in "Uncle's Dream"). This laughter comes to the fore in the straightforward or half-concealed parodies which are scattered through all of Dostoevsky's novels.[115]

■

We shall pause on several other characteristics of carnivalization in Dostoevsky's novels.

Carnivalization is not an external and immobile framework which is applied to a ready-made content, but rather an unusually flexible form of artistic vision, a sort of heuristic principle which makes possible the discovery of new and as yet unseen things. By *relativizing* everything that was externally stable and already formed, carnivalization, with its pathos of change and renewal, permitted Dostoevsky to penetrate into the deepest strata of man and of human relationships. It was an amazingly productive means of artistically capturing the developing relationships under capitalism at a time when previously current moral principles, beliefs and forms of life were turning into "rotten strings," and the ambivalent, unfinalizable nature of man and of human *thought,* which until then had been hidden, was laid bare. Not only people and their actions, but also *ideas* broke out of their self-enclosed hierarchical nests and began to collide in the familiar contact of the "absolute" (i.e. fully unlimited) dialog. Capitalism brings together people and ideas just as the "pander" Socrates had once done on the market square of Athens. In all of Dostoevsky's novels, beginning with *Crime and Punishment,* the dialog is consistently *carnivalized.*

In *Crime and Punishment* we find other manifestations of carnivalization as well. Everything in this novel—people's fates, their experiences and ideas—approaches its own borders, everything is, as it were, prepared to become its own opposite (although not in an abstract-dialectical sense), everything is taken to the extreme, to its limit. There is nothing in the novel which could become stabilized, nothing which could justifiably settle down contentedly within itself and enter into the normal course of biographical time and develop in it (at the end of the novel Dostoevsky indicates the possibility of such a development for Razumikhin and Dunya, but of course he does not depict it—such a life lies outside his artistic world). Everything requires change and rebirth. Everything is depicted in the moment of

[139]

uncompleted transition.

It is characteristic that the very setting of the novel's action—*Petersburg* (its role in the novel is enormous)—is on the border of existence and nonexistence, of reality and a phantasmagoria which is about to dissipate and vanish like a fog. Petersburg too is seemingly devoid of inner grounds for a justified stabilization; it too is on the threshold.[116]

In *Crime and Punishment* Gogol's works no longer served as the source of carnivalization. We feel here in part a Balzacian type of carnivalization, and in part the elements of the social-adventure novel (Soulié and Sue). But perhaps the most essential and profound source of carnivalization for this novel was Pushkin's *The Queen of Spades.*

We shall pause for an analysis of only a single small episode of the novel, which will enable us to reveal certain important characteristics of carnivalization in Dostoevsky, and at the same time to clarify our assertion concerning Pushkin's influence.

After his meeting with Porfiry and the appearance of the mysterious trades-man, who pronounces the word "Killer!", Raskolnikov has a *dream* in which he *again* kills the old woman. We shall quote the end of this dream:

> He stood over her: "She is afraid!" he thought, and then he silently freed the axe from its loop and smashed the old woman in the darkness, once and then again. But strangely, as if she were made of wood, she did not even stir under the blows. He was frightened; he bent down closer to get a look at her, but she bent her head even lower. Then he crouched all the way down to the floor and looked up into her face; he looked and went numb: the old girl was sitting there and *laughing—she was overcome with soft, inaudible laughter,* which she was trying with all her might to restrain, so that he would not hear her. Suddenly it seemed to him that the door to the bedroom opened a tiny bit and that *there too someone began to laugh* and to whisper. He was overpowered by rage: he began to smite the old woman in the head with all his might, but with every blow of the axe the *laughter* and whispers from the bedroom grew *louder and louder,* and the old girl heaved with laughter. He jumped up to run away, but *the whole foyer was already full of people, the stairway doors* were wide open and *on the landing, on the stairs and all the way down*—nothing but people, shoulder to shoulder, and they were all *looking*—but they all fell quiet and waited, silently!...He wanted to scream—and he woke up. (V, 288)

Several points are of interest here.

1. We are already familiar with the first point: Dostoevsky's use of the fan-tastical logic of dream. We recall his words: "*...you leap over* space and time, over the *laws of existence and reason,* stopping only on those points which cause your *heart to dream.*" *("The Dream of a Ridiculous Man.")* This logic of dream allowed

for the creation of the image of the *laughing old woman murder victim* and for the *combination of laughter with death and murder.* But the ambivalent logic of carnival also allows for this. We have before us a typical carnival combination.

The image of the laughing old woman in Dostoevsky echoes Pushkin's image of the old countess winking from the coffin and the Queen of Spades winking from the face of the playing card (the Queen of Spades is, incidentally, a sort of *carnivalistic double* for the old countess). This is an *essential* correspondence of two images, not an accidental external similarity, since it is presented against the background of the general correspondence of these two works *(The Queen of Spades* and *Crime and Punishment),* a correspondence of the whole atmosphere of images and of basic ideological content: "Napoleonism" on the specific basis of young Russian capitalism; in both cases this concrete historical phenomenon is given a second *carnivalistic plane* which recedes into the infinite ideological distance *(smyslovaia dal').* And the motivation for these two corresponding fantastic images (laughing dead women) is similar: *insanity* in Pushkin and a *delirious dream* in Dostoevsky.

2. In Raskolnikov's dream it is not only the murdered old woman (actually she is not murdered in the dream, since it turns out to be impossible to kill her) who laughs, but also people somewhere else, in the bedroom, who constantly laugh louder and louder. Then a crowd appears, a multitude of people, both on the *stairway* and *below;* in relation to this crowd passing below him, Raskolnikov is located *at the head of the stairs.* We have before us the image of a carnival impostor-king being subjected to the discrowning ridicule of the entire folk on the public square. The square is a symbol of belonging to the whole folk *(vsenarodnost'),* and at the end of the novel Raskolnikov, before giving himself up at the police station, appears on the square and bows deep down to the earth before the folk *(narod).* In *Queen of Spades* there is nothing which *completely* corresponds to this discrowning by the whole people which "came in a dream to Raskolnikov's heart," but even so there is a distant correspondence: Germann faints in the presence of the folk at the countess' grave. We find a closer correspondence to Raskolnikov's dream in another of Pushkin's works, *Boris Godunov.* We have in mind the Impostor's thrice-recurring prophetic *dream* (the scene in the cell at the Chudova monastery):

> I dreamed a *stairway steep*
> Had led me to the tower; and from that *height*
> Moscow appeared to me of anthill size;
> *Below, the folk* swarmed on the *square,*
> And, *laughing,* pointed up at me;
> *Embarrassment and fear came over me,*
> And as I fell headlong, I woke...

Here we have the very same carnival logic of an impostor's *elevation,* his comical *discrowning* by the whole folk on the square, and his *downward* fall.

3. In Raskolnikov's dream *space* takes on additional meaning in the spirit of carnival symbolism. *Up, down, the stair, the threshold, the foyer,* and the *landing* acquire the meaning of "a point" in which *crisis,* radical change, or an unexpected turn of fate takes place, where decisions are taken, where demarcation lines are crossed, where people are renewed or perish.

Action in Dostoevsky's works takes place primarily in these "points." Dostoevsky almost never makes use of the interior space of houses or rooms, far from his borders, i.e. far from the threshold, except, of course, for scandalous scenes and discrownings, when interior space (the drawing room or the hall) becomes a substitute for the square. Dostoevsky "leaps over" all that is homey and settled and stable and far from the threshold, the inner space of houses, apartments and rooms, because the life which he depicts is not played out in that kind of space. Dostoevsky was least of all an estate-domestic-room-apartment-family writer. In homey interior space, far from the threshold, people live a biographical life in biographical time: they are born, they experience childhood and youth, enter into marriage, give birth to children, grow old, and die. And Dostoevsky "leaps over" that kind of biographical time, too. On the threshold and on the square the only possible time is *crisis time,* in which the *instant* is equal to years, decades, even to "a billion years" (as in "The Dream of a Ridiculous Man").

If we move now from Raskolnikov's *dream* to the things which happen in the novel when the characters are awake, we will be convinced that the threshold and its substitutes are its basic "points" of action.

In the first place, Raskolnikov lives in essence on the *threshold:* his narrow room, "the coffin" (here a carnival symbol), opens directly onto the *stairway landing,* and he never locks his door, even when he goes out (i.e. his room is unenclosed inner space). In this "coffin" it is impossible to live a biographical life— in it one can only experience a crisis, make an ultimate decision, die or be born anew (as in the graves in "Bobok" or in the "ridiculous man's" coffin). Marmeladov's family also lives on the threshold, in a walk-through room *(proxodnaia komnata)* which opens directly onto a stairway (there, on the threshold, Raskolnikov meets the members of the family for the first time when he brings the drunken Marmeladov home). He experiences terrifying moments on the threshold of the old usuress whom he has murdered, when the people who have come to visit her are standing on the other side of the door, on the stairway landing, ringing the bell. He comes again to this place and rings the bell himself, in order to experience these moments anew. The scene of his half-confession to Razumikhin, expressed only by glances, without words, takes place on the threshold in the corridor by a lamp. His conversations with Sonya take place on the threshold, near the door leading to the neighboring apartment (with Svidrigailov eavesdropping on the other side). It goes without saying that there is no need to enumerate all of the *"performances" ("deistva")* which take place in this novel on or near the threshold, or which exude the living sensation of the threshold.

The threshold, the foyer, the corridor, the landing, the stair, its steps, doors which open onto stairs, garden gates, and aside from this—the city: squares, streets, facades, taverns, dens, bridges, gutters. That is the space in this novel. In essence the interiors—alien to the threshold—of drawing rooms, dining rooms, halls, studies and bedrooms in which biographical life unfolds and in which events take place in the novels of Turgenev, Tolstoy, Goncharov and others, does not exist at all. Of course we observe this same organization of space in Dostoevsky's other novels.

■

We find a somewhat different shade of carnivalization in the novella *The Gambler.*

In the first place, it depicts the life of "Russians abroad," a special category of person which interested Dostoevsky. These are people cut off from their homeland and its folk, their life ceases to be determined by the norms of people living in their own country, their behavior is no longer regulated by the position which they occupied in the homeland, they are not firmly attached to their milieu. The general, the teacher in the general's house (the story's hero), the roguish Des Grieux, Polina, the courtesan Blanche, the Englishman Astley, and the others who came together in the little German town of Roulettenburg make up a kind of *carnival collective* which considers itself to be to a certain degree outside the norms and the order of ordinary life. Their interrelationships and their behavior become unusual, eccentric and scandalous (they live constantly in an atmosphere of scandal).

In the second place, the center of the life depicted in the novella is the *game of roulette.* This second aspect is decisive and determines the shade of carnivalization in this work.

The nature of gambling (dice, cards, roulette, etc.) is a carnival nature. This was clearly recognized in antiquity, in the Middle Ages, and during the Renaissance. The symbols of gambling were always part of the image system of carnival symbols.

People from various (hierarchical) situations in life, crowded around the roulette table, are made equal by the rules of the game and are equal in the eyes of fortune, of chance. Their behavior at the roulette table does not correspond to the role which they play in ordinary life. The atmosphere of gambling is an atmosphere of quick and sudden changes of fate, of instantaneous rises and falls, i.e. of crownings and discrownings. The *stake* in the game is similar to a *crisis:* the player feels that he is on the *threshold.* And gambling time is special time— here too one minute is equal to years.

The game of roulette extends its carnivalizing influence over all of life that comes into contact with it, over almost the whole town, which Dostoevsky did not accidentally name Roulettenburg.

In the intensified carnivalized atmosphere the characters of the story's main heroes are revealed—the characters of Alexey Ivanovich and Polina are ambivalent, crisis characters, unfinalizable, eccentric, full of the most unexpected possibilities. In a letter written in 1863 Dostoevsky thus characterized the *plan* of

Alexey Ivanovich's image (in the final version of 1866 this image was changed considerably):

> "I take a spontaneous nature, a man of considerable development, however, but *in everything incomplete,* a man *who has lost his faith* but **does not dare to be an unbeliever**, *who rebels against the authorities, but at the same time fears them...* The main point is that all his vital juices, strengths, anger and audacity have been expended on **roulette**. He is a gambler, but *not an ordinary gambler,* just as *Pushkin's miserly knight is not an ordinary miser..."*

As we have said, the final image of Alexey Ivanovich differs rather considerably from this plan, but the ambivalence mentioned in the plan not only remains, it is heightened sharply, and the incompletedness becomes consistent *unfinalizability;* in addition, the hero's character is revealed not only in gambling and in scandals and eccentricities of a carnival type, but also in his profoundly ambivalent and crisis-ridden passion for Polina.

Dostoevsky's mention of Pushkin's *The Miserly Knight* is not, of course, an accidental juxtaposition. *The Miserly Knight* exercises a very significant influence on all of Dostoevsky's subsequent works, particularly on *A Raw Youth* and *The Brothers Karamazov* (a maximally intensified and universalized treatment of the theme of patricide).

We quote another excerpt from the same letter to Dostoevsky:

> "If *House of the Dead* attracted the public's attention because it depicted convicts, whom no one had **graphically** depicted before *House of the Dead,* then this story will without a doubt attract attention as a **graphic** and highly detailed *depiction of the game of roulette... House of the Dead* was curious. *But this is a description of a sort of hell,* a sort of 'prison bath-house.' "[117]

At first glance it might seem strange and far-fetched to compare the game of roulette with penal servitude and *The Gambler* with *House of the Dead.* In fact this comparison is profoundly relevant. Both the convict's life and the gambler's life, despite all their differences in content, are "life withdrawn from life" (i.e. from the usual, general life). In this sense both convicts and gamblers are carnivalized collectives.[118] The convict's *time* and the gambler's *time* are, despite their profound differences, identical *types of time,* similar to the "final moments of consciousness" before execution or suicide, in general similar to crisis time. This is all time on the *threshold,* not biographical time experienced in the interior spaces of life, far from the threshold. It is remarkable that Dostoevsky equates both gambling at roulette and penal servitude to *hell,* or as we would say, to the carnivalized nether world of the "Menippean satire" ("prison bath-house" presents this symbol with outstanding external clarity). The juxta-

[144]

positions which Dostoevsky made are characteristic in the utmost, and at the same time have the sound of a typical carnival mésalliance.

■

In the novel *The Idiot* carnivalization is manifested simultaneously with great external clarity and with the enormous inner depth of the carnival attitude to the world (in part thanks to the direct influence of Cervantes' *Don Quixote*).

The carnivalistically ambivalent image of the "Idiot," Prince Myshkin, stands at the center of the novel. He is a person in a special, *higher sense,* and does not occupy any *position* in life which might define his behavior and limit his *pure humanity.* From the point of view of the normal logic of life Prince Myshkin's entire behavior and all of his experiences are incongruous and extremely eccentric. Such, for example, is his brotherly love for his rival, a person who makes an attempt on his life and becomes the murderer of the woman he loves; in addition, this brotherly love toward Rogozhin reaches its apogee immediately after Nastasya Filippovna's murder and fills Myshkin's "final moments of consciousness" (before he sinks into complete idiocy). The final scene of *The Idiot*— the last meeting of Myshkin and Rogozhin beside Nastasya Filippovna's corpse— is one of the most striking in all of Dostoevsky's work.

Equally paradoxical from the point of view of the normal logic of life is Myshkin's attempt to *combine in life* his love for Nastasya Filippovna and for Aglaya. Myshkin's relationship to the other characters is also outside the logic of life: to Ganya Ivolgin, Ippolit, Burdovsky, Lebedev, and others. One might say that Myshkin cannot enter completely into life, cannot become completely embodied, or accept the definitiveness in life that limits the personality *(ogranichivaiushchaia cheloveka zhiznennaia opredelennost')*. He remains, as it were, on a tangent to the circle of life. It is as if he lacks the *flesh of life* which would allow him to occupy a specific place in life (thereby displacing others from that place), and therefore he remains on a tangent to life. But precisely for that reason he is able to *"pierce"* the flesh of life of others and to penetrate their deepest "I."

Myshkin's withdrawnness from the usual relationships of life and the constant *incongruousness* of his personality and his behavior have the character of integrity, almost of naivete—he is precisely an "idiot."

The novel's heroine, Nastasya Filippovna, also deviates from the normal logic and relationships of life. She too always and in everything acts *in spite of* her position in life. But *hysteria* is characteristic of her; she possesses no naive integrity. She is a "madwoman."

It is around these two central figures of the novel—the "idiot" and the "madwoman"—that life is carnivalized and turned into an "inside-out world": traditional plot situations change radically in meaning, and a dynamic carnival game of sharp contrasts and unexpected changes and transitions develops; secondary characters in the novel take on carnival overtones and form carnival pairs.

The carnivalistic-fantastic atmosphere permeates the entire novel. But with Myshkin at its center this atmosphere is *bright,* almost *cheerful.* Around Nastasya Filippovna the atmosphere is *gloomy* and *infernal.* Myshkin is in the carnival *heaven,* and Nastasya Filippovna is in the carnival *hell;* but heaven and hell in the novel intersect, intertwine in diverse ways, and are reflected in one another according to the laws of profound carnival ambivalence. All of this enables Dostoevsky to expose a different side of life to himself and to the reader, searching out and depicting certain new, unknown depths and possibilities in it.

We are interested here not in the depths of life that Dostoevsky *saw,* but only in the *form of his vision* and the role of the elements of carnivalization in that form.

We shall pause a while longer on the carnivalizing function of Prince Myshkin's image.

Wherever Prince Myshkin appears, hierarchical barriers between people suddenly become penetrable, an inner contact is formed between them, and the frankness of carnival is born. His personality possesses the special capacity for relativizing everything that separates people, giving a *false seriousness* to life.

The action of the novel begins in a third-class railway car, where "two passengers found themselves face to face by the window"—Myshkin and Rogozhin. We have already had occasion to mention that the third-class railway car, like the deck of a ship in the antique menippea, is a substitue for the *square,* where people of various positions find themselves in familiar contact with one another. Thus the *penniless prince* and the *millionaire merchant* were thrown together. The carnivalistic contrast is emphasized even in their clothing: Myshkin has on half-boots and a sleeveless cloak of foreign make with an enormous cowl, and Rogozhin has on a sheepskin coat and high-topped boots.

> "They struck up a conversation. The willingness of the *fair-haired* young man in the Swiss cloak to answer all his *swarthy* neighbor's questions was truly amazing and betrayed not the slightest inkling as to the thoughtlessness, impropriety and idleness of some of the questions." (VI, 7)

Myshkin's amazing willingness to unbosom himself gives rise to reciprocal frankness on the part of the suspicious and reticent Rogozhin and prompts him to relate the story of his passion for Nastasya Filippovna with absolute carnivalistic frankness.

This is the first carnivalized episode of the novel.

The second episode takes place in the *foyer* of the Epanchins' home, where Myshkin, while waiting to be received, carries on a conversation with the *butler* on the inappropriate subject of capital punishment and the condemned man's final moral torments. And he succeeds in entering into inner contact with this limited and stuffy servant.

He also carnivalistically penetrates the social barriers in his first meeting

[146]

with General Epanchin.

The carnivalization of the following episode is of interest: in General Epanchin's wife's living room Myshkin tells of the *final moments of consciousness* of a man condemned to death (an autobiographical retelling of Dostoevsky's own experience). The theme of the *threshold* intrudes into the interior space, far removed from the threshold, of the living room. No less out of place here is Myshkin's amazing story of Marya. This whole episode is filled with carnivalistic frankness; the strange and in fact, suspicious, *stranger*—Prince Myshkin—is with carnivalistic unexpectedness and swiftness transformed into an intimate friend of the family. The Epanchins' house is drawn into Myshkin's carnival atmosphere. Of course this process is abetted by the child-like, eccentric character of Mrs. Epanchin herself.

The following episode, which takes place in the Ivolgins' apartment, is distinguished by even more pronounced external and internal carnivalization. From the very beginning it develops in an atmosphere of scandal, which lays bare the souls of almost all its participants. Such carnivalistic figures as Ferdyshchenko and General Ivolgin appear. Typical carnival mystifications and mésalliances occur. Characteristic is the short, heavily carnivalized scene in the foyer, or on the *threshold,* when Nastasya Filippovna, who has arrived unexpectedly, mistakes the prince for a servant and rudely abuses him ("oaf," "you should be fired," "what an idiot!"). This abuse, which contributes to the intensification of the carnival atmosphere of the scene, is not at all in keeping with the way in which Nastasya Filippovna treats servants in reality. The scene in the foyer prepares for the final scene of mystification in the living room, where Nastasya Filippovna plays the role of the callous, cynical courtesan. Then the exaggeratedly carnivalistic scene of the scandal takes place: the appearance of the tipsy general with his carnival story, his exposure, the appearance of Rogozhin's motley and drunken party, Ganya's clash with his sister, the slap in the face administered to the prince, the provoking behavior of the petty carnival demon Ferdyshchenko, etc. The Ivolgins' living room is turned into the carnival square, on which Myshkin's carnival paradise for the first time intersects and intertwines with Nastasya Filippovna's carnival nether world.

After the scandal, the prince's soul-searching conversation with Ganya and the latter's frank confession take place; then follows the carnivalistic ride through Petersburg with the drunken general, and finally, the evening at Nastasya Filippovna's and the cataclysmic scandal-catastrophe, which we have already analyzed. So ends the first part, and with it the first day of the novel's action.

The action of the first part began at dawn and closed late in the evening. This is, of course, not the single day of the classical tragedy ("from the rising to the setting of the sun"). We have here neither tragical time (although it is time of a similar type), nor epical, nor biographical time. This is a day in special carnival time, which is as if divorced from historical time and which is governed by its own carnival laws and can accommodate an unlimited number of radical changes and metamorphoses.[119] Dostoevsky needed precisely this sort of time—not carnivalistic in the strict sense, but rather carnivalized time—to carry out his particular artistic tasks. The events depicted by Dostoevsky on the *threshold* or on the *square,* with their profound inner significance, and such heroes as Raskolnikov, Myshkin, Stavrogin, and Ivan Karamazov could not have been revealed in normal biographical and historical time. And polyphony itself, as an event of the interaction of full-fledged and innerly unfinalized consciousnesses, requires a different artistic conception of time and space, a "non-Euclidean" conception, to use Dostoevsky's own expression.

■

This concludes our analysis of carnivalization in Dostoevsky's works.

In Dostoevsky's next three novels we find the same characteristics of carnivalization,[120] although in a more complex and profound form (especially in *The Brothers Karamazov).* In concluding the present chapter we shall touch upon one more aspect, which is most clearly expressed in the last novels.

We have spoken of the characteristics of the structure of the carnival image: it strives to encompass and unite within itself both poles of evolution or both members of an antithesis: birth-death, youth-age, top-bottom, face-backside, praise-abuse, affirmation-negation, the tragical-the comical, etc., and the upper pole of a two-in-one image is reflected in the lower, after the manner of the figures on playing cards. It could be expressed thus: opposites meet, look at one another, are reflected in one another, know and understand one another.

And one could define the principle of Dostoevsky's art in this same way. In his world everything lives on the very border of its opposite. Love lives on the very border of hate, which it knows and understands, and hate lives on the border of love, and also understands it (Versilov's love-hate, Katerina Ivanovna's love for Dmitry Karamazov; Ivan's love for Katerina Ivanovna and Dmitry's love for Grushenka are to a certain degree of this same type). Faith lives on the very border of atheism, sees its reflection in atheism and understands it, and atheism lives on the border of faith and understands it.[121] Loftiness and nobility live on the border of degradation and baseness (Dmitry Karamazov). Love of life is neighbor to the thirst for self-destruction (Kirillov). Purity and chastity understand vice and voluptuousness (Alyosha Karamazov).

We are, of course, rather crudely simplifying the very complex and subtle ambivalence of Dostoevsky's last novels. In Dostoevsky's world all people and all things must know one another and know about one another, must enter into contact, come together face to face, and *talk* to one another. Everything must be mutually reflected and mutually elucidated dialogically. Therefore all things that are distant and separated must be brought together in a single *"point"* in space and time. And for this the *freedom* of carnival and carnival's artistic conception of space and time are needed.

Carnivalization made possible the creation of the *open* structure of the great dialog and allowed people's social interaction to be carried over into the sphere of the spirit and the intellect, which had always been primarily the sphere of a single, unified monological consciousness or of a unified and indivisible spirit, whose development took place within its own limits (as in Romanticism). The carnival attitude helps Dostoevsky overcome gnoseological as well as ethical solipsism. A single person, remaining alone with himself, cannot even tie the ends together in the deepest and most intimate spheres of his own spiritual life; he cannot manage without *another* consciousness. One person can never find complete fulness in himself alone.

In addition, carnivalization makes it possible to extend the narrow stage of personal life in a specific, limited time to the dimensions of the universal *stage* of the *mystery play*. This was Dostoevsky's goal in his later novels, especially in *The Brothers Karamazov*.

In *The Devils,* before their heart-to-heart talk begins, Shatov says to Stavrogin:

> "We are two *human beings* and we have met in *infinity...* for the *last time in this world.* Drop that tone of yours and take up a *human* one! For once in your life speak in a human voice." (VII, 260-261)

All *decisive* encounters of man with man and consciousness with consciousness take place in Dostoevsky's novels "in infinity" and "for the last time" (in the final moments of crisis), i.e. they take place in the time and space of carnival or the mystery play.

■

The task of our work is to reveal the inimitable uniqueness of Dostoevsky's poetics, to reveal the "Dostoevsky in Dostoevsky." But if a *synchronic* task such as this is properly carried out, it should help us to feel out and to trace Dostoevsky's tradition of genre all the way back to its sources in antiquity. This has been our goal in the present chapter, although we have done so in a rather general, almost schematic form. It seems to us that our diachronic analysis confirms the results of our synchronic one. More precisely: the results of the two analyses mutually check and confirm one another.

It goes without saying that we have not in the slightest way detracted from the profound originality and individual uniqueness of Dostoevsky's work by connecting him with a specific tradition. Dostoevsky is the creator of *true polyphony,* which did not and could not exist in the "Socratic dialog," the antique "Menippean satire," the medieval mystery play, in Shakespeare and Cervantes, in Voltaire and Diderot, or in Balzac and Hugo. But this line of development in European literature did *fundamentally* pave the way for polyphony. This whole tradition, beginning with the "Socratic dialog" and the menippea, was reborn and renewed in Dostoevsky in the uniquely original and innovative form of the polyphonic novel.

[149]

CHAPTER FIVE

THE WORD IN DOSTOEVSKY

1. Types of the prose word. The word in Dostoevsky.

A few preliminary remarks on methodology.

We have titled this chapter "The *Word* in Dostoevsky" because we have in mind the *word,* i.e. language in its concrete and living totality, as opposed to language as the specific subject matter of linguistics, which, quite legitimately and necessarily, is detached from certain aspects of the concrete life of the word. But precisely those aspects of the life of the word from which linguistics detaches itself are of paramount importance for our purposes. Therefore the analyses which follow cannot be called linguistic in the strict sense of the word. They belong to metalinguistics, by which we mean the study of those aspects of the life of the word which—quite legitimately—fall outside the bounds of linguistics, and which have not as yet taken their places within specific individual disciplines. Metalinguistics cannot, of course, ignore linguistics, and must utilize its results. Linguistics and metalinguistics study one and the same concrete, extremely complex and many-sided phenomenon—the word, but they study it from different angles and different viewpoints. They must supplement one another, but must not be confused. In practice the borders between them are very often violated.

From the point of view of *pure* linguistics, no really essential differences can be discerned between the monological and the polyphonic utilization of the word in belles lettres. For example, in Dostoevsky's multi-voiced novel there is significantly less linguistic differentiation, i.e. fewer distinct linguistic styles, territorial and social dialects, professional slang words, etc., than in the work of many monological writers: of L. Tolstoy, Pisemsky, Leskov and others. It might even seem that the heroes of Dostoevsky's novels all speak the same language—the language of their author. Many people, including L. Tolstoy, have reproached Dostoevsky for this monotony of language.

But the point is that characters' linguistic differentiation and clear-cut "characteristics of speech" have the greatest significance precisely for the creation of objectivized, finalized images of people. The more objectified a character is, the more sharply his verbal physiognomy stands out. The significance of linguistic variety and of characteristics of speech does remain in the polyphonic novel, but it becomes smaller, and, what is most important, the artistic functions of these phenomena change. The point is not the mere presence of specific linguistic styles, social dialects, etc., a presence which is measured by purely linguistic criteria; the point is the *dialogical angle* at which they (the styles, dialects, etc.) are juxtaposed or counterposed in the work. But that dialogical angle cannot be measured by means of purely linguistic criteria, because dialogical relationships, although they belong to the province of the *word,* fall outside the province of its purely linguistic study.

Dialogical relationships (including the dialogical relationships of the speaker to his own word) are a matter for metalinguistics. It is precisely these relationships, which determine the characteristics of the verbal structure of Dostoevsky's works, which interest us here.

In language as the subject matter of linguistics there are and can be no dialogical relationships: they are possible neither among elements in a system of language (among words in a dictionary, among morphemes, etc.), nor among elements of a "text" in a strictly linguistic approach. They cannot exist among units of a single level, nor among elements of different levels. Neither can they exist, of course, among syntactic units, among prepositions, for example, in a strict linguistic approach.

There can be no dialogical relationships among texts, again in a strictly linguistic approach to those texts. Any purely linguistic juxtaposition or grouping of any given texts must necessarily detach itself from any dialogical relationships which may exist among those texts seen as complete utterances.

Linguistics of course recognizes the compositional form of "dialogical speech" and studies its syntactic and lexico-semantic characteristics. But it studies them as purely linguistic phenomena, i.e. in the plane of language, and is quite incapable of treating the specifics of dialogical relationships between speeches (*repliki*). Therefore, when studying "dialogical speech," linguistics must utilize the results of metalinguistics.

Dialogical relationships are, then, extra-linguistic phenomena. But they must not be separated from the province of the *word,* i.e. from language as a concrete, integral phenomenon. Language is alive only in the dialogical intercourse of those who make use of it. Dialogical intercourse is the genuine sphere of the *life* of language. Language's entire life, in whatever area it is used (in everyday life, in business, science, art, etc.), is permeated by dialogical relationships. Linguistics studies "language" and its specific logic in its *commonality (obshchnost')* as that factor which makes dialogical intercourse *possible,* but it consistently refrains from studying those dialogical relationships themselves. Those relationships lie within the province of the word, since the word is by nature dialogical, and therefore they must be studied by metalinguistics, which reaches beyond the boundaries of linguistics and has its own independent subject matter and its own tasks.

Dialogical relationships are not reducible to logical or concrete semantic relationships, which are in and of *themselves* devoid of any dialogical aspect. In order for dialogical relationships to arise among them, they must clothe themselves in the word, become utterances, and become the positions of various subjects, expressed in the word.

"Life is good." "Life is not good." We have before us two judgements which have a specific logical form and a specific concrete semantic content (philosophical judgements on the value of life). There exists between these two judgements a specific logical relationship: the one is the negation of the other. But there is and can be no dialogical relationship between them, they do not dispute with one another (although they can supply the subject matter and the logical basis for disputation). Both of these judgements must be embodied in order for a dialogical relationship between them or toward them to arise. Thus, as thesis and antithesis, these two judgements can be united in a single utterance of a single subject, an utterance which expresses that subject's unified dialectical position on a given question. In that case no dialogical relationships arise. But if the two judgements are divided between two different utterances of two different subjects, then dialogical relationships arise between them.

"Life is good." "Life is good." Here we have two completely identical judgements, or, essentially, one single judgement written (or pronounced) *twice,* with "twice" referring only to its verbal embodiment, and not to the judgement itself. We can, it is true, speak here of the logical relationship of identity between two judgements. But if this judgement is expressed in two utterances of two different subjects, then dialogical relationships arise between them (agreement, corroboration).

Dialogical relationships are totally impossible without logical and concrete semantic relationships, but they are not reducible to them; they have their own specificity.

As has already been stated, in order to become dialogical, logical and concrete semantic *(predmetno-smyslovye)* relationships must be embodied, i.e. they must enter into a different sphere of existence: they must become a *word,* i.e. an utterance, and have an *author,* i.e. the creator of the given utterance, whose position is expressed.

In this sense every utterance has its author, who is heard in the utterance as its creator. We can know absolutely nothing about the actual author as he exists outside the utterance. The forms of actual authorship can be very diverse. A given work can be the product of a collective effort, can be created by the successive efforts of a series of generations, etc.—in any case we hear in it a unified creative will, a specific position to which we can react dialogically. A dialogical reaction personifies every utterance to which it reacts.

Dialogical relationships are possible not only between (relatively) entire utterances; the dialogical approach can be applied to any meaningful part of an utterance, even to an individual word, if that word is perceived not as an impersonal word of language, but as the sign of another person's semantic position, as the representative of another person's utterance, i.e. if we hear in that word another person's voice. Thus dialogical relationships can penetrate an utterance, or even an individual word, so long as two voices collide within it (the microdialog, of which we had occasion to speak earlier).

On the other hand, dialogical relationships are possible among linguistic styles, social dialects, etc., if those phenomena are perceived as semantic positions, as a sort of linguistic *Weltanschauung,* i.e. if they are perceived outside the realm of linguistic investigation.

Finally, it is possible to have dialogical relationships to one of our own

[152]

utterances, to its individual parts, and to an individual word within it, if we in some way separate ourselves from them, if we speak with an inner reservation, if we maintain distance from them, as if limiting or dividing our authorship in two.

In conclusion we would recall that in the broadest sense dialogical relationships are possible also between intelligible phenomena of unlike types, if those phenomena are expressed in some sort of *symbolic (znakovoi)* material. For example, dialogical relationships are possible between images of various art forms. But such relationships fall outside the bounds of metalinguistics.

The chief subject matter of our investigation, its chief hero, so to speak, will be the *double-voiced word,* which inevitably arises under the conditions of dialogical intercourse, i.e. under the conditions of the genuine life of the word. Linguistics does not recognize this double-voiced word. But it is precisely what, in our opinion, should become one of the chief objects of study for metalinguistics.

This concludes our preliminary methodological remarks. Our further concrete analyses will make clear what we have in mind.

■

There exists a group of artistic-verbal *(khudozhestvenno-rechevye)* phenomena which has long attracted the attention of both literary scholars and linguists. These phenomena by nature fall outside the bounds of linguistics, i.e. they are metalinguistic phenomena. They are stylization, parody, *skaz*[122] and dialog (i.e. dialog expressed within a work's composition, broken down into the speeches of characters).

A single trait is common to all of these phenomena, despite their essential differences: in all of them the word has a double-directedness—it is directed both toward the object of speech, like an ordinary word, and toward *another word,* toward *another person's speech.* If we are not aware of the existence of this second context of the other person's speech and begin to perceive stylization or parody in the same way that ordinary speech—which is directed only toward its object—is perceived, then we will not understand the essence of these phenomena: we will mistake stylization for the style itself, and will perceive parody merely as a poor work of art.

This double-directedness is less obvious in *skaz* and in the dialog (within the bounds of a single speech). *Skaz* may indeed sometimes have only a single direction —towards its object. A speech in a dialog may also strive for direct, object-oriented significance. But in the majority of cases both *skaz* and the speech in a dialog are oriented toward another person's speech: *skaz* stylizes that speech, and the dialog speech takes it into account, replies to it, or anticipates it.

These phenomena have a profound fundamental significance. They require a totally new approach to speech, an approach which does not fit within the bounds of the usual stylistic and linguistic examinations. The usual approach regards the word within the bounds of a *single monological context.* The word is defined in relation to its object (the study of tropes, for example) or in relation to other words within the same context or the same speech (stylistics in the narrow sense). Lexicology does, it is true, recognize a somewhat different attitude toward the word. The lexical nuance of a word, of an archaism or a provincialism, for example, indicates some other context in which the given word *normally* functions (ancient literature, provincial speech), but that other context is linguistic and not a context of speech (in the strict sense), it is not another person's utterance, but rather the impersonal material of language, not organized into a concrete utterance. If the lexical nuance is even to a slight degree individualized, i.e. if it indicates some specific utterance of another person, from which the word in question is borrowed or in the spirit of which the word in question is constructed, then we have before us either stylization, parody, or an analogous phenomenon. Thus lexicology, too, in essence remains within the bounds of a single monological context and recognizes only the word's linear directedness towards its object, without taking into account another person's word or a second context.

The very fact of the existence of double-directed words, words which contain as an integral part of themselves a relationship toward another person's utterance, makes it necessary for us to give a complete and exhaustive classification of words from the point of view of this new principle, which is taken into account neither by stylistics, nor by lexicology, nor by semantics. It is not difficult to demonstrate that, aside from object-oriented words and words which are directed toward another person's word, there exists yet another type. But double-directed words (ones which take into account the word of another person), including such phenomena as stylization, parody and dialog are also in need of differentiation. It is imperative that we point out their essential varieties (from the point of view of this principle). Further, the question will inevitably arise of the possibility and the methods of combining within a single context words which belong to different types. In this connection there arise new stylistic questions which as yet have not been taken into consideration by stylistics. It is precisely these problems that are of paramount importance for an understanding of the style of prose speech.[123]

Alongside the direct, linear, object-oriented word, which denominates, informs, expresses or represents, and is intended for direct, object-oriented comprehension (the first type of word), we observe the represented or objectivized word as well (the second type). The most typical and widespread form of the represented, objectivized word is the *direct speech of characters*. It has direct object-oriented meaning, but it does not lie in the same plane with the author's speech, residing instead at a perspective distance from it. It is not only understood from the point of view of its object, it becomes itself an object as a characteristic, typical, or picturesque word.

Where there appears within the author's context the direct speech of, let us say, a certain hero, we have before us two speech centers and two speech unities within a single context: the unity of the author's utterance and the unity of the hero's utterance. But that second unity is not independent, it is subordinate to and included in the first as one of its elements. The stylistic treatment is not the same for both utterances. The hero's word is treated as the word of another person, as the word of an individual whose character and type are predetermined, i.e. it is treated as the object of the author's understanding, and not from the point of view of its own object-oriented directedness. The author's word, on the contrary, is treated stylistically from the point of view of its direct object-oriented significance. It must conform to its object (cognitive, poetic, or otherwise). It must be expressive, powerful, significant, elegant, etc., from the point of view of its direct, object-oriented task, namely to signify, express, convey or represent something. And its stylistic treatment is directed toward a purely object-oriented understanding. If the author's word is treated in such a way that its typicality for a specific individual, a specific social status or a specific artistic manner is apparent, then we have already a stylization: either an ordinary literary stylization or a stylized *skaz*. We shall speak later of this *third* type.

The direct object-oriented word recognizes only itself and its object, to which it seeks to conform in the highest degree possible. If in the process it imitates or takes a lesson from someone else, nothing is changed in the slightest: it is like the scaffolding which is not part of the architect's plan, although it is indispensable and is taken into consideration by the builder. The fact that another person's word is imitated and that the words of other persons, clearly recognizable to the literary historian and to every competent reader, are present is not of concern to the word itself. If it were, i.e. if the word itself contained a deliberate reference to another person's word, then we would have before us again a word of the third type, not of the first.

The stylistic treatment of the objectivized word, i.e. of the hero's word, is subordinated as to an ultimate authority to the stylistic tasks of the author's context, of which it is an objectivized element. This gives rise to a series of stylistic problems connected with the introduction and organic inclusion of the hero's direct speech into the author's context. The ultimate semantic authority, and consequently the ultimate stylistic authority as well, is contained in the direct speech of the author.

An ultimate semantic authority, which requires a purely object-oriented understanding, does, of course, exist in every literary work, but it is not always represented by the direct authorial word. The latter can be absent altogether, being replaced compositionally by the narrator's word, or in the drama may lack a compositional equivalent. In this case the entire verbal material of the work belongs to the second or third type of word. The drama is almost always built of objectivized, represented words. In Pushkin's *Tales of Belkin,* for example, the story (Belkin's words) is built of words of the third type; the heroes' words belong, of course, to the second type. The absence of the direct object-oriented word is a common phenomenon. The ultimate semantic authority—the author's intention—is realized not in his direct word, but with the help of the words of others, created and distributed in a specific way as belonging to others.

The degree of objectivization of the hero's represented word can vary. It would suffice to compare the words of Tolstoy's Prince Andrey with the words of Gogol's heroes, those of Akaky Akakievich, for example. To the degree that the direct object-orientation of the hero's words is intensified and their objectivization is correspondingly weakened, the interrelationship between the author's speech and that of the hero begins to approach the interrelationship between two speeches in a dialog. The perspective relationship between them is weakened and they can occupy a single plane. This is, however, only a tendency, a striving toward a limit which is never reached.

A scientific article, in which various authors' utterances on a given question are quoted, some to be refuted and others, on the contrary, to be corroborated and supplemented, is an example of a dialogical interrelationship among directly significant words within the bounds of a single context. The relations of agreement—disagreement, corroboration—supplementatation, question—answer, etc. are purely dialogical relationships, although not, of course, between words, sentences, or other elements of a single utterance, but rather between whole utterances. In a dramatic dialog or in a dramaticized dialog which is introduced into the author's context, these relationships tie together represented, objectivized utterances and therefore are themselves objectivized. This is not a collision of two ultimate semantic authorities, but rather an objectivized (thematic) collision of two represented positions which is wholly subordinate to the author's ultimate authority. The monological context is neither broken nor weakened.

The weakening or destruction of the monological context occurs only when two equally and directly object-oriented utterances come together. Two equally and directly object-oriented words within a single context cannot stand side by side without dialogically intersecting, regardless of whether they corroborate one another, mutually supplement one another, or, on the contrary, contradict one another or have any other sort of dialogical relationship (the relationship of question and answer, for example). Two equal-weighted words which speak to the same subject, once they have come together, must inevitably become oriented one to another. Two embodied thoughts cannot lie side by side like two objects—they must come into inner contact, i.e. must enter into a semantic bond.

The direct, linear, fully significant word is oriented toward its object and is the ultimate semantic authority within its given context. The objectivized word is also oriented only toward an object, but at the same time it is itself the object of its author's intention. But this foreign intention does not penetrate inside the objectivized word; it takes it rather as a whole and, without altering the word's sense or tone, subordinates it to its own tasks. It does not invest the word with another object-oriented meaning. It is as if the word is not aware of the fact that is has become an object; it is like a person who goes about his business and is not aware of the fact that he is being watched. The objectivized word sounds as though it were a direct, single-voiced word. In words of the first and of the second types there is in fact only a single voice. These are *single-voiced words*.

But an author can also make use of another person's word for his own purposes by inserting a new semantic orientation into a word which already has—and retains—its own orientation. In that case such a word, by virtue of its task, must be perceived as belonging to another person. Then two semantic orientations, two voices, are present in a single word. The parodistic word is of this type, as are stylization and the stylized *skaz*. We shall now move on to the characterization of the third type of word.

Stylization makes the assumption that a certain style has existed, i.e. it assumes that the body of stylistic devices which it reproduces had at some time direct significance, that it expressed an ultimate semantic authority. Only a word of the first type can be the object of stylization. Stylization forces another person's (artistically) subject-oriented intention *(chuzhoi predmetnyi zamysel)* to serve its [stylization's] own purposes, i.e. its new intentions. The stylizer uses another person's word as another person's *(pol'zuetsia chuzoe slovo kak chuzhim)* thereby casting a slight shadow of objectivization on that word. The word does not, however, become his object. The body of devices of another person's speech is important to the stylizer precisely as the expression of a particular point of view. He works with the other person's point of view. Therefore a certain shadow of objectivization falls on that point of view itself, and as a result it becomes conditional *(uslovnoe*—i.e. no longer absolute or independent—trans.). The objectivized speech of the hero is never conditional. The hero always speaks in earnest. The author's attitude does not penetrate inside his speech, the author views it from without.

The conditional word is always a double-voiced word. Only that which was at some time unconditional, in earnest, can become conditional. The original direct and unconditional meaning now serves new purposes which gain control of it from within and make it conditional. This is the difference between stylization and imitation. Imitation does not make the imitated form conditional, since it takes it seriously, it makes it its own, it seeks to master another person's word. The voices merge completely, and if we do hear the other voice, it is by no means because the imitator intended us to do so.

Thus, although there is a clear semantic borderline between stylization and imitation, historically there exist between them extremely subtle and sometimes imperceptible transitions. To the degree that a style's seriousness is weakened in the hands of an epigone, its devices become more and more conditional and imitation becomes semi-stylization. On the other hand, stylization can become imitation if the stylizer's enthusiasm for his model breaks down the distance between them and weakens the deliberate sensation that the reproduced style is indeed that of *another person.* For it was precisely that distance which created the conditionality in the first place.

Analogous to stylization is the narrator's story, which acts as a compositional surrogate for the author's word. The narrator's story can be developed in the forms of the literary word (Belkin and the narrator-chronicler in Dostoevsky) or in the forms of the spoken word—*skaz* in the simple sense of "tale" (from *skazat'*—to say, tell—trans.). Here, too, another person's verbal manner is used by the author as a point of view, a position, which he needs in order to tell the story. But here the shadow of objectivization which falls on the narrator's word is much heavier than in stylization, and the conditionality is much weaker. Of course both can vary greatly. But the narrator's word can never be purely objectivized, even when he is

[157]

himself one of the characters and tells only a part of the story. For the author, not only the narrator's individual and typical manner of thinking, experiencing and speaking is important, but above all his manner of seeing and depicting: therein lies his immediate purpose as narrator, as surrogate for the author. Therefore, just as in stylization, the author's attitude penetrates into the narrator's word, making it to a greater or lesser degree conditional. The author does not show us the narrator's word (as the objectivized word of a hero), but makes use of it from within for his own purposes, causing us to clearly feel the distance between him and this word which is foreign to him.

The element of *skaz*, i.e. the orientation toward spoken language, is necessarily inherent in every narrated story. The narrator, even if he writes his story and gives it a certain literary treatment, is nonetheless not a professional literator, he does not have a definite style, but only a socially and individually determined manner of telling a story, which tends toward the oral *skaz*. If he has a definite literary style which is reproduced by the author in the narrator's name, then we have before us a stylization and not a narrated story (stylization can be introduced and motivated in various ways).

Both the narrated story and even the pure *skaz* can lose all their conditionality and become the direct authorial word, directly expressing the author's intention. This is almost always the case with *skaz* in Turgenev. When introducing a narrator Turgenev in the majority of instances does not at all stylize the *other person's* individual and socially determined manner of narrating. For example, the story in *Andrey Kolosov* is the story of an intelligent man of letters of Turgenev's circle. He would have told the story the same way himself, and would have told of the most serious things in his life. There is no orientation here toward the socially foreign narrative tone and manner of seeing and communicating what is seen. Nor is there an orientation toward an individual-characteristic manner. Turgenev's *skaz* is of independent significance and contains a single voice which directly expresses the author's intention. We have here a simple compositional device. The narration in *First Love* has a similar character (it is presented in written form by the narrator).[124]

The same cannot be said of the narrator Belkin: he is important to Pushkin as another person's voice, above all as a socially defined person with a corresponding spiritual level and approach to the world, but also as an individual-characteristic image. Consequently the author's intention is refracted in the narrator's word; the word here is double-voiced.

The problem of *skaz* was first raised in our literary scholarship by B. M. Eikhenbaum.[125] He perceives *skaz* exclusively as the *orientation toward the oral form of narration,* the orientation toward spoken language and the corresponding linguistic characteristics (oral intonation, the syntactic construction of spoken language, the corresponding vocabulary, etc.). He does not consider at all that in the majority of instances *skaz* is first of all the orientation toward the *speech of another person,* and only as a consequence of that fact is also the orientation toward spoken language.

For an elaboration of the historical-literary problem of *skaz,* the concept of *skaz* which we have proposed seems much more relevant. It seems to us that in the majority of instances *skaz* is first of all the orientation toward the *speech of another person,* and only as a consequence of that fact is also the orientation toward spoken language.

For an elaboration of the historical-literary problem of *skaz,* the concept of *skaz* which we have proposed seems much more relevant. It seems to us that in the majority of instances *skaz* is introduced precisely for the sake of a *foreign voice,* a socially-defined voice which brings with it a whole series of points of view and values which are necessary to the author. Actually, it is a narrator who is introduced, and a narrator is not a man of letters; in most cases he belongs to the lower social strata, to the folk (which is just what the author needs) and brings with him spoken language.

The direct authorial word is not possible in all epochs and not every epoch possesses a style, since style assumes the presence of authoritative points of view and authoritative, established ideological values. In such epochs the author can either take the path of stylization or resort to extra-literary forms of narration which possess a particular manner of seeing and depicting the world. Where there is no adequate form for the direct expression of the author's thoughts, he must resort to refracting them in another person's word. Sometimes the author's artistic tasks themselves are such that they can be realized only by means of the double-voiced word (as we shall see, such was precisely the case with Dostoevsky).

It seems to us that Leskov resorted to the narrator for the sake of a socially foreign word and a socially foreign *Weltanschauung,* and only secondarily for the sake of the oral *skaz* (since he was interested in the folkloric word). Turgenev, on the contrary, sought in the narrator precisely an oral form of narration, but for the *direct* expression of his intentions. For him the orientation toward spoken language is characteristic, and the orientation toward another person's word is not. Turgenev was not fond of refracting his thoughts in another person's word, and he was not good at doing so. The double-voiced word did not turn out well for him (cf. the satirical and parodical sections of *Smoke,* for example). For that reason he chose a narrator from his own social circle. Such a narrator, not sustaining an oral *skaz* to the end, had inevitably to speak in a literary language. Turgenev wanted only to enliven his literary speech with oral intonations.

This is not the place to substantiate all of the literary-historical assertions that we have made. Let them remain assumptions. But on one point we do insist: the strict differentiation in the *skaz* between orientation toward another person's word and orientation toward spoken language is absolutely indispensable. To see only spoken language in the *skaz* is to miss the most important point. Moreover, a whole series of intonational, syntactical and other *linguistic* phenomena in *skaz* is explained (in light of the author's orientation toward the speech of another person) precisely by its double-voicedness and by the intertwining of two voices and two accents. Our analysis of the narrated story in Dostoevsky will convince us of this. Similar phenomena do not exist, for example, in Turgenev, although his narrators' tendency toward spoken language is stronger than that of Dostoevsky's narrators.

The form of the *Icherzählung* (the first-person story) is analagous to the narrator's story: sometimes it is determined by the orientation toward another person's word, and sometimes it can, like the story in Turgenev, approach and finally merge with the direct authorial word, i.e. it operates with the single-voiced word of the first type.

It must be kept in mind that compositional forms do not of themselves answer the question as to what type of word is present. Such definitions as *Icherzählung,* narrator's story, author's story, etc., are purely compositional definitions. These compositional forms do, it is true, tend toward a particular type of word, but are not necessarily connected with it.

All the manifestations of the third type of word which we have thus far discussed—stylization, narrated story and *Icherzählung*—share a common trait, by virtue of which they constitute a special (the first) variety of the third type. That common trait is that the author's intention makes use of another person's word in the direction of its own aspirations. Stylization stylizes another style in the direction of that style's own tasks. It merely makes those tasks conditional. Also the narrator's story, in refracting the author's intention, does not diverge from its own straight path and remains faithful to the tones and intonations which are truly typical for it. Having penetrated into another person's word and having made itself at home in it, the author's idea does not collide with the other person's idea, but rather follows the direction of that idea, merely making that direction conditional.

The parody is a different matter. As in stylization, the author speaks through another person's word, but in contrast to stylization, he introduces a semantic direction into that word which is diametrically opposed to its original direction. The second voice, which has made its home in the other person's word, collides in a hostile fashion with the original owner and forces him to serve purposes diametrically opposed to his own. The word becomes the arena of conflict between two voices. Therefore the merging of voices, as can occur in stylization or in the narrator's story (in Turgenev, for example), is impossible in the parody: the voices here are not only detached and distanced, they are hostilely counterposed. Therefore the deliberate perceptibility of the other person's word in the parody must be particularly sharp and distinct. The author's intentions, on the other hand, must be more individualized and filled with content. Another person's style can be parodied in various directions and new accents can be introduced into it, while it can be stylized essentially only in a single direction—in the direction of its own original task.

The parodistic word can be extremely diverse. Another person's style can be parodied as a style; another person's social-typical or individual-characterological manner of seeing, thinking and speaking can be parodied. Furthermore, parody can be more, or less, deep: one can parody only superficial verbal forms, or one can parody the deepest principles of the other person's word. Furthermore, the parodistic word itself can be employed by the author in various ways: parody can be an end in itself (the literary parody as a genre, for example), but it can also serve

[160]

other, positive purposes (Ariosto's parodistic style, or Pushkin's, for example). But despite all of the parodistic word's possible variants, the relationship between the author's aspiration and that of the other person remains the same: these two aspirations are directed toward different ends, in contrast to stylization, the narrated story, and analogous forms, in which both aspirations are directed toward a single end.

Therefore the differentiation between the parodistic and the simple *skaz* is extremely essential. The conflict of two voices in the parodistic *skaz* gives rise to very specific linguistic phenomena, which we have mentioned above. To ignore in the *skaz* the orientation toward the other person's word and, consequently, its double-voicedness is to be ignorant of the complex interrelationships which can exist between voices within the *skaz* word, when those voices become directed toward different ends. In the majority of cases a slight parodical nuance is inherent in the modern *skaz*. As we shall see, parodistic elements of a special type are always present in Dostoevsky's stories.

The ironical use, and in general any ambiguous use of another person's word, is analogous to the parodistic word, since in such cases the other person's word is being used to communicate aspirations which are hostile to it. In practical everyday speech, such use of another person's word is extremely widespread, especially in the dialog, where one speaker very often repeats word for word a statement of another speaker, investing it with a new valuation and accenting it in his own way: with an expression of doubt, indignation, irony, mockery or ridicule, etc.

In his book on the characteristics of the Italian spoken language, Leo Spitzer says:

> When we reproduce in our speech a small chunk of our interlocutor's utterance, already by virtue of the change of speakers a change in tone inevitably occurs: *on our lips the "other's" words always sound foreign to us, and very often have an intonation of ridicule, exaggeration, or mockery....* I would mention here the facetious or sharply ironical repetition of the verb of the interlocutor's question in the ensuing answer. In this situation it can be observed that we often resort not only to grammatically correct, but also to quite daring, sometimes simply impossible constructions in order to at any price repeat a chunk of our interlocutor's speech and to impart an ironical tint to it.[126]

Another person's words, when introduced into our speech, inevitably take on a new aspect—our understanding and our valuation; i.e. the other person's words become double-voiced. But the interrelationship between the two voices can vary. Alone the repetition of another person's statement in the form of a question leads to a collision of two interpretations in a single word: we are not only asking a question, we are problematizing another person's statement. Our practical everyday speech is full of the words of other people: we merge our voice completely with some of them, forgetting whose they are; others we take as authoritative, using them to support our own words; still others we people with aspirations of our own which are foreign or hostile to them.

Now we move on to the last variety of the third type. In stylization and in parody, i.e. in the two other varieties of the third type, the author makes use of another person's words for the expression of his own intentions. In the third variety the other person's word remains beyond the bounds of the author's speech, but the author's speech takes it into consideration and relates to it. Here the other person's word is not reproduced with a new interpretation, but it influences and in one way or another determines the author's word while itself remaining outside it. Such is the word in the hidden polemic and in the majority of cases in the dialog speech *(dialogicheskaia replika)*.

In the hidden polemic the author's word is directed toward its object, as is any other word, but in addition, every statement about the object is so constructed that, besides expressing its object-oriented meaning, it strikes a blow at the other person's word about the same topic and at the other person's statement about the same object. Directed at its object, the word collides within the object itself with the other person's word. The other person's word is not reproduced, it is merely implied, but the entire structure of the speech would be completely different if this reaction to the implied word were not present. In stylization the reproduced actual model—the other person's style—also remains outside the author's context, it is implied. Also, in the parody the parodied, specific actual word is only implied. But in the parody the author's word either tries to pass itself off as the word of another person, or tries to pass off another person's word as its own. In any case, it works directly with another person's word, while the implied model (the actual word of another person) only provides the material and acts as a document confirming the fact that the author is in fact reproducing a specific word of another person. In the hidden polemic the other person's word is antagonized, and this antagonization determines the author's word no less than the object under discussion itself. This causes a radical change in the semantics of the word: alongside its object-oriented meaning there appears a second meaning—the directedness toward the other person's word. It is impossible to fully and fundamentally understand such a word if only its direct, object-oriented significance is taken into consideration. A word's polemical coloration is manifested in other purely linguistic phenomena as well: in intonation and in syntactical construction.

It is sometimes difficult in concrete cases to draw a distinct line between hidden polemics and obvious, open ones. But the semantic differences are quite essential. The obvious polemic has as its object simply the word of the other person which it is refuting. In the hidden polemic the word is directed toward an ordinary object, which it denominates, depicts and expresses, only obliquely taking swipes at the other person's word, colliding with it as it were in the object itself. Thus the other person's word begins to influence the author's word from within. Therefore the hidden-polemical word is double-voiced, although the interrelationship of the two voices within it is a special one. The other person's thought does not personally make its way inside the word, but rather is reflected in it and determines its tone and its meaning. The word is intensely aware of the presence alongside it of another person's word speaking about the same object, and that awareness determines its structure.

The innerly polemical word—a word with a sideward glance *(ogliadka)* at another person's hostile word—is extremely widespread, both in practical, everyday speech and in literary speech, and possesses enormous style-determining significance. In practical everyday speech all cutting remarks—"jabs" and "needles"—belong to this category. But all self-deprecating, florid speeches which repudiate themselves in advance and have a thousand reservations, concessions, loopholes, etc. belong to this category, too. Such a speech as it were cringes in the presence or in the anticipation of another person's word, answer, or objection. The individual manner in which a person constructs his speech is to a large degree determined by his characteristic awareness of the other person's word and his means of reacting to that word.

In literary speech the significance of the hidden polemic is enormous. Actually there is an element of inner polemic in every style, the difference being only in its degree and character. Any literary word is more or less keenly aware of its listener, reader, or critic, and reflects in itself his anticipated objections, assessments and points of view. In addition, the literary word is aware of the presence of another literary word and another style alongside it. The element of the so-called reaction to the foregoing literary style which is present in every new style is also in its way an inner polemic or, so to speak, a hidden anti-stylization of the other style, and often combines with an obvious parody of that style. The style-determining significance of the inner polemic is extremely great in the autobiography and in the confessional *Icherzählung.* It suffices to mention Rousseau's *Confession.*

A speech in any essential and profound dialog is analagous to the hidden polemic. Every word in such a dialog speech is directed toward its object, but at the same time reacts intensely to the word of the other person, answering it and anticipating it. The element of answer and anticipation penetrates deeply into the intensely dialogical word. Such a word envelopes and draws into itself the speeches of the other people and intensely reworks them. The semantics of the dialogical word are quite special. Unfortunately the subtle changes in meaning which occur as a result of intense dialogicality have not as yet been studied. If the opposite word *(Gegenrede)* is taken into consideration, there occur specific changes in the structure of the dialogical word which make it internally eventful *(sobytiinoe)* and illuminate the word's object in a new way, revealing in it new aspects which are inaccessible to the monological word.

The phenomenon of hidden dialogicality, which is not synonymous with the phenomenon of the hidden polemic, is particularly significant and important for our purposes. Let us imagine a dialog of two people in which the speeches of the second are omitted, but in such a way that the sense is in no way done violence. The second interlocutor is invisibly present, his words are absent, but the profound traces of those words determine all of the first interlocutor's words. Although only one person is speaking, we feel that this is a conversation, and a most intense one at that, since every word that is present answers and reacts with its every fiber to the invisible interlocutor, it points outside itself, beyond its own borders to the other person's unspoken word. We shall see that this hidden dialog occupies a very important place in Dostoevsky's works and that it is very profoundly and subtly developed.

As we see, this third variety differs greatly from the first two varieties of the third type. This final variety can be called *active* in contrast to the preceeding *passive* varieties. In stylization, in the narrated story and in the parody the other person's word is in fact a passive tool in the hand of the author. He takes, so to speak, the other person's meek and helpless word and installs in it his own interpretation, forcing it to serve his new purposes. In the hidden polemic and the dialog, however, the other person's word exerts an active influence and inspiration on the author's speech, forcing it to change accordingly.

A heightening of the activity of the other person's word is, however, also possible in all the manifestations of the second variety of the third type. When the parody feels the resistance, strength and depth of the parodied word of the other person, it is complicated by tones of the hidden polemic. Such a parody has a different sound. The parodied word is more active and exercises a counterforce against the author's intention. The internal dialogization of the parodied word occurs. Similar phenomena occur when the hidden polemic is coupled with the narrated story, and in general in all phenomena of the third type when the aspirations of the author's word and the other person's word are directed toward different objects.

In single-directed words[127] (in stylization, in the single-directed narration) the author's voice and that of the other person tend to merge to the degree that the objectivization of the other person's word is reduced (and we know that objectivization is to a certain degree inherent in all words of the third type). The distance between them is lost; stylization becomes style; the narrator is turned into a mere compositional convention. In hetero-directed words,[128] however, a reduction of the objectivization of the other person's word and a corresponding heightening of the activity of its own aspirations inevitably lead to inner dialogization of that word. In such a word the author's thought no longer overwhelmingly dominates the other person's thought, the word loses its composure and confidence and becomes agitated, innerly undecided and two-faced. Such a word is not only double-voiced, it is double-accented as well, and it is difficult to intonate, since a loud, vigorous intonation excessively monologizes the word and cannot do justice to the other person's voice in it.

This inner dialogization, which is connected with the reduction of objectivization in hetero-directed words of the third type, is not, of course, a new variety of this type. It is merely a tendency inherent in all manifestations of the type (given the conditions of hetero-directedness). Taken to its extreme, this tendency leads to the division of the double-voiced word into two words, two

[164]

F. M. Dostoevsky in 1876

I. The direct word, aimed directly at its object; the expression of the speaker's ultimate semantic authority

II. The objectivized word (the word of a represented character)
1. Predominance of social-typical characteristics
2. Predominance of individual-characterological characteristics

III. The word oriented toward another person's word (the double-voiced word)
1. The single-directed double-voiced word:
   a) stylization
   b) the narrator's story
   c) the non-objectivized word of the hero-(partial) carrier of the author's intentions
   d) the *Icherzählung*

When objectivization is reduced, these variants tend toward the merging of voices, i.e., toward the word of the first type.

2. The hetero-directed double-voiced word:
   a) the parody with all its nuances
   b) the parodistic narration
   c) the parodistic *Icherzählung*
   d) the word of the parodistically represented hero
   e) any reproduction of another person's word with a change of accent

When objectivization is reduced and the other person's idea is activated, these variants become internally dialogized and tend to break down into two words (two voices) of the first type.

3. The active type (the reflected word of the other person):
   a) the hidden internal polemic
   b) the polemically colored auto-biography and confession
   c) any word with a sideward glance at another person's word
   d) the speech in a dialog
   e) the hidden dialog

The other person's word exerts influence from within; the most diverse forms of interrelation-ship with the other person's word are possible, as are vary-ing degrees of its deforming influence.

completely detached independent voices. The other tendency, inherent in single-directed words, when taken to its extreme leads to the complete merging of voices when the objectivization of the other person's word is reduced, and consequently results in a single-voiced word of the first type. All manifestations of the third type operate between these two boundaries.

We have, of course, by no means exhausted all the possible manifestations of the double-voiced word and in general of all the possible means of orientation toward the other person's word, which complicate the ordinary orientation of speech toward its object. A more profound and subtle classification, with a greater number of variants and, perhaps, of types, is possible. But for our purposes the present classification seems sufficient.

We shall give a schematic representation of it on the preceeding page.

The classification given opposite is, of course, of an abstract character. A concrete word may belong simultaneously to various varieties and even types. Moreover, the interrelationships with the other person's word in a concrete living context have a dynamic, not a static character: the interrelationship of voices within the word can change drastically, a single-directed word can transform itself into a hetero-directed one, the inner dialogization can be intensified or weakened, a passive type can become activated, etc.

The examination of the word from the point of view of its relation to the word of another person is, it seems to us, of exceptionally great significance for an understanding of artistic prose. Poetic speech in the narrow sense requires uniformity of all words and their reduction to a common denominator, which can either be a word of the first type or can belong to certain weakened variants of the other types. Of course even under these conditions works which do not reduce their entire verbal material to a common denominator are possible, but in the 19th century are rare and isolated cases. To this category belongs, for example, the "prosaic" lyric of Heine, Barbey, to some extent Nekrasov, and others (the drastic "prosification" of the lyric occurs only in the 20th century). The possibility of employing within a single work words of various types in their extreme expressions without reducing them to a common denominator is one of the most essential characteristics of prose. Herein lies the most profound distinction between prose style and poetic style. But in poetry, too, a whole series of fundamental problems cannot be solved without examining the word from the point of view of another person's word, since various types of word require various stylistic treatments in poetry.

Contemporary stylistics, which ignores this area of examination, is in essence a stylistics only of the first type of word, i.e. of the direct, object-oriented authorial word. Contemporary stylistics, whose roots reach back into the poetics of classicism, can still not free itself from the specific orientations and limitations of those poetics. The poetics of classicism are oriented toward the direct, object-oriented single-voiced word, though with a certain slant in the direction of the conditional stylized word. The half-conditional, half-stylized word sets the tone in classical poetics. And to this day stylistics is oriented toward this half-conditional direct word, which in fact is for it identical with the poetic word as such. For classicism there exists only the word of language, belonging to no one, the material word *(veshchnoe slovo),* which is part of the poetic vocabulary, and is transferred directly from the treasurehouse of the poetic language to the mono-logical context of the given poetic utterance. Thus stylistics, which grew out of the soil of classicism, recognizes only the life of the word in a single, self-enclosed context. It ignores the changes which the word goes through in the process of its transference from one concrete utterance to another and in the process of the mutual orientation of those utterances. It recognizes only those changes which occur in the process of the word's transference from the system of language to the monological poetic utterance. The life and functions of a word in the *style* of a concrete utterance are perceived on the background of its life and functions in the *language.* The inner dialogical relationships of a word to that same word in another person's context or on another person's lips are ignored. Stylistics continues to develop within this framework right up to the present time.

Romanticism brought with it the direct, fully significant word, without any slant toward conditionality. Characteristic of romanticism is the direct authorial word, expressive to the point of self-oblivion, which does not allow itself to be cooled down by refraction through another person's verbal milieu. In romantic poetics the second, and particularly the last variant of the third type were of rather great significance,[129] but nonetheless the directly expressive word taken to its extreme (i.e. the word of the first type) dominated to such a degree that any significant progress in the realm of our question was impossible on the basis of Romanticism as well. In this respect the hegemony of the poetics of classicism went almost unchallenged. Even so, contemporary stylistics is inade-quate even for Romanticism.

Prose, and especially the novel, is completely out of the reach of such a stylistics. It can halfway successfully elaborate only small segments of prose literature, and the least characteristic and significant ones, at that. For the prose artist the world is full of the words of other people, among which he orients himself and for the specific characteristics of which he must have a keen ear. He must introduce them into the plane of his own word, and must do so in such a way that that plane is not destroyed.[130] He works with a very rich verbal pallete, and he works brilliantly with it.

And in interpreting prose we very subtly orient ourselves among all the types and variants of the word which we have discussed. Moreover, in life itself we very keenly and subtly hear all of these nuances in the speech of the people around us, and we ourselves work very well with all the colors of our verbal pallete. We very subtly perceive the smallest change in intonation and the slightest interruption of voices in the practical, everyday word of another person. No verbal sideward glances, reservations, loop-holes, hints or thrusts escape our ear, nor are they foreign to our own lips. It is therefore all the more astounding that all of these things have as yet not been given a clear-cut theoretical basis or the evaluation due them!

On the basis of abstract linguistic categories we gain a theoretical understanding only of the stylistic interrelationships of elements within the limits of
a self-enclosed utterance. Only such single-voiced phenomena are within the
reach of superficial linguistic stylistics which, despite its linguistic value, is as yet
capable within the realm of artistic creativity only of registering on the verbal
periphery of a work the traces and residue of artistic tasks which it does not
understand. The genuine life of the word in prose does not fit within these
boundaries. And they are too narrow for poetry as well.[131]

Stylistics should be based not only, and even *not as much* on linguistics
as on *metalinguistics,* which studies the word not within the system of language
and not in a "text" which is removed from dialogical intercourse, but rather precisely within the sphere of dialogical intercourse itself, i.e. within the sphere of
the genuine life of the word. The word is not a thing, but rather the eternally
mobile, eternally changing medium of dialogical intercourse. It never coincides
with a single consciousness or a single voice. The life of the word is in its transferral from one mouth to another, one context to another, one social collective
to another, and one generation to another. In the process the word does not
forget where it has been and can never wholly free itself from the dominion of
the contexts of which it has been a part.

When each member of a collective of speakers takes possession of a word,
it is not a neutral word of language, free from the aspirations and valuations of
others, uninhabited by foreign voices. No, he receives the word from the voice
of another, and the word is filled with that voice. The word arrives in his context from another context which is saturated with other people's interpretations.
His own thought finds the word already inhabited. Therefore the orientation of
the word among words, the various perceptions of the other person's word and
the various means of reacting to it are, perhaps, the most essential problems of
the metalinguistic study of every kind of word, including the artistic. Every trend
in every epoch has its own characteristic perception of the word and its own
range of verbal possibilities. The ultimate semantic authority of a creative writer
is by no means capable in every historical situation of being expressed in the
direct, unrefracted, unconditional authorial word. When one's own personal
"final" word does not exist, then every creative plan, every thought, feeling and
experience must be refracted through the medium of another person's word,
style and manner, with which it is impossible to directly merge without reservation, distance and refraction.[132]

If a given epoch has at its disposal an at all authoritative and mature medium
of refraction, then the conditional word in one or another of its variants will
prevail, with a greater or lesser degree of conditionality. If such a medium does
not exist, then the prevalent word will be the hetero-directed double-voiced
word, i.e. the parodistic word in all its variants, or a special type of half-conditional, half-ironical word (the word of late Classicism). In such epochs, particularly in times when the conditional word dominates, the direct, unconditional, unrefracted word seems barbarous, raw, and wild. The cultured word is

the word which is refracted through the authoritative and mature medium.

What sort of word dominates in a given moment in a given epoch, what forms of refraction of the word exist, what serves as a medium of refraction? All of these questions are of first-rate importance for the study of the artistic word. Here, of course, we can only hurriedly and in passing mention these problems, without proving them and without elaborating them on the basis of concrete material—this is not the place for the basic examination of these problems.

Let us return to Dostoevsky.

Dostoevsky's works are amazing first of all for the extraordinary diversity of types and variants of word present in them, these types and variants being expressed in their most extreme form. The hetero-directed double-voiced word clearly predominates, being at the same time an internally dialogized, reflected word of another person: the hidden polemic, the polemically colored confession and the hidden dialog. There is almost no word in Dostoevsky which does not take an intense sideward glance at another person's word. At the same time, there are almost no objectivized words in Dostoevsky, since the heroes' speeches are constructed in a way which deprives them of all objectivization. The constant, sharp alteration of the most varied types of word is also amazing in Dostoevsky. Sudden, unexpected transitions from parody to inner polemic, from polemic to hidden dialog, from hidden dialog to the stylization of serene hagiographic tones, thence again to the parodistic story, and finally to an extraordinarily intense open dialog make up the disturbed verbal surface of these works. All of this is intertwined with the deliberately dull thread of the documentarily factual word, whose beginnings and ends are difficult to catch; but the bright reflections or heavy shadows of other nearby utterances also fall on this dry documentary word and give it, too, a peculiar and ambiguous tone.

The main thing is, of course, not alone diversity and sudden changes of verbal types and the predominance among them of double-voiced internally dialogized words. Dostoevsky's uniqueness is in the special distribution of these verbal types and variants among the basic compositional elements of a work.

How and in what elements of the verbal whole is the author's ultimate semantic authority realized? For the monological novel this question is very easily answered. Whatever types of word the novelist-monologist may introduce and whatever their compositional distribution may be, the author's interpretations and evaluations must dominate all others and must comprise a compact and unambiguous whole. Any intensification of another person's intonation in a particular word or a particular segment of a work is only a game allowed by the author to insure that his own direct or refracted word subsequently seems the more energetic. Every struggle of two voices for possession of and dominance in the word in which they appear is decided in advance—it is a sham struggle; all fully significant authorial interpretations are sooner or later gathered together in a single verbal center and in a single consciousness, and all accents are gathered together in a single voice.

[168]

Dostoevsky's artistic task is completely different. He has no fear of the most extreme activization of hetero-directed accents within a double-voiced word; on the contrary, such activization is precisely what he needs, for the plurality of voices must not be done away with, but rather must triumph in his novel.

The stylistic significance of the *other person's word* in Dostoevsky's works is enormous. The other person's word lives an intense life in them. For Dostoevsky the basic stylistic bonds are not bonds between words in the plane of a single monological utterance; basic, rather, are the dynamic, intense bonds between utterances and between independent, full-fledged verbal and semantic centers which are not subordinated to the verbal-semantic dictatorship of a monological, unified style and tone.

We shall investigate the word in Dostoevsky, its life within the work and its function in the realization of the polyphonic task in connection with those compositional units in which the word functions: in the hero's monological self-utterance, in the story—in the narrator's story or in the story told by the author—and finally in the dialog carried on among the heroes. This will be the order in which we carry out our investigation.

2. The hero's monological word and the narrational word in Dostoevsky's novellas *(povesti)*.

Dostoevsky began with the *refracting word*—with the epistolary form. Apropos of *Poor Folk* he writes to his brother:

"They (the public and the critics—M.B.) have become accustomed to seeing the author's ugly mug in everything; I didn't show mine. It doesn't occur to them that Devushkin is speaking, and not I, and that he cannot speak in any other way. They find the novel drawn out, but there is not a superfluous word in it."[133]

Makar Devushkin and Varenka Dobroselova are speaking, the author merely distributes their words: his intentions and aspirations are refracted in the words of the hero and the heroine. The epistolary form is a variant of the *Icherzählung*. The word here is double-voiced and in the majority of cases single-directed. As such it is the compositional surrogate of the author's word, which is absent here. We shall see that the author's conception is very subtly and carefully refracted in the words of the hero-narrators, although the entire work is filled with both obvious and hidden parodies, with both obvious and hidden (authorial) polemics.

But for the present we are interested in Makar Devushkin's speech only as the monological utterance of a hero, and not as the speech of the narrator in the *Icherzählung,* a function which it does fulfill here (since no word-carriers other than the heroes are present). The word of any narrator, employed by the author for the realization of his artistic plan, itself belongs to some specific type, aside

from that type which is defined by its function as narration. Of what type
is Devushkin's monological utterance?

The epistolary form in and of itself does not predetermine the type of word
which will be found in it. In general this form allows for broad verbal possibilities, but it is most favorable for the last variant of the third type of word, i.e. for
the reflected word of another person *(otrazhennoe chuzhoe slovo)*. Characteristic
of the letter is the writer's acute awareness of his interlocutor, the addressee to
whom it is directed. The letter, like the speech in a dialog, is directed to a specific person, and it takes into account his possible reply. This reckoning with the
absentee interlocutor can be more, or less, intensive. In Dostoevsky it has an extremely intensive character.

In his first work Dostoevsky develops a verbal style, very characteristic of
his entire oeuvre, determined by the intense anticipation of the other person's
word. The significance of this style in his subsequent work is enormous: the most
important confessional self-utterances of the heroes are permeated by a highly intense relationship to the anticipated words of others about them and to others'
reaction to their own words about themselves. Not only the tone and style, but
also the internal semantic structure of these self-utterances is determined by the
anticipated word of the other person, from the reservations and loopholes which
stem from Golyadkin's easily offended nature to the ethical and metaphysical
loopholes of Ivan Karamazov. The "servile" variant of this style began to develop
in *Poor Folk*—the cringing word with a timid and bashful sideward glance and
stifled cry of defiance.

This sideward glance is manifested above all in halting speech and its interruptions with the reservations characteristic of this style.

"I live in the kitchen, or, more correctly speaking, here next to the
kitchen is a little room (and I would like to point out that our kitchen is
clean and bright, a very good one), a small nook, a humble little corner...
that is, to put it even better, the kitchen is large, with three windows, and
along one wall there is a partition, so it is as if there were another room, a
supernumerary one; it is all roomy and convenient, and there is a window,
and it is all—in a word, it is convenient. Well, so, this is my little corner. Well
now, my dear, don't think that there is anything strange here, some mysterious significance—Aha, he lives in the kitchen!—that is, you see, I do
live in this room behind the partition, but that doesn't matter; I keep to
myself, away from the others, I live in a small way, I live quietly. I have a
bed, a table, a chest of drawers, a couple of chairs, and an icon on the wall.
True, there are better apartments, perhaps even much better ones, but then
convenience is the main thing; I live like this for convenience sake, and don't
go thinking that it is for any other reason." (I, 82)

After almost every word Devushkin takes a sideward glance at his absentee
interlocutor, he is afraid that she will think that he is complaining, he tries in

advance to destroy the impression which the news that he lives in the kitchen will create, he does not want to trouble his interlocutor, etc. The repetition of words is caused by the desire to intensify their accent or to give them a new nuance in light of the interlocutor's possible reaction.

In the excerpt which we have quoted, the reflected word is the potential word of the addressee—Varenka Dobroselova. In the majority of instances Makar Devushkin's speech about himself is determined by the reflected word of this "other person, this stranger" *(chuzhoi chelovek)*. Here is how he defines this stranger. He asks Varvara Dobroselova:

> "And what will you do out there among strangers? Don't you know yet what a stranger is?...No, you've asked me a question, so I'll tell you what a stranger is. I know him, my dear, I know him well; I've had to eat his bread. He is mean, Varenka, mean, he is so mean, your poor little heart won't be able to stand the way he torments it with his reproaches and rebukes and his evil glance." (I, 140)

The poor, but "ambitious" man, such as Makar Devushkin, according to Dostoevsky's plan constantly feels other people's "evil glance" directed toward him, a glance which is either reproachful or—perhaps even worse in his eyes— mocking (for the heroes of the prouder type the worst glance of all is the compassionate one). Devushkin's speech cringes under this glance. He, like the hero from the underground, is constantly listening in on other people's words about him.

> "The poor man, he is demanding; he looks at God's world differently, and he looks askance at every passerby, he casts a troubled gaze about him and he listens closely to every word—isn't it him they are talking about?" (I, 153)

The sideward glance at the socially foreign word defines not only the style and tone of Makar Devushkin's speech, but his very manner of thinking and experiencing, of seeing and understanding himself and the little world which surrounds him, as well. In Dostoevsky's artistic world there is always a profound organic bond between the superficial elements of a character's verbal manner, his way of expressing himself, and the ultimate foundations of his *Weltanschauung*. The whole person is presented in every one of his manifestations. The orientation of one person to another person's word and consciousnes is, in essence, the basic theme of all of Dostoevsky's works. The hero's attitude toward himself is inseparably bound up with his attitude towards others and with their attitude toward him. His consciousness of self is always perceived against the background of others' consciousness of him—"I for myself" against the background of "I for others." For this reason the hero's word about himself takes shape under the constant influence of another person's word about him.

This theme develops in various forms in various works, with varying content and on various spiritual levels. In *Poor Folk* the poor man's self-consciousness unfolds against the background of a socially foreign consciousness of him. His self-affirmation has the sound of an uninterrupted hidden polemic or hidden dialog with another person, a stranger, on the subject of himself. In Dostoevsky's first works this is expressed rather simply and directly—the dialog has not yet gone inside, into the very atoms of thought and experience, so to speak. The heroes' world is still small, and they have not yet become ideologists. Their social servility itself makes their inner sideward glance and inner polemic direct and clear-cut, without the complex internal loopholes which grow into whole ideological constructions that we see in Dostoevsky's final works. But the profound dialogicality and polemicism of self-consciousness and self-affirmation are already here revealed with complete clarity.

"The other day in a private conversation Evstafy Ivanovich said that the most important civic virtue is the ability to make a lot of money. He was joking (I know he was joking), it was a moral lesson that one shouldn't be a burden to anyone else, but I'm not a burden to anyone! I have my own piece of bread; true, it is a modest piece of bread, sometimes it's even stale, but it is mine, I win it with my own labor and use it lawfully and blamelessly. But what can one do? I know myself that my copying is not much of a job, but, still, I am proud of it: I work, I spill my sweat. Well, and really, so what if I just copy! Is it a sin to copy, or something? 'He just copies!...' What is so dishonorable about that? I realize now that I am needed, that I am indispensable, and that I shouldn't let their nonsense disturb me. Well, so I'm a rat, if they find some resemblance! But that rat is necessary, that rat accomplishes something, they're all supported by that rat, and that rat will get its reward—that's the kind of rat it is! But enough on this subject, my dear; I didn't want to talk about that, I just got a little carried away. All the same, it is nice to do oneself justice now and then."
(I, 125-126)

Makar Devushkin's self-consciousness is revealed in an even sharper polemic when he recognizes himself in Gogol's *The Overcoat;* he perceives it as another person's word about him personally, and he seeks to polemically destroy that word as being inapplicable to him.

But let us now take a closer look at the construction of this "word with a sideward glance."

Already in the first excerpt, where Devushkin casts his sideward glances at Verenka Dobroselova as he informs her of his new room, we notice the peculiar interruptions of speech which define its syntactical and accentual construction. The other person's words as it were wedge their way into his speech, and although they are in reality not there, their influence brings about a radical reorganization of that speech. The other person's words are not present, but they cast a shadow on his speech, and that shadow is real. But sometimes the speech of another person, in addition to its influence on the accentual and syntactical structure, leaves behind a word or two, and sometimes a whole sentence, in Makar Devushkin's speech:

> "Well now, my dear, don't think that there is anything strange here, some mysterious significance—'Aha, he lives in the *kitchen!*'—that is, you see, I do live in this room behind the partition, but that doesn't matter..."
> (I, 82)

The word "kitchen" bursts into Devushkin's speech from out of the other person's possible speech as it is anticipated by him. This word is presented with the other person's accent, which Devushkin polemically exaggerates somewhat. He does not accept this accent, although he cannot help recognizing its power, and he tries to evade it by means of all sorts of reservations, partial concessions and extenuations, which distort the structure of his speech. The smooth surface of his speech is furrowed by ripples fanning out from the other person's word, which has taken root in that speech. Apart from this obviously foreign word with its obviously foreign accent, the majority of words in the quoted passage are chosen by the speaker from two points of view simultaneously: as he himself understands them and wants others to understand them, and as others might in fact understand them. Here the other person's accent is only sketched in, but it already gives rise to reservations or hesitations in his speech.

The encroachment of words and especially of accents from the speech of others into Makar Devushkin's speech is even more marked and obvious in the second of the passages which we have quoted. Here the word containing the other person's polemically exaggerated accent is even enclosed in quotation marks: "He just copies!..." In the immediately preceeding lines the word "copy" is repeated three times. In each of these three instances the other person's potential accent is present in the word "copy," but it is suppressed by Devushkin's own accent; however, it becomes constantly stronger, until it finally breaks through and takes on the form of the direct speech of the other person. Thus we are presented here with the gradations of the gradual intensification of the other person's accent: "I know myself that my *copying* is not much of a job... (a reservation follows—M.B.). Well, and really, so what if I just *copy!* Is it a sin to *copy* or something? 'He just *copies!...*' " We have indicated the other person's accent, which gradually grows stronger and finally completely takes over the word, which is enclosed in quotation marks. Even so, in this last, obviously foreign word Devushkin's own voice is present, too, as he polemically exaggerates the other person's accent. To the degree that the other person's accent is intensified, Devushkin's counter-accent is also intensified.

We can thus descriptively define all the phenomena which we have discussed: the hero's self-consciousness was penetrated by another person's consciousness of him, and another person's word about him was thrown into the hero's self-utterance; the consciousness and the word of the other person give rise to specific phenomena which define the thematic development of the self-consciousness, its breaking points, loopholes and protests on the one hand, and the hero's speech with its accentual interruptions, syntactical breaking points, repetitions, reservations and prolixity on the other.

Or we can give another graphic definition and explanation of the same phenomena: let us imagine that in a very intense dialog two speeches—a word and a counter-word,—instead of following one after the other and proceeding from two different mouths, are overlaid one on the other and merge into a *single* utterance coming from a *single* mouth. These speeches move in opposite directions and collide with one another; thus their overlapping and their merging into a single utterance lead to their intense interference *(pereboi)*. The collision of entire single-accented, unified speeches is transformed within a new utterance (which results from the merging of those speeches) into the sharp interference of voices contradictory in every detail and every atom of that utterance. The dialogical collision has gone inward, into the subtlest structural elements of speech (which are also the elements of consciousness).

The passage which we have quoted could be roughly paraphrased in the following crude dialog of Makar Devushkin with the "stranger:"

> Stranger: One must know how to make a lot of money. One shouldn't be a burden to anyone. But you are a burden to others.
> Makar Devushkin: I'm not a burden to anyone. I've got my own piece of bread.
> Stranger: But what a piece it is! Today it's there, and tomorrow it's gone. And most likely a stale piece, at that!
> Makar Devushkin: True, it is a modest piece of bread, sometimes it's even stale, but it is mine, I win it with my own labor and use it lawfully and blamelessly.
> Stranger: But what kind of labor! All you do is copy. You're not capable of anything else.
> Makar Devushkin: Well, what can one do! I know myself that my copying is not much of a job, but, still, I am proud of it!
> Stranger: Oh, there's something to be proud of, all right! Copying! It's disgraceful!
> Makar Devushkin: Well, and really, so what if I just copy!...etc.

It is as if as a result of the overlapping and merging of the speeches of this dialog in a single voice that this self-utterance of Devushkin came to be.

Of course this imagined dialog is terribly primitive, just as the content of Devushkin's consciousness is still primitive. For he is in the final analysis an Akaky Akakievich who is illuminated by a self-consciousness and has discovered speech and a "refined style" *(vyrabatyvaiushchii slog)*. But on the other hand, as a result of its primitiveness and crudeness, the formal structure of his self-consciousness and self-utterance is extremely clear and lucid. That is why we are examining it in such detail. All of the important self-utterances of Dostoevsky's later heroes could also be developed into dialogs, since they all, as it were, arose out of two merged speeches, but in them the interference of voices goes so deep, into such subtle elements of thought and word, that to develop them into an obvious and crude dialog, as we have just done with Devushkin's self-utterance, is, of course, completely impossible.

The phenomena which we have discussed, produced by the word of another person within the hero's speech, are in *Poor Folk* presented in the stylistic accouterments of the speech of a petty Petersburg clerk. The structural characteristics of the "word with a sideward glance," the hidden polemical and internally dialogical word are refracted here in the strictly and skillfully sustained social-typical verbal manner of Devushkin.[134] For this reason all of these phenomena of language—reservations, repetitions, diminutives, diverse particles and interjections—in the form in which they appear here are impossible in the mouths of other heroes of Dostoevsky who belong to other social worlds. The same phenomena appear in a different social-typical and individual-characterological verbal form. But their essence remains the same: the crossing and intersection in every element of the consciousness and the word of two consciousnesses, two points of view, two evaluations —the intra-atomic interference of voices, so to speak.

Golyadkin's word is constructed within the same social-typical verbal milieu, but it has a different individual-characterological manner. In *The Double* the characteristics of consciousness and speech which we have discussed are to be found in a more extreme and clear-cut form than in any other of Dostoevsky's works. The tendencies which began already in Makar Devushkin are here developed with extraordinary daring and consistency to their semantic limits on the basis of the same deliberately primitive, simple and crude ideological material.

Dostoevsky himself, in a letter to his brother written while he was working on *The Double,* gave a parodistic stylization of the verbal and semantic system of Golyadkin's word. As would be the case in any parodistic stylization, the basic characteristics and tendencies of Golyadkin's word are plainly and crudely made visible here.

> **Yakov Petrovich Golyadkin** holds his own completely. He's a terrible scoundrel and there is no approaching him; he refuses to move forward, pretending that, you see, he's not ready yet, that for the present he's his own man, he's alright, nothing is the matter, but that if it comes to that, then he can do that, too, why not, what's to prevent it? He is just like everyone else, he's nothing special, just like everyone else. What's it to him! He's a scoundrel, a terrible scoundrel! He'll never agree to end his career before the middle of November. He's already just spoken with his excellency, and he just may (and why shouldn't he) announce his retirement.[135]

As we shall see, this style, in which the hero is parodied, is the same style in which the story of the novella is told. But we shall turn to the story later.

The influence of the other person's word on Golyadkin's speech is completely obvious. We immediately feel that his speech, like Devushkin's, is adequate not just to itself and to its object. However, Golyadkin's interrelationship with the word and the consciousness of the other person is somewhat different than Devushkin's. Therefore the phenomena in Golyadkin's style which result from the other person's word are also of a different sort.

Golyadkin's speech above all seeks to simulate total independence from the other person's word: "he's his own man, he's alright." This simulation of independence and indifference also leads to endless repetitions, reservations and prolixity, here directed toward himself, and not outside himself toward the other person: he tries to convince and reassure and comfort himself, playing the role of the other person in relation to himself. Golyadkin's self-comforting dialogs with himself are the most widespread phenomenon in the novella. Along with the simulation of indifference goes another attitude toward the other person's word: the desire to hide from it, to avoid calling attention to oneself, to get lost in the crowd, to become inconspicuous: "He's just like everyone else, he's nothing special, just like everyone else." But now he is trying to convince not himself, but the other person, of this. Finally, the third attitude toward the other person's word involves Golyadkin's yielding to it, subordinating himself to it, and submissively adopting it, as if he himself were of the same opinion and sincerely agreed with it: "if it comes to that, then he can do that, too, why not, what's to prevent it?"

These are the three general lines in Golyadkin's orientation, and they are complicated by other secondary, but rather important ones. Each of these three lines in and of itself gives rise to very complex phenomena in Golyadkin's consciousness and in his word.

We shall concentrate above all on his simulation of independence and composure.

As we have said, the pages of *The Double* are full of the hero's dialogs with himself. One might say that Golyadkin's entire inner life develops dialogically. We quote two examples of such dialogs:

"But, still, will it be right?" continued our hero, alighting from the coach near the entrance to a certain five-storied house on the Liteinaya, beside which he had ordered his carriage to halt. "Will it be right? Will it be proper? Will it be appropriate? But really why all the fuss," he continued as he climbed the steps, catching his breath and checking the thumping of his heart, which was in the habit of thumping on other people's stairways. "Why the fuss? I'm on my own business, there's nothing reprehensible here at all...I would be silly to hide myself. I'll just pretend that nothing's the matter, that I just happened by...He'll see that everything's as it should be."
(I, 215)

The second example of interior dialog is much more complex and acute. It takes place after the appearance of Golyadkin's double, i.e. after the second voice has become objectivized for him within his own field of vision.

> Mr. Golyadkin's delight thus expressed itself, though at the same time something was still tickling in his head, not exactly melancholy, but now and then it tugged so at his heart that he was almost inconsolable. "Still and all, we'll wait until morning before rejoicing. But really, why all the fuss? Well, we'll think it over, we'll see. Well, let's think it over, my young friend, let's think it over. Well, in the first place, he's a person just like you, exactly the same. Well, what does it matter? Should I cry about it or something, just because he's a person like that? What's it to me? It doesn't involve me; I'll go my merry way, and that'll be all there is to it! That's the way he wants it, and that's all there is to it! Let him do his job! Well, it's a miracle and an oddity, they say that there are Siamese twins...Well, but why do they have to be Siamese? Let's assume that they are twins, but great men have sometimes been odd-looking, too. It's even known from history that the famous Suvorov crowed like a rooster...Well, yes, that was for political reasons; and great generals...but what are generals, anyway? I'm my own man, that's all there is to it, I don't need anybody, and in my innocence I have nothing but contempt for the enemy. I'm not an intriguer, and I'm proud of it. I'm pure, I'm straightforward, orderly, pleasant, and gentle..." (I, 268-269)

The first question to arise is that of the function of Golyadkin's dialog with himself in his spiritual life. The answer can be briefly formulated thus: *the dialog allows him to substitute his own voice for the voice of another person.*

The function of Golyadkin's second voice as a substitute is felt everywhere. Without understanding this it is impossible to understand his interior dialogs. Golyadkin addresses himself as if addressing another person ("my young friend"), he praises himself as only another person could, he verbally caresses himself with tender familiarity: "Yakov Petrovich, my dear fellow *(golubchik)*, you little Golyadka, you—you have just the right name!," and he reassures and comforts himself with the authoritative tone of an older, more confident person. But this second voice of Golyadkin's, confident and calmly self-satisfied, cannot possibly merge with his first voice, the uncertain, timid one; the dialog cannot turn into an integral and confident monolog of a single Golyadkin. Moreover, that second voice is to such a degree unable to merge with the first one and feels so threateningly independent that teasing, mocking, traitorous tones begin to appear in place of comforting, reassuring ones. With amazing tact and art, in a way almost imperceptible to the reader, Dostoevsky transfers Golyadkin's second voice from the interior dialog to the telling of the story itself: it takes on the sound of the voice of the narrator. But we shall speak of the narration a bit later.

Golyadkin's second voice must make up for the fact that he receives too little recognition from other people. Golyadkin wants to get by without such recognition, to get by on his own, so to speak. But this "on his own" inevitably takes on the form "you and I, my friend Golyadkin," i.e. it takes on a dialogical form. In fact, Golyadkin lives only in the other person, he lives in his reflection in the other person: "will it be proper," "will it be appropriate?" And this question is always answered from the possible, conjectured point of view of the other person: Golyadkin *will pretend* that nothing is the matter, that he just happened by, and the other person will see "that everything's as it should be." Everything depends on the reaction of the other person, on his word and his answer. The confidence of Golyadkin's second voice cannot take complete possession of him and in fact substitute for an actual other person. The other person's word is the most important thing for him.

> Although Mr. Golyadkin said all of these things (about his independence— M.B.) as clearly and confidently as could be, weighing and calculating every word for the surest effect, he was now looking uneasily, very uneasily, most uneasily at Krestyan Ivanovich. He was all eyes, and he timidly awaited Krestyan Ivanovich's answer with annoying, melancholy impatience. (I, 220-221)

In the second quoted interior-dialog excerpt the function of the second voice as a substitute is completely obvious. But in addition, a third voice appears here, the direct voice of another, which interrupts the second, the substitute voice. Thus we have here phenomena which are completely analogous to those which we analyzed in Devushkin's speech—foreign (i.e. *chuzhie*—belonging to another person— trans.) and half-foreign words and the corresponding accentual interferences:

> "Well, it's a miracle and an oddity, they say that there are Siamese twins... Well, but why do they have to be Siamese? Let's assume that they are twins, but great men have sometimes been odd-looking, too. It's even known from history that the great Suvorov crowed like a rooster...Well, yes, that was for political reasons; and great generals...but what are generals?" (I, 268)

Everywhere, but especially in those places where ellipses appear, the antici- pated speeches of other people wedge themselves in. This passage, too, could be elaborated in the form of a dialog, but here the dialog is much more complex. While in Devushkin's speech a single, integral voice polemicized with the "other person," here there are two voices: one is confident, too confident, and the other is too timid, it relents in everything, capitulating totally.[136]
Golyadkin's second voice—the one which substitutes for that of another person, his first voice—the one which first hides itself from the other person's word ("I'm like everyone else, I'm alright"), then gives in to it ("but if that's the case, then I'm prepared"), and finally the voice of the other which sounds constantly within him, are interrelated in such a complex way that they provide sufficient material for the entire plot *(intriga)* and permit the construction of the whole novella to be based on them alone. The actual event, namely the unsuccessful

courtship of Klara Olsufevna, and all the attendant circumstances are in fact not represented in the novella—they serve merely as the stimulus which sets the inner voices in motion, they merely intensify and make immediate the inner conflict which is the real object of representation in the novella.

Except for Golyadkin and his double, none of the characters takes any actual part whatever in the plot, which unfolds totally within the bounds of Golyadkin's self-consciousness; the other characters merely provide the raw material, the fuel, as it were, necessary for the intense work of that self-consciousness. The external, intentionally obscure plot (everything of importance has taken place before the novella begins) also serves as the firm, barely discernible carcass for Golyadkin's inner plot. The novella relates how Golyadkin wanted to get along without the other person's consciousness and without recognition by the other person, wanted to avoid the other person and to assert his own self, and what resulted therefrom. Dostoevsky intended *The Double* to be a "confession"[137] (not in a personal sense, of course), i.e. the representation of an event which occurs within the bounds of the self-consciousness. *The Double* is the *first dramatical confession* among Dostoevsky's works.

Thus, at the basis of the plot lies Golyadkin's attempt, in view of the total non-recognition of his personality on the part of others, to find for himself a substitute for the other person. Golyadkin plays at being an independent person; his consciousness plays at being confident and self-sufficient. The new, violent collision with the other person during the party when Golyadkin is publicly devastated, intensifies his divarication. Golyadkin's second voice over-exerts itself in the desperate simulation of self-sufficiency, in order to save his face. Golyadkin's second voice cannot merge with him; on the contrary, the traitorous tones of ridicule grow louder and louder in it. It provokes and teases Golyadkin, it casts off his mask. The double appears. The inner conflict is dramatized; Golyadkin's intrigue with the double begins.

The double speaks in the words of Golyadkin himself, bringing in no new words or tones. At first he pretends to be a cringing, capitulating Golyadkin. When Golyadkin brings the double home with him, the latter looks and behaves like the first, the uncertain voice in Golyadkin's interior dialog ("Will it be appropriate, will it be proper," etc.):

> The guest (the double—M.B.) was, obviously, extremely embarrassed, he was very timid, he submissively followed his host's every movement, he tried to catch his glances in order, so it seemed, to divine his thoughts from them. All of his gestures expressed something abased, downtrodden and terrified, so that, if the comparison will be permitted, in that moment he bore a fair resemblance to a person, who for lack of his own clothes, has put on someone else's: the sleeves crawl up his arms and the waist comes almost up to his neck, and he is constantly either straightening the tiny vest, shuffling sideways and getting out of the way, trying to hide somewhere, or glancing at people's faces and listening carefully to hear if they are talking about him

or laughing at him or are ashamed for him—the fellow grows red, the fellow is flustered, and his pride suffers... (I, 270-271)

This is a characterization of the cringing, self-effacing Golyadkin. The double also speaks in the tones and the style of Golyadkin's first voice. The part of the second—the confident and tenderly reassuring—voice in relation to the double is played by Golyadkin himself, who this time as it were merges completely with this voice:

"You and I, Yakov Petrovich, shall live like a fish with water, like blood brothers; we, my friend, shall be crafty, we together shall be crafty; we shall think up intrigues to spite them, to spite them we shall think up intrigues. And don't you trust any of them. Because I know you, Yakov Petrovich, and I understand your character: you'll go and tell everything, you're a truthful soul! You must keep away from all of them, old boy." (I, 276) 138

But subsequently the roles change: the traitorous double takes over the tone of Golyadkin's second voice, parodistically exaggerating its tender familiarity. Already at their next meeting at the office the double takes on this tone and sustains it to the end of the novella, himself now and then emphasizing the identity of his expressions with the words of Golyadkin (i.e. the ones Golyadkin said during their first conversation). During one of their meetings at the office the double, familiarly poking Golyadkin, "with the most venomous and broadly suggestive smile, said to him: 'Oh no you don't Yakov Petrovich, old boy, oh no you don't! You and I'll be crafty, Yakov Petrovich, we'll be crafty.' " Or a little later, before their face-to-face confrontation in the café:

"Well, so then, as you say, my good fellow," said Mr. Golyadkin Jr., getting out of the droshky and shamelessly patting our hero on the shoulder, "you're such a buddy; for you, Yakov Petrovich, I'd go through thick and thin (as you, Yakov Petrovich, once justly saw fit to remark). He is a rascal, though, he'll do to you whatever comes into his head!" (I, 337)

This transferral of words from one mouth to another, in which their tone and ultimate meaning are changed, while their content remains the same, is one of Dostoevsky's basic devices. He causes his heroes to recognize themselves, their idea, their own word, their orientation, and their gesture in another person, in whom all of these manifestations take on a different integral and ultimate meaning and a different sound, the sound of parody or ridicule.139

As we have said, almost all of Dostoevsky's major heroes have a partial double in another person or even in several other people (Stavrogin and Ivan Karamazov). In his final work Dostoevsky again returned to the device of fully embodying the second voice, though on a more profound and subtle basis. In its externally formal plan Ivan Karamazov's dialog with the devil is analogous with the interior dialogs which Golyadkin carries on with himself and with his double; despite the dissimilarity in situation and in ideological content, in both instances essentially the same artistic problem is being solved.

Thus Golyadkin's intrigue with his double develops as a dramatized crisis of his self-consciousness, as a dramatized confession. The action does not go beyond the bounds of the self-consciousness, since the characters are merely subdivided elements of that self-consciousness. The actors are the three voices into which Golyadkin's voice and consciousness have dissociated: his "I for myself," which cannot do without the other person and without recognition by him; his fictitious "I for the other person" (reflection in the other person), i.e. Golyadkin's second substitute-voice; and, finally, the voice of the other person which does not recognize Golyadkin, and which at the same time has no real existence outside him, since there are no other characters of equal stature in the work.[140] The result is a peculiar mystery play or, more precisely, a morality play, in which the actors are not whole people, but rather the spiritual forces battling within them, a morality play, however, devoid of any formalism or abstract allegoricalness.

But who tells the story in *The Double*? What is the position of the narrator and what is his voice like?

Also in the narration we find not a single element which goes beyond the bounds of Golyadkin's self-consciousness, not a single word or a single tone which could not be a part of his interior dialog with himself or of his dialog with his double. The narrator picks up Golyadkin's words and thoughts, the words of his *second voice,* intensifies the teasing, taunting tones present in them, and in these tones depicts Golyadkin's every act, gesture and movement. We have already mentioned that Golyadkin's second voice, by means of imperceptible transitions, merges with the voice of the narrator; the impression is created that the *narration is dialogically directed toward Golyadkin himself,* it rings in his ears as the taunting voice of another person, the voice of his double, although formally the narration is directed toward the reader.

This is how the narrator describes Golyadkin's behavior at the most fateful moment in his adventures, when he tries to crash the ball given by Olsufy Ivanovich:

> We should better turn our attention to Mr. Golyadkin, the true and only hero of this our most veracious story.
>
> At the moment he is, to put it mildly, in a very strange situation. He, ladies and gentlemen, is also here, that is he is not at the ball, but he is almost at the ball; he, ladies and gentlemen, is all right; he may be his own man, but at this moment he is on a somewhat less than straight and narrow path; he is now—it seems strange even to say it—he is now standing in a passageway on the back stairs of Olsufy Ivanovich's house. But it's alright that he is standing here, it is nothing special. He is, ladies and gentlemen, standing in a corner, jammed into a little space, if not a very warm one, at least very dark, hiding partly behind a huge cabinet and some old screens, in the middle of all sorts of rubbish, trash and junk, waiting for the proper time, and at the

[181]

moment just observing the general course of events in the capacity of an outside spectator. He is, ladies and gentlemen, just observing now; but, ladies and gentlemen, he, too, could make an entrance...why shouldn't he make an entrance? He only has to step out, and he will make his entrance, and make it very adroitly, at that. (I, 239-240)

In the construction of this narration we observe the interference of two voices, the same kind of merging of two speeches that we observed already in Makar Devushkin's utterances. But here the roles have been changed; here it is as if the other person's speech has swallowed up the speech of the hero. The narration glitters with Golyadkin's own words: "He's all right," "he's his own man," etc. But the narrator gives these words an intonation of ridicule, ridicule and in part reproach, directed at Golyadkin himself and constructed in such a form as to touch his sore spots and provoke him. This taunting narration imperceptibly turns into the speech of Golyadkin himself. The question "why shouldn't he make an entrance?" belongs to Golyadkin himself, but it is spoken in the teasing, egging-on intonation of the narrator. But this intonation, too, is essentially not foreign to Golyadkin's own consciousness. All of these things could ring in his own head, as his second voice. In essence, the author could insert quotation marks at any point without changing the tone, the voice or the construction of the sentence.
Somewhat further on he does precisely that:

So, ladies and gentlemen, he is waiting quietly, now, and has been doing so for exactly two-and-one-half hours. And why shouldn't he wait? Villèle himself waited. "But what does Villèle have to do with it?" thought Mr. Golyadkin. "There's no Villèle here! But what should I do now...should I up and make my appearance? Ach, you nobody, you!" (I, 241)

But why not insert quotation marks two sentences earlier, before the words, "And why shouldn't," or still earlier, changing, "So, ladies and gentlemen, he" to "Golyadkin, old boy," or some other form of Golyadkin addressing himself? The quotation marks are, of course, not inserted at random. They are inserted in such a way as to make the transition particularly subtle and imperceptible. Villèle's name appears in the narrator's last sentence and in the hero's first. Golyadkin's words seem to continue the narration without interruption and to answer it within the interior dialog. "Villèle himself waited," " 'But what does Villèle have to do with it?' " These are in fact speeches from Golyadkin's interior dialog with himself which have become separated, one going into the narration and the other remaining with Golyadkin. This is the reverse of the phenomenon which we observed earlier: the interferrential merging of two speeches. But the result is the same: a double-voiced interferrential construction with all the accompanying phenomena. And the arena of action is the same: a single self-consciousness. The difference is that this consciousness is ruled by the word of another person which has taken up residence in it. We shall quote another example with the same kind of vacillating

[182]

border between the narration and the hero's word. Golyadkin has made up his mind and at last has entered the hall where the ball is going on; he appears before Klara Olsufevna:

> Without the slightest doubt, without batting an eye, he would at this moment have been most happy to fall through a hole in the earth; but what's done is done...What could he do? "If it doesn't work out—stand firm; if it does—stand firm, too. Mr. Golyadkin was, naturally, no intriguer, nor a master at polishing the parquet with his boots...." So it happened. In addition, the Jesuits somehow had a hand in the affair...Mr. Golyadkin was, however, in no mood for them! (I, 242-243)

This passage is interesting because it contains no direct speech belonging to Mr. Golyadkin, and therefore there is no basis for the quotation marks. The portion of the narration included here in quotation marks was apparently mistakenly set off by the editor. Dostoevsky probably set off only the proverb, "If it doesn't work out, stand firm; if it does, stand firm too" *(Ne udastsia—derzhis', a udastsia— krepis' ")*. The following sentence is given in the third person, although it obviously belongs to Golyadkin himself. Further, the pauses indicated by ellipses also belong to Golyadkin's interior speech. According to their accents, the sentences preceding and following these ellipses are related to one another as speeches in an interior dialog. The two adjacent sentences concerning the Jesuits are quite analogous to the above-quoted sentences about Villèle, which were separated by quotation marks.

Finally, one more excerpt in which, perhaps, the opposite mistake has crept in—quotation marks have been omitted where, grammatically, they should have been included. Golyadkin, having been ejected from the ball, runs home in a snow storm and meets a passerby who later turns out to be his double:

> Not that he was afraid that he was a dangerous person, but then, perhaps... "Who knows who this fellow is, out so late," flashed through Mr. Golyadkin's mind. "Maybe he's just out late like I am, but then maybe he's not here for no reason, maybe he has a purpose, to cross my path and bump into me." (I, 252)

Here the ellipsis serves as a divider between the narration and Golyadkin's direct interior speech, which is given in the first person *("my path," "catch me")*. But the two are so closely merged here that one really does not want to put in the quotation marks. This sentence must be read with a single voice, albeit with an innerly dialogized one. The transition from the narration to the hero's speech is amazingly successfully executed: we feel, as it were, a wave of a single current of speech which carries us, with no dams or barriers, from the narration into the hero's soul, and from it back into the narration; we feel that we are, in essence, moving within the circle of a single consciousness.

It would be possible to cite many more examples proving that the narration is a direct continuation and development of Golyadkin's second voice and that it is dialogically addressed to the hero, but the examples which we have cited are sufficient. Thus the entire work is constructed as a total interior dialog of three voices within the bounds of a single dissociated consciousness. Every essential element of the work lies in the point of intersection of these three voices and of their sharp, agonizing interference. To make use of our image, we can say that, while this is not yet polyphony, it is no longer homophony. One and the same word, idea, phenomenon passes through three voices, and has a different sound in each one. One and the same totality of words, tones and inner orientations passes through Golyadkin's external speech, through the narrator's speech, and through the speech of the double; these three voices are situated face to face and speak not about one another, but with one another. The three voices sing the same song, but not in unison—each has its own part.

But these three voices have not yet become completely independent, real voices, they are not yet three full-fledged consciousnesses. That takes place only in Dostoevsky's novels. In *The Double* the monological word, adequate only to itself and its object, is not present. Every word is dialogically dissociated, every word contains an interference of voices, but the genuine dialog of unmerged consciousnesses which appears later in the novels is here not yet present. The rudiment of counterpoint is already here: it is hinted at in the very structure of the word. The analyses which we have made are, as it were, already contrapuntal analyses (figuratively speaking, of course). But these new bonds have not yet gone beyond the bounds of monological material.

The provoking, taunting voice of the narrator and the voice of the double ring relentlessly in Golyadkin's ears. The narrator shouts his very own words and thoughts into his ear, but in a different, a hopelessly foreign, hopelessly censorious and mocking tone. This second voice is present in every one of Dostoevsky's heroes, but as we have said, in his final novel it again takes on the form of independent existence. The devil shouts Ivan Karamazov's very own words into his ear in a mocking commentary on his decision to confess in court, repeating his intimate thoughts in a foreign tone. We shall not discuss Ivan's actual dialog with the devil, since we will concern ourselves with the principles of the genuine dialog later on. But we shall quote the story which Ivan excitedly relates to Alyosha immediately after his dialog with the devil. Its structure is analogous to the structure of *The Double* as we have analyzed it. The same principle of the combination of voices is present here, though here everything is deeper and more complex. In this story Ivan passes his own personal thoughts and decisions through two voices simultaneously; he communicates them in two different tonalities. In the quoted excerpt we shall omit Alyosha's replies, since his real voice does not yet fit into our scheme. We are for now interested only in the intra-atomic counterpoint of voices and their combination only within the bounds of a single dissociated consciousness (i.e. a microdialog).

"He teased me! And cleverly, you know, cleverly:'Conscience! What is conscience? I create it myself. Why do I torment myself? Out of habit. Out of a universal human habit seven thousand years old. When we get out of the habit, we will be gods.' That's what he said, that's what he said!...''

"Yes, but he is evil. He laughed at me. He was insolent, Alyosha," said Ivan with an offended shudder. "And he slandered me, he slandered me in many ways. He lied about me to my face. 'Oh, you are going to perform an heroic deed of virtue, you are going to announce that you killed your father, that you incited that lackey to kill your father...' "

That's what he says, he, and he knows it. 'You are going to perform an heroic deed of virtue, but you do not believe in virtue—that is what torments and enrages you, that is why you are so vindictive.' He told me these things about myself, and he knows what he is talking about...."

"No, he knows how to torture, he is cruel," continued Ivan, not listening. "I always had the feeling I knew why he was coming. 'Let us assume that you went out of pride, but still there was the hope that they would find Smerdyakov out and send him to prison, exonerate Mitya, and only *morally* condemn you (he laughed here, do you hear it?), and others would praise you. But then Smeryakov died, hanged himself—well, now who is going to take your word alone in court? But still you are going, you are going, you will go anyway, you have resolved to go. But why are you going now?' This is terrible, Alyosha, I can't endure such questions. Who dares to ask me such questions!" (X, 184-185)

All the loopholes of Ivan's thoughts, all his sideward glances at the other person's word and the other person's consciousness, all his attempts to avoid the other person's word and to replace it in his soul with his own self-affirmation *(samoutverzhdenie)*, all the reservations of his conscience which create an interference in his every thought, his every word and experience, all these things are brought to a focus and intensified here in the completed speeches of the devil. The difference between Ivan's words and the devil's replies is not one of content, but merely one of tone, of accent. But this change of accent alters their whole ultimate meaning. The devil as it were transfers to the main clause that which in Ivan's sentence was merely a subordinate clause and was pronounced in a low voice with no independent accent; he in turn transforms the content of the main clause into an unaccented subordinate clause. The devil turns Ivan's reservation regarding the main motif of his decision into the main motif, while the main motif becomes a mere reservation. The result is a profoundly tense and extremely eventful combination of voices, but one which at the same time is not based on any opposition whatever in content or theme.

But, of course, this complete dialogization of Ivan's self-consciousness is, as is always the case in Dostoevsky, prepared gradually. The other person's word stealthily, little by little, penetrates the speech and consciousness of the hero: now in the form of a pause where none would occur in monologically secure speech, now in the form of an accent which is foreign to the speaker and thus breaks up his sentence, now in the form of the abnormally raised, exaggerated or hysterical tone of the speaker, etc. The process of the gradual dialogical dissociation of Ivan's consciousness begins with his first words and his whole inner orientation in Zosima's cell, and is drawn out through his conversations with Alyosha, with his father, and especially with Smerdyakov (before his departure for Chermashnya), and, finally, through his three meetings with Smerdyakov after the murder; this process is more profound and ideologically complex than in the case of Golyadkin, but structurally the two are completely analogous.

The phenomenon of a foreign voice whispering the hero's own words into his ear (with a rearranged accent) and the resultant uniquely inimitable combination of hetero-directed words and voices within a single word or a single speech and the intersection of two consciousnesses within a single consciousness are present—in one form or another, to one degree or another, in one ideological direction or another—in each of Dostoevsky's works. This contrapuntal combination of hetero-directed words within the bounds of a single consciousness also serves for him as the basis, the soil, on which he introduces other actual voices, too. But we shall turn our attention to this question later on. At this point we wish to quote a passage from Dostoevsky in which he presents with astounding artistic power a musical image of the interrelation of voices which we have analyzed. This page from *A Raw Youth* is all the more interesting since, except in this passage, Dostoevsky almost nowhere in his works discusses music.

Trishatov is telling the raw youth of his love for music and elaborates for him a plan for an opera:

"Listen, do you love music? I love it terribly. I'll play you something when I come to visit you. I play the piano very well, and I studied for a very long time. I studied seriously. If I were to write an opera, I would, you know, take the plot from *Faust*. I like the theme very much. I am constantly creating the scene in the cathedral, just imagining it in my head. A Gothic cathedral, the interior, choirs, hymns, Gretchen enters and, you know—medieval choirs, so that you can hear the fifteenth century. Gretchen is in anguish, first a recitative, a soft, but terrible, agonizing one, and the choirs thunder somberly, severely, without sympathy:
Dies irae, dies illa!
And suddenly—the voice of the devil, the song of the devil. He is invisible, just his song, alongside the hymns, together with the hymns, almost coinciding with them, but still completely different from them—this would have to be done somehow. The song is long, indefatigable—this is the tenor. It begins softly, tenderly: 'Do you remember, Gretchen, how you, still innocent, still a baby, would come with your mother to this cathedral and babble prayers from an old book?' But the song becomes ever stronger, more passionate and impetuous; the notes get higher: there are tears, hopeless undying agony in them, and, finally, despair: 'There is no forgiveness, Gretchen, there is no forgiveness for you here!' Gretchen wants to pray, but only shrieks

burst from her breast—you know, when the breast is convulsed from weeping—
and Satan's song goes on, piercing deeper and deeper into the soul, like a
spear, ever higher, and suddenly it is nearly broken off by a cry: 'It is the
end, accursed one!' Gretchen falls on her knees, wrings her hands—and then
comes her prayer, something very short, a semi-recitative, but naive, completely unpolished, something utterly medieval, four lines, just four lines in
all—there are a few such notes in Stradella—and with the final note—she
swoons! Confusion. People lift her up and carry her—and then suddenly a
thundering chorus. It is like a clap of voices, an inspired, triumphant, overwhelming chorus, something like our Dori-no-si-ma-chin-mi—so that everything rattles on its foundations, and then it all turns into a rapturous, exultant
exclamation: Hosanna!—Like the cry of the entire universe, and she is carried
away, carried, and then the curtain falls!" (VIII, 482-483)

A part of this musical plan, in the form of literary works, was, undisputably,
realized by Dostoevsky, and realized more than once, using diverse material.[141]
But let us return to Golyadkin—we have not yet finished with him; more
precisely, we have not yet finished with the word of the narrator. In his article
"Stil' peterburgskoi poemy' Dvoinik' " ("The Style of the Petersburg Poem *The
Double*") V. Vinogradov gives a definition of the narration in *The Double* which is
analogous to ours, though it proceeds from a completely different point of view—
namely from the point of view of linguistic sylistics.[142]
Here is Vinogradov's basic assertion:

The introduction of the "little words" *("slovechki")* and expressions of
Golyadkin's speech into the narrational *skaz* achieves an effect whereby Golyadkin himself from time to time begins to seem to be hidden behind the mask
of the narrator as he (Golyadkin) relates his adventures. In *The Double* the
convergence of Mr. Golyadkin's conversational speech with the narrational
skaz of the storyteller is increased also because the Golyadkin style remains
unchanged in indirect speech, thus falling into the realm of the author's re-
sponsibililty. And since Golyadkin says one and the same thing not only with
his language, but with his glance, his look, his gestures and movements as
well, it is easy to understand why almost all descriptions (which point significantly at Mr. Golyadkin's "usual habit") swarm with un-set-off quotations
from his speeches.

Citing a series of examples of the coincidence of the narrator's speech with
that of Golyadkin, Vinogradov continues:

The quantity of excerpts could be significantly increased, but those
which we have quoted, being a combination of Mr. Golyadkin's self-definitions
and the little verbal brush strokes of an outside observer, clearly enough
emphasize the idea that the "Petersburg Poem" at least in many parts, takes

on the form of a story about Golyadkin told by his "double," i.e. "by a person with his language and his concepts." The reason for the failure of *The Double* also lay in the use of this innovative device.[143]

Vinogradov's analysis is sound and astute and his conclusions are correct, but of course he remains within the bounds of his accepted method, and the most important and essential points simply do not fit within those bounds.

It seems to us that V. Vinogradov was not able to perceive the real peculiarity of *The Double*'s syntax, since its syntactical system is determined not by *skaz* in and of itself and not by the conversational dialect of the civil servant or by official bureacratic phraseology, but above all by the collision and the interference of various accents within the bounds of a single syntactical whole, i.e. precisely by the fact that this whole, being one, encompasses the accents of two voices. Furthermore, he does not comprehend or point out the fact that the narration is *dialogically addressed* to Golyadkin, which can be seen in certain very clear external signs, for example in the fact that the first sentence of Golyadkin's speech is very often an obvious reply to a foregoing sentence in the narration. Finally, he does not understand the basic bond between the narration and Golyadkin's interior dialog: the narration does not, after all, reproduce Golyadkin's speech in general, but rather directly continues only the speech of his second voice.

In general, it is impossible to approach the strictly artistic task of style while remaining within the bounds of linguistic stylistics. No one formal linguistic definition of a word can cover its artistic functions in a work. The true style-determining factors remain outside the field of vision of linguistic stylistics.

There is in the style of the narration in *The Double* yet another very essential feature which Vinogradov correctly noted, but did not explain. "Motor images," he says, "predominate in the narrational *skaz,* and its primary stylistic device is the registration of movements, regardless of their recurrence."[144]

Indeed, the narration registers with the most tedious exactness all of the hero's minutest movements, not sparing endless repetitions. It is as if the narrator were riveted to his hero and cannot back far enough away from him to give a summarizing, integrated image of his deeds and actions. Such a generalizing image would lie outside the hero's own field of vision, and in general such an image assumes the existence of some firm position on the outside. The narrator is not in possession of such a position, he does not have the required perspective for an artistically finalizing encompassment of the hero's image and his acts as a whole.[145]

The characteristic nature of the narration in *The Double* is retained, with certain modifications, throughout the course of all of Dostoevsky's subsequent creative work. Narration *(rasskaz)* in Dostoevsky is always narration without perspective. To use a term of art criticism we might say that in Dostoevsky there exists no "perspective representation" *("dalevoi obraz")* of the hero and the event. The narrator finds himself in immediate proximity to the hero and to the event which is taking place, and he represents them from this maximally close, aperspective point of view. True, Dostoevsky's chroniclers write their notes after the events have come to an end, i.e. from an apparent temporal perspective. The narrator of *The Devils,* quite often says e.g., "now that all of this is over with," "now, as we recall all of this," etc., but in fact he constructs his narration without any significant perspective whatever.

On the other hand, in contrast to the narration in *The Double,* Dostoevsky's later narrations do not at all register the hero's minute movements, are not in the least drawn out, and are completely devoid of all repetition. The narration in Dostoevsky's later period is brief, dry, and even somewhat abstract (especially when it gives information about foregone events). But the brevity and dryness of the narration in the later works, "sometimes equalling *Gil Blas",* stems not from perspective, but, on the contrary, from its lack. This deliberate lack of perspective is predetermined by Dostoevsky's entire artistic intention, for, as we know, a firm, finalized image of the hero and the event is excluded in advance from that intention.

But let us return once again to the narration in *The Double.* Aside from its relationship to the speech of the hero, which we have already explained, we note yet another parodistic tendency in it. Elements of literary parody are present in the narration of *The Double,* just as they are present in Devushkin's letters.

Already in *Poor Folk* the author made use of his hero's voice as a refractor of his parodistic intentions. He achieved this by various means: the parodies were either motivated by the subject matter and simply introduced into Devushkin's letters (the excerpts from the works of Rotozyaev: a parody on the society novel, the historical novel of the time, and, finally, on the naturalists), or the parodistic strokes were presented in the very structure of the novella ("Tereza and Faldoni", for example). Finally, the author introduces into the novella the polemic with Gogol, which is refracted directly in the hero's voice; it is a parodistically colored voice (Devushkin's reading of "The Overcoat" and his outraged reaction to it. In the following episode involving the general who helps the hero there is present a hidden contraposition to the episode with "the important personage" in Gogol's "The Overcoat").[146]

In *The Double* a parodistic stylization of the "high-style" in *Dead Souls* is refracted in the voice of the narrator; and in general there are scattered throughout *The Double* parodistic and semi-parodistic reminiscences of various of Gogol's works. It should be mentioned that these parodistic tones in the narration are directly intertwined with the mimicking of Golyadkin.

The introduction of the parodistic and polemical element into the narration makes it more multi-voiced and interferential and less coincident with itself and its object. On the other hand, literary parody strengthens the element of literary conventionality within the narrator's word, thus depriving it still more of its independence and finalizing power in relation to the hero. Also in the subsequent works the element of literary conventionality and its exposure in one form or another always served to increase the direct significance *(polnoznachnost')* and independence of the hero's position. In this sense literary conventionality in

[189]

Dostoevsky's plan did not only not reduce the idea content and significance of his novel, but, on the contrary, could only increase it (as was, by the way, the case with Jean Paul and even with Sterne). The destruction in Dostoevsky's works of the ordinary monological orientation led him to completely exclude from his structure certain elements of that monological orientation, and to carefully neutralize others. One of the means of that neutralization was literary conventionality, i.e. the introduction of the conventional word into the narration or into the principles of structure: the stylized or the parodistic word.[147]

The phenomenon of dialogically addressing the narration to the hero was still present, of course, in Dostoevsky's subsequent works, but it was modified, it became more complex and profound. It is no longer the narrator's every word that is addressed to the hero, but rather the narration as a whole, its whole orientation. The speech within the narration is in the majority of cases dry and lusterless: "documentary style" is the best definition for it. But it is a documentation as a whole in its basic function—an indication, provoking documentation, addressed to the hero, speaking as if to him and not about him, speaking with its entire mass, not with its individual elements. True, even in the final works certain heroes were illuminated in a style which directly parodied and taunted them and sounded like an exaggerated speech taken from their interior dialog. The narration in *The Devils,* for example, is so constructed in relation to Stepan Trofimovich, but only in relation to him. Isolated notes of this taunting style are scattered in other novels, too. They are present in *The Brothers Karamazov.* But in general they are considerably weakened. Dostoevsky's basic tendency in his later period was to make his style and tone dry and precise, to neutralize it. But wherever dry, documentary, neutralized narration is exchanged for sharply accented tones colored with value judgements, those tones are in every case addressed to the hero and are born of the speeches in his potential interior dialog with himself.

■

From *The Double* we shall jump to *Notes from the Underground,* passing over the whole series of works which preceed *Notes.*

Notes from the Underground is a confessional *Icherzählung.* Originally this work was to have been entitled *A Confession.*[148]

It is indeed a true confession. Of course we do not here understand "confession" in the personal sense. The author's intention is here refracted, as in any *Icherzählung;* it is not a personal document, but a work of art.

The extreme and acute interior dialogization is the first thing to amaze us in the "underground man's confession: it contains literally not a single monologically firm, undissociated word. From the very first sentence the hero's speech begins to cringe and crack under the influence of the anticipated word of the other person, with which he, from the very first step, enters into a most intense interior polemic.

"I am a sick man...I am an evil man. I am an unattractive man." Thus begins

the confession. The elipsis and the sharp change of tone following it are porten-
tious. The hero began with a rather plaintive tone—"I am a sick man"—but immediately grew angry at himself for that tone: as if he were complaining and is in
need of sympathy, as if he were looking for that sympathy in others, as if he needed
another person! This is an abrupt dialogical turning point, a typical break in
accent which is characteristic of the entire style of *Notes:* it is as if the hero wants
to say: Perhaps my first words caused you to think that I'm looking for your
sympathy. Well, I'm an evil man, I'm an unattractive man. So there!

This intensification of the negative tone (to spite the other person) under
the influence of the other person's anticipated reaction is characteristic. These
breaks in tone always lead to an accumulation of ever-intensifying invectives or,
at least, words unflattering to the other person. For example:

> "To live beyond forty years of age is indecent, vulgar, immoral! Who
> lives longer than forty years—answer me truthfully, honestly? I'll tell you
> who does: fools and rascals do. I'll tell all the elders that to their faces, all
> of those honorable, silver-haired, sweet-smelling elders! I'll tell the whole
> world to its face! I have a right to talk like this because I'll live to sixty
> myself. I'll survive to seventy! I'll survive to eighty!...Wait a minute!Let
> me catch my breath..." (IV, 135)

In the first words of the confession the internal polemic with the other
person is hidden. But the other person's word is invisibly present, determining
the style of the speech from within. But already midway into the second paragraph the polemic breaks out into the open: the other person's anticipated reply
takes root in the narration, though for the time in a weakened form. "No, no,
it's out of malice that I don't want to get well. Now you probably won't understand this. Well, but I understand."

At the end of the third paragraph a very characteristic anticipation of the
other person's reaction is already present: "Doesn't it seem to you, ladies and
gentlemen, that I'm repenting of something to you, that I'm asking your forgiveness for something?...I'm sure that it seems so...But I assure you that I don't
care what you think..."

At the end of the following paragraph comes the polemical attack on the
"honorable elders" which we have already quoted. The next paragraph begins
directly with the anticipated reply to the foregoing paragraph:

> "You surely think, ladies and gentlemen, that I want to amuse you. Well,
> you're mistaken. I'm not nearly such a jolly fellow as you think, or as you
> perhaps think; and if you're irritated by all this chatter (and I feel already that
> you are irritated) and you get a notion to ask me just who the hell I am,
> anyway, I'll answer you: I'm a certain collegiate assessor."

The following paragraph again concludes with an anticipated reply: "I bet you think I'm writing all this out of arrogance, that I want to be funny at the expense of the men of action, and that I'm rattling my sabre out of vulgar arrogance, like my officer."

Subsequently such paragraph endings become more rare, but even so all the basic semantic sections of the novella are exacerbated toward the end by the open anticipation of the other person's reply.

Thus the novella's entire style is under the powerful, all-determining influence of the other person's word, which either acts upon the speech secretly from within, as at the beginning of the novella, or, as the anticipated reply of the other person, takes root directly in its fabric, as in the endings which we have quoted. There is not a single word in the novella which coincides with itself and its object, i.e. there is not a single monological word. We shall see that the "underground man's" intense relationship to the consciousness of the other person is complicated by a no less intense dialogical relationship to himself. But first we shall make a brief structural analysis of the anticipation of the other person's replies.

This anticipation possesses a distinctive structural characteristic: it tends to become a vicious circle *(durnaia beskonechnost')*. The tendency of these anticipations comes down to the necessity to retain for oneself the final word. This final word must express the hero's complete independence from the views and the word of the other person, his absolute indifference toward the other person's opinion and assessment. More than anything else he fears that people will think that he is repenting before another person, that he is asking someone's forgiveness, that he is submitting to someone's judgement or assessment, that his self-affirmation is in need of confirmation and recognition by another person. And it is in this direction that he anticipates the other person's reply. But precisely through the anticipation of the other person's reply and his answer to it he again demonstrates to the other person (and to himself) that he is dependent on him. He *fears* that the other person will think that he *fears* his opinion. But through this fear he demonstrates his dependence on the other person's consciousness and his inability to be content with his own self-definition. His refutation confirms precisely that which he wanted to refute, and he knows it. Hence the endless circle into which the word and the consciousness of the hero fall: "Doesn't it seem to you, ladies and gentlemen, that I'm repenting of something to you?... I'm sure that it seems so...But I assure you that I don't care what you think..."

During the drinking bout, after being insulted by his companions, the "underground man" wants to show them that he pays no attention to them:

"I smiled contemptuously and paced about on the other side of the room, directly opposite the couch, along the wall, from the table to the stove and back. I wanted with all my might to show them that I could get along without them; I purposely made a racket with my boots, clacking my heels. But it was all in vain. *They* were the ones who were paying no attention."
(IV, 199)

The hero from the underground recognizes all of this himself and understands full well the inescapability of the circle in which his relationship to the other person moves. This relationship to the other person's consciousness gives rise to a peculiar perpetuum mobile of his internal polemic with the other person and with himself, an endless dialog in which one speech begets a second, the second a third, and so on ad infinitum, with none of this producing any forward motion.

Here is an example of this endless perpetuum mobile of the dialogized self-consciousness:

> "You will say that it is vulgar and base to drag all of this (the hero's dreams—M.B.) out into the market place after all the raptures and tears I've admitted to. But why is it base? Do you really think that I'm ashamed of all this, or that it is any stupider than anything in your own lives, ladies and gentlemen? And besides, believe me, some of the things I dreamed up were not at all bad...It didn't all take place on Lake Como. But actually you are right; it is really both vulgar and base. And basest of all is the fact that I tried to justify myself to you just now. And baser yet is that I'm making this remark. But anyway, that's enough, or we'll never finish; one thing will be baser than the next..." (IV, 181)

We have before us an example of a vicious-circle dialog that can neither be finished nor finalized. The formal significance of such inescapable dialogical oppositions in Dostoevsky's works is very great. But in the subsequent works this opposition is nowhere given in such naked and abstractly clear-cut or, one could say simply, mathematical form.[149]

As a result of the "underground man's" relationship to the other person's consciousness and his word—extraordinary dependence on it coupled with extreme hostility toward it and with non-acceptance of its judgement—his narration acquires a certain very essential artistic characteristic. This is a deliberate uncomeliness of style which is, however, subject to a particular artistic logic. His word does not and cannot flaunt its beauty, since it has no one to whom to flaunt it. For it does not naively coincide with itself and its object. It is addressed to the other person and to the speaker himself (in his interior dialog with himself). In both of these directions the last thing it wants to do is to flaunt its beauty and to be "artistic" in the usual sense of the word. In relation to the other person it strives to be deliberately inelegant, to be in every respect obnoxious to him and his tastes. But it occupies the same position in relation to the speaker himself, since one's relationship to oneself is inextricably intertwined with one's relationship to others. Therefore the word is pointedly cynical, calculatedly cynical, though anguished as well. It strives toward *iurodstvo* ("God's—fool—ness."—trans.), and *iurodstvo* is a sort of form, a sort of aestheticism, though, as it were, in reverse.

As a result of this, prosaism in the representation of his inner life attains extreme proportions. On the basis of its material and its theme the first part of *Notes from the Underground* is lyrical. From a formal point of view it is just as much a prose lyric of emotional and spiritual quest and emotional unfulfilledness *(dushevnaia nevoploshchennost')* as, for example, Turgenev's "Phantoms" or "Enough", as any lyrical page from a confessional *Icherzählung,* as a page from *Werther.* But this is a peculiar lyricism, analogous to a lyrical expression of a toothache.

Such an expression of a toothache, an expression with an internal polemical orientation toward the listener and toward the sufferer himself, is mentioned by the hero from the underground himself, and he mentions it not, of course, by chance. He suggests listening to the groans of "an educated man of the 19th century" who is suffering from toothache for the second or third day. He tries to reveal the peculiar voluptuousness in the cynical expression of this pain, in its expression before "the public."

> "His groans become somehow wretched, mean and nasty, and they continue night and day. And he knows himself that his moaning does no good; he knows better than anyone that he is tormenting and annoying himself and others for nothing; he knows that even the public for which he is making such an effort, and his whole family, too, are sick and tired of listening to him and don't believe him for a minute and know that he could moan differently, more simply, without all those trills and embellishments, and that he is carrying on so simply out of spite and malice. Well, and his voluptuousness consists of all these little ignominies and of his consciousness of them. 'So,' he says, 'I'm bothering you, I'm breaking your heart, I'm keeping the whole house awake. Well, don't sleep, then, feel every minute that my teeth ache. I'm no longer the hero to you that I tried to seem before, I'm just a nasty little man, a scoundrel. Well, so be it! I'm very glad that you've found me out. Are you sick of hearing my miserable little moans? Well, go ahead and be sick of it; I'll cut a trill that's even more wretched in a minute...!' (IV, 144)

Of course the comparison of the structure of the "underground man's" confession with an expression of a toothache is itself a parodistic exaggeration, and in that sense is cynical. But the orientation in relation to the listener and to oneself in the expression of a toothache "with trills and embellishments" nonetheless very accurately reflects the orientation of the word in a confession, although, we repeat, it reflects it not objectively, but rather in a taunting parodistically exaggerated style, in the same way that the narration of *The Double* reflected Golyadkin's inner speech.

The sullying and destruction of one's own image in the eyes of another person as a last desperate effort to free oneself from the dominion of the other person's consciousness and to break through to oneself for oneself—this is in fact the orientation of the "underground man's" whole confession. It is for this reason that he makes his own word about himself deliberately ugly. He wants to annihilate in himself any desire to look like a hero in other peoples' eyes (and in his own): "I'm no longer the hero to you that I tried to seem before, I'm just a nasty little man, a scoundrel..."

To do this one must banish all epical and lyrical "heroizing" tones from one's word, making it *cynically* objective. It is impossible for the hero from the underground to soberly and objectively define himself without exaggeration and taunting, since such a soberly prosaic definition would require a word without a sideward glance and a word without a loophole; but his verbal palette contains neither the one nor the other. True, he is constantly trying to break through to such a word, trying to break through to spiritual sobriety, but the path leading there in his case passes through cynicism and *iurodstvo.* He has neither liberated himself from the dominion of the other person's consciousness, nor accepted that dominion over himself,[150] he is still just struggling with it, he polemizes bitterly with it, unable to accept it, but also unable to reject it. In his effort to stamp out his image and his word in the other person and for the other person is present not only the desire for a sober self-definition, but also the desire to spite the other person; that in turn causes him to overdo his sobriety, tauntingly exaggerating it to the point of cynicism and *iurodstvo:* "Are you sick of hearing my miserable little moans? Well, go ahead and be sick of it; I'll cut a trill that's even more wretched in a minute..."

But the word of the hero from the underground is not only a word with a sideward glance, but, as we have said, a word with a loophole as well. The influence of the loophole on the style of his confession is so great that that style cannot be understood without taking into consideration the loophole's formal function. In general, the word with a loophole has enormous significance in Dostoevsky's works, especially in the later ones. Now we shall move on to another aspect of the structure of *Notes from the Underground:* the hero's relationship to himself, and to his interior dialog with himself, which throughout the entire work intertwines and combines with his dialog with the other person.

What is a loophole of the consciousness and of the word?

A loophole is the retention for oneself of the possibility to alter the final, ultimate sense of one's word. If the word leaves this loophole open, then that fact must inevitably be reflected in its structure. This possible other sense, i.e. the open loophole, accompanies the word like a shadow. According to its sense, the word with a loophole must be the last word, and it presents itself as such, but in fact it is only the next-to-last word, and is followed by only a conditional, not a final, period.

For example, the confessional self-definition with a loophole (the most widespread form in Dostoevsky) is, according to its sense, the speaker's last word about himself, his final definition of himself, while in fact it inwardly reckons with the other person's answering, counterposed assessment of him. He who is confessing and condemning himself in fact only wants to provoke praise and acceptance by the other person. In condemning himself he wants and demands that the other person dispute his self-definition, but he leaves himself a loophole for the eventuality that the other person will indeed suddenly agree with him, with his self-definition, not making use of his privilege as the other person.

This is how the underground hero expresses his "literary" dreams:

"I, for example, triumph over everyone; they are all, naturally, grovelling in the dust and are *forced to voluntarily* recognize my perfection, and I forgive them all. I, a famous poet and gentleman in waiting, fall in love; I come into untold millions and on the spot I donate them for the good of the human race, at the same time *confessing to the whole world all my shameful deeds, which are, of course, not just shameful, but are full of all sorts of 'beautiful and sublime' things, too, a bit in the style of Manfred. Everyone is weeping and kissing me (what sort of asses would they be if they didn't),* and then I set off, barefoot and hungry, to preach new ideas and rout the reactionaries at Austerlitz." (IV, 181)

Here he ironically tells of his dreams of heroic deeds with a loophole and of his confession with a loophole. He casts his dreams in a parodistic light. But his next words betray the fact that this, his penitent admission of his dreams, also has its loophole, and that he himself is prepared to find in the dreams and in his very admission of them something, if not Manfredian, then at least out of the realm of "the beautiful and the sublime"; if someone takes it into his head to agree with him that they are indeed just vulgar and base, then:

"You will say that it is vulgar and base to drag all of this out into the market place after all the raptures and tears I've admitted to. But why is it base? Do you really think that I'm ashamed of all this, or that it is any stupider than anything in your own lives, ladies and gentlemen? And besides, believe me, some of the things I dreamed up were not at all bad..."

This passage, which we quoted earlier, recedes into the vicious circle of the self-consciousness with a sideward glance.

The loophole creates a special type of fictive final word about oneself; its tone is unclosed and it peers importunately into the other person's eyes, demanding a sincere refutation. We shall see that the word with a loophole was especially sharply expressed in Ippolit's confession, but that it is, essentially, to a greater or lesser degree inherent in all the confessional self-utterances of all of Dostoevsky's heroes.[151] The loophole makes all of the heroes' self-definitions unstable; the word in their self-definitions does not take on a firm meaning—it is ready, like a chameleon, to change its tone and its ultimate meaning at a moment's notice.

The loophole makes the hero ambiguous and elusive for himself as well. He must travel a long path in order to break through to himself. The loophole profoundly distorts his attitude toward himself. The hero does not know whose opinion, whose assertion is in the final analysis the ultimate judgement about him: his own penitent, critical one or, on the contrary, the one which he desires and coaxes from the other person, the one which accepts and justifies him. Nastasya Filippovna's entire image, for example, is built almost exclusively on this single motif. While she considers herself guilty and fallen, she considers that the other person, being another person, must justify her and cannot consider her guilty. She sincerely disputes Myshkin, who justifies her in everything, but she equally sincerely hates and rejects everyone who agrees with her self-censure and considers her a fallen woman. In the final analysis Nastasya Filippovna does not know what her own word about herself is: does she really consider herself a fallen woman or, on the contrary, does she justify herself? Self-censure and self-justification divided between two voices—I censure myself, the other person justifies me—but anticipated by a single voice, create in that voice interferences and inner duality. The anticipated and demanded justification by the other person merges with self-censure, and two tones begin to sound at once within the voice, causing sharp interferences and sudden transitions. Such is Nastasya Filippovna's voice, such is the style of her word. Her whole inner life (and, as we shall see, her outward life as well) is reduced to the quest for herself and her unbifurcated voice behind the two voices which have made their home in her.

The "underground man" carries on with himself the same kind of endless dialog that he carries on with the other person. He is not able to completely merge with himself in a unified monological voice, leaving the other person's voice wholly outside himself (without a loophole, regardless of what the other voice may say), since, as is the case with Golyadkin, his voice must also function as the surrogate for the other person. He cannot come to an agreement with himself, but neither can he stop talking with himself. The style of his word about himself is alien to the period and alien to finalization, both in its individual elements and as a whole. This is a style of internally endless speech which can be mechanically cut short, but cannot be organically completed.

But Dostoevsky was able precisely for that reason to give his work a conclusion so organic and so in keeping with his hero; he concludes by bringing to the fore the hero's tendency, established in his notes, toward internal endlessness.

> "But that's enough; I don't want to write 'from the Underground' any longer..."
> The 'notes' of this paradoxer do not, however, end here. He could not restrain himself, and he continued on. But we, too, think that we can stop here. (IV, 244)

In conclusion we shall mention two other characteristics of the "underground man." Not only his word, but his face as well is accompanied by a sideward glance and a loophole and all the other phenomena that proceed therefrom. It is as though the interference of voices penetrates into his body, depriving him of his self-sufficiency and unambiguousness. The "underground man" hates his face, because in it he feels the dominion of the other person over him, the dominion of his assessments and opinions. He looks at his own face with the eyes of the other person. And that foreign view interferentially merges with his own view and creates in him a peculiar hatred for his own face:

"I hated my face, for instance, I found it vile and even suspected it of having a sort of depraved expression, and therefore every time I showed up at work I tried agonizingly to be as independent as possible so as not to be suspected of depravity, and I tried to express as much nobility as possible with my face. 'Let it be an ugly face,' I thought, 'but to make up for that let it be noble, expressive, and, above all, **extremely** intelligent.' But I was probably painfully aware that my face could never express all that perfection. But the most awful thing is that I found it positively stupid. I would have settled for intelligence. I would even have agreed to a depraved expression, if only my face could have been considered terribly intelligent." (IV, 168)

Just as he makes his word about himself purposely uncomely, he welcomes the uncomeliness of his face:

"I accidentally caught sight of myself in the mirror. My face was agitated and it seemed to me repugnant in the extreme: pale, nasty, depraved, and my hair all dishevelled. 'So be it, I'm glad of it,' I thought, 'I'm glad that I'll seem repugnant to her; that suits me fine.' " (IV, 206)

His polemic with the other person on the subject of himself is complicated in *Notes from the Underground* by his polemic with the other person on the subject of the world and of society. The hero from the underground, in contrast to Devushkin and Golyadkin, is an ideologist.

In his ideological world we can easily discover the same phenomena that are present in his word about himself. His word about the world is both openly and furtively polemical; in addition, it polemizes not only with other people and other ideologies, but also with the object of its thinking itself—with the world and its order. Also in his word about the world he hears, as it were, two voices, between which he cannot find himself and his own world, since his definition of the world also contains a loophole. The world, nature and society seem to him full of interferences, just as the body became interferential in his eyes. In his every thought about them there is a struggle of voices, assessments, points of view. He senses in everything above all the *will of the other person,* the will which predefines him. He perceives the world order, nature with its mechanistic inevitability, and the social order all from the point of view of this foreign will. His thought is developed and constructed as the *thought of a person personally insulted by the world order,* personally debased by its blind inevitability. This lends his ideological word a profoundly intimate and passionate character and allows it to become tightly

[198]

intertwined with his word about himself. It seems (and this was Dostoevsky's intention) that essentially only a single word is present and that the hero will arrive at his world only by arriving at himself. His word about the world, like his word about himself, is deeply dialogical; he rebukes the world order, and even the mechanistic inevitability of nature, as if he were speaking not about the world, but with it. We shall further discuss these characteristics of the ideological word when we move on to the hero-ideologists, especially Ivan Karamazov, in whom these traits are particularly sharp and clear-cut.

The word of the "underground man" is through and through a word-address *(slovo-obrashchenie)*. For him, to speak means to address someone; to speak about himself means to address himself with his own word, to speak about someone else means to address the world. But, while speaking with himself, with another person, with the world, he simultaneously addresses a third party: he squints his eyes toward the side, toward the listener, the witness, the judge.[152] This simultaneous triple-directedness of his word and the fact that it can conceive of no object without addressing it creates the extraordinarily lively, restless, agitated and, we would say, importunate character of that word. It cannot be viewed as a lyrical or epical "detached" word which contentedly coincides with itself and its object; no, one above all reacts to it, answers it, is drawn into its game; it is capable of agitating and touching one, almost like the personal appeal of a living person. It destroys the barrier between the hero and the reader, though not as a result of its topicality or its direct philosophical significance, but rather thanks to its formal structure as we have analyzed it.

The element of *address* is inherent to every word in Dostoevsky, to the narrative word as much as to the hero's word. In Dostoevsky's world there is in general nothing material, there is no thing or object—there are only subjects. And therefore there is no word-judgement, no word about an object, no secondhand object word *(zaochnoe predmetnoe slovo)*—there is only the word-address, a word which comes into dialogical contact with another word, a word about a word addressed to a word.

3. The hero's word and the narrative word in Dostoevsky's novels.

We now move on to the novels. We shall concentrate more briefly on them, since the new material which they bring with them is manifested in dialog rather than in the monological utterance of the heroes, which here only becomes more complex and subtle, but in general is not enriched by essentially new structural elements.

Raskolnikov's monological word is amazing in its extreme inner dialogization and its lively personal appeal to everything about which it thinks and speaks. For Raskolnikov, too, to conceive of an object means to address it. He does not think about phenomena, he speaks with them.

He addresses himself in the same way (often saying "you" as if speaking to another person), he tries to convince himself, taunts, exposes and mocks

[199]

himself, etc. Here is an example of such a dialog with himself:

> " 'It won't happen? And what will you do to keep it from happening?
> Forbid it? And what right do you have? What can you promise them on
> your part in order to have such a right? To dedicate your whole fate and
> future to them, once you've **completed your studies and found a position**?
> We've heard all that, and it's nothing but **words**, but what about now?
> Something has to be done right now, do you understand that? And what
> are you doing now? You're sponging on them. They get their money by
> pawning their hundred-rouble pension with the Messrs. Svidrigailov! How
> are you going to protect them from the Svidrigailovs, from Afanasy Ivano-
> vich Vakhrushin, you future millionaire, you, you Zeus, you commander
> of their destinies? In ten years? In ten years your mother will have gone
> blind from sewing kerchiefs, and most likely from tears, too; she'll waste
> away from hunger. And your sister? Well, just imagine what can happen
> to your sister ten years from now, or during those ten years. Can you
> guess?'
> Thus he teased and tormented himself with such questions, even
> deriving a certain enjoyment from them." (V, 50)

Such is the nature of his dialog with himself throughout the course of the
entire novel. True, the questions change and the tone changes, but the structure
remains the same. It is characteristic that his inner speech is filled with other
peoples' words which he has heard or read in the immediate past: from his
mother's letter, from the speeches of Lukin, Dunechka and Svidrigailov mentioned in the letter, from the speech of Marmeladov which he has just heard, from
the words of Sonechka which he hears from Marmeladov, etc. He floods his inner
speech with the words of others, complicating them with his own accents or
simply reaccenting them, and entering into an impassioned polemic with them.
Thus his inner speech is constructed like a succession of living, impassioned replies to all of the words of other people which he has heard and which have
touched him, words gleaned from the experience of the immediate past. He addresses everyone with whom he polemizes as "you," and he returns their own
words to almost all of them, with an altered tone and accent. And every individual, every new person immediately becomes for him a symbol and his name a
generic term: the Svidrigailovs, the Luzhins, the Sonechkas, etc. "Hey, you,
Svidrigailov! What do you want here?" he shouts to a dandy who was trying to
proposition a drunken girl. Sonechka, with whom he is acquainted from Marmeladov's stories, constantly figures in his inner speech as the symbol of unnecessary
and senseless sacrifice. Dunya figures in a similar way, but with a different nuance,
and the symbol of Luzhin has its meaning, too.

Every individual enters into his inner speech, however, not as a character or
type, not as an actor in the plot of his life (sister, sister's fiancé, etc.), but rather
as the symbol of a certain orientation to life and an ideological position, as the

symbol of a specific solution in life to the same ideological questions which torment him. A person need only show himself within Raskolnikov's field of vision to immediately become for him an embodied solution to his own problem, a solution which differs from the one at which he himself has arrived; therefore everyone touches a sore spot and takes on a firm role in his inner speech. He correlates all of these individuals one to another, he juxtaposes or counterposes them, forces them to answer one another, react to one another or expose one another. As a result, his inner speech unfolds like a philosophical drama in which the actors are personified, realized-in-life points of view toward life and the world.

All the voices which Raskolnikov introduces into his inner speech come into a peculiar sort of contact such as is impossible among voices in an actual dialog. Thanks to the fact that they reverberate within a single consciousness, they become as it were reciprocally permeable one to another. They are brought together, caused to overlap, they partially intersect one another, creating corresponding interferences in the region of intersection.

We mentioned earlier that in Dostoevsky there is no evolution of ideas, not even within the bounds of the consciousness of the individual heroes (with only the rarest exceptions). The hero's consciousness always receives semantic material full-blown, not in the form of individual thoughts and propositions, but rather in the form of human semantic orientations, in the form of voices, among which it remains only to make a choice. The internal ideological struggle waged by the hero is a struggle for the choice among already-present semantic possibilities, whose quantity remains almost unchanged throughout the entire novel. The motifs "I didn't know that," "I didn't see that," "that was only later revealed to me" are absent from Dostoevsky's world. His hero knows and sees everything from the very outset. Therefore the heroes (or the narrator, speaking about the heroes) so often announce after a catastrophe that they knew and foresaw everything in advance. "Our hero let out a cry and clutched at his head. Alas! He had foreseen this for a long time." Thus concludes *The Double*. The "underground man" constantly emphasizes that he knew and foresaw everything. "I saw everything myself, all my despair was open to view!" exclaims the hero of "A Gentle Creature." As we shall see in a moment, the hero does, it is true, very often hide that which he knows from himself and pretends to himself that he does not see what is in fact constantly before his very eyes. But in such cases the characteristics which we have mentioned merely stand out all the more clearly.

Almost no evolution of thoughts under the influence of new material takes place. Only the choice is important, the answer to the question, "Who am I?," "With whom am I?" To find one's own voice and to orient it among other voices, to combine it with some of them and to counterpose it to others, or to separate one's voice from another voice, with which it is inseparably merged—these are the problems solved by the heroes throughout the novel. And this determines the hero's word. It must find itself and reveal itself among other words, within a most intense mutual orientation with them. And all of these words are usually presented in their entirety from the very outset. In the process of the whole internal and external action of the novel they are merely distributed in various ways in relation to one another, entering into various combinations, but their quantity, given from the very outset, remains unchanged. We could express it thus: from the very outset a certain stable and contentually unchanging semantic diversity is given, and within it there occurs merely the rearrangement of accents. Already before the murder Raskolnikov recognizes Sonya's voice from Marmeladov's stories, and he decides on the spot to go to her. From the very outset her voice and her word fall within Raskolnikov's field of vision and join in his interior dialog.

"By the way, Sonya," says Raskolnikov, after he finally confesses to her, "when I was lying in the darkness and all those things came to me, was it the devil who was tempting me? Hm?"

"Be quiet! Don't make fun, you blasphemer, you don't understand anything, not a thing! Oh God! He can't understand anything, not a thing!"

"Be quiet, Sonya, I'm not making fun at all, I know myself that the devil was dragging me on. Be quiet, Sonya, be quiet!" he repeated gloomily and insistently. "I know it all. *I thought it over and whispered it to myself as I lay there in the darkness ..... I argued it all out with myself, down to the last detail, and I know it all, everything!* And how sick I was then of all that blabbering! I wanted to forget everything and start over, Sonya, and to stop blabbering! ... I had to find out something else, something else was goading me on: *I had to find out, and find out quickly, if I was a louse like everyone else, or a man.* Could I step over or not? Did I have the courage to stoop down and take it, or not? Was I some quivering creature, or did I have the **right**.... I just wanted to prove one thing to you: *that the devil dragged me on then, and afterwards he explained to me that I did not have the right to go there because I was exactly the same kind of louse as everyone else! He laughed at me, and now I've come to you!* Greet your guest! If I weren't a louse, would I come to you? Listen: when I went to the old woman that time, I just dropped by to give it a **try...** That you must know!" (V, 436-438)

All of the voices, including Sonya's, reverberated in Raskolnikov's whispers already as he lay alone in the darkness. He was searching for himself among them (and the crime was only a test of himself), he was orienting his accents. Now their reorientation is taking place; the dialog, from which we have quoted an excerpt, takes place at a moment of transition within the process of rearranging the accents. The voices in Raskolnikov's soul have already shifted and intersect in different places. But even so, the interference-free voice of the hero will not be heard within the bounds of the novel; its possibility is merely hinted at in the epilog.

This, of course, does not nearly exhaust the characteristics of Raskolnikov's word and the full variety of stylistic phenomena inherent in it. We shall yet return to the extraordinarily intense life of that word in the dialogs with Porfiry.

We shall concentrate even more briefly on *The Idiot,* since it contains almost no essentially new stylistic phenomena.

Ippolit's confession ("My Urgent Explanation") is a classic example of the confession with a loophole, just as his attempted suicide itself was planned as a suicide with a loophole. Ippolit's plan is on the whole correctly defined by Myshkin. In answering Aglaya, who assumes that Ippolit wanted to shoot himself so that she would then read his confession, Myshkin says:

"That is...how can I explain it? It is very difficult to say. But he probably wanted everyone to crowd around him and tell him that they are very fond of him and respect him very much, and they would all start to beg him to remain among the living. It is very possible that you were on his mind more than anyone else, since he mentioned you at such a time...although perhaps he didn't know himself that you were on his mind." (VI, 484)

This is, of course, no crude calculation, but rather a loophole which Ippolit's will leaves open for itself and which confuses his relationship to himself as much as his relationship to others.[153] Therefore Ippolit's voice is just as internally unfinalized and just as unfamiliar with the period [.] as the "underground man's" voice. It was no accident that his final word (which his confession was intended to be) in fact turned out to be not at all the final one, since his suicide did not succeed.

Ippolit's hidden orientation toward being recognized by other people, which determines the entire tone and style of the whole, is contradicted by his open pronouncements, which determine the content of his confession: independence from and indifference to the judgement of others and the manifestation of self-willedness.

"I don't want to depart," he says, "without leaving behind a word of response, a free word, not a forced one, and not to justify myself—oh, no! I won't beg forgiveness from anyone for anything. But just because I want to." (VI, 468)

His entire image is based on this contradiction, which defines his every thought and his every word.

This personal word of Ippolit about himself is intertwined with an ideological word which, as in the "underground man", is a protest addressed to the universe; his suicide is intended to be the expression of this protest. His thinking about the world develops in the form of a dialog with some higher power which has mistreated him.

The mutual orientation of Myshkin's speech with the word of the other person is also very intense, though it has a somewhat different character. Myshkin's internal speech develops dialogically in relation to himself as well as in relation to the other person. He also speaks not about himself and not about the other person, but with himself and with the other person, and the agitation of these interior dialogs is great. But he is guided rather by fear of his own word (in relation to the other person) than by fear of the other person's word. His reservations and hesitations, etc., can be explained in the majority of cases precisely by this fear, which begins with simple tactfulness to others and extends to the profound and fundamental fear to pronounce a decisive, ultimate word about another person. He fears his own thoughts, suspicions and assumptions about the other person. In this respect his interior dialog, which takes place just before Rogozhin's attempt on his life, is typical.

True, according to Dostoevsky's plan Myshkin is already the carrier of the *penetrant word (proniknovennoe slovo)*, i.e. of a word which is capable of actively and confidently intervening in the interior dialog of another person, helping that person to recognize his own voice. At a moment when the interference of voices within Nastasya Filippovna is at its sharpest, in the scene in Ganichka's apartment where she desperately plays out the role of the "fallen woman", Myshkin introduces an almost decisive tone into her interior dialog:

> "Aren't you ashamed? Are you really the kind of person you've been presenting yourself as? Can that be?" the prince cried suddenly, with profound, heartfelt reproach.
>
> Nastasya Filippovna was surprised, and she smiled ironically, but as if trying to hide something behind her smile, and she was somehow confused; she glanced at Ganya and left the living room. But before reaching the hallway she suddenly returned, quickly went up to Nina Alexandrova, took her hand and raised it to her lips.
>
> She flushed suddenly, "He is right, I am really not that kind of person," she whispered quickly and fervently, and turning, she went out, this time so quickly that no one had a chance to realize why she had returned. (VI, 136)

He is able to say similar words, and with the same effect, to Ganya and Rogozhin and Elizaveta Prokofievna and others. But Myshkin's penetrant word, his appeal to one of the other person's voices, to the genuine voice, is, according to Dostoevsky's plan, never decisive. It is devoid of a certain ultimate confidence and sovereignty, and he often simply lets it drop. The firm and integral monological word is foreign to him, too. The inner dialogism of his word is as great and as agitated as in the case of the other heroes.

We now move on to *The Devils*. We shall concentrate only on Stavrogin's confession.

The style of Stavrogin's confession attracted the attention of Leonid Grossman, who devoted an article to it titled *"Stilistika Stavrogina (K izucheniiu novoi glavy 'Besov')"* ["Stavrogin's Style (Toward a Study of a New Chapter of *The Devils)"*] [154]

Here is a summary of his analysis:

Such is the unusual and subtle compositional system of Stavrogin's

[204]

"Confession." The acute self-analysis of the criminal consciousness and
the merciless recording of all of its tiniest ramifications required within
the very tone of the story some new principle for the stratification of the
word and the division of smooth, integral speech. Throughout almost the
entire story the principle of the dissociation of the harmonious narrational style can be felt. The murderously analytic theme of the confession of a
terrible sinner required just such a dismembered and, so to speak, constantly disintegrating embodiment. The synthetically finished, smooth and
balanced speech of a literary description would have corresponded least
of all to this chaotically terrifying and excitedly unstable world of the
criminal spirit. The monstrous ugliness and inexhaustible horror of Stavrogin's reminiscences required this derangement of the traditional word.
The nightmarishness of the theme sought new examples of the distorted
and irritating phrase.

"Stavrogin's Confession" is a marvelous stylistic experiment, in which
the classical prose of the Russian novel was for the first time shaken up,
distorted and moved in the direction of unknown future achievements.
Criteria for assessing all the prophetic devices of this disorganized style can
be found only against the background of contemporary European art."[155]

L. Grossman understood the style of Stavrogin's confession as a monological expression of his consciousness; this style, in his opinion, is adequate to the
theme, i.e. to the crime itself, and to Stavrogin's soul. Thus Grossman applied
the principles of ordinary stylistics to the confession, taking into account only
the direct word, the word which recognizes only itself and its object. In fact the
style of Stavrogin's confession is determined above all by its internally dialogical
orientation in relation to the other person. Precisely this sideward glance at the
other person determines the breaks in its style and its whole specific mien. This
is exactly what Tikhon had in mind when he began directly with an "esthetic
critique" of the confession's style. It is characteristic that Grossman ignores the
most important points in Tikhon's critique and discusses only secondary ones.
Tikhon's critique is very important since it without doubt expresses the artistic
intention of Dostoevsky himself.

What is for Tikhon the chief shortcoming of the confession?

Tikhon's first words upon reading Stavrogin's notes were:

"Would it be possible to make a few changes in this document?"
"What for? It is written sincerely," answered Stavrogin.
"Something in the style..." [156]

Thus the style and its uncomeliness surprised Tikhon above all in the confession. We quote an excerpt from their dialog, in which the true essence of
Stavrogin's style is revealed:

"*You seem to want to depict yourself more coarsely than your heart would wish you to...,*" said Tikhon, growing ever bolder. The "document" had obviously made a strong impression on him.

"To depict? I repeat: I did not 'depict myself,' and in particular I was not 'affecting' anything."

Tikhon quickly lowered his eyes.

"This document proceeds directly from the needs of a mortally wounded heart—do I understand you correctly?" he said insistently and with unusual fervor. "Yes, this is the heart's confession and its natural need, which has overcome you, and you have entered on a noble path, an unexampled path. *But you seem to already despise and disdain in advance all who will read what is described here, and you call them to battle.* You are not ashamed to admit your crime, so *why are you ashamed of your confession?*"

"Ashamed?"

"You are ashamed and afraid!"

"Afraid?"

"Mortally. *Let them look at me, you say; well, but you yourself, how will you look at them?* Certain places in your account are emphasized by the style, as if you were admiring your psychology, and you grasp at every trifle in order to *astound the reader* with the insensitivity which does not exist in you. *What is this if not a prideful challenge from a guilty man to his judge?*"[157]

Stavrogin's confession, like that of Ippolit and the "underground man", is a confession intensely oriented toward the other person, who is indispensable to the hero, but whom he at the same time despises and whose judgement he does not accept. Therefore Stavrogin's confession, like the other confessions which we have discussed, is devoid of the power to finalize and tends toward the same vicious circle to which the "underground man's" speech so clearly tended. Without recognition and affirmation by the other person Stavrogin is incapable of accepting himself, but at the same time he does not want to accept the other person's judgement of him.

"But for me there will remain those people who know everything and will look at me, and I will look at them. I want everyone to look at me. If that will make things easier for me, I do not know. This is for me a last resort."

And at the same time the style of his confession is dictated by his hatred and non-acceptance of this "everyone."

Stavrogin's attitude toward himself and toward the other person is locked into the same endless circle in which the "underground man" wandered, "paying no attention to his comrades", but at the same time clacking his heels so that they would without fail finally notice that he was paying no attention to them. This is presented on the basis of different material here, material far removed from the comic. But Stavrogin's position is nonetheless comical. "Even in the *form* of this greatest of confessions there is something *funny*," says Tikhon.

But, turning to the "Confession" itself, we must admit that in the outward characteristics of its style it differs sharply from *Notes from the Underground*. Not a single foreign accent and not a single foreign *(chuzhoe)* word interrupts its fabric. Not a single reservation, not a single repetition, not a single elipsis. It is as if no external signs of the overwhelming influence of the other person's word were present. The word of the other person has indeed penetrated inward, into the very atoms of the structure to such a degree, and the conflicting speeches overlap so solidly, that the word appears externally to be monological. But nonetheless, even an unsensitive ear catches the sharp and irreconcilable interference of voices which Tikhon also immediately pointed out.

The style is above all determined by the cynical, pointedly deliberate disregard of the other person. The sentences are rudely choppy and cynically precise. This is not sober austerity and precision, it is not documentation in the usual sense, since realistic documentation is directed toward its object and, despite its stylistic dryness, strives to be adequate to all sides of that object. Stavrogin strives to present his word without a valuational accent, to make it intentionally wooden, and to eliminate all human tones in it. He wants everyone to look at him, but at the same time he makes his confession wearing a deathly, motionless mask. That is why he reworks every sentence in such a way that his personal tone is not revealed in it and his repentant, or even simply agitated, accent does not slip through. That is why he breaks up his sentences, since the normal sentence too supply and delicately transmits the human voice.

We shall cite a single example:

"I, Nikolai Stavrogin, a retired officer, in the year 186...resided in Petersburg, living a life of debauchery, which gave me no pleasure. For a time I had three different apartments. In one of them, where Marya Lebyadkina, now my lawful wife, was also quartered, I lived alone in the rooms with a table and a servant. I rented the other apartments by the month for love affairs: in one of them I entertained a certain lady who was in love with me, and in the other—her housemaid, and for a time I was quite taken up with the intention of arranging a rendezvous in such a way that the two of them would meet at my place. Knowing both of their characters, [I] expected a great deal of enjoyment from this joke."[158]

The sentences seem to be broken off at the point where a living human voice begins. It is as if Stavrogin turns away from us every time he has tossed a word our way. It is remarkable that he even attempts to omit the word "I" when speaking of himself, when "I" is not simply the formal subject of the verb, when it should carry a particularly strong and personal accent (in the first and the last

sentence of the quoted excerpt, for example). All of the syntactical characteristics mentioned by Grossman—the broken-off sentence, the intentionally lack-
luster or intentionally cynical word, etc.—are in essence manifestations of Stavrogin's basic effort to pointedly and challengingly eliminate the living, personal
accent from his word and to speak with his back turned toward the listener. Of
course alongside this element we would also find in Stavrogin's "Confession"
certain of the phenomena which we encountered in the foregoing monological
utterances of other heroes, though they appear in a weaker form, and in any
case are subordinated to the basic dominant tendency.

The narration of *A Raw Youth*, especially at the beginning, seems to take
us back to *Notes from the Underground:* the same hidden and open polemic
with the reader, the same reservations and elipses, the same inclusion of anticipated replies, the same dialogization of all relationships to oneself and to the
other person are present. The same traits, of course, characterize the word of the
raw youth as a hero.

Several other phenomena are also revealed in Versilov's word. But in fact
it, too, lacks genuine seemliness. It is constructed in such a way as to intentionally and pointedly, with a restrainedly disdainful challenge to the other person,
mute out all personal tones and accents. This incenses and insults the raw
youth, who is eager to hear Versilov's own voice. With amazing mastery Dostoevsky causes that voice, too, to break through and reveal itself and its new and
unexpected accents. For a long time Versilov stubbornly avoids meeting the raw
youth face to face, without the verbal mask which he has developed and which
he constantly wears with such finesse. Here is one of the meetings where Versilov's voice breaks through.

> "These stairs...," mumbled Versilov, drawing out his words, appar-
> ently in order to break the silence, and apparently fearing that I would say
> something, "these stairs, I'm not used to them, and you're on the third
> floor, but still, I'll find my way...Don't trouble yourself, my boy, you'll
> catch cold yet..."
> We had already reached the exit, but I still followed along behind
> him. He opened the door; the wind darted in and put out my candle. With
> that I suddenly caught at his hand; the darkness was utter. He shivered,
> but remained silent. I pressed myself to his hand and suddenly began to
> kiss it avidly, several times, many times.
> "My dear boy, why is it you're so fond of me?" he said, but this
> time in a completely different voice. His voice quivered and something
> completely new sounded in it, as if it were not he who was speaking.
> (VIII, 229-230)

But the interference of two voices in Versilov's voice is particularly sharp
and strong in relation to Akhmakova (love-hate) and in part to the Raw Youth's
mother. This interference results in the total temporal disintegration of these

voices, i.e. it results in doubleness *(dvoinichestvo)*.

In *The Brothers Karamazov* a new element in the structure of the hero's monological speech appears, and we must consider it briefly, although it is in the dialog that it is actually fully revealed.

We have said that Dostoevsky's heroes know everything from the very outset, and that they merely choose among semantic material that is already completely at hand. But at times they conceal from themselves that which they in fact already know and see. The simplest expression of this is in the dual thoughts characteristic of all of Dostoevsky's heroes (even of Myshkin and Alyosha). One thought is the obvious one, which determines the *content* of their speech, and the other is the hidden one, which nonetheless determines the *structure* of their speech, on which it casts its shadow.

The novella *A Gentle Creature* is built directly on the motif of conscious not knowing. The hero conceals from himself and carefully eliminates from his own word something which is constantly before his eyes. His whole monolog is directed toward forcing himself to finally see and admit that which he in essence knows and sees from the very outset. Two-thirds of this monolog are devoted to the hero's desperate attempt to avoid that which, as an invisibly present "truth", innerly determines his thought and speech. At first he tries to "gather his thoughts in a point" which lies beyond that truth. But in the final analysis he is forced to gather them together in that, for him, terrible point of "truth."

This stylistic motif is most profoundly developed in the speeches of Ivan Karamazov. First his desire for his father's death, and then his participation in the murder are the facts which invisibly determine his word, though of course in close and uninterrupted connection with his dualistic orientation in the world. The process of Ivan's inner life which is depicted in the novel is to a significant degree the process of his recognizing and confirming for himself and for others what he in essence has known all along.

We repeat, this process unfolds mainly in the dialogs, and above all in his dialogs with Smerdyakov. Smerdyakov gradually gains control over that particular one of Ivan's voices which Ivan conceals from himself. Smerdyakov is able to control that voice precisely because Ivan's consciousness does not look in that direction and does not want to look there. He finally gets from Ivan the deed and the word which he needs. Ivan leaves for Chermashnya, where Smerdyakov has been tenaciously trying to send him.

> As he was getting into the carriage, Smerdyakov ran up to straighten the rug.
>
> "Do you see...I'm going to Chermashnya..." somehow suddenly burst from Ivan Fedorovich's lips, again as it had happened yesterday, flying out of its own accord, together with a sort of nervous chuckle. He remembered this a long time after.
>
> "Well, then, it's true what people say about it being worthwhile to talk to intelligent people," answered Smerdyakov resolutely, gazing pene-

trantly at Ivan Fedorovich." (IX, 351)

The content of the following parts of the novel consists in the process of the self-elucidation and gradual admission of that which he in essence knew, of that which his second voice had been saying. This process remained unfinished. It was interrupted by Ivan's mental illness.

Ivan's ideological word, its personal orientation and its dialogical appeal to its object stand out with extraordinary vividness and clarity. It is not a judgement about the world, it is his personal non-acceptance of the world, his rejection of it, directed to God as the culprit responsible for the world order. But Ivan's ideological word develops, as it were, in a dual dialog: he inserts into his dialog with Alyosha the dialog (more exactly, dialogized monolog) which he has created between the Grand Inquisitor and Christ.

We shall touch upon one other variety of word in Dostoevsky—the hagiographic word. It appears in the speeches of Khromozhka, of Makar Dolgoruky, and, finally, in the Life of Zosima. It appeared perhaps for the first time in the tales of Myshkin (especially in the episode with Marya). The hagiographic word is a word without a sideward glance, confidently adequate to itself and its object. But this word in Dostoevsky is, of course, stylized. The monologically firm and confident voice of the hero essentially never appears in his works, but a certain tendency toward it is obviously to be felt in certain infrequent instances. When, in Dostoevsky's plan, the hero comes close to the truth about himself, is reconciled with the other person, and takes possession of his own genuine voice, his style and tone begin to change. When, for example, the hero of *A Gentle Creature,* according to the plan, arrives at the truth: "The truth irresistibly edifies his mind and heart. Toward the end even the tone of the story changes in comparison to its disorderly beginning." (From Dostoevsky's foreword).

Here is the hero's altered voice on the last page of the novella:

"She was blind, blind! She is dead, she does not hear! You have no idea what a paradise I would have built to protect you! Paradise was in my soul, I would have planted it all around you! You wouldn't have loved me,— well, so be it, what of it? Everything would have been *so* and would have remained *so.* If only you had told me like a friend, we would have become happy and would have laughed happily, gazing in each other's eyes. That's how we would have lived. And if you had loved another, well, so be it, so be it! You would have walked with him and laughed, and I would have watched from across the street...O, let anything happen, just let her open her eyes, if only once! For a single second, just one! Let her look at me as she did then, when she stood before me and swore to be my faithful wife! O, she would understand everything in a single glance." (X, 419)

Analogous words about paradise, in the same style, but with tones of fulfillment, ring in the speeches of "the youth, the brother of the elder Zosima," in Zosima's own speeches after his victory over himself (the episode with the orderly and the duel), and, finally in the speeches of the "mysterious visitor" after he has made his confession. But all of these speeches are to a greater or lesser degree subordinated to the stylized tones of the religious-hagiographic or religious-confessional style. In the narration itself these tones appear only a single time: in *The Brothers Karamazov* in the chapter "Cana of Galilee."

A special place is occupied by the *penetrant word,* which has its own functions in Dostoevsky's works. In his plan it is intended to be a firmly monological, intact word, a word without a sideward glance, without a loophole, without an internal polemic. But this word is possible only in an actual dialog with another person.

In general, the reconciliation and merging of voices, even within the bounds of a single consciousness, cannot—according to Dostoevsky's plan and in accordance with his basic ideological premises—be a monological act; it assumes that the hero's voice will join in the chorus. But for this to take place, the fictive voices, which interrupt and mock a person's true voice, must be subdued and muffled. On the level of Dostoevsky's social ideology this took the form of his demanding that the intelligentsia merge with the folk: "Humble yourself, you prideful man, and above all subdue your pride. Humble yourself, you idle man, and above all begin to toil in the fields of the folk." On the level of his religious ideology this meant to join in the chorus and shout "Hosanna!" In this chorus the word is transferred from mouth to mouth in identical tones of praise, joy and happiness. But in the plan of his novels it is not the polyphony of reconciled voices that unfolds, but rather the polyphony of struggling, innerly cloven voices. These latter were presented not on the level of his narrowly ideological aspirations, but rather in the reality of the time. The social and religious utopia characteristic of his ideological views did not swallow up or dissolve his objectively artistic vision.

A few words on the narrator's style.

In the final works, too, the narrator's word is not, in comparison with the heroes' word, accompanied by any new tones or any essential orientations. It is, as before, a word among words. In general, the narration gravitates between two boundaries: between the dryly informative, documentary, in no way representational word and the word of the hero. But where the narration strives toward the hero's word, it presents it with a shifted or altered accent (mockingly, polemically, ironically), and only in the rarest of instances does it strive to merge in a single accent with it.

In every novel the narrator's word gravitates between these two boundaries.

The influence of these two boundaries is clearly visible even in the titles of the chapters: some of the titles are lifted directly from the words of a hero (but as chapter titles these words take on, of course, a different accent); others are given in the style of a hero; others have a strictly informative character; yet others are of a literary-conventional nature. Here is an example of each instance from *The Brothers Karamazov:* Chapter 4 (Book II): "For What Reason Does

Such a Person Live?" (Dmitry's words); Chapter 2 (Book I): "The First Son is Turned Out" (in the style of Fyodor Pavlovich); Chapter 1 (Book I): "Fyodor Pavlovich Karamazov" (an informative title); Chapter 6 (Book V): "An As Yet Quite Unclear Chapter" (a literary-convential title). The chapter titles of *The Brothers Karamazov* compromise a microcosm of the whole variety of tones and styles in the novel.

This variety of tones and styles is not reduced to a common denominator in any of the novels. There is nowhere a dominant word, be it the word of the author or the central hero's word. Unity of style in this monological sense does not exist in Dostoevsky's novels. As for the structuring of the narration as a whole, it is, as we know, dialogically addressed to the hero. This is because the complete dialogization of all elements of the work, with no exceptions, is an essential aspect of the author's plan.

At those times when the narration does not intervene as the voice of the other person in the heroes' interior dialog, where it does not enter into an inter-ferential union with the speech of one or another of them, it presents a fact without a voice, without an intonation, or with a conventional intonation. The dry, informative, documentary word is, as it were, a voiceless word, the raw material for a voice. But this voiceless and accentless fact is presented in such a way that it can enter the field of vision of the hero himself and can become the material for his own voice, the material for his own judgement of himself. The author does not invest it with his own judgement, his own assessment. Therefore the narrator has no surplus in his field of vision, no perspective.

Thus certain words participate directly and openly in the hero's interior dialog, while others have the potential to participate: the author constructs them so that the consciousness and voice of the hero himself can take control of them; their accent is not predetermined, a place is left open for it.

So, in Dostoevsky's works there exists no ultimate, finalizing, once-and-for-all definite word. And therefore there exists no firm image for the hero, answering the question "who is *he?*" There exist only the questions "who am *I?*" and "who are *you?*" But these questions, too, are asked within an uninter-rupted and unfinalized interior dialog. The word of the hero and the word about the hero are defined by his open dialogical relationship to himself and to the other person. The author's word cannot envelop the hero and his word from all sides, enclose them and finalize them from without. It can only address itself to them. All definitions and all points of view are swallowed up by the dialog and are drawn into its evolution. The secondhand word which neutrally and objectively constructs the hero's finalized image without intervening in his in-terior dialog is foreign to Dostoevsky. The "secondhand" word which gives a final summary of the personality does not enter into his plan. That which is firm, dead, finished, mute, and has already pronounced its final word does not exist in Dostoevsky's world.

4. Dialog in Dostoevsky

In Dostoevsky the self-consciousness of the hero is completely dialogized: its every aspect is turned outward, it is intensively addressed to itself, to another person, to a third person. Outside this living directedness toward itself and toward the other person it does not exist, even for itself. In this sense one could say that in Dostoevsky the person is the *subject of address (sub' 'ekt obrashcheniia)*. One cannot speak about him, one can only address oneself to him. Those "depths of the human soul," whose representation Dostoevsky considered the main task of his realism "in a higher sense," are revealed only through the intense address. It is impossible to master the inner man, to see and understand him, by making him the object of an impersonal, neutral analysis, nor is it possible to master him by merging with him or by feeling one's way into him. No, he can be approached and revealed, or, rather, he can be caused to reveal himself, only dialogically, by means of communication with him. And it is possible to represent the inner man, as Dostoevsky understood him, only by representing his communication with another person. The "man in man" is revealed, both for himself and for others, only in communication, in the interaction of one person with another.

It is quite understandable that the dialog must lie at the center of Dostoevsky's artistic world, and the dialog not as a means, but as an end in itself. Dialog is for him not the threshold to action, but the action itself. Nor is it a means of revealing, of exposing the already-formed character of a person; no, here the person is not only outwardly manifested, he becomes for the first time that which he is, not only—we repeat—as far as others are concerned, but for himself, as well. To be means to communicate dialogically. When the dialog is finished, all is finished. Therefore the dialog, in essence, cannot and must not come to an end. On the level of his religious-utopian *Weltanschauung* Dostoevsky carries the dialog over into eternity, thinking of it as an eternal co-rejoicing, co-admiration, con-cord. On the level of the novel this is presented as the unfinalizability of the dialog, or, originally, as the dialog's vicious circle.

Everything in Dostoevsky's novels gravitates toward the dialog, toward dialogical opposition, as the center point. Everything else is the means, the dialog is the end. One voice alone concludes nothing and decides nothing. Two voices is the minimum for life, the minimum for existence.

The potential endlessness of the dialog in Dostoevsky's plan in and of itself settles the question of why such a dialog cannot be a decisive part of the plot, since a plot-related *(siuzhetnyi)* dialog strives just as inevitably toward a conclusion as does the plot-related event of which it is, in essence, a part. Therefore, as we have already said, in Dostoevsky the dialog always stands outside the plot, i.e. it is inwardly independent of the plot-determined interrelationships of the speakers, although its path is, of course, prepared by the plot. For example, Myshkin's dialog with Rogozhin is a "person to person" dialog, but is by no means a dialog of two rivals, although rivalry is precisely what has brought them together. The nucleus of the dialog always stands outside the plot, however intensely related to the plot it may be (Aglaya's dialog with Nastasya Filippovna, for example). On the other hand, the shell of the dialog is always profoundly related to the plot. Only in Dostoevsky's early work were the dialogs somewhat abstract and not firmly anchored in the framework of the plot.

The basic theme of the dialog in Dostoevsky is very simple: the opposition of person to person, as the opposition of the "I" to the "other person."

In the early work this "other" is also of a rather abstract nature: it is the other as such. "I am alone, and they are everyone else," thought the "underground man" to himself in his youth. But he continues to think in essentially the same way in his subsequent life as well. For him the world is divided into two camps: in the one is "I," in the other are "they," i.e. all "others," whoever they may be. Every person exists for him above all as "the other." And this definition of the person directly conditions his entire attitude toward him. He reduces all people to a common denominator—"the other." He refers his school comrades, his fellow workers, the servant Apollon, the woman who falls in love with him, and even the creator of the world order, with whom he polemizes, to this category, and he reacts to them above all as "others" in relation to himself.

This abstractness is determined by the whole plan of the work. The life of the hero from the underground is devoid of any plot whatsoever. A life in which there are friends, brothers, parents, wives, rivals, lovers, etc., and in which he himself could be a brother, son or husband is experienced by him only in his dreams. In his actual life these real human categories do not exist. Therefore the interior and exterior dialogs in this work are so abstract and classically clear-cut that they are comparable only to the dialogs in Racine. The endlessness of the exterior dialog stands out here with the same mathematical clarity as the endlessness of the interior dialog. An actual "other person" can enter into the "underground man's" world only as that "other" with whom he is already involved in his endless interior polemic. Every actual foreign voice inevitably merges with the foreign voice which is already ringing in the hero's ears. And the actual word of the "other person" is also drawn into the perpetuum mobile, as are all of his anticipated replies. The hero tyranically demands from it complete recogniztion and affirmation of himself, but at the same time he does not accept that recognition and affirmation, since he is the weak, the passive party in it: he is the one who is understood, accepted, forgiven. That his pride cannot tolerate.

"And I'll never forgive you those tears which I couldn't hold back from you just now, like an abashed old woman! Nor will I ever forgive you for what I'm confessing to you now!" he cries out as he confesses to the girl who loves him. "Do you realize that now, having said these things to you, I will hate you because you were here and you heard? A person says such things only once in a lifetime, and then only when he's hysterical!...What more do you want? And why are you still hanging around after all this, torturing me? Why don't you go away?" (IV, 237-238)

But she did not go away. Something much worse happened. She understood him and accepted him as he was. He could not endure her sympathy and acceptance.

> "The thought entered my wrought-up head that the roles had now been switched once and for all, that she was now the heroine and I was exactly the same kind of devastated creature that she appeared to me to be on that night—four days ago....And all this came to me in those minutes when I was lying facedown on the couch!
> My God, did I really envy her then?
> I don't know, I still can't decide, and then, of course, I was even less capable of understanding than I am now. I cannot exist without having tyrannical power over someone...But...but you can't explain anything with reason, so, consequently, there's no sense in reasoning." (IV, 239)

The "underground man" remains in his inescapable opposition to the "other person." A real human voice is no more capable of finalizing his endless interior dialog than is the anticipated reply of another person.

We have already said that the interior dialog (i.e. the microdialog) and the principles of its construction served as the basis on which Dostoevsky originally introduced other actual voices. We must now more carefully examine the interrelationship of the interior and the exterior, compositionally expressed dialog, since it contains the essence of Dostoevsky's handling of dialog.

We have seen that in *The Double* the second hero (the double) was directly introduced by Dostoevsky as the personified second interior voice of Golyadkin himself. The narrator's voice had the same function. On the other hand, Golyadkin's interior voice itself was only a substitute, a specific surrogate for the actual voice of another person. Thanks to this circumstance, a close bond was achieved between the voices, and their dialog became extremely (and, here, one-sidedly) intense. The other person's (the double's) reply could not touch Golyadkin's sore spot, since it was nothing more than his own word placed in the mouth of another, though it was, so to speak, turned inside-out and had its accent shifted and maliciously distorted.

This same principle of the combination of voices is retained, in a more complex and profound form, throughout all of Dostoevsky's subsequent work. To it he is obliged for the extraordinary power of his dialogs. Dostoevsky always introduces two heroes in such a way that each is intimately connected with the interior voice of the other, although that voice is no longer ever the direct personification of the other hero (with the exception of Ivan Karamazov's devil). Therefore in their dialog the speeches of the one touch and even partially coincide with the speeches of the other's interior dialog. The profound essential bond or the partial coincidence of one hero's words with the interior, secret word of another hero is an indispensable element in all of Dostoevsky's essential dialogs; the most important dialogs are built directly on this element.

[215]

We shall quote a brief, but very vivid dialog from *The Brothers Karamazov*.

Ivan Karamazov still believes absolutely in Dmitry's guilt. But in the depth of his soul, as yet almost unbeknownst to him, the question of his own guilt begins to arise. The inner struggle in his soul is an extremely intense one. It is at this moment that the following dialog with Alyosha occurs.

Alyosha categorically denies Dmitry's guilt.

"Who do you think is the murderer?" he (Ivan—M.B.) asked apparently, coldly somehow, even with a certain note of arrogance in the tone of his question.

"You know yourself who did it," said Alyosha quietly and penetrantly.

"Who? That fable about that crazy idiot epileptic? About Smerdykov?" Alyosha suddenly felt that he was trembling all over.

"You know yourself who did it," broke feebly from his lips. He gasped for breath.

"Well who, who?" cried Ivan, now almost ferociously. His restraint had suddenly disappeared.

"I only know one thing," in the same near-whisper. "It was **not you** who killed father."

" 'Not you!' What do you mean, not you?" Ivan was dumbfounded.

"You did not kill father, you did not do it!" repeated Alyosha firmly. The silence lasted half a minute.

"I know myself that I didn't do it. Are you delirious?" said Ivan, smiling palely and crookedly. His eyes bored into Alyosha. They both stood again by the lantern.

"No, Ivan, you've told yourself several times that you're the murderer."

"When did I say so?...I was in Moscow....When did I say so?" murmured Ivan, completely at a loss.

"You often told yourself so when you were left alone in these two terrible months," continued Alyosha, again speaking softly and distinctly. But now he was speaking as if outside himself, as if not of his own will, but rather obeying some irresistable command. "You accused yourself and admitted to yourself that the murderer is none other than yourself. But you did not kill him, you're mistaken, you are not the murderer, do you hear me, not you! God has sent me to tell you so." (X, 117-118)

Here Dostoevsky's device is exposed and revealed with complete clarity in the content itself. Alyosha openly states that he is answering a question that Ivan had asked himself in his interior dialog. This excerpt is also a typical example of the penetrant word and its artistic role in the dialog. The following is very important. Ivan's own secret words coming from the lips of another person call forth in him repulsion and hatred for Alyosha, precisely because they have touched his sore spot, because they do indeed answer his question. Now he refuses to accept any discussion of his own inner affair by outsiders. Alyosha understands this perfectly well, but he foresees that Ivan—the "profound conscience"—will sooner or later inevitably give himself a categorically affirmative answer: I killed him. And according to Dostoevsky's plan it is impossible to give any other answer. So Alyosha's word, precisely because it is the word of *another person,* must make itself useful:

> "Brother," began Alyosha again in a trembling voice, "I've told you this because you will take my word, I know you will. I've told you once and for all: not you! Do you hear, once and for all. God laid the burden of telling you on my soul, even if you hate me from this hour on and forever more...."
> (X, 118)

Alyosha's words, which intersect with Ivan's interior speech, must be juxtaposed with the words of the devil, which also repeat the words and thoughts of Ivan himself. The devil introduced into Ivan's interior dialog the accents of mockery and hopeless condemnation, in the same manner as the voice of the devil in Trishatov's projected opera, where the devil's song is heard "alongside the hymns, together with the hymns, almost coinciding with them, but still completely different from them." The devil speaks as Ivan, but at the same time as "another," hostilely exaggerating and distorting his accents. "You are I, I myself," Ivan tells the devil, "only with a different mug." Alyosha also introduces foreign accents into Ivan's interior dialog, but exactly in the opposite direction. Alyosha, as "another person," introduces tones of love and reconciliation which on Ivan's own lips are, of course, impossible. Alyosha's speech and the speech of the devil, both repeating Ivan's words, lend those words diametrically opposite accents. One intensifies one speech in his interior dialog, and the other—a different speech.

This distribution of the heroes and this interrelationship of the heroes' words is extremely typical of Dostoevsky. In Dostoevsky's dialogs it is not two integral monological voices which collide and conflict, but rather two cloven voices (one is in any case cloven). The overt speeches of the one answer the covert speeches of the other. The contraposition of two heroes to another one, the two both being connected with the counterposed speeches in the interior dialog of the first, is a most typical grouping for Dostoevsky.

For a correct understanding of Dostoevsky's intention it is very important to take into account his assessment of the role of the other person as "the other," since his basic artistic effects are achieved by passing a single word through several voices, all of which are counterposed one to another. As a parallel to the dialog between Alyosha and Ivan which we have just quoted, we quote an excerpt from a letter of Dostoevsky to G.A. Kovner (1877):

> Not quite to my liking are the two lines of your letter in which you say that you feel no remorse for the act which you committed in the bank. There exists something higher than rational arguments and all possible extenuating circumstances, something to which everyone must subordinate

himself (i.e. something similar, again, to a **banner**). It may be that you are intelligent enough to not be offended by the frankness of my **unsolicited** remark. In the first place, I am no better than you or anyone else (and this is in no way false modesty—what reason would I have for it?), and secondly, if I excuse you in my own way in my heart (as I invite you to excuse me), it is in any case better if I excuse you than if you excuse yourself."[159]

The distribution of the characters in *The Idiot* is analagous to this. Here we have two main groups: Nastasya Filippovna, Myshkin and Rogozhin make up one group, and Myshkin, Nastasya Filippovna and Aglaya make up the other. We shall concern ourselves only with the second.

As we have seen, Nastasya Filippovna's voice has split into one voice which pronounces her guilt, a "fallen woman," and another which excuses and accepts her. Her speeches are full of the interferential combination of these two voices: first one, then the other dominates, but neither can ultimately defeat the other. The accents of each voice are intensified by or interfere with the actual voices of other people. The voices which censure her force her to exaggerate the accents of her own accusatory voice in order to spite those other people. Therefore her confession begins to sound like Stavrogin's confession or—stylistically more closely related—the confession of the "underground man." When she comes to Ganya's apartment, where, as she knows, she is condemned by those present, she plays the role of the courtesan out of spite, and it is only Myshkin's voice, intersecting in the opposite direction with her interior dialog, which forces her to radically alter that tone and to respectfully kiss the hand of Ganya's mother, whom she has just been mocking. Myshkin's place, and that of his actual voice, in Nastasya Filippovna's life is also defined by his connection with one of the speeches in her interior dialog.

> "Haven't I dreamed of you myself? You're right, I dreamed a long time ago, already there in the country with him, where I lived five years absolutely alone; I used to think and think and dream and dream—I constantly imagined someone like you, kind, honest, good, and just as foolish as you, who would all of a sudden come and say: 'You are innocent, Nastasya Filippovna, and I adore you!' Yes, I used to dream like that, and it almost drove me mad...." (VI, 197)

She heard this anticipated speech of another person in the actual voice of Myshkin, who repeats it almost word for word on that fateful evening at Nastasya Filippovna's.

Rogozhin is constructed differently. From the very outset he becomes for Nastasya Filippovna the symbol for the embodiment of her second voice. "I'm a Rogozhin type," she repeats more than once. To go carousing with Rogozhin or to go away with him means for her to wholly embody and realize her second voice. Rogozhin's drinking bouts and his attempts to barter and buy her are maliciously exaggerated symbols of her fallenness. This is unjust to Rogozhin, since he, especially at the beginning, is by no means inclined to condemn her, although on the other hand he is capable of hating her. Rogozhin has the knife, and she knows it. Such is the structure of this group. The actual voices of Myshkin and Rogozhin intertwine and intersect with the voices of Nastasya Filipovna's interior dialog. The interferences of her voices are turned into the interferences of her interrelationships with Myshkin and Rogozhin within the plot: her repeated flights from the altar with Myshkin to Rogozhin, and from him back to Myshkin, and her hate and love for Aglaya.[160]

Ivan Karamazov's dialogs with Smerdyakov have a different nature. Here Dostoevsky attains the summit of his mastery in creating dialog.

The mutual orientation of Ivan and Smerdyakov is very complex. We have already said that certain of Ivan's speeches at the beginning of the novel are determined, invisibly and half-covertly even for himself, by the desire for his father's death. Smerdyakov, however, apprehends this covert voice, and he does so with absolute clarity and certitude.[161]

According to Dostoevsky's plan, Ivan desires the murder of his father, but he desires it with the condition that he himself remain not only externally, but also *internally* uninvolved in it. He wants the murder to occur as an inevitability of fate, not only *independently of his will, but against it.* "You should know," he says to Alyosha, "that I will always defend him (father—M.B.). But as far as my desires are concerned, in this case I reserve for myself complete freedom of movement." The interior-dialogical dissociation of Ivan's will could be imagined in the form of the two following speeches, for example:

"I do not desire father's death. If it happens, it will be against my will."

"But I desire that the murder take place against my will, because then I will be internally uninvolved in it and will have nothing for which to reproach myself."

This is how Ivan's interior dialog with himself is constructed. Smerdyakov divines, or rather, clearly hears the second speech in this dialog, but he comprehends the loop-hope contained in it in his own way: as Ivan's effort not to give him any evidence to prove his complicity in the crime, as the extreme external and internal caution of an "intelligent person," who avoids all direct words which could expose him, and with whom it is therefore "worthwhile to talk," since one can converse with him by means of innuendos alone. Before the murder Ivan's voice appears to Smerdyakov to be completely integral and undivided. Ivan's desire for the death of his father seems to Smerdyakov to be the completely simple and natural conclusion drawn from his ideological views, from his assertion that "all is permitted." Smerdyakov does not hear the first speech in Ivan's interior dialog, and to the end he does not believe that Ivan's first voice indeed seriously did not desire the death of his father. According to Dostoevsky's plan that voice was indeed serious, and this gives Alyosha grounds for excusing Ivan, despite the fact that he knows very well of the existence of the second, the "Smerdyakovian" voice in him.

Smerdyakov confidently and firmly takes possession of Ivan's will, or rather, he invests that will with concrete forms of expression. Through Smerdyakov Ivan's interior speech is transformed from a desire to a deed. Smerdyakov's dialogs with Ivan before the latter's departure for Chermashnya are astounding in the artistic effect they achieve by embodying the conversation between Smerdyakov's overt, conscious will (disguised only by innuendos) and the covert will of Ivan (hidden even from Ivan himself), as if over the head of Ivan's conscious will. Smerdyakov speaks directly and confidently, addressing himself with his innuendos and equivocations to Ivan's second voice; his words intersect with the second speech in Ivan's interior dialog. Ivan's first voice answers him. That is why Ivan's words, which Smerdyakov understands as an allegory with the opposite meaning, are in fact not allegorical at all. They are Ivan's direct words. But this voice, the one which answers Smerdyakov, is now and then interrupted by a covert speech from his second voice. There occurs an interference, thanks to which Smerdyakov remains fully convinced that Ivan is in agreement with the murder.

These interferences in Ivan's voice are very subtle and are expressed not so much in words as in pauses which are incongruous with the meaning, in changes of tone which are incomprehensible from the point of view of his first voice, in unexpected and incongruous laughter, etc. If the voice with which Ivan answers Smerdyakov were his one and only, unified voice, i.e. if it were a purely monological voice, all of these phenomena would be impossible. They are the result of two voices within a single voice, of two speeches within a single speech. Ivan's dialogs with Smerdyakov before the murder are constructed in this manner.

After the murder the structure of the dialogs is different. Now Smerdyakov forces Ivan to gradually, at first vaguely and ambiguously, then clearly and distinctly, recognize his own covert will in another person. That which seemed to him to be a consciously inactive desire, well-hidden even from himself, and therefore innocent, was, as it turns out, for Smerdyakov the clear and distinct expression of will which motivated his actions. It turns out that Ivan's second voice called and commanded, and Smerdyakov was merely the executor of his will, his "faithful servant Licharda." In the first two dialogs Ivan becomes convinced that he was in fact inwardly involved in the murder, since he had indeed desired it and had unmistakably expressed that will. In the final dialog he discovers his own actual, external involvement in the murder, as well.

We shall direct our attention to the following point. At first Smerdyakov perceived Ivan's voice as an integral monological voice. He hearkened to his preachments on the permissibility of all things as to the word of a called and self-confident teacher. He did not at first understand that Ivan's voice was divaricated and that his convincing and confident tone was intended to convince himself, and not at all as the completely convinced transmission of his views to another.

Analagous is the relationship of Shatov, Kirillov and Petr Verkhovensky to

[220]

Stavrogin. Each of them follows Stavrogin as a teacher, accepting his voice as integral and confident. They all think that he spoke with them as a mentor speaks with his pupils; in fact he made them participants in his endless interior dialog, in which he was trying to convince himself, not them. Now Stavrogin hears his own words from each of them, but with a firm, monologized accent. He himself can now repeat these words only with an accent of mockery, not conviction. He was unable to convince himself of anything, and it is painful for him to listen to people who have been convinced by him. This is the basis of the construction of Stavrogin's dialogs with each of his three followers.

"Do you know (says Shatov to Stavrogin—M.B.) which is now the only "God-bearing" people on earth, destined to renew and redeem the world in the name of a new god, and which alone holds the keys to life and the new word...Do you know which is that people and what is its name?"

"Judging by your manner, I am supposed without fail to conclude, and, it would seem, the sooner the better, that it is the Russian people...."

"And you are already laughing—oh, what a tribe!" Shatov was about to jump up.

"Keep calm, I beg you; on the contrary, I was expecting precisely something of this sort."

"You expected something of this sort? And aren't you familiar with these words yourself?"

"Quite familiar; I can foresee all too clearly what you are leading up to. Your whole phrase and even the expression "God-bearing" people is only the conclusion of our conversation which took place abroad over two years ago, shortly before your departure for America...At least as far as I can now recall."

"It is entirely your phrase, not mine. It is your own, and it is not merely the conclusion of our conversation. 'Our' conversation did not exist at all: there was a teacher declaiming enormous words and a pupil, raised from the dead. I am that pupil and you are the teacher." (VII, 261-262)

The tone of conviction with which Stavrogin spoke at that time, when he was abroad, about the 'God-bearing' people, the tone of "the teacher declaiming enormous words," is to be explained by the fact that he was indeed still trying to convince only himself. His words with their convincing accent were addressed to himself, they were a speech from his interior dialog pronounced aloud: ' I wasn't joking with you then; in trying to convince you I was, perhaps, even more concerned for myself than I was for you,' said Stavrogin enigmatically."

Accents of profound conviction in the speeches of Dostoevsky's heroes are in the huge majority of instances merely the result of the fact that the words are a part of an interior dialog and are intended to convince the speaker himself.

[221]

The intensification of the convincing tone is evidence of the internal opposition of the hero's other voice. A word completely independent of these internal struggles is almost never found in Dostoevsky.

Stavrogin also hears his own voice, with an altered accent, in the speeches of Kirillov and Verkhovensky: in Kirillov the accent is one of maniacal conviction, and in Petr Verkhovensky it is one of cynical exaggeration.

Raskolnikov's dialogs with Porfiry constitute a special type of dialog, although externally they are extremely similar to Ivan's dialogs with Smerdyakov before the murder of Fedor Pavlovich. Porfiry speaks in inuendos, addressing himself to Raskolnikov's covert voice. Raskolnikov seeks to play his role calculatingly and precisely. Porfiry's goal is to force Raskolnikov's inner voice to break out into the open and to create interferences in his calculatingly and skillfully acted-out speeches. That is why real words and intonations from Raskolnikov's actual voice are constantly breaking into the words and intonations of his role. Porfiry too sometimes allows his genuine face—that of a confident person—to peek out from behind the role of the unsuspecting investigator which he has taken on; and among the fictive speeches of both interlocutors, two real speeches, two real words, two real human opinions unexpectedly meet and intersect with one another. As a result of this, the dialog is from time to time transferred from one plane—that of role-playing—to another—that of reality,—but only for a brief moment. And it is only in the final dialog that the effective destruction of the role-playing plane and the word's complete and ultimate emergence into the plane of reality occur.

Here is that unexpected breakthrough into the plane of reality. At the beginning of his final conversation with Raskolnikov, after Mikolka's confession, Porfiry Petrovich ostensibly retracts all of his suspicions, but then, unexpectedly for Raskolnikov, he announces that Mikolka could not possibly have been the killer:

"...But why are we talking about Mikolka, my dear Rodion Romanovich? There is no Mikolka here!"

These last words, after all that had been said before and that had sounded so like a retraction, were too unexpected. Raskolnikov began to shake all over, as if he had been pierced through.

"So...who...killed her...then?" he asked in a choking voice, unable to restrain himself. Even Porfiry Petrovich fell back in his chair, as if he had been caught equally off guard by the question.

"What do you mean, who killed her?.." he repeated, as if he could not believe his ears, "why *you* killed her, Rodion Romanovich! You killed her...," he added, almost in a whisper, with absolute conviction in his voice.

Raskolnikov jumped up from the couch, meant to stand for several seconds, and sat down again, without saying a word. Tiny convulsions suddenly ran across his entire face...

"It wasn't I who killed her," Raskolnikov was about to whisper, like a frightened child caught in the act of committing a misdeed. (V, 476)

The confessional dialog possesses enormous significance in Dostoevsky. The role of the other person as "the other," regardless of who he may be, stands out particularly distinctly here. Let us concentrate briefly on Stavrogin's dialog with Tikhon, an extremely pure example of the confessional dialog.

Stavrogin's whole orientation in this dialog is determined by his dualistic attitude toward the "other person": the inability to do without his judgement and forgiveness, and the simultaneous hostility toward him and the opposition to his judgement and forgiveness. This determines all the interferences in his speeches, gestures and facial expression, the abrupt changes in his mood and tone, his incessant reservations *(ogovorki)*, his anticipation of Tikhon's replies and his sharp refutations of those imagined replies. It is as if Tikhon were speaking with two persons who have been interferentially merged into one. Tikhon is confronted with two voices, into whose inner struggle he is drawn as a participant.

> After the opening greetings, which were for some reason pronounced with obvious mutual awkwardness, hurriedly and even carelessly, Tikhon led his guest into his study and, with apparent haste, had him sit down on the couch, in front of a table, and then he seated himself next to him in a wicker chair. With that, amazingly, Nikolai Vsevolodovich became completely confused. It was as if he were resolving with all his strength to do something extraordinary and irrefutable, but at the same time almost impossible for him. He looked about the study for a moment, without seeming to notice what he was looking at, and he lost himself in thought, without, perhaps, knowing what he was thinking about. He was aroused by the silence, and it suddenly seemed to him as if Tikhon were sitting with bashfully downcast eyes, a completely superfluous sort of smile on his lips. This instantaneously aroused in him aversion and a feeling of rebelliousness; he wanted to get up and leave. In his opinion Tikhon was thoroughly intoxicated, but then the latter suddenly raised his eyes and looked at him with such a firm and meaningful glance, and at the same time with such an unexpected and enigmatic expression, that he nearly gave a start. And things suddenly seemed altogether different to him, as if Tikhon already knew why he had come, as if he were informed in advance (although there was no one in the world who could possibly know his reason) and if Tikhon did not speak first, it was because he wanted to spare him, it was because he was afraid of humiliating him.[162]

The abrupt changes in Stavrogin's mood and tone determine the entire subsequent dialog. First one, then the other voice wins out, but most often Stavrogin's speech is constructed as the interferential merging of two voices.

These revelations (of Stavrogin's visitation by the devil—M.B.) were weird and confused, as if they were indeed coming from a madman. But at the same time Nikolai Vsevolodovich spoke with such strange frankness, the like of which he had never before displayed, and with such completely uncharacteristic ingenuousness, that, so it seemed, the person who he had been had suddenly and unexpectedly disappeared completely. He was not at all ashamed of revealing the dread with which he spoke of his apparition. But this was all only momentary, and was gone as suddenly as it had appeared.

"It's all nonsense," he recollected quickly and with embarrassed vexation. "I'll go see a doctor."

And a bit further on:

"But this is all nonsense. I'll go see a doctor. It's all nonsense, awful nonsense. It is just I myself in various forms, that's all. Since I added that... phrase just now, you probably think that I'm still in doubt and that I'm not sure that it is I, and not in fact a devil."[163]

At first one of Stavrogin's voices wins out completely, and it seems that "the person he had been had suddenly and unexpectedly disappeared." But then the second voice again steps forward and causes an abrupt change of tone and breaks off his speech. A typical anticipation of Tikhon's reaction takes place, along with all of the accompanying phenomena, with which we are already familiar.

Finally, before he hands over the pages of his confession to Tikhon, Stavrogin's second voice abruptly interrupts his speech and disrupts his intentions, proclaiming its independence from and contempt for the other voice, thus directly contradicting the very intention of his confession and the very tone of his proclamation.

"Listen, I can't stand spies and psychologists, at least ones who go boring into my soul. I haven't invited anyone into my soul, I don't need anyone, I can get along by myself. You think that I'm afraid of you," he raised his voice and lifted his head challengingly, "you are totally convinced that I've come to you to divulge a 'terrible' secret, and you're awaiting it with all the monkish curiosity which you're capable of. Well, then, rest assured that I'm not going to divulge anything to you, no secret, because I am completely capable of getting along without you."

The structure of this speech and its position within the entire dialog are fully analogous with the phenomena which we have analyzed in *Notes from the Underground.* The tendency to become entrapped in a vicious circle in relation to the "other person" is manifested here in perhaps an even more acute form.

Tikhon knows that he is supposed to be for Stavrogin the representative of the "other person" as such, and that his voice stands opposed not to Stavrogin's monological voice, but rather that it forces its way into his interior dialog, where the position of "the other" is as if predetermined.

"Answer the question, but truthfully, answer me alone, just me," said Tikhon in a totally different voice, "If someone were to forgive you for this (Tikhon pointed toward the pages of the confession), and not someone whom you respect or fear, but a stranger, a person whom you would never recognize as he reads your strange confession silently to himself, would that make things easier for you, or wouldn't it matter?"

"It would be easier," answered Stavrogin in an undertone. "If you were to forgive me, it would be much easier for me," he added with downcast eyes.

"On the condition that you forgive me, too," said Tikhon emphatically. [164]

The functions in the dialog of the other person as such, devoid of any social or real-life concretization, stand out here in all clarity. This other person, "a stranger, a person whom you would never recognize," fulfills his functions in the dialog outside the plot and independently of his definition in the plot, as a pure "man in man," a representative of "all others" for the "I". As a result of this construction of "the other," communication takes on a special character which is beyond all real and concrete social forms (of family, social status, class and biography).[165] We shall pause to consider yet another passage, in which the function of "the other" as such, whoever he may be, is revealed with extreme clarity.

On the eve of his public confession, after admitting his crime to Zosima, the "mysterious guest" returns to Zosima during the night, for the purpose of killing him. He was led to this by pure hatred for "the other" as such. He describes the state of his mind thus:

I left you then and went out into the darkness, and I wandered about the streets, struggling with myself. And suddenly I began to hate you so fiercely that my heart almost could not bear it. I thought "He is the only one holding me now, he is my only judge, and I cannot back out of my execution tomorrow, because he knows everything." And it wasn't as though I thought that you would betray me (that never entered my mind), but I thought: "How will I be able to look at him if I don't denounce myself?" Even if you were a million miles away, but still alive, the thought that you are alive and that you know everything and sit in judgement of me would have been intolerable. I hated you just as if you were the cause of all this and it were all your fault.(IX, 390-391)

The voice of an actual "other" in the confessional dialogs is always given ilogous, pointedly plot-external construction. But this very same construction of "the other" determines the form of all of Dostoevsky's essential dialogs, though not in such a naked form: they are prepared for by the plot, but their culminating points—the peaks of the dialogs—rise above the plot in the abstract sphere of the pure relationship of man to man.

With that we conclude our investigation of the types of dialog, although we have by no means exhausted all of them. Moreover, each type has numerous variants which we have not touched upon at all. But the principle of their construction is everywhere the same. The *intersection, consonance, or interference of speeches in the overt dialog with the speeches in the heroes' interior dialogs* are everywhere present. *The specific totality of ideas, thoughts and words* is everywhere *passed through several unmerged voices, taking on a different sound in each.* The object of the author's aspirations is not at all this totality of ideas in and of itself, as something neutral and identical with itself. No, the object is precisely *the act of passing the themes through many and varied voices,* it is, so to speak, the fundamental, irrescindable *multivoicedness and varivoicedness* of the theme. The distribution of voices itself and their interaction is important to Dostoevsky.

■

Thus the external dialog, expressed within the composition, is inseparably connected with the interior dialog, i.e. with the microdialog, and is to a certain degree dependent upon it. And both are also inseparably connected with the great dialog of the novel as a whole, by which they are encompassed. Dostoevsky's novels are totally dialogical.

As we have seen, the dialogical attitude toward the world permeates all of Dostoevsky's other works, beginning with *Poor Folk.* Thus the *dialogical nature of the word* is revealed in his works with enormous power and acute tangibility. His works provide extraordinarily fertile material for the metalinguistic study of this nature of the word, and in particular of the diverse variants of the *double-voiced word* and its influence on the various aspects of the structure of speech.

Like every great artist of the word, Dostoevsky was able to perceive and to convey to the creative artistic consciousness new aspects of the word and new depths in it which had been very weakly and faintly made use of by other artists before him. Important for Dostoevsky are not only the ordinary representational and expressive functions of the word which are important to every artist, and not only the ability to recreate in an objectified way the social and individual distinctiveness of the characters' speeches—for him the most important thing is the dialogical interrelationships of those speeches, regardless of their linguistic characteristics. For the main object of his representation is the word itself, and specifically the *fully significant (polnoznachnoe) word.* Dostoevsky's works consist of a word about a word and addressed to a word. The represented word and the representational word meet on equal terms on a single level. They penetrate one another and overlap one another from various dialogical angles. As a result of this meeting, new aspects and new functions of the word are revealed and come to the fore. In the present chapter we have attempted to characterize those new aspects and functions.

CONCLUSION

We have sought in this work to reveal Dostoevsky's uniqueness *as an artist* who developed new forms of artistic vision, thus discovering and perceiving new aspects of the human being and his life. Our attention has been concentrated on that new artistic position which made it possible for him to broaden the horizon of artistic vision and to look at man from a different artistic angle of vision.

While continuing the "dialogical line" in the development of European prose, Dostoevsky created a new variant of the novelistic genre—the polyphonic novel, whose innovative characteristics we have attempted to elucidate in our work. We consider the creation of the polyphonic novel an enormous step forward not only in the development of novelistic prose, i.e. of all the genres developing within the orbit of the novel, but in general in the development of the *artistic thinking* of mankind. It seems to us that it is possible to speak directly of a special *polyphonic mode of artistic thinking,* which extends beyond the bounds of the novelistic genre. This mode of thinking opens up aspects of man—above all the *thinking human consciousness and the dialogical sphere of man's existence*—which cannot be *artistically* mastered from a *monological position.*

At the present time in the West Dostoevsky's novel is perhaps the most influential literary model. The disciples of Dostoevsky the artist include people professing utterly diverse ideologies, often profoundly alien to Dostoevsky's own ideology: they are enthralled by his artistic will and by the new principle of artistic thinking which he discovered.

But does this mean that the polyphonic novel, having been discovered, supplants all the monological forms of the novel, making them obsolete and of no further use? Of course not. A new-born genre never supplants or replaces other already-existing genres. Every new genre merely suppliments the old ones, it merely widens the circle of already-existing genres. For each genre has a sphere of existence in which it is predominant and irreplaceable. Therefore the appearance on the scene of the polyphonic novel does not nullify or in any way limit the further productive development of the monological forms of the novel (the biographical, historical, social, or epical novel, etc.), since there will continue to exist and expand spheres of human and natural existence which require objectivized, finalizing forms of artistic cognition. But, we repeat once more, *the thinking human consciousness and the dialogical sphere of that consciousness's existence* in all their depth and specificity are inaccessible to the monological artistic approach. They become the object of a genuinely artistic representation only in Dostoevsky's polyphonic novel.

Thus, no new artistic genre nullifies or replaces old ones. But at the same time, every essential and significant new genre, once it has arrived on the scene, exerts an influence on the whole range of old genres: a new genre heightens the consciousness of the old genres, so to speak; it causes them to better perceive their possibilities and their boundaries, i.e. it helps them to overcome their *naiveté*. Such was, for example, the influence of the novel, as a new genre, on all of the old literary genres: on the novella, the narrative poem *(poema)*, the drama, the lyric. In addition, a new genre can exert a positive influence on the old ones, to the degree, of course, that their nature as genres allows; thus one can, for example, speak of a certain "novelization" of the old genres during the age of the novel's flowering. In the majority of instances the influence of new genres on old ones contributes to their renewal and enrichment.[166] This can, of course, be extended to the polyphonic novel, too. Against the background of Dostoevsky's works, many old monological literary forms begin to look naive and simplistic. In this respect the influence of Dostoevsky's polyphonic novel on monological literary forms has been very fruitful.

The polyphonic novel makes new demands of esthetic thought as well. Raised on the monological forms of artistic vision and thoroughly steeped in them, esthetic thought tends to absolutize those forms and to fail to see their limits.

This explains why the tendency to monologize Dostoevsky's novels is still so strong, even today. It can be seen in critics' attempts to provide the heroes with finalizing definitions, to find without fail a specific monological authorial idea, to always look for superficial verisimilitude, etc. Such people ignore or deny the fundamental unfinalizedness and dialogical openness, i.e. the very essence, of Dostoevsky's artistic world.

The *scientific* consciousness of contemporary man has learned to orient itself in the complex circumstances of "the probability of the universe;" no "uncertainties" are capable of confusing this scientific consciousness, for it knows how to calculate and account for them. It has long since grown accustomed to the Einsteinian world with its multitudinous systems of measurement, etc. But in the realm of *artistic* cognition people continue now and then to demand the crudest, most primitive certainty *(opredelennost')*, which cannot possibly be true.

We must renounce our old monological habits in order to become comfortable in the new artistic sphere which Dostoevsky discovered and to orient ourselves in that incomparably more complex *artistic model of the world* which he created.

CHAPTER I

1. B. M. Engel'gardt, "Ideologicheskii roman Dostoevskogo" (Dostoevsky's Ideological Novel") in: *F. M. Dostoevskii. Stat'i i materialy (F. M. Dostoevsky. Articles and Materials)* (Moscow-Leningrad, 1924), p. 71.

2. Julius Meier-Grafe, *Dostoevski der Dichter* (Berlin, 1926), p. 189, quoted from T. L. Motyleva's thorough article "Dostoevskii i mirovaia literatura (K postanovke voprosa)" ["Dostoevsky and World Literature (Toward a Formulation of the Question)"], published in the collection *Tvorchestvo F. M. Dostoevskogo (F. M. Dostoevsky's Work)* (Moscow, 1959), p. 29.

3. i.e., as practical motivation for everyday events.

4. This does not mean, of course, that Dostoevsky is isolated in the history of the novel or that the polyphonic novel which he created had no forebears. But we must restrain ourselves here from tackling historical questions. In order to correctly localize Dostoevsky historically and to discover his *essential* bonds with his predecessors and his contemporaries, it is first of all necessary to reveal his distinctive qualities, it is necessary to show the Dostoevsky in Dostoevsky—even if such a definition of his distinctive qualities, in the absence of a broad historical investigation, will be of only a preliminary and orientational character. Without such a preliminary orientation, historical investigations degenerate into a disconnected series of chance comparisons. Not until the fourth chapter of our book will we touch upon the question of the traditions of genre from which Dostoevsky sprang, i.e., the question of *historical poetics.*

5. See his work "Dostoevskii i roman-tragediia" ("Dostoevsky and the Novel-Tragedy") in the book *Borozdy i mezhi (Furrows and Boundaries)* Moscow, 1916).

6. See *Borozdy i mezhi*, pp. 33-34.

7. We shall in due course give a critical analysis of Ivanov's definition.

8. Vyacheslav Ivanov makes a typical methodological mistake here: he makes a direct transition from the author's *Weltanschauung* to the content of his works, skipping over the form. In other instances Ivanov better understands the interrelationship between *Weltanschauung* and form.

9. Such, for example, is Ivanov's assertion that Dostoevsky's heroes are multiple doubles of the author himself, who has been regenerated and has, as it were, cast off his earthly shell, while at the same time remaining alive. (See *Borozdy i mezhi*, pp. 39-40).

10. S. Askol'dov, "Religiozno-eticheskoe znachenie Dostoevskogo" ("The Religious-ethical Meaning of Dostoevsky") in *F. M. Dostoevskii. Stat'i i materialy,* Book I, (Moscow-Leningrad, 1922).

11. *Ibid.*, p. 2.

12. *Ibid.*, p. 5.

13. *Ibid.,* p. 10.

14. *Ibid.,* p. 9.

15. *F. M. Dostoevskii. Stat'i i materialy,* Book II.

16. Leonid Grossman, *Poetika Dostoevskogo (Dostoevsky's Poetics)* (Moscow, 1925), p. 165.

17. *Ibid.,* pp. 174-175.

18. *Ibid.,* p. 178.

19. Leonid Grossman, *Put' Dostoevskogo* (Leningrad, 1924), pp. 9-10.

20. *Ibid.,* p. 17.

21. The heterogeneity of material of which Grossman speaks is simply inconceivable in the drama.

22. And therefore Vyacheslav Ivanov's formula "novel-tragedy" is also incorrect.

23. Grossman, *Put' Dostoevskogo,* p. 10.

24. We shall return to the mystery play, as well as to the Platonic philosophical dialog, in connection with the problem of the genre tradition from which Dostoevsky sprang.

25. We are speaking, of course, not of antimony nor of the opposition of abstract ideas, but of the concrete opposition of integral personalities in the events of the novel.

26. Otto Kaus, *Dostoewski und sein Schicksal* (Berlin, 1923), p. 36.

27. *Ibid.,* p. 63.

28. *F. M. Dostoevskii. Stat'i i materialy,* Book II, p. 48.

29. *Ibid.,* pp. 67-68.

30. *Ibid.,* p. 90.

31. *Ibid.,* p. 93.

32. *Ibid.*

33. The themes of the first plane: (1) the Russian superman *(Crime and Punishment);* (2) the Russian Faust (Ivan Karamazov), etc. The themes of the second plane: (1) *The Idiot;* (2) passion in the captivity of the sensual "I" (Stavrogin), etc. The themes of the third plane: the Russian righteous man *(pravednik)* (Zosima, Alyosha). See Engel'gardt, p. 98ff.

34. *Ibid.,* p. 96.

35. For Ivan Karamazov, as the author of "A Philosophical Poem," the idea is also the principle of the representation of the world, but then all of Dostoevsky's heroes are potential authors.

36. Dostoevsky's only plan for a biographical novel, *Zhitie velikogo greshnika (The Life of a Great Sinner),* limited to the history of the development of a consciousness, remained unfulfilled or, more precisely, disintegrated into a series of polyphonic novels in the process of its fulfillment. See V. Komarovich, "Nepisannaia poema Dostoevskogo" ("Dostoevsky's Unwritten Poem") in *F. M. Dostoevskii. Stat'i i materialy.,* Book I (1922).

37. But, as we have said, without the dramatic prerequisite of a unified monological world.

38. Concerning this characteristic of Goethe see G. Simmel, *Goethe* (Russian translation, 1928) and F. Gundolf, *Goethe,* 1916.

39. Pictures out of the past are present only in Dostoevsky's early works (Varenka Dobroselova's childhood, for example).

40. L. Grossman speaks pertinently on Dostoevsky's predilection for the newspaper: "Dostoevsky never shared the aversion to the newspaper page characteristic of other people of his turn of mind, or their contemptuous disgust for the daily press, as openly expressed by Hoffmann, Schopenhauer, or Flaubert. In contrast to them, Dostoevsky liked to bury himself in newspaper reports, and he criticized the indifference of contemporary authors to these 'most real and oddest of facts,' and he was able, with a real journalist's instinct, to establish a unifed picture of the current historical moment out of the fragmentary, trivial details of the day. In 1867 he asked one of the people with whom he corresponded: 'Do you get any of the newspapers? For heaven's sake, read them! One can't do otherwise today, not to be fashionable, but so that the visible connection of all public and private affairs should become ever stronger and clearer...'" (Leonid Grossman, *Poetika Dostoevskogo,* p. 176).

41. *F. M. Dostoevskii. Stat'i i materialy,* Book II, p. 105.

42. Lunacharskii's article was originally published in the journal *Novyi mir,* 1929, No. 10. It has been reprinted several times. We shall quote it from the book *F. M. Dostoevskii v russkoi kritike (F. M. Dostoevsky in Russian Criticism)* (1965), pp. 403-429. Lunacharskii's article was written in connection with the first edition of our book on Dostoevsky.

43. *Ibid.,* p. 405.

44. *Ibid.,* p. 406.

45. *Ibid.,* p. 410.

46. *Ibid.,* p. 411.

47. *Ibid.,* p. 427.

48. *Ibid.,* p. 428.

49. *Ibid.,* p. 429.

50. See, for example, A. S. Dolinin's valuable work *V tvorcheskoi laboratorii Dostoevskogo (istoriia sozdaniia romana Podrostok) [In Dostoevsky's Creative Laboratory (The History of the Creation of the Novel A Raw Youth)]* (Moscow, 1947).

51. V. Kirpotin, *F. M. Dostoevskii* (Moscow, 1947), pp. 63-64.

52. *Ibid.,* pp. 64-65.

53. *Ibid.,* pp. 66-67.

54. Viktor Shklovskii, *Za i protiv. Zametki o Dostoevskom* (Moscow, 1957).

55. *Voprosy literatury (Questions of Literature),* 1960, No. 4, p. 98.

56. Shklovskii, p. 258.

57. *Ibid.,* pp. 171-172.

58. Lunacharsky gives an analogous characterization of Dostoevsky's creative process: "...Dostoevsky, if not in the final execution of the novel, then at least *at the stage of its original conception and during its gradual growth—* did not work with a preconceived structural plan...rather, we are indeed involved here with polyphony, of a type in which *absolutely free personalities* are combined and intertwined. Dostoevsky himself was, perhaps, extremely and intensely interested in discovering the outcome of the ideological and ethical conflict of the characters which he had created (or, more exactly, which had created themselves in him)." *(F. M. Dostoevskii v russkoi kritike,* p. 405.)

59. Shklovsky, p. 223.

60. The majority of authors do not accept the concept of the polyphonic novel.

61. *Tvorchestvo F. M. Dostoevskogo* (Moscow, 1959), pp. 341-342.

62. *Ibid.,* p. 342.

CHAPTER II

63. Devushkin, on his way to the general, sees himself in a mirror: "I was so thunderstruck that my lips trembled, and my legs too. And with good reason, my dear. First of all, I was ashamed; I glanced to the right into the mirror, and what I saw there was simply enough to drive you mad...His excellency immediately noticed the figure I cut, and especially my suit. I remembered what I had seen in the mirror: I dashed after my lost button!" (F. M. Dostoevsky, *Sobranie sochinenii v desiati tomax [Collected Works in Ten Volumes],* vol. I. (Moscow, 1956-1958), p. 186. Further quotations from Dostoevsky's literary works, except where otherwise noted, will be taken from this edition and will be indicated by volume and page number.)

Devushkin sees in the mirror that which Gogol depicted in his description of Akaky Akakievich's coat and general appearance, but which Akaky himself did not see and did not perceive. The heroes' constant agonizing reflection on their appearance performs for them the functions of the mirror. Golyadkin's mirror is his double.

64. Dostoevsky also often gives external portraits of his heroes, either directly from the authorial viewpoint, through a narrator, or through other characters. But these external portraits do not have the function of finalizing the hero and do not create a fixed and pre-determining image. The functions of one or another of the hero's traits do not, of course, depend exclusively on the basic literary methods by which those traits are portrayed (by means of the hero's self-characterization, directly from the author, by oblique means, etc.).

65. "Mister Prokharchin" also remains within the bounds of the same

Gogolian material, as did, apparently, "The Shaved Whiskers" *("Sbritye baken-bardy")*, which Dostoevsky destroyed. But in writing "Whiskers" Dostoevsky realized that his new principle, applied to the same old Gogolian material, would be redundant, and that it was necessary to master new material. In 1846 he wrote to his brother: "I am not writing 'Shaved Whiskers,' either. I've dropped the whole thing. Because it is nothing but a repetition of what I have said before. Now brighter, livelier, more original thoughts are crying out to be expressed. Upon finishing 'Shaved Whiskers' all of this came to me spontaneously. In my situation monotony is ruin." (F.M. Dostoevsky, *Pis'ma (Letters)*, v. 1, Moscow—Leningrad, 1928, p. 100). He then begins work on *Netochka Nezvanova* and "The Landlady," i.e. he seeks to apply his new principle to a different aspect of the same Gogolian world ("The Portrait" and in part "A Terrible Vengeance").

66. Oscar Wilde accurately understood and defined the inner unfinalizability of Dostoevsky's heroes as their leading characteristic. T.L. Motyleva in her book *Dostoevskii i mirovaia literatura (Dostoevsky and World Literature)* says of Wilde: "Wilde saw the greatest contribution of Dostoevsky the artist in the fact that he 'never completely explains his characters.' In Wilde's words Dostoevsky's heroes 'always amaze us by what they say or do, and they conceal within themselves to the end the eternal secret of existence.' " *(Tvorchestvo F.M. Dostoevskogo*, p. 32.)

67. *Dokumenty po istorii literatury i obshchestvennosti (Documents Concerning the History of Literature and Society)*, No. 1, "F.M. Dostoevskii," (Moscow, 1922), p. 13.

68. *Biografiia, pis'ma i zametki iz zapisnoi knigi F.M. Dostoevskogo (Biography, Letters and Notes from the Notebook of F. M. Dostoevsky)*, (St. Petersburg, 1883), p. 373.

69. In "The Diary of a Writer" for 1877 Dostoevsky says in regard to *Anna Karenina:* "It is clear and obvious that evil lurks deeper in humanity than the socialist healers suppose; that evil cannot be avoided, regardless of the social arrangement; that the human soul will remain as it is; that abnormality and sin spring from the soul itself; and, finally, that the laws of the human spirit are still so unknown, so undiscovered by science, so *undefined* and so mysterious, that there are no, and as yet can be no healers, nor even **final** judges. But there is one who says: 'Vengeance is mine and I will repay.' " (F. M. Dostoevsky, *Polnoe sobranie xudozhestvennyx proizvedenii (The Complete Fiction)*, B. Tomashevsky and K. Khalabaev, eds., vol. XI, Moscow—Leningrad, 1929, p. 210).

70. V. Ermilov, *F. M. Dostoevskii* (Moscow, 1956).

71. Since *meaning* "lives" not in that time which has a "yesterday," a "today," and a "tomorrow," i.e. not in the time in which the heroes "lived" and in which the biographical life of the author unfolds.

72. Quoted in V. V. Vinogradov, *O iazyke xudozhestvennoi literatury*, pp. 141-142.

73. *Ibid.*, p. 140.

74. Murder (described from within the murderer's field of vision), suicide and insanity are characteristic for Dostoevsky's world. Normal deaths are rare in his work, and he usually mentions them only in passing.

CHAPTER III

75. Plato's idealism is not purely monological. It becomes so only in the neo-Kantian interpretation. Neither is the Platonic dialog a pedagogical one, although monologism is strong in it. We shall discuss the Platonic dialogs in greater detail in connection with Dostoevsky's genre traditions. (See Chapter 4.)

76. *Zapisnye tetradi F. M. Dostoevskogo (F. M. Dostoevsky's Notebooks),* (Moscow-Leningrad, 1935), p. 179. L. P. Grossman speaks very well to this point, using Dostoevsky's own words: "The artist 'hears, senses, even sees' that 'new elements arise which thirst after a new word,' Dostoevsky wrote much later; they must be captured and expressed." (L. P. Grossman, *"Dostoevskii-xudozhnik"* ("Dostoevsky the Artist") in the collection *Tvorchestvo F. M. Dostoevskogo (F. M. Dostoevsky's Art)* (Moscow, 1959), p. 366.

77. This book, published during the time when Dostoevsky was working on *Crime and Punishment,* found great resonance in Russia. On this subject see F. I. Evnin's article"Roman *Prestuplenie i nakazanie"* ("The Novel *Crime and Punishment"*) in *Tvochestvo F. M. Dostoevskogo,* pp. 153-157.

78. On this subject see Evnin's article "Roman *Besy"* ("The Novel *The Possessed"*), *Ibid.,* pp. 228-229.

79. On This subject see A. S. Dolinin's book *V tvorcheskoi laboratorii Dostoevskogo (In Dostoevsky's Creative Laboratory)* (Moscow, 1947).

80. F. M. Dostoevsky, *Polnoe sobranie xudozhestvennyx proizvedenii (Complete Literary Works)* (Moscow-Leningrad, 1929), vol. XI, pp. 11-15.

81. Here we do not, of course, have in mind finalized, closed images of reality (type, character, temperament), but rather the open image-word *(obraz-slovo).* Such an ideal authoritative image, one which is not contemplated, but followed, occurred to Dostoevsky as the farthest limit of his artistic plans, but it was never realized in his works.

82. *Biografiia, pis'ma i zametki iz zapisnoi knizhki F. M. Dostoevskogo (Biography, Letters and Notes from F. M. Dostoevsky's Notebook)* (St. Petersburg, 1883), pp. 371-372, 374.

83. *Dokumenty po istorii literatury i obshchestvennosti (Documents on the History of Literature and Society),* No. 1, F. M. Dostoevskii (Moscow, Central Archive of the RSFSR, 1922), pp. 71-72.

84. F. M. Dostoevskii, *Pis'ma,* vol. II, (1930), p. 170.

85. *Ibid.*

86. In the letter to Maikov Dostoevsky says: "In the second story I want to set forth Tikhon Zadonsky as the main figure, under another name, of course, but

Notes for pp. 82-118.

this bishop will live quietly in a monastery...Perhaps I shall make a stately, **positive,** holy figure of him. He is not a Kostanzhoglo or the German in *Oblomov* (I've forgotten his name)...nor is he a Lopukhov or a Rakhmetov. *Actually I won't create anything.* I'll simply present the real Tikhon, whom I've long since taken joyfully into my heart." *(Pis'ma, voL II, p. 264).*

    87. *Pis'ma,* vol. IV (Moscow, 1959), p. 5.

CHAPTER IV

    88. Leonid Grossman, *Poetika Dostoevskogo* (Moscow, 1925), pp. 53, 56-57.

    89. *Ibid.,* pp. 61, 62.

    90. His satires have not survived, but their titles are mentioned by Diogenes Laertius.

    91. The phenomenon of reduced laughter *(reducirovannyi smex)* has rather great significance in world literature. Reduced laughter has no direct expression, it does not, so to speak, "ring out," but traces of it remain and can be discerned in the structure of the image and the word. Paraphrasing Gogol, one can speak of "laughter which is invisisble to the world." We shall meet it in Dostoevsky's works."

    92. In *Eumenides* (fragments) Varro depicts such passions as ambition and acquisitiveness as insanity.

    93. Two lives—the official and the carnivalistic—existed in antiquity, too, but there was never such a sharp break between them (especially in Greece).

    94. My work *Rabelais and the Folk Culture of the Middle Ages and the Renaissance* (1940), which is at present being prepared for publication, is devoted to the carnivalistic folk culture of the Middle Ages and the Renaissance (and, in part, of antiquity). It includes a special bibliography on this question.

    95. Dostoevsky was very well acquainted not only with the canonical Christian literature, but also with the Apocrypha.

    96. Mention must be made here of the enormous influence exerted by the novella *The Widow of Ephesus* (from the *Satyricon*) on the Middle Ages and the Renaissance. This inserted novella is one of antiquity's greatest menippea.

    97. The application of such terms as "epopée," "tragedy," and "idyll" to modern literature has become generally accepted and customary, and we are not at all disturbed when *War and Peace* is called an epopée, *Boris Godunov* a tragedy, or *Old-World Landowners* an idyll. But the term "menippea" is unfamiliar (especially in our literary scholarship), and therefore its application to works of modern literature (to Dostoevsky, for example) may seem somewhat strange and strained.

    98. He appears again in *The Diary of a Writer* in "A Certain Person's Half-Letter."

    99. In the 18th century *Conversations in the Kingdom of the Dead* were written by Sumarokov, and even by A. V. Suvorov, the future general (cf. his *Razgovor v tsarstve mertvyx mezhdu Aleksandrom Makedonskim i Gerostratom—*

Notes for pp. 118-134.

Conversation in the Kingdom of the Dead between Alexander the Great and Herostrat, 1755).

100. It is true that this sort of juxtaposition does not carry the force of proof. All of these points of similarity could have been engendered by the logic of the genre itself, particularly by the logic of carnivalistic discrowning, debasement and mésalliance.

101. The possibility that Dostoevsky was acquainted with Varro's satires is not to be discounted, although it is doubtful. A complete scholarly edition of Varro's fragments was published in 1865 (Riese, *Varronis Saturarum Menippearum reliquiae.* Leipzig, 1865). The book aroused interest not only in narrowly philological circles, and Dostoevsky could have gained a secondhand acquaintance with it during his stay abroad, or perhaps through his Russian philologist friends.

102. F. M. Dostoevskii, *Polnoe sobranie xudozhestvennyx proizvedenii,* vol. XIII (Moscow-Leningrad, 1930), p. 523.

103. General Pervoedov (whose name means "the first to eat"—trans.) even in the grave is not able to lose the awareness of his officerial dignity, in whose name he categorically protests against Klinevich's proposal ("not to be ashamed of anything"), announcing: "I have served my monarch." There is an analogous situation in *The Devils:* General Drozdov, finding himself among the nihilists, for whom the very word "general" is a derogatory sobriquet, defends his dignity as a general with the very same words. Both episodes are handled in a comical way.

104. *Sorokoviny*—the Russian Orthodox commemoration of the passage of forty days from the time of death (trans.).

105. Even from such competent and well-meaning contemporaries as A. N. Maikov.

106. "And suddenly I *called out,* not with my voice, for I could not move, but with my whole being, to the *master of all that was happening to me.*" (X, 428)

107. Concerning the sources of the genre and the themes of "The Grand Inquisitor" (Voltaire's *Histoire de Jenni, ou L'Athée et le Sage,* Victor Hugo's *Le Christe au Vatican)* see the works of L. P. Grossman.

108. Gogol was still subject to the fundamental, direct influence of Ukrainian carnivalistic folklore.

109. Grimmelshausen does not fit within the limits of the Renaissance, but his work reflects the direct and profound influence of carnival to no lesser degree than that of Shakespeare and Cervantes.

110. It cannot, of course, be denied that a certain degree of special charm is present in all of the contemporary forms of carnival life. It suffices to name *Hemingway,* whose generally heavily carnivalized work was strongly influenced by contemporary forms and celebrations of the carnival type (by the bullfight in particular). He had a very keen ear for everything carnivalistic in contemporary life.

111. F. M. Dostoevskii, *Polnoe sobranie xudozhestvennyx proizvedenii,* vol. XIII (Moscow-Leningrad, 1930), pp. 158-159.

112. Dostoevsky's model was Gogol, namely the ambivalent tone of "The Story of how Ivan Ivanovich Quarreled with Ivan Nikiferovich."

113. *Kamarinskaia*—a Russian folk dance and also the accompanying song (trans.).

114. During this period Dostoevsky was even working on a large comic epopee, of which "Uncle's Dream" is an episode (according to his own statement in a letter). As far as we know, Dostoevsky subsequently never returned to a plan for a large, purely comical work.

115. Thomas Mann's novel *Doktor Faustus,* which reflects Dostoevsky's powerful influence, is also thoroughly permeated with reduced ambivalent laughter which sometimes breaks through to the surface, particularly in the story of the narrator Zeitbloom. T. Mann himself says in the history of the creation of the novel: "More humor, more grimacing by the biographer (i.e. by Zeitbloom—M. B.), more *self-mockery, so that he does not become pathetic*—as much as possible of all that sort of thing!" (T. Mann, *"Istoriia* **Doktora Faustusa.** *Roman odnogo romana," Sobranie Sochinenii* ["The History of *Doktor Faustus.* The Novel of a Novel," in *Collected Works*] [Moscow, 1960], vol. 9, p. 224). Reduced laughter, predominantly of a parodistic type, is in general characteristic of all of T. Mann's work. In comparing his own style with that of Bruno Frank, Mann makes a very characteristic admission: "He (i.e. B. Frank—M. B.) uses Zeitbloom's humanistic narrative style *completely seriously,* as his own style. But, *if we are talking about style, I recognize, actually, only the parody."* (*ibid.,* p. 235).

We must mention that T. Mann's work is profoundly carnivalized. Carnivalization can be seen in its most vivid external form in his novel *Die Bekentnisse des Hochstaplers Felix Krull* (where a sort of philosophy of carnival and of carnival ambivalence is put into the mouth of Professor Kuckuck).

116. The carnivalistic perception of Petersburg first appears in Dostoevsky in the novella *A Weak Heart* (1847), and was subsequently extensively developed in regard to Dostoevsky's entire early work in "Petersburg Dreams in Verse and Prose."

117. F. M. Dostoevskii, *Pis'ma,* v. I, pp. 333-334.

118. Also in prison people of various positions, who in normal life would not be able to meet on equal terms in a single plane, find themselves in familiar contact.

119. For example, the penniless prince, who in the morning has nowhere to lay his head, becomes by the end of the day a millionaire.

120. In the novel *The Devils,* for example, that part of life which is penetrated by the devils is depicted as a carnival nether world. The crowning-discrowning theme deeply permeates the entire novel (Stavrogin's discrowning by Khromonozhka, for example, or Petr Verkhovensky's idea to proclaim Stavrogin "Tsarevich Ivan"). *The Devils* affords very abudant material for an analysis of external carnivalization. *The Brothers Karamazov* is also very rich in external carnival accessories.

121. In his conversation with the devil, Ivan Karamazov asks him:

"You clown! But have you ever tried to tempt someone who eats lo-
custs and has been praying for 17 years in the desert and is grown over with
moss?"

"My friend, that's all I've been doing. You may forget about whole
worlds, but you latch onto someone like that, because the diamond is a very
precious stone; *one such soul is sometimes worth a whole constellation—
we've got our own arithmetic.* What a sweet victory! And some of those
people are, I swear, no less cultivated than you, though you won't believe
it: *they can contemplate such abysses of faith and unbelief at one and the
same time,* that sometimes it seems as though it would take only another
hair, and they would go flying 'head over heels,' as the actor Gorbunov says."
(X, 174)

It should be noted that Ivan's conversation with the devil is full of images of
cosmic space and time: "quadrillions of kilometers," "billions of years," "whole
constellations," etc. All of these cosmic magnitudes are mixed together with elements of immediate contemporaneity ("the actor Gorbunov") and with commonplace everyday details, all of which are organically combined under the conditions
of carnival time.

CHAPTER V

122. *Skaz*—a narrative told by a fictitious narrator in the language typical to
him, containing the distinctive peculiarities of his own (as opposed to the author's)
speech (trans.).

123. We will not illustrate with examples of all the types and varieties of
word in the classification given below, since we shall in due course present voluminous material from Dostoevsky for each of the instances under discussion.

124. B. M. Eikhenbaum quite correctly, but from a different point of view,
noted this characteristic of Turgenev's story: "The form of the authorially motivated
introduction of a special narrator, to whom the narration is entrusted, is extremely
widespread. However, very often this form has a quite conditional character (as in
Maupassant or Turgenev), bearing witness only to the vigor of the tradition of the
narrator as a special character in the novella. In such cases the narrator remains the
same as the author and the motivation of his presence plays the role of a simple
introduction." (B. M. Eikhenbaum, *Literatura,* Leningrad, 1927, p. 217).

125. First in the article *"Kak sdelana* **Shinel'"** ("How *The Overcoat* Is Made"),
in *Poetika* (1919). Later particularly in the article *"Leskov i sovremennaia proza"*
("Leskov and Contemporary Prose") (See *Literatura,* p. 210 ff.).

126. Leo Spitzer, *Italienische Umgangssprache* (Leipzig, 1922), pp. 175-176.

Notes for pp. 164-180.

127. *Odnonapravlennye slova*—i.e. words in which the author's voice and the other person's voice are directed toward the same object (trans.).

128. *Raznonapravlennye slova*—i.e. words in which the author's voice and the other person's voice are directed toward different objects (trans.).

129. In connection with the interest in "folk-ness" *(narodnost')* (not as an ethnographic category), the various forms of *skaz* take on enormous significance in Romanticism as a means of refracting another person's word while maintaining a low degree of objectivization. For Classicism, however, the "folk word" (in the sense of another person's social-typical and individual-characteristic word) was a purely objectivized word (in the lower genres). Among the words of the third type the internally polemical *Icherzählung* (particularly of the confessional type) was of particularly great significance in Romanticism.

130. The majority of prose genres, and the novel in particular, are constructive: they are made up of *entire utterances,* although these utterances are not full-fledged and are subordinated to monological unity.

131. The brilliant works of V. V. Vinogradov stand out sharply from all the rest of contemporary linguistic stylistics, both Soviet and foreign; he reveals, on the basis of voluminous material, the whole fundamental contradictoriness *(razno-rechivost')* and multistyledness of artistic prose and the whole complexity of the authorial position ("the author's image") in it, although, as it seems to us, Vinogradov somewhat underestimates the significance of dialogical relationships among verbal styles (inasmuch as such relationships exceed the bounds of linguistics).

132. We recall Thomas Mann's very characteristic admission quoted in footnote 115.

133. F. M. Dostoevskii, *Pis'ma*, vol. 1, p. 86.

134. In his book *O iazyke xudozhestvennoi literatury (On Literary Language)* V. V. Vinogradov gives a brilliant analysis of Makar Devushkin's speech as the speech of a specific *social character* (pp. 477-492).

135. F. M. Dostoevskii, *Pis'ma,* vol. I, p. 81.

136. The rudiments of the interior dialog were, it is true, present already in Devushkin.

137. While at work on *Netochka Nezvanova* Dostoevsky writes to his brother: "But soon you shall read *Netochka Nezvanova.* It will be a confession, like *Golyadkin,* only of a different tone and kind." (*Pis'ma*, vol. 1, p. 108).

138. Not long before Golyadkin had said to himself: "That's just like you!... you're so happy, you'll start singing in a minute! You're a truthful soul!"

139. In *Crime and Punishment,* for example, Svidrigailov (Raskolnikov's partial double) repeats literally Raskolnikov's most intimate words, which he had said to Sonya, and he repeats them with a meaningful wink. We quote this passage in its entirety:

"Ach! You're such a distrustful person!" laughed Svidrigailov. "Didn't I say that I don't need this money? Well, simply for humanitarian reasons,

can't you believe it? After all, she was not a 'louse,' (he poked his
finger toward the corner where the dead woman lay) like some old useress.
Well, you'll agree, well, 'Should Luzhin really go on living and doing awful
things, or should she die?' And if I don't help, then 'Polechka, for example,
will go down the same path...' "

He said this with a look of **winking**, jolly roguishness, without taking
his eyes off Raskolnikov. Raskolnikov grew pale and went cold at hearing his
own expressions, which he had used in his conversation with Sonya. (V, 455)

140. Other equal consciousnesses appear only in the novels.

141. In Thomas Mann's novel *Doktor Faustus* a great deal was suggested by
Dostoevsky, including namely Dostoevsky's *polyphony.* I shall quote an excerpt
from the description of one of the works of the composer Adrian Leverkühn which
is very close to Trishatov's "musical idea:" "Adrian Leverkühn is always great at
*making things that are alike different....*So it is here—but nowhere so profound, so
mysterious and so great as here. Every word that evokes the idea of "the other
side," of metamorphosis in a mystical sense, i.e. of transubstantiation—transformation, transfiguration—is to be welcomed here as being exactly appropriate. The
horror which came before is, to be sure, completely transformed in the indescrib-
able childrens' choir, it is totally reinstrumented and rerhythmized, but *there is not
a single note in the whirring, whirring song of the spheres and the angels which
could not be heard in strict correspondence in the laughter of hell."* (Thomas Mann,
Doktor Faustus, Moscow, 1959, pp. 440-441).

142. Belinsky was the first to note this characteristic of *The Double's* narration, but he offered no explanation of it.

143. *F. M. Dostoevskii. Stat'i i materialy,* Book I, pp. 241, 242.

144. *Ibid.,* p. 248.

145. This perspective is lacking even for the generalizing "authorial" construction of the hero's indirect speech.

146. V. Vinogradov makes very valuable literary-historical remarks concerning
literary parody and literary polemic in *Poor Folk* in his article in the collection of
essays *Tvorcheskii put' Dostoevskogo (Dostoevsky's Creative Path),* edited by N. L.
Brodskii (Leningrad, 1924).

147. All of these stylistic characteristics are also connected with the carnival
tradition and with reduced ambivalent laughter.

148. *Notes from the Underground* were originally announced by Dostoevsky
in *Vremia* under that title.

149. This is explained by the genre characteristic of *Notes* as a "Menippean
satire."

150. Its acceptance would, according to Dostoevsky, calm down his word and
purify it.

151. We shall indicate the exceptions below.

152. We recall the characterization which Dostoevsky himself gave to the

hero's speech in "A Gentle Creature": "...first he speaks to himself, then addresses himself as if to an invisible listener, a judge. And so it always is in reality." (X, 379)

153. Myshkin correctly defines this also: "...besides, perhaps he didn't think that at all, but only wanted it...he wanted to be together with people for the last time, he wanted to earn their respect and love." (VI, 484-485)

154. In the book *Poetika Dostoevskogo* (Moscow, 1925). The article was originally published in the second volume of *Dostoevskii. Stat'i i materialy,* edited by D. S. Dolinin (Moscow-Leningrad, 1924).

155. Leonid Grossman, *Poetika Dostoevskogo* (Moscow, 1925), p. 162.

156. *Dokumenty po istorii literatury i obshchestvennosti (Documents Concerning the History of Literature and Society),* issue No. 1, *F. M. Dostoevskii* (Moscow, 1922), p. 32.

157. *Ibid.,* p. 33.

158. *Ibid.,* p. 15.

159. F. M. Dostoevskii, *Pis'ma,* vol. 3, p. 256.

160. In his article *"Tematicheskaia kompozitsiia romana* Idiot" ("The Thematic Composition of the Novel *The Idiot*") A. P. Skaftymov quite correctly perceived the role of the "other" (in relation to the "I") in the distribution of the characters in Dostoevsky. He says, "In both Nastasya Filippovna and in Ippolit (and in all of his prideful characters) Dostoevsky reveals the torments of melancholy and loneliness expressed in the inexorable craving for love and sympathy, and thereby expresses the point of view that, in the face of intimate inner feelings, man **cannot accept himself** and, unable to sanctify himself, he causes himself pain and seeks sanction and sanctification in the heart of another. The image of Marya in Prince Myshkin's story has the function of purification through forgiveness."

He defines the structure of Nastasya Filippovna in relation to Myshkin as follows: "Thus the inner meaning of Nastasya Filippovna's unstable relationship to Prince Myshkin is revealed by the author himself: though she is attracted to him (the thirst after an ideal, after love and forgiveness), she is repelled by him, now because of her own feelings of unworthiness (consciousness of guilt, purity of spirit), now because of her pride (the inability to forget herself and accept love and forgiveness)." (In *"Tvorcheskii put' Dostoevskogo"* [*Dostoevsky's Creative Path*] edited by N. L. Brodskii [Leningrad, 1924], p. 153 and 148.)

A. F. Skaftymov remains, however, on the level of a purely psychological analysis. He does not reveal the genuinely artistic significance of this element in the structure of the group of heroes and the dialog.

161. Alyosha, too, clearly perceives this voice of Ivan from the very outset. We shall quote one of his small dialogs with Ivan which takes place after the murder. In general this dialog is analogous in structure to the dialog between them which we have already analyzed, although it does differ from it in certain respects.

"Do you remember (asks Ivan—M. B.) when Dmitry burst into the house after dinner and hit father, and I said to you later outside that I reserve the 'right to wish'—well, did you think then that I wished for father's death, or not?"

"Yes, I thought so," answered Alyosha softly.

"That's the way it was, too, there was nothing left to the imagination. But didn't you think that what I wanted was for 'one filthy bastard to do away with the other one,' that is for Dmitry to kill father, and the sooner the better ...and that I had nothing against giving him a little help, either!"

Alyosha grew slightly pale and silently looked his brother in the eye.

"Answer!" cried Ivan. "I want to know with all my might what you thought then. I need the truth, the truth!" He gasped for air, already in advance fixing a sort of malicious gaze on Alyosha.

"Forgive me for thinking that," whispered Alyosha, and said no more, not adding a single 'extenuating circumstance.' (X, 130-131)

162. *"Dokumenty po istorii literatury i obshchestvennosti"* (*Documents Concerning the History of Literature and Society*), Issue No. 1, *"F. M. Dostoevskii"* (Moscow, 1922), p. 6.

163. *Ibid.,* pp. 8-9.

164. *Ibid.,* p. 35. It is interesting to compare this passage with the excerpt we have quoted from Dostoevsky's letter to Kovner.

165. This is, as we know, a departure into the space and time of carnival and the mystery play, in which the ultimate event in the interaction of consciousnesses takes place in Dostoevsky's novels.

CONCLUSION

166. If they do not die a "natural death" of their own accord.

INDEX

adventure novel, 83-86
Aeschines, 89
Alexamenos, 89
Antisthenes, 89, 90, 92, 98
Apollonius of Tyana, 99
Apuleius, 93, 94, 97, 98, 110; *Metamorphoses (The Golden Ass)*, 93, 110, 118
Ariosto, 161
Aristotle, 92
Askoldov, S., 8-10, 47, footnotes 10-14
Augustine, 96, 98
Bakhtin, M. M., 27, footnote 94
Balzac, 27, 29, 79, 132-134, 140, 149
Barbey, 165
Belinsky, V., 40, footnote 142
Belkin, A., 32
Bergerac, Cyrano de, 123
Bernard, Claude, 34, 50
Bilinkis, Ia., 32
Biografiia, pis'ma i zametki iz zapisnoi knigi F. M. Dostoevskogo (Biography, Letters and Notes from F. M. Dostoevsky's Notebook), footnotes 68, 82
Bion Borysthenes, 92, 94, 95, 98
Boccaccio, 131
Boethius *(De Consolatione Philosophiae)*, 93, 110
Boileau, 118
Byron, 4, 68
Calderon, 123
capitalism, 15, 16, 29, 30, 139, 141
carnival, carnivalization, 88, 89, 92, 93, 100-116, 118, 120-122, 124, 131-149, footnotes 93, 94, 100, 110, 115, 116, 120, 121, 147, 165
Catechism of a Revolutionary, 74
Cervantes, 28, 105, 108, 112, 131, 132, 135, 138, 145, 149, footnote 109
Chaadaev, P., 74, 75
Chateaubriand, 68
Chernyshevsky, 53-56, 122
Christ, 80, 81, 111, 130, 210
Christiansen, Broder, 17
Cicero, 92
Citizen, The (Grazhdanin), 75, 117
Claudius, 95
Critias, 87
Criton, 89
cynics, 125

INDEX

[245]

INDEX

INDEX

INDEX